STECK-VAUG

Spelling

Teacher's Edition
Level 5

John R. Pescosolido, Ph.D.
Professor Emeritus
Central Connecticut State University
New Britain, Connecticut

Consultants

Felice M. Rockoff
Reading Teacher
New York City Public Schools
New York, New York

Theodore J. Thibodeau
Assistant Superintendent
Attleboro Public Schools
Attleboro, Massachusetts

Anna L. Ulrich
Adjunct Professor
College of Santa Fe
Albuquerque, New Mexico

Anita Uphaus
Coordinator of Early Childhood Programs
Austin Independent School District
Austin, Texas

STECK-VAUGHN®
COMPANY
ELEMENTARY • SECONDARY • ADULT • LIBRARY

Acknowledgments

Executive Editor: Diane Sharpe
Project Editor: Amanda Johnson
Design Manager: Richard Balsam
Designers: Jim Cauthron
Danielle Szabo

Product Development: Cottage Communications
Typesetting: Publishers' Design and Production Services, Inc.

Writers: Linda Ekblad (pp. 62, 140, 152); Kathleen Fischer (p. 126); Bobbi Katz (pp. 158, 190); Susan Katz (pp. 38, 108); Jackie Podhaizer (p. 30); Stuart Podhaizer (Etymologies); Gena Reisner (pp. 12, 44, 70, 82, 94); Joan Rosenblatt (pp. 24, 56, 88, 114, 120, 134, 146, 166, 178); Linda Rogers (pp. 102, 172); Lorraine Sotiriou (pp. 6, 18, 50, 76, 184)

Artists: Andrea Baruffi, Maxie Chambliss, Brian Cody, Holly Cooper, Arlene Dubanevich, Julie Durrell, Allan Eitzen, Jon Friedman, John Gamache, Jon Goodell, David Griffin, Carol Grosvenor, Konrad Hack, Meryl Henderson, Pamela Higgins, Joan Holub, Will Kefauver, Tom Leonard, Susan Lexa, Shelly Matheis, Carolyn McHenry, Kimble Pendleton Mead, Linda Miyamoto, Marcy Ramsey, Jerry Smath, Joel Snyder, Arvis Stewart, Pat Traub, John Wallner, Kay Wilson

---

Grateful acknowledgment is made to the following for the use of copyrighted materials. Every effort has been made to obtain permission to use previously published material. Any errors or omissions are unintentional.

ISBN 0-8114-9283-4

4 5 6 7 8 9 PO 04 03 02 01 00

TABLE OF CONTENTS

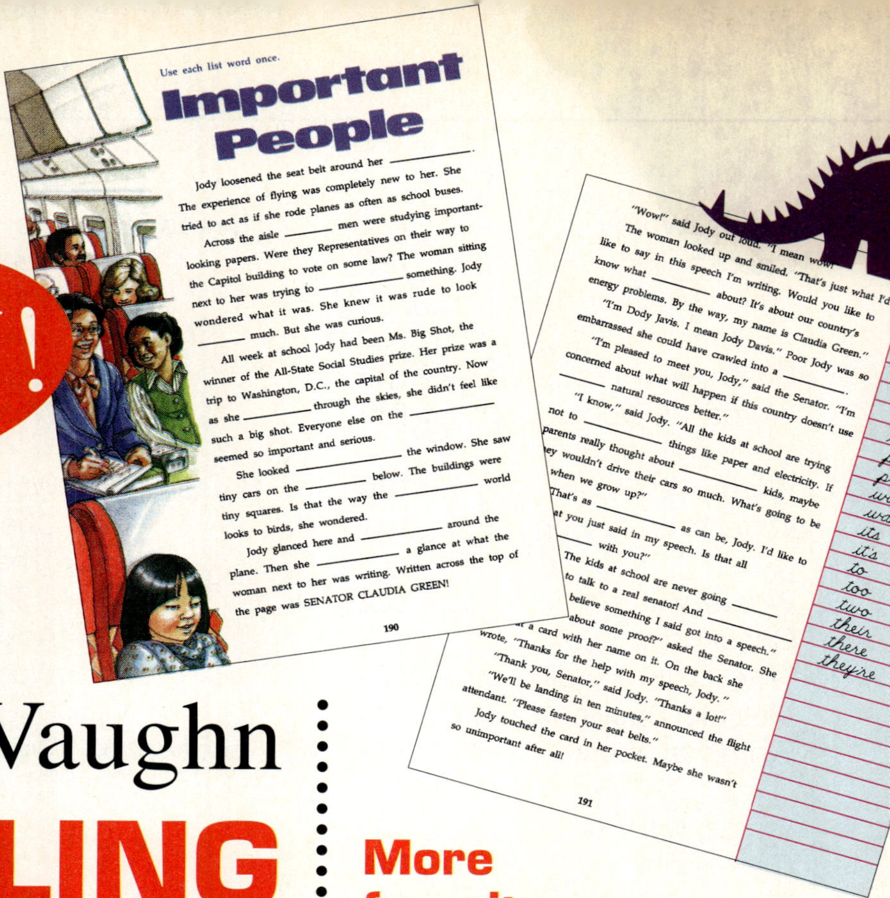
Use each list word once.

Important People

Jody loosened the seat belt around her ____. The experience of flying was completely new to her. She tried to act as if she rode planes as often as school buses.

Across the aisle ____ men were studying important-looking papers. Were they Representatives on their way to the Capitol building to vote on some law? The woman sitting next to her was trying to ____ something. Jody wondered what it was. She knew it was rude to look ____ much. But she was curious.

All week at school Jody had been Ms. Big Shot, the winner of the All-State Social Studies prize. Her prize was a trip to Washington, D.C., the capital of the country. Now as she ____ through the skies, she didn't feel like such a big shot. Everyone else on the ____ seemed so important and serious.

She looked ____ the window. She saw tiny cars on the ____ below. The buildings were tiny squares. Is that the way the ____ world looks to birds, she wondered.

Jody glanced here and ____ around the plane. Then she ____ a glance at what the woman next to her was writing. Written across the top of the page was SENATOR CLAUDIA GREEN!

190

"Wow!" said Jody out loud. "I mean wow!"

The woman looked up and smiled. "That's just what I'd like to say in this speech I'm writing. Would you like to know what ____ about? It's about our country's energy problems. By the way, my name is Claudia Green."

"I'm Dody Javis. I mean Jody Davis." Poor Jody was so embarrassed she could have crawled into a ____.

"I'm pleased to meet you, Jody," said the Senator. "I'm concerned about what will happen if this country doesn't use ____ natural resources better."

"I know," said Jody. "All the kids at school are trying not to ____ things like paper and electricity. If parents really thought about ____ kids, maybe ey wouldn't drive their cars so much. What's going to be when we grow up?"

That's as ____ as can be, Jody. I'd like to at you just said in my speech. Is that all ____ with you?"

The kids at school are never going ____ to talk to a real senator! And ____ believe something I said got into a speech."

about some proof?" asked the Senator. She a card with her name on it. On the back she wrote, "Thanks for the help with my speech, Jody."

"Thank you, Senator," said Jody. "Thanks a lot!"

"We'll be landing in ten minutes," announced the flight attendant. "Please fasten your seat belts."

Jody touched the card in her pocket. Maybe she wasn't so unimportant after all!

191

threw
through
right
write
hole
whole
road
rode
plain
plane
waist
waste
its
it's
to
too
two
their
there
they're

Cloze selections allow students to use spelling words in meaningful context.

NEW!

Steck-Vaughn SPELLING

Integrates spelling with reading, writing, and language arts!

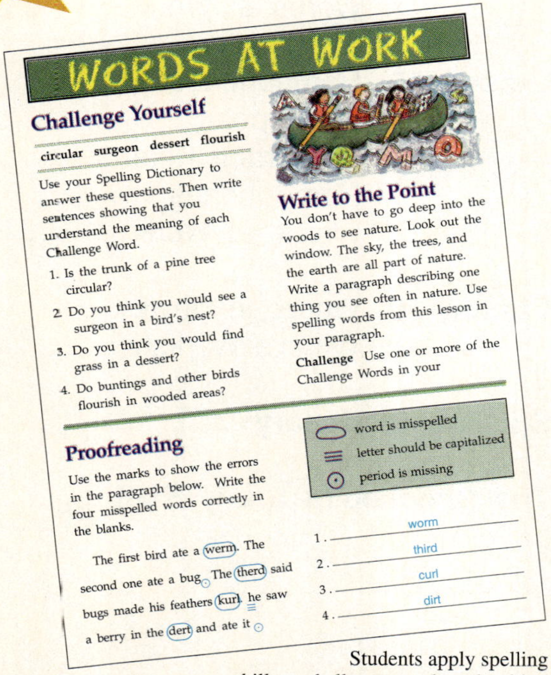
WORDS AT WORK

Challenge Yourself

circular surgeon dessert flourish

Use your Spelling Dictionary to answer these questions. Then write sentences showing that you understand the meaning of each Challenge Word.

1. Is the trunk of a pine tree circular?
2. Do you think you would see a surgeon in a bird's nest?
3. Do you think you would find grass in a dessert?
4. Do buntings and other birds flourish in wooded areas?

Write to the Point

You don't have to go deep into the woods to see nature. Look out the window. The sky, the trees, and the earth are all part of nature. Write a paragraph describing one thing you see often in nature. Use spelling words from this lesson in your paragraph.

Challenge Use one or more of the Challenge Words in your

Proofreading

Use the marks to show the errors in the paragraph below. Write the four misspelled words correctly in the blanks.

word is misspelled
letter should be capitalized
period is missing

The first bird ate a werm. The second one ate a bug The therd said bugs made his feathers kurl. he saw a berry in the dert and ate it

1. worm
2. third
3. curl
4. dirt

Students apply spelling skills to challenge words and writing activities.

More favorite features for teachers!

The all-new *Steck-Vaughn Spelling* has more of the features teachers love. The holistic approach integrates spelling with reading, writing, and language arts. ***Words at Work* activities reinforce list words in context.** Word meaning, proofreading, and dictionary skills get extra emphasis. **Challenge Words extend each lesson!** It's an ideal environment for expanding vocabulary and improving spelling accuracy.

Consistent instruction, enrichment, maintenance, and review!

Steck-Vaughn Spelling builds skills through a consistent pattern of instruction, enrichment, maintenance, and review. Each new word is analyzed on the basis of structure, sound, and meaning, and then reinforced through reading, writing, proofreading, and dictionary activities. The colorful format, compelling stories, and creative exercises keep student motivation high.

- Word lists built around similar sounds and spelling patterns emphasize spelling rules.

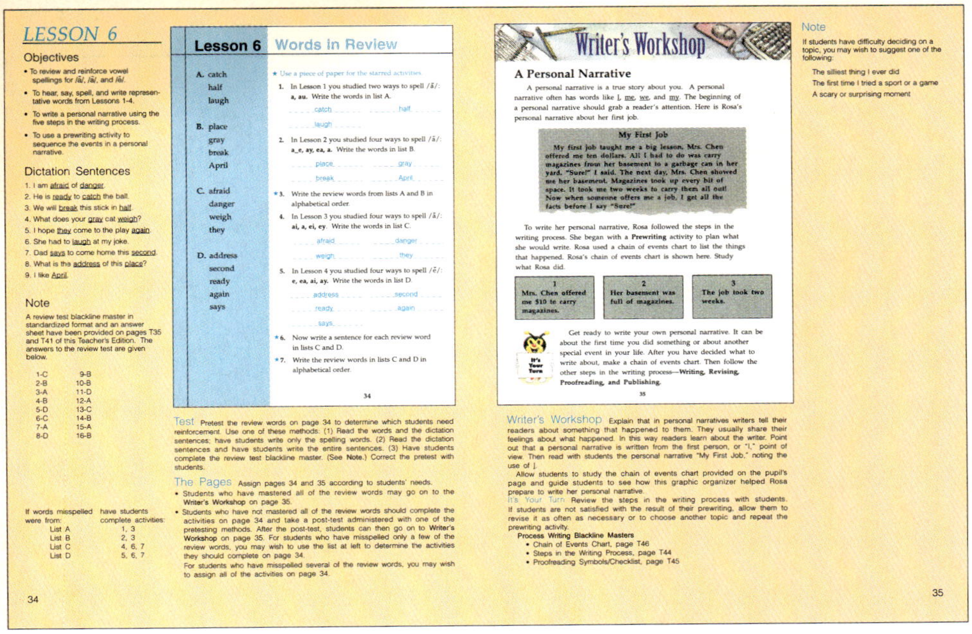

LESSON 6

Objectives

- To review and reinforce vowel spellings for /ă/, /ā/, and /ĕ/.
- To hear, say, spell, and write representative words from Lessons 1-4.
- To write a personal narrative using the five steps in the writing process.
- To use a prewriting activity to sequence the events in a personal narrative.

Dictation Sentences

1. I am afraid of danger.
2. He is ready to catch the ball.
3. We will break this stick in half.
4. What does your gray cat weigh?
5. I hope they come to the play again.
6. She had to laugh at my joke.
7. Dad says to come home this second.
8. What is the address of this place?
9. I like April.

Note

A review test blackline master in standardized format and an answer sheet have been provided on pages T35 and T41 of this Teacher's Edition. The answers to the review test are given below.

1-C	9-B
2-B	10-B
3-A	11-D
4-B	12-A
5-D	13-C
6-C	14-B
7-A	15-A
8-D	16-B

If words misspelled were from:	have students complete activities:
List A	1, 3
List B	2, 3
List C	4, 6, 7
List D	5, 6, 7

34

Lesson 6 Words in Review

A. catch, half, laugh

B. place, gray, break, April

C. afraid, danger, weigh, they

D. address, second, ready, again, says

★ Use a piece of paper for the starred activities.

1. In Lesson 1 you studied two ways to spell /ă/: **a, au.** Write the words in list A.
   catch half
   laugh
2. In Lesson 2 you studied four ways to spell /ā/: **a_e, ay, ea, a.** Write the words in list B.
   place gray
   break April

★3. Write the review words from lists A and B in alphabetical order.

4. In Lesson 3 you studied four ways to spell /ā/: **ai, a, ei, ey.** Write the words in list C.
   afraid danger
   weigh they
5. In Lesson 4 you studied four ways to spell /ĕ/: **e, ea, ai, ay.** Write the words in list D.
   address second
   ready again
   says

★6. Now write a sentence for each review word in lists C and D.

★7. Write the review words in lists C and D in alphabetical order.

34

Test Pretest the review words on page 34 to determine which students need reinforcement. Use one of these methods: (1) Read the words and the dictation sentences; have students write only the spelling words. (2) Read the dictation sentences and have students write the entire sentences. (3) Have students complete the review test blackline master. (See **Note**.) Correct the pretest with students.

The Pages Assign pages 34 and 35 according to students' needs.

- Students who have mastered all of the review words may go on to the **Writer's Workshop** on page 35.
- Students who have not mastered all of the review words should complete the activities on page 34 and take a post-test administered with one of the pretesting methods. After the post-test, students can then go on to **Writer's Workshop** on page 35. For students who have misspelled only a few of the review words, you may wish to use the list at left to determine the activities they should complete on page 34.
  For students who have misspelled several of the review words, you may wish to assign all of the activities on page 34.

Writer's Workshop

A Personal Narrative

A personal narrative is a true story about you. A personal narrative often has words like I, me, we, and my. The beginning of a personal narrative should grab a reader's attention. Here is Rosa's personal narrative about her first job.

My First Job

My first job taught me a big lesson. Mrs. Chen offered me ten dollars. All I had to do was carry magazines from her basement to a garbage can in her yard. "Sure!" I said. The next day, Mrs. Chen showed me her basement. Magazines took up every bit of space. It took me two weeks to carry them all out! Now when someone offers me a job, I get all the facts before I say "Sure!"

To write her personal narrative, Rosa followed the steps in the writing process. She began with a **Prewriting** activity to plan what she would write. Rosa used a chain of events chart to list the things that happened. Rosa's chain of events chart is shown here. Study what Rosa did.

1	2	3
Mrs. Chen offered me $10 to carry magazines.	Her basement was full of magazines.	The job took two weeks.

It's Your Turn

Get ready to write your own personal narrative. It can be about the first time you did something or about another special event in your life. After you have decided what to write about, make a chain of events chart. Then follow the other steps in the writing process—**Writing, Revising, Proofreading, and Publishing.**

35

Writer's Workshop Explain that in personal narratives writers tell their readers about something that happened to them. They usually share their feelings about what happened. In this way readers learn about the writer. Point out that a personal narrative is written from the first person, or "I," point of view. Then read with students the personal narrative "My First Job," noting the use of I.

Allow students to study the chain of events chart provided on the pupil's page and guide students to see how this graphic organizer helped Rosa prepare to write her personal narrative.

It's Your Turn Review the steps in the writing process with students. If students are not satisfied with the result of their prewriting, allow them to revise it as often as necessary or to choose another topic and repeat the prewriting activity.

Process Writing Blackline Masters

- Chain of Events Chart, page T46
- Steps in the Writing Process, page T44
- Proofreading Symbols/Checklist, page T45

Note

If students have difficulty deciding on a topic, you may wish to suggest one of the following:

The silliest thing I ever did
The first time I tried a sport or a game
A scary or surprising moment

35

With each review lesson, students engage in a process writing activity. Student models provide a springboard to prewriting.

- *Checkpoint* activities using the bound-in dictionary encourage students to explore word meanings and origins, and invite interaction in multicultural classrooms.
- Two-page cloze reading selections encourage students to use spelling words in context.
- Language arts activities extend spelling into grammar, usage, mechanics, and dictionary skills.
- Challenge Words introduced in each lesson share the same phonetic sound or structural feature as list words but are more difficult in meaning.
- New *Words at Work* pages incorporate list words into thematically related writing and proofreading activities.
- A review every sixth lesson reinforces lessons and assesses progress.
- A *Writer's Workshop* with each review lesson challenges students to complete an extended writing activity using writing process skills.

Teaching resources at your fingertips!

Resourceful Teacher's Editions include reduced, annotated student pages, detailed lesson plans, word lists, handwriting models, record-keeping charts, a Scope and Sequence, and other new features.

- New strategic assessment section provides tools for error analysis and strategies to help students master frequently misspelled words.
- New blackline masters support family involvement and the writing process.

What you want is what you get!

We asked hundreds of teachers all over the country what they wanted in a spelling series.

Steck-Vaughn Spelling is the answer.

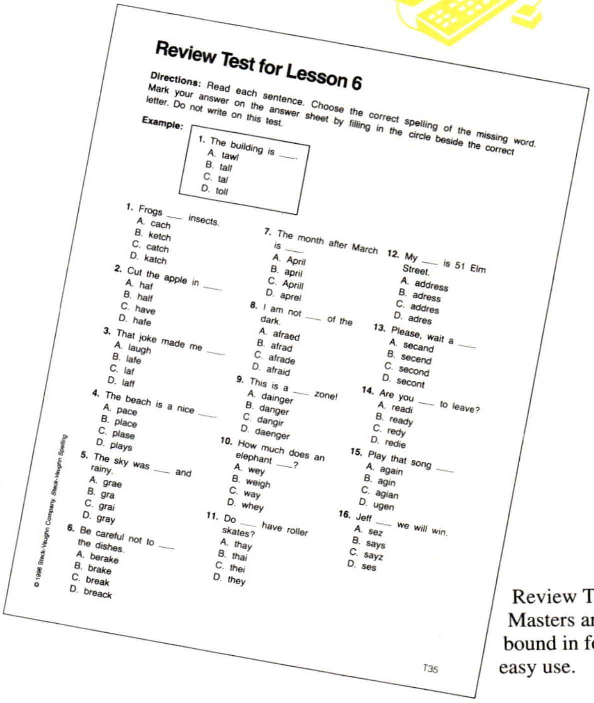

Review Test for Lesson 6

Directions: Read each sentence. Choose the correct spelling of the missing word. Mark your answer on the answer sheet by filling in the circle beside the correct letter. Do not write on this test.

Example:

1. The building is ___.
   A. tawl
   B. tall
   C. tal
   D. toll

1. Frogs ___ insects.
   A. cach
   B. ketch
   C. catch
   D. katch
2. Cut the apple in ___.
   A. haf
   B. half
   C. have
   D. hafe
3. That joke made me ___.
   A. laugh
   B. lafe
   C. laf
   D. laff
4. The beach is a nice ___.
   A. pace
   B. place
   C. plase
   D. plays
5. The sky was ___ and rainy.
   A. grae
   B. gra
   C. grai
   D. gray
6. Be careful not to ___ the dishes.
   A. berake
   B. brake
   C. break
   D. breack
7. The month after March is ___.
   A. April
   B. april
   C. Aprill
   D. aprel
8. I am not ___ of the dark.
   A. afraed
   B. afrad
   C. afrade
   D. afraid
9. This is a ___ zone!
   A. dainger
   B. danger
   C. dangir
   D. daenger
10. How much does an elephant ___?
    A. wey
    B. weigh
    C. way
    D. whey
11. Do ___ have roller skates?
    A. thay
    B. thai
    C. thei
    D. they
12. My ___ is 51 Elm Street.
    A. address
    B. adress
    C. addres
    D. adres
13. Please, wait a ___.
    A. secand
    B. secend
    C. second
    D. secont
14. Are you ___ to leave?
    A. readi
    B. ready
    C. redy
    D. redie
15. Play that song ___.
    A. again
    B. agin
    C. agian
    D. ugen
16. Jeff ___ we will win.
    A. sez
    B. says
    C. sayz
    D. ses

T35

Review Test Masters are bound in for easy use.

SERIES OVERVIEW

Spelling is a skill that many students cannot master without hard work. Hard work alone, however, is usually not enough. Students need a well-constructed plan to help them gain strong spelling skills. *Steck-Vaughn Spelling* was created to offer such guidance. On the following pages you will find a comprehensive and systematic approach that recognizes the importance of spelling as well as its inherent connection to writing. Based on research conducted over several decades, *Steck-Vaughn Spelling* presents an integrated language arts approach to the study of spelling. Six-page lessons afford ample opportunities to use words in a variety of writing and language arts assignments.

The Lesson

Throughout the core of the program, each six-page instructional lesson begins with a word analysis page, which introduces a list of words derived from analysis of research on spelling difficulty and word frequency in students' writing. Sources consulted include *The American Heritage Word Frequency Book*, by Carroll, Davies, and Richman; *Computational Analysis of Present-Day American English*, by Kucera and Francis; *The New Iowa Spelling Scale*, by Green; *The Spelling Encyclopedia of Educational Research*, by Horn; and *Phoneme-Grapheme Correspondences as Clues to Spelling Improvement*, by Hanna and Hanna. Other studies used were those by Dolch, Horn, Dale and O'Rourke, Gates, Loomer, and Rinsland. The words are organized to facilitate analysis of sounds and letters as students study and write each word. The word analysis page is followed by **Checkpoint**, a series of meaning-based prompts in the forms of definitions, context clues, analogies, synonyms, antonyms, and word plays for writing each word a second time. At this point an optional and independent self-assessment tool, the **Checkpoint Study Plan**, is recommended.

The next two pages, the story pages, are devoted to a carefully structured reading passage. In levels 7 and 8, the passage is provided on blackline masters. The passage allows students to work with meaning in the cloze-style format often used in testing. Students must use context clues as they complete the passage using words from the lesson list, which is reprinted adjacent to the passage.

Attention is then given to the related language arts areas of grammar, usage, mechanics, and dictionary skills. Using the spelling words, students engage in a variety of activities that reinforce instruction in these areas.

Each instructional lesson concludes with **Words at Work**, a highly motivating series of activities in which students can extend and apply what they have learned in the lesson. In the **Challenge Yourself** section, students have the opportunity to build their reading vocabulary by studying several Challenge Words. The Challenge Words share the same phonetic or structural elements as the lesson words but range approximately two grade levels above the level of the list words. In **Write to the Point**, students have an opportunity to apply their spelling skills in a brief writing assignment thematically related to the earlier reading passage. Finally, students practice proofreading for spelling, capitalization, punctuation, and similar errors, using sentences or a paragraph that is also thematically tied to the reading passage.

Level 1 follows a special pattern. This level begins with a series of readiness lessons based on a story or poem and designed to help students master basic phoneme-grapheme relationships. The instructional lessons that follow include an activity page with an abbreviated word list, two story pages on which students identify list words and complete sentences about the story, and a final page that integrates spelling with language arts activities.

Maintenance and Review

The phonetic and structural principles that form the focus of the lessons are maintained and reviewed from level to level through increasingly difficult words, sometimes in an affixed form. In addition, beginning in level 2, every sixth lesson reviews representative words from previous lessons. Flexible blackline masters available in the **Activity Masters** booklets provide three options for use: review, maintenance, and enrichment. The **Teacher's Edition** also provides an additional review in standardized test format.

Writing and Enrichment

The **Challenge Yourself** feature of each concluding lesson page allows students to extend the phonetic and structural principles of the lesson to words with similar phonetic or structural elements. By combining the use of the **Spelling Dictionary** and a variety of context-related clues, students unlock the meanings of more challenging words and have the opportunity to use these words in a "quick write" assignment.

Each of the six review lessons provides a more formal writing assignment drawn from a variety of writing types: narratives, letters, description, explanation, evaluation, and persuasion. The type of writing as well as a prewriting activity is modeled for students. Students then follow the steps in the writing process to complete the writing assignment. The fully developed prewriting activities usually include the use of a graphic organizer.

Comprehensive Teacher Aids

Steck-Vaughn Spelling contains a wealth of material with which you can strengthen and enrich your lessons.

Pupil's Edition

- **Checkpoint Study Plan** for self-assessment allows students to study and practice spelling independently.
- **Spelling Dictionary** includes all lesson words and Challenge Words.

Teacher's Edition

- **Reduced annotated student pages** display correct answers and facilitate instruction.
- **Detailed lesson plans** feature a warm-up activity to introduce pages, guidelines for teaching, and suggestions for follow-up activities.
- **Clear objectives** for each part of the lesson state the concepts and skills that students should achieve.
- **Spelling Dictionary** facilitates teaching spelling and dictionary skills.
- **Word lists** include all lesson words and Challenge Words for a grade level as well as the words from the levels immediately above and below.
- **Scope and Sequence** chart displays the instructional content for a grade level, along with the content of the levels immediately above and below it.
- **Class Recordkeeping Chart** provides a convenient resource for tracking students' progress.

Blackline Masters

- **Review Tests** in standardized testing format provide a consumable alternative to the sentence dictation test.
- **Family Involvement Letters** in English and Spanish facilitate communication with students' families and offer specific activities for important at-home support.
- **Steps in the Writing Process** serves as a reference for students while they are working on writing assignments.
- **Proofreading Symbols/Checklist** guides students through the proofreading step of the writing process.
- **Graphic Organizers** help students generate and arrange ideas before they write a first draft.

Blackline Masters Booklets

- **Activity Masters** booklets for levels 2 through 8 include games, puzzles, and similar activities to motivate students to analyze words.
- **Comprehension Masters** booklets for levels 7 and 8 allow students to use the spelling words in a meaningful context.

Evaluation and Assessment

Specific self-assessment opportunities occur twice during each instructional lesson. In **Checkpoint** students check their work and determine which words need study.

The Teacher's Edition provides **Sample Sentences** for pre- and/or post-testing. Embedded in each sentence is a single spelling word. A second set of sentences, labeled **Dictation Sentences**, may incorporate several spelling words into each sentence. Because the vocabulary of these sentences has been controlled, teachers may require students to write the entire sentences. **Dictation Sentences** are also included in the review lessons. As mentioned above, alternative **Review Tests** in standardized format appear as blackline masters in the Teacher's Edition.

ESL and Special Needs

Steck-Vaughn Spelling offers several advantages for students for whom English is a second language and for students with special needs. The **Checkpoint** step in each lesson provides focused attention to word meaning. In addition the reading passage that follows each **Checkpoint** lends itself easily to oral practice with the spelling words in a meaningful and motivating context. In the Teacher's Edition, the **Spelling Strategy** for each instructional lesson discusses possible causes for misspelling and offers one or more activities to address the problem.

SAMPLE TEACHER'S EDITION PAGE

An easy-to-use, helpful teacher's edition accompanies each student edition in *Steck-Vaughn Spelling*. These teacher's guides provide thorough, consistent lesson plans and supplementary activities to meet individual needs. Each teacher's edition contains the following features:

- Sample pages from the student edition with notes explaining the purpose of each page
- A section on testing and classroom management
- A recordkeeping chart for noting students' progress
- A scope and sequence chart listing the instructional content for a particular level, as well as for the levels immediately above and below it
- A word list including all the spelling words at that level, as well as the words in the levels immediately above and below it
- Blackline masters consisting of review tests in standardized testing format, family involvement letters (English and Spanish), and writing process aids (five steps, graphic organizers, and proofreading)

Lesson pages include these features:

1. Each student page is shown in reduced form.
2. Correct responses are printed in blue on the student page.
3. Clear, consistently placed objectives specify exactly what students should accomplish for each lesson.
4. Sample sentences are provided for every lesson.
5. A lesson plan for each page is presented beneath the reduced student page. Lessons are presented in three sections: Preparation, The Page, and Follow-Up. These sections include warm-up exercises to help the teacher introduce the activities, guidelines for page instruction, and suggestions for extension activities. At the conclusion of each lesson, helpful advice is provided for checking student progress and assigning short writing and proofreading activities thematically tied to the story pages, as well as an optional Challenge Word activity.
6. Notes offer additional information and suggestions for enrichment, maintenance, individualized study, and testing.

LESSON 1

Objectives ③

- To hear and say words with /ă/.
- To write words with /ă/ with attention to letter sequence and sound/symbol relationships.
- To write each spelling word at least once.
- To recognize that /ă/ may be spelled a and au.

④

Sample Sentences

1. The boats made rapid progress down the river.
2. There is a traffic jam on Third Street.
3. I'll pick up the nails with a magnet.
4. If we all act together, we can succeed.
5. The magician did many magic tricks.
6. Did you read the last chapter of this book?
7. Then the magician pulled a rabbit out of a hat.
8. Dave ate a snack of fruit and milk.
9. Many raincoats are made of plastic.
10. This cup has a crack in it.
11. I like to watch that educational program on television.
12. The earth is the third planet from the sun.
13. The lamp fell with a crash.
14. Ron cooked the dessert, and Manuel made the salad.
15. Cars are made in that factory.
16. What kind of bread do you use to make a sandwich?
17. I ate half the cherry pie.
18. Our cow had a calf last week.
19. My uncle and my aunt are coming to the party.
20. Her funny jokes made us all collapse with laughter.

Note ⑥

- The sample sentences may be used for pretesting.
- The first page of every lesson highlights the letter order of each spelling word and the special sound/symbol relationships. Words in this lesson are grouped according to spellings of /ă/:
  a
  au

Lesson 1 Words with /ă/

Listen for /ă/ in each word. ①

rapid
traffic
magnet
act
magic
chapter
rabbit
snack
plastic
crack
program
planet
crash
salad
factory
sandwich
half
calf

aunt
laughter

②

1. Write the two words that begin with a vowel.
   act aunt
2. Write the three words that begin with the letter p.
   plastic program
   planet
3. Which word begins and ends like market?
   magnet
4. Which word begins and ends like funny? factory
5. Write one word that begins with the letters ch and one that ends with ch.
   chapter sandwich
6. Which word ends with the letters sh? crash
7. Write the two words that end with the letter d.
   rapid salad
8. Which five words end with /k/? Circle the letters that spell /k/. traffic magic
   snack plastic
   crack
9. Which two words have /f/ in the middle? Circle the letters that spell /f/.
   traffic laughter
10. In which word is /b/ spelled bb? rabbit
11. Write the two words in which you see the letter l but don't hear /l/. half calf
12. Which two words have the same spelling of /ă/ as laugh?
    aunt laughter
13. Write the word in which you hear /j/ but don't see the letter j. magic

---

⑤

Preparation Have students read aloud the title of the lesson on page 4. Remind them that symbols inside the brackets stand for speech sounds, not letters. Write /ă/ on the board. Tell students this is the vowel sound they hear in pat. Read each spelling word aloud. Have students repeat and then spell each word aloud.

Note these special sound/symbol relationships: sandwich contains a d, which most people do not pronounce; aunt is pronounced /ănt/ or /änt/ but is always spelled aunt. Note that in the first 18 words, /ă/ is spelled a, and in the last two, au. (See **Note**.)

Read the sample sentences. Have students point to each spelling word as you read the sentence for it.

The Page Guide students through the exercises on page 4. Have volunteers write the answers on the board and have students correct their own work. For exercise 8, note that /k/ means the sound and not the letter. Remind students that /k/ may be spelled k, ck, or c.

Follow-Up Have students head columns on a sheet of paper with the following letters: a, c, f, h, l, m, p, r, s, t. Then have them write the spelling word or words that begin with each letter. Have volunteers write the answers on the board and have students correct their own work.

SAMPLE STUDENT LESSON

First Page

The first page of every lesson has these features:

1. A title introduces the lesson and identifies the sound to be studied.
2. Instructions direct the student to say each spelling word and listen for the vowel sound.
3. Twenty list words are in each lesson, grouped accorcing to the different spellings of the sound presented.
4. Exercises require students to examine the sound/symbol relationships in the list words.

Lesson 7 Words with /ē/ (1)

Listen for /ē/ in each word. (2)

(3)

delivery
hobby
angry
tardy
fancy
merry
pretty
penalty
ugly
liberty
empty
shady
busy

complete
theme
athlete
trapeze
evening
compete

believe

(4)

1. Write the two words that begin with /k/.
2. Which three words begin with the letter t? Circle the word that has one syllable.
3. Which word begins with the letters sh?
4. Which word begins and ends like factory?
5. Which four words begin and end with a vowel?
6. Which word begins with a vowel and ends with a consonant?
7. Which word has the same spelling of /ē/ as relieve?
8. Which two words contain the /z/ sound?
9. Write the two words that have three syllables.
10. Write the word that has four syllables.
11. Write the three words in which a double consonant letter spells one sound.
    bb ______ rr ______
    tt ______
12. Which two words contain the letters th?

36

Word-Analysis Page

The first page of every lesson introduces the sound to be studied and words containing that sound. The words are grouped according to different spellings of the sound. Periodically, the lesson teaches such skills as adding suffixes, compound words, and special vocabulary.

Checkpoint (1)

Write a spelling word for each clue.
Then use the Checkpoint Study Plan on page 224.

1. If he is mad, he is ___.
2. If your day is filled with activity, you are ___.
3. Discover is to discovery as deliver is to ___.
4. After sundown, it is ___. (2)
5. The opposite of full is ___.
6. Jolly, happy, and ___ go together.
7. A subject or topic may be called a ___.
8. Another word for late is ___.
9. The opposite of plain is ___.
10. Under the trees we found a ___ spot.
11. If I break a rule, I must pay a ___.
12. Collecting stamps is a ___.
13. She is ___ enough to win a beauty contest.
14. Something with no part left out is ___.
15. An acrobat might do stunts on a ___.
16. The opposite of beautiful is ___.
17. If you are free, you have ___.
18. To pretend is to make ___.
19. To take part in a contest is to ___.

(3)

20. The ancient Greeks were enthusiastic sports fans. They held many contests in running, boxing, and wrestling. The winner of these contests was given a prize. The prize was called the *athlon* in Greek. The contest for the prize was called the *athlos*. The name for a person who competed for the prize comes from these words. We use the word today to describe someone who participates in sports. Can you guess it? ___

(4)

37

SAMPLE STUDENT LESSON

Second Page

The Checkpoint page has these features:

(1) Instructions direct students to choose and write list words in response to clues and then to use the Checkpoint Study Plan on the last page of the book.

(2) Nineteen puzzle-like clues incorporate definitions, context clues, synonyms, antonyms, analogies, word plays, and riddles. Students write list words in response to these clues.

(3) Each Checkpoint page relates the etymology of a "mystery" list word.

(4) The etymology clue is illustrated.

Checkpoint Page

The second page of each lesson, the Checkpoint page, has two important purposes. First, it shifts the focus of the lesson from word structure to word meaning and usage. Students write each spelling word in response to puzzle-like clues and an etymology clue. This page is also used with the Checkpoint Study Plan on the last page of each student edition for self-testing and independent study.

SAMPLE STUDENT LESSON

Third and Fourth Pages

Story pages of each lesson have these features:

1. Exercise directions are short and easy to understand.
2. The story title is in large, appealing type.
3. The story uses all or most of the week's spelling words. Any remaining list words are used to complete sentences that relate to the story.
4. Interesting, attractive art accompanies each story to enhance students' interest and to aid comprehension.
5. The list words are provided in cursive writing large enough for students to use as handwriting models.

Use each list word once. (1)

(2)

The Ambassadors

Samantha waited for the ambassadors from the planet Ixod to arrive. It was a hot day, so she waited on the __________ side of the landing pad. Samantha had made sure she was on time to greet the visitors. The (3) Ixodians did not like anyone to be __________.

What a sight the Ixodians were as they left their ship. They were tall and rainbow-colored. Each Ixodian uniform came __________ with a red helmet. Samantha thought the ambassadors looked very __________.

"Welcome," Samantha said. "I have planned lots of fun for you. I hope you will have a very __________ time. I thought you would like to rest while you wait for the __________ of your things. Then this __________ we will go to a magic show."

Xio, the Ixodian leader said, "Samantha, please feel at __________ to show us what you think we will like." However, the Ixodians were very quiet during the show. They never seemed surprised by the magic.

"Circus clowns" was the __________ for the next day's entertainment. Samantha took her guests to a store that sold clown puppets. There were puppets with sad faces and puppets with mean, __________ faces. There were clown dolls with colorful, __________ costumes. The Ixodians seemed to have seen the puppets before. Later, at the circus,

(4)

Story Pages

On the third and fourth pages of each lesson, students choose and write spelling words to complete a continuous-text selection. In addition to providing another opportunity for students to practice writing and spelling list words, these pages offer a change of pace and a chance for students to improve their understanding of word usage and meaning. Stories on these pages were checked for readability. The Spache, Fry, Dale-Chall, and Degrees of Reading Power formulas were applied by an independent laboratory.

the ambassadors didn't bat an eyelash at the funny clown on the tightrope. Even the man on the flying ______________ didn't excite the Ixodians.

Samantha did not want to be upset or ______________. She decided to ask Xio what the problem was. She found him watching TV.

"Xio! What are you doing?" she asked.

"I'm watching a football game," he explained. "I have always been an ______________, and football has long been a ______________ of mine. I love it so much I don't even wear my future-predicting helmet while I watch the game."

Samantha could not ______________ her ears. "Do you mean your helmet tells you everything that is going to happen before it happens? That's why your people seem so lifeless and ______________. Now I know how to make your people enjoy their visit more."

Xio listened. Then Xio and Samantha gathered the Ixodians together.

"Today," Samantha said, "you are going to learn to play football. But first, please remove your red helmets and put on these football helmets instead."

The Ixodians did as asked. They learned how to make a goal and how not to cause a ______________. They were kept ______________ cheering each other on.

When it was time to go, Xio said to Samantha, "Someday Ixod may ______________ against Earth in an intergalactic football game. But for now, you have taught my people that life is much more interesting when you don't always know what lies ahead."

39

delivery
hobby
angry
tardy
fancy
merry
pretty
penalty
ugly
liberty
empty
shady
busy
complete
theme (5)
athlete
trapeze
evening
compete
believe

Enrichment

A note in the teacher's edition suggests which activity master to assign for additional practice and enrichment.

Maintenance and Review

A note in the teacher's edition suggests which activity master to assign for review and maintenance of the previous week's lesson. In addition, another review and maintenance activity is included in the teacher's edition.

SAMPLE STUDENT LESSON

Fifth Page

The fifth page of every lesson has these features:

1. A title identifies the language arts skill.
2. Text explains the language arts skill. Students are always given explicit skill instruction before completing the exercise.
3. Exercise directions are set off by large, colored stars. Each star indicates a change of activity.
4. Exercises integrate spelling words with a language arts activity.

Parts of a Dictionary Entry ①

The words that are listed in alphabetical order under the guide words in a dictionary are called entry words. They are printed in dark type with a dot between the syllables. A dictionary entry includes the entry word, the sound spelling, the part of speech, the definition or meaning of the word, and anything else important about the word. ②

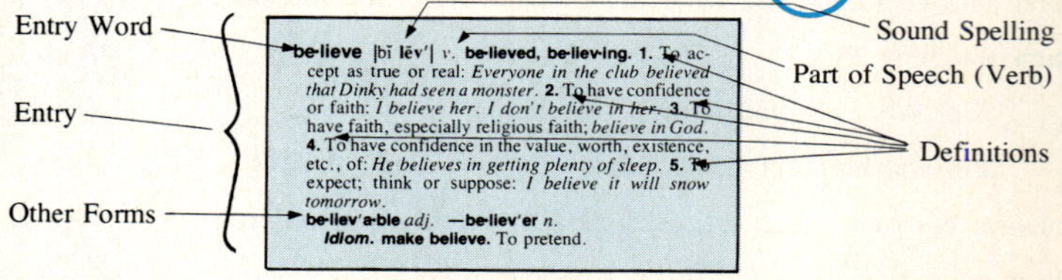

Many words have more than one meaning. To decide how a word is used in a sentence, a dictionary and context clues must be used.

★ Read the above entry and answer these questions. ③

1. What is the entry word in the above entry? ______

2. How many meanings does the dictionary show for this entry word? ______

★ Write the number of the definition used in each of these sentences.

3. Our teacher believes in homework. ______

4. I believe everything Grandma tells me. ______

5. Ted believes the rain will stop before the game. ______

★ Write the following words in alphabetical order. Then look them up in the Spelling Dictionary. Write the number of meanings each word has.

shady **angry** **trapeze** **complete** **fancy** ④

Word	Number of Meanings
6. ______	______
7. ______	______
8. ______	______
9. ______	______
10. ______	______

40

Language Arts Page

The fifth page of each lesson focuses on such language arts skills as capitalization, punctuation, grammar, usage, and dictionary study.

WORDS AT WORK

Challenge Yourself ①

canopy **recede** **utility** **siege**

Write what you think each underlined Challenge Word means. Check your Spelling Dictionary to see if you were right. Then write sentences showing that you understand the meaning of each Challenge Word.

1. Marta's bed has a white lace canopy over it.
2. If we have a drought, the water in the river will recede.
3. We get utility bills for water, telephone, and electricity.
4. The enemy held the town under siege, so no one was allowed to leave.

Write to the Point ②

Imagine that you are directing a movie about aliens from outer space who have landed on Earth. Write a paragraph describing these beings. Create a name for these unusual beings and their home planet. What do the aliens look like? How do they move? How do they communicate? Use spelling words from this lesson in your description.

Challenge Use one or more of the Challenge Words in your description.

Proofreading ③

Use the proofreading marks to show the errors in the paragraph below. Write the five misspelled words correctly in the blanks.

⬭	word is misspelled
? ^	question mark is missing
^	word is missing

Can you believe it Friday evning I was in the library, buzy reading about life other planets. Suddenly, to my compleet surprise, a Martian sat down in the emty seat beside me. He pretty uggly but seemed quite nice.

1. ______________________
2. ______________________
3. ______________________
4. ______________________
5. ______________________

41

Sixth Page

The Words at Work page of every lesson includes these features:

① Four Challenge Words with the same sound or structural element as the list words are provided in an optional Challenge Yourself feature.

② A writing assignment provides students with an opportunity to use the list words and the Challenge Words in a brief writing activity on a topic thematically tied to the selection on the story pages.

③ The concluding exercise allows students to practice proofreading for spelling and appropriate language mechanics skills in paragraphs also thematically tied to the selection on the story pages.

Words at Work Page

Following a teacher-directed post-test, the Words at Work page of each lesson provides students with an opportunity to extend and apply the skills presented in the lesson.

An optional Challenge Yourself activity presents four new words with the same sound or structural element as the list words. Students use context and the Spelling Dictionary to unlock the meanings of these new words. In Write to the Point, students have an opportunity to use the list words and the Challenge Yourself words in a brief, informal writing assignment. This activity may be assigned to the entire class. All students also may be assigned the proofreading exercise that concludes this page.

SAMPLE REVIEW LESSON

First Page

Each review page includes these features:

1. Lesson number and title are included.
2. Twenty list words from the previous five lessons are grouped according to sounds.
3. Exercises direct students to write list words in response to sound-symbol clues.
4. Exercises direct students to write list words in response to language arts activities.
5. Starred exercises indicate that students will use their own paper.

Lesson 12 Words in Review ①

A. piano
complete
speech ②
believe
empty
evening
reason
liberty
breathe
freeze

B. damage
mystery
except
insist
business
discuss
message
different
guilty
review

★ You will need a piece of paper for these review activities.

1. In Lessons 7 and 8 you studied seven different ways to spell /ē/: **y, e_e, ie, ee, ea, ea_e, i.** Write the words in list A.

④ ★ **2.** Look up each review word from list A in the Spelling Dictionary. Write the first definition of each word.

3. In Lessons 9 and 10 you studied six different ways to spell /ĭ/: **i, e, ui, a, y, u.** Write the words in list B. ③

⑤ ★ **4.** Use each review word from list B in a sentence.

★ **5.** Write all 20 review words in alphabetical order.

Your teacher may give you a test. Answer these questions when you have finished.

6. Did you spell all the words correctly? ____________

7. Did you leave out a letter? ____________

8. Did you write the wrong letter? ____________

9. Did you miss the spelling of a vowel sound? ____________

66

Review and Writer's Workshop Pages

Every sixth lesson in the student edition is a two-page review lesson. The first review page presents representative words from the previous lessons. The words were chosen because of their frequency of use and spelling difficulty. The second page provides a carefully structured writing assignment keyed to the types of writing commonly studied at this level. The type of writing is clearly identified and explained. A model further assists students in drafting a response to the assignment.

A Narrative

①

A narrative is a story. Every good story has a beginning, a middle, and an end. In the beginning the main character and the problem that the main character must solve are introduced. In the middle of the story, the main character tries to solve the problem. The end of the story tells how the problem is solved. Notice how Diego introduces the main character and the problem in the beginning of his story "The Hardest Race."

②

The Hardest Race

Luke knew he should be training for the big race next week, but he didn't feel like it. Usually he loved to race. He spent all his free time getting into shape. This time it was different, though, because Luke would be racing against his best friend, Carlos. Luke knew how much Carlos wanted to win. After all, Luke had helped Carlos practice for a whole year. Winning against Carlos wouldn't be any fun, but losing might feel even worse.

To write his story, Diego followed the steps in the writing process. First he decided what kind of story he wanted to write and who the main character would be. Then he used a story map as a **Prewriting** activity. The map helped Diego plan the three main ingredients of the plot of his story—the beginning, the middle, and the end. The map also helped him put the events of his story in an order that made sense. Diego's story map is shown here. Study what Diego did.

③

Beginning

Luke must race against his best friend, Carlos.

Middle

Luke wins the race.

End

Carlos is a good sport.

Get ready to write your own story. You can write a realistic story like Diego's, a mystery, a fairy tale, or any kind of story you wish. After you have decided what to write about, make a story map. Then follow the other steps in the writing process—**Writing, Revising, Proofreading,** and **Publishing.**

67

SAMPLE REVIEW LESSON

Second Page

The second page of every review lesson provides a carefully structured writing assignment with these features:

① The type of writing is identified and explained at the beginning of the lesson.

② A model student response to the writing assignment is provided.

③ A prewriting activity, usually incorporating a graphic organizer, is explained and modeled. In most cases a blackline master in the teacher's edition is provided for duplication and distribution to students.

Writer's Workshop Page

These pages may be used in a variety of ways. Following a teacher-directed pretest, students can be assigned work according to spelling needs. Poor spellers may be assigned all or part of the first page before attempting the Writer's Workshop on the second page, while good spellers may go directly to the Writer's Workshop. A student who was absent for a weekly test may complete the first-page section for that week before progressing to the Writer's Workshop.

A post-test may be administered with the same testing method as the pretest or with the blackline master in standardized testing format.

DICTIONARY

Each student edition of *Steck-Vaughn Spelling* contains a Spelling Dictionary at the back of the text. It contains all the words taught in each level.

At level 1, a picture dictionary begins the developmental dictionary strand. An exemplifying sentence using the previously studied characters and words accompanies each boldface list word. When read in sequence, the sentences for each entry letter form a little story. The story is illustrated with colorful pictures.

The level 2 dictionary is an illustrated, beginning dictionary. Each boldface entry word has a pronunciation, one or more numbered definitions, and a simple, exemplifying sentence. Affixed forms are also given. Guide words and full-color illustrations are on each page.

The dictionary entries are more full in levels 3 through 6 and list pronunciations, parts of speech, common meanings, and when pertinent, affixed endings and irregular forms in a two-column format.

The entries in levels 7 and 8 are taken directly from *The American Heritage Student Dictionary* and contain more extensive definitions. All pronunciations and abbreviations in *Steck-Vaughn Spelling* are from *The American Heritage Dictionary*. A page from the Spelling Dictionary in this level is shown.

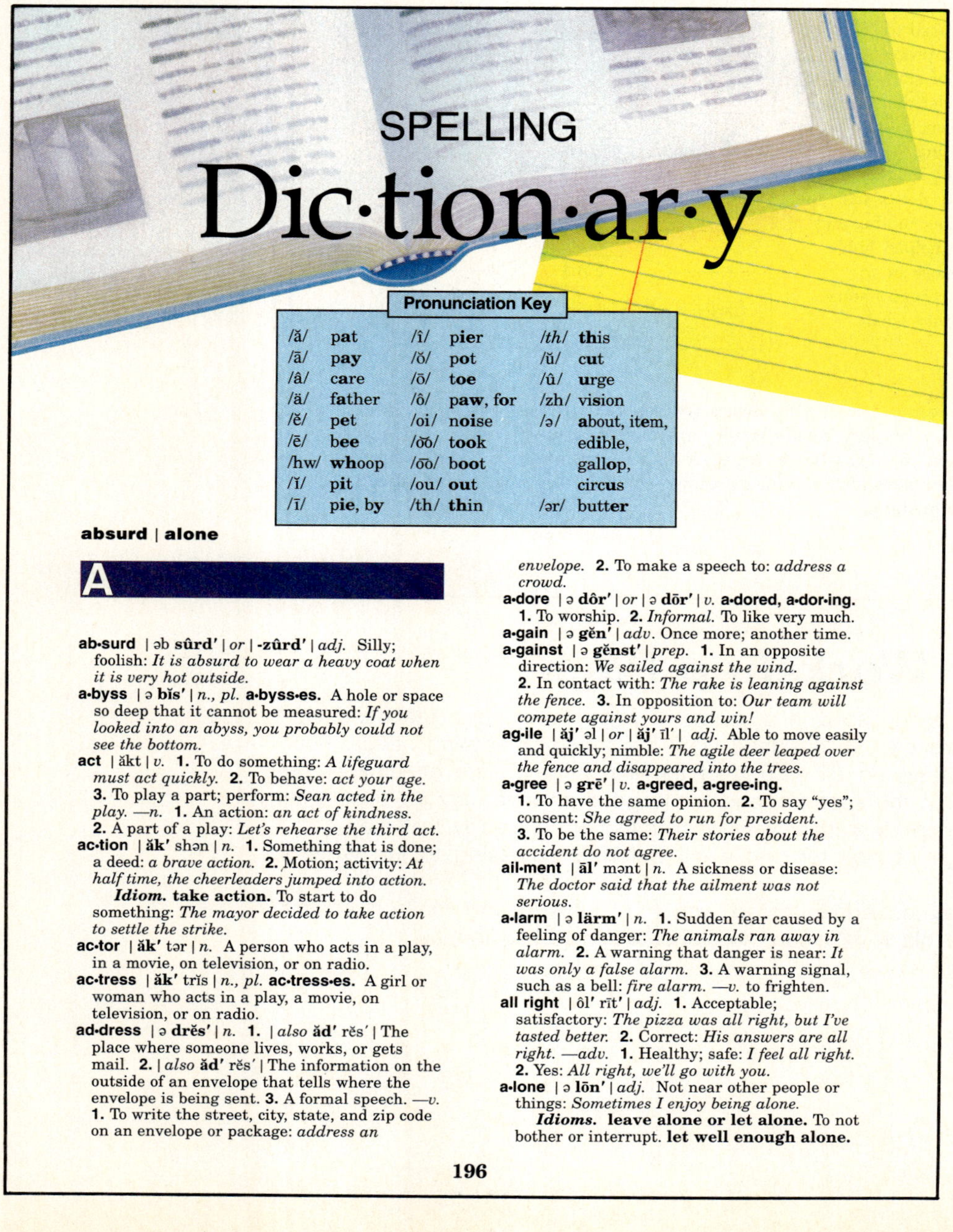

SPELLING

Dic·tion·ar·y

Pronunciation Key

/ă/	**pat**	/î/	**pier**	/th/	**this**
/ā/	**pay**	/ŏ/	**pot**	/ŭ/	**cut**
/â/	**care**	/ō/	**toe**	/û/	**urge**
/ä/	**father**	/ô/	**paw, for**	/zh/	**vision**
/ĕ/	**pet**	/oi/	**noise**	/ə/	**about, item,**
/ē/	**bee**	/ŏŏ/	**took**		**edible,**
/hw/	**whoop**	/ōō/	**boot**		**gallop,**
/ĭ/	**pit**	/ou/	**out**		**circus**
/ī/	**pie, by**	/th/	**thin**	/ər/	**butter**

absurd | alone

A

ab·surd | əb **sûrd'** | *or* | **-zûrd'** | *adj.* Silly; foolish: *It is absurd to wear a heavy coat when it is very hot outside.*

a·byss | ə **bĭs'** | *n., pl.* **a·byss·es.** A hole or space so deep that it cannot be measured: *If you looked into an abyss, you probably could not see the bottom.*

act | ăkt | *v.* **1.** To do something: *A lifeguard must act quickly.* **2.** To behave: *act your age.* **3.** To play a part; perform: *Sean acted in the play.* —*n.* **1.** An action: *an act of kindness.* **2.** A part of a play: *Let's rehearse the third act.*

ac·tion | **ăk'** shən | *n.* **1.** Something that is done; a deed: *a brave action.* **2.** Motion; activity: *At half time, the cheerleaders jumped into action.* ***Idiom.* take action.** To start to do something: *The mayor decided to take action to settle the strike.*

ac·tor | **ăk'** tər | *n.* A person who acts in a play, in a movie, on television, or on radio.

ac·tress | **ăk'** trĭs | *n., pl.* **ac·tress·es.** A girl or woman who acts in a play, a movie, on television, or on radio.

ad·dress | ə **drĕs'** | *n.* **1.** | *also* **ăd'** rĕs′ | The place where someone lives, works, or gets mail. **2.** | *also* **ăd'** rĕs′ | The information on the outside of an envelope that tells where the envelope is being sent. **3.** A formal speech. —*v.* **1.** To write the street, city, state, and zip code on an envelope or package: *address an envelope.* **2.** To make a speech to: *address a crowd.*

a·dore | ə **dôr'** | *or* | ə **dōr'** | *v.* **a·dored, a·dor·ing.** **1.** To worship. **2.** *Informal.* To like very much.

a·gain | ə **gĕn'** | *adv.* Once more; another time.

a·gainst | ə **gĕnst'** | *prep.* **1.** In an opposite direction: *We sailed against the wind.* **2.** In contact with: *The rake is leaning against the fence.* **3.** In opposition to: *Our team will compete against yours and win!*

ag·ile | **ăj'** əl | *or* | **ăj'** īl′ | *adj.* Able to move easily and quickly; nimble: *The agile deer leaped over the fence and disappeared into the trees.*

a·gree | ə **grē'** | *v.* **a·greed, a·gree·ing.** **1.** To have the same opinion. **2.** To say "yes"; consent: *She agreed to run for president.* **3.** To be the same: *Their stories about the accident do not agree.*

ail·ment | **āl'** mənt | *n.* A sickness or disease: *The doctor said that the ailment was not serious.*

a·larm | ə **lärm'** | *n.* **1.** Sudden fear caused by a feeling of danger: *The animals ran away in alarm.* **2.** A warning that danger is near: *It was only a false alarm.* **3.** A warning signal, such as a bell: *fire alarm.* —*v.* to frighten.

all right | ôl′ rīt' | *adj.* **1.** Acceptable; satisfactory: *The pizza was all right, but I've tasted better.* **2.** Correct: *His answers are all right.* —*adv.* **1.** Healthy; safe: *I feel all right.* **2.** Yes: *All right, we'll go with you.*

a·lone | ə **lōn'** | *adj.* Not near other people or things: *Sometimes I enjoy being alone.* ***Idioms.* leave alone or let alone.** To not bother or interrupt. **let well enough alone.**

196

INDIVIDUALIZED STUDY

Steck-Vaughn Spelling encourages individualized study through the use of a special feature called the Checkpoint Study Plan. Students should use the plan in the following way:

- The second page of each lesson is called the Checkpoint page. Students write their spelling words in response to puzzle-like clues that involve definitions, synonyms, antonyms, analogies, context clues, and word plays. A final item asks students to write a list word after reading about its etymology or similar interesting information.
- Every Checkpoint page refers students to the Checkpoint Study Plan when they have correctly answered all the questions. The Checkpoint Study Plan is given on the last page in each student edition.
- Students number their papers according to the number of questions on the Checkpoint lesson page.
- Students read the clues on the Checkpoint lesson page, spell the answers aloud, and write the answers.
- Students then refer to their first set of answers.
- Students check their second answers against their first answers, circle the number beside any words they misspelled on their second set of answers, and write the correct spelling next to any misspelled words.
- Students then fold their papers so that only the numbers show. For each number that is circled, students go through the study process again.

The first few times that students are referred to the Checkpoint Study Plan, the teacher shows them how to use this study aid. Students need to realize that their answers to the Checkpoint lesson page must be correct before they can use the Checkpoint Study Plan. After the first week or two, this should become a self-directed activity.

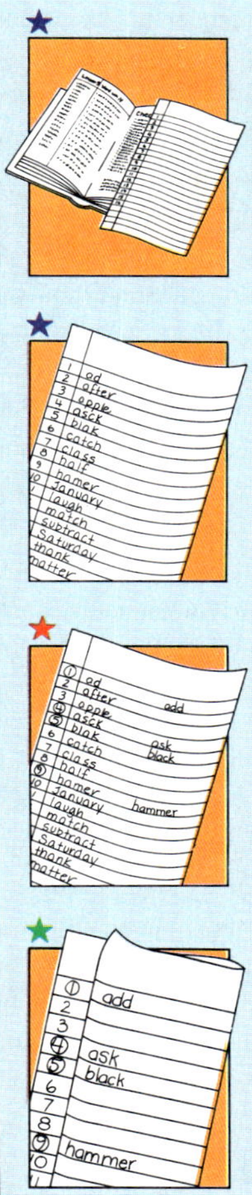

THE CHECKPOINT Study Plan

When you have finished a Checkpoint page and you know that you have the correct answers, use the Checkpoint page and this Study Plan to test yourself.

★ Cover your answers to the Checkpoint page with a piece of paper. Number the paper 1 through 16. For each spelling clue, do steps 1, 2, and 3.

1 Read the clue and say the answer.

2 Spell the answer aloud.

3 Write the answer

★ Uncover your first answers and do steps 4, 5, and 6.

4 Check your answers.

5 Circle the number of each misspelled word.

6 Write the correct spelling next to each incorrect word.

★ To study, cover your answers again, and fold the paper so that only the numbers show. For each circled number, repeat steps 1 through 6.

224

TESTING, CLASSROOM MANAGEMENT, AND RECORDKEEPING

Achieving spelling competency is a highly individual process. A responsible spelling program must ensure frequent and consistent checkpoints so that individual students can ascertain their own strengths and weaknesses on a regular basis. In levels 3 through 8 of *Steck-Vaughn Spelling*, each lesson provides options for pretesting, self-assessment, and post-testing. The six review lessons in each text at levels 3 through 8 also provide for maintenance, diagnostic evaluation, and reinforcement. (No formal testing is suggested in level 1; testing in review lessons is optional at level 2.)

TESTING

Steck-Vaughn Spelling incorporates test-study-test methods. Several options provide students and teachers with a means of measuring achievement and ascertaining which words to emphasize in their study and teaching.

Pretesting and Self-Assessment

Before assigning the first page of a lesson, teachers may administer an optional pretest using the sample sentences given in the teacher's edition for each lesson. The test may be scored by students so that they are aware of words to study. In addition, every Checkpoint page in levels 2 through 8 provides a self-assessment tool. By using the Checkpoint Study Plan, students find out which list words they need to study further. After the first few weeks of teacher direction, the Checkpoint Study Plan becomes a self-directed activity.

Post-testing

After the optional lesson pretest and the Checkpoint self-evaluation in levels 2 through 8, students work with other activities and gain practice in writing the spelling words. After completing the language arts page, students take a teacher-directed post-test. Then they proceed to the Words at Work page, which provides opportunities for students to extend and apply what they have learned.

Maintenance and Review

In levels 2 through 8, a two-page review lesson occurs after every fifth lesson. The teacher tests students on spelling mastery and then assigns students reinforcement or enrichment activities or a combination of these activities, according to individual progress. Students who missed words complete the activities that correspond to the words missed on the first review page. The format of the first review page allows teachers to have students work individually, completing only those activities that pertain to their individual needs. These students are then tested again to ensure that they have grasped the various spellings. When students demonstrate mastery, they can proceed to the second page of the review lesson. This page requires students to apply their spelling skills in a formal writing assignment using a process writing approach.

Midyear and End-of-Year Test

Midyear tests may be administered using list words from review lessons 6, 12, and 18. For end-of-year testing, words from all review lessons (6, 12, 18, 24, 30, and 36) may be used.

CLASSROOM MANAGEMENT

Steck-Vaughn Spelling is a highly flexible program, especially since pretesting and self-assessment assignments allow for a high degree of individualization. The following suggestions are offered for pacing:

Level 1

The first level is divided into two parts—readiness lessons and spelling lessons. The readiness lessons cover consonant and vowel recognition and discrimination. The spelling lessons consist of 20 four-page lessons. The order in which teachers use the consonant and vowel lessons is optional and may be determined by the order in which the letters are taught in the basal reading program. Pages are perforated so that lessons may be taught in a preferred order. Each vowel or consonant lesson is self-contained and not dependent on any specific lesson order. Students usually complete the consonant and vowel lessons by January or February.

The second part of level 1 contains formal spelling lessons. Most teachers find that one lesson a week is comfortable pacing.

Levels 2 Through 8

Since most schools operate on a thirty-six-week academic year, *Steck-Vaughn Spelling* bases its instructional format on thirty-six lessons. Each lesson can be covered in one week, using three, four, or five classroom periods per week. For example:

Levels 2 Through 8 Lesson Pacing

<table>
<tr><th></th><th>Five-Day Plan</th><th>Four-Day Plan</th><th>Three-Day Plan</th></tr>
<tr><td>Word Analysis page</td><td>One day</td><td rowspan="2">One day</td><td rowspan="2">One day</td></tr>
<tr><td>Checkpoint page</td><td>One day</td></tr>
<tr><td>Story pages (or story masters)</td><td>One day</td><td>One day</td><td rowspan="2">One day</td></tr>
<tr><td>Language arts page</td><td>One day</td><td>One day</td></tr>
<tr><td>Test and Words at Work page</td><td>One day</td><td>One day</td><td>One day</td></tr>
<tr><td>Review pages</td><td colspan="3">Ongoing after initial individual assignments</td></tr>
</table>

RECORDKEEPING

A blackline master of a Class Recordkeeping Chart is provided on the following page. The chart has space for students' names and for recording the pretest and final post-test score for each lesson and review. Space is also provided for a midyear and a final score for teachers who wish to administer such tests.

CLASS RECORDKEEPING CHART

Student Name	Lesson Number																																					
	1	2	3	4	5	6	7	8	9	10	11	12	13	14	15	16	17	18		19	20	21	22	23	24	25	26	27	28	29	30	31	32	33	34	35	36	

SCOPE AND SEQUENCE

The skills identified in the Scope and Sequence may be found in the lessons indicated for each grade level.

Vowel Spellings	Level 4	Level 5	Level 6
/ă/			
a	1,6	1,6,34	1,6
au	1,6	1,6	1,6
/â/			
a	28,30	27,30	
ai	28,30		
e	28,30		
ei	28,30		
ey	28,30		
/ā/			
a		2,6,34	2,6
a-e	2,6	2,6	2,6
ai	2,6	2,6,35	2,6
ay		2,6	2,6
ea	2,6	2,6	
ei	2,6	2,6	2,6
ey			2,6
/ä/			
a	28,30	27,30	27,30
ea	28,30		
ua			27,30
/ĕ/			
ai	3,6		3,6
e	3,6	3,4,6	3,6
ea	3,6	3,6	3,6
ie	3,6	3,6	
ue	3,6		3,6
/ē/			
e	7,12		7,12
ea	4,6	8,12	7,12,35
ea-e		8,12	
ee	4,6	8,12	7
e-e	7,12	7,12	7
ei			7,12
eo	7,12		
i	7,12	8,12	7,12
ie		7,12	7,12

Vowel Spellings (cont.)	Level 4	Level 5	Level 6
i-e	7,12		7
y	7,12	7,12,29	7,12,20,21,23,31
/ĭ/			
a	8,12	10,12	13,14,18
e		9,12	13,18
i	8,12	9,10,12	13,18
u		10,12	
ui	8,12	9,12	
y	8,12	10,12	13,18
/ī/			
i	9,10,12	13,18,35	15,18
ie	9,12		
i-e	10,12	13,18	15,18
ui-e		13,18	
uy	10,12		
y	9,12		15,18
y-e			15,18
/î/			
ea	31,36		
e	31,36		
ee	31,36		
/ŏ/			
a	13,18	14,18	19,24
o	13,18	14,18	19,24
ow			19,24
/ō/			
eau			20,24
ew		15,18	
o	14,18	16,18,34	20,24
oa	14,18	16,18	20,24
oe	14,18		
o-e	15,18	15,18,35	20,24
ou	15,18	16,18	20,24
ow	15,18	15,18	20,24
owe		15,18	

Vowel Spellings (cont.)	Level 4	Level 5	Level 6
/ô/			
a	26,27,30	20,24,25,30	21,24
au	26,30	20,24	21,24
aw	27,30	20,24	21,24
o	26,27,30	20,24,25,30	21,24
oa		25,30	21,24
ou	26,30	20,24,25,30	21,24
/oi/			
oi	25,30	22,24	
oy	25,30	22,24	28
/ou/			
ou	22,24		25,30
ow	22,24		25,30
/o͝o/			
o	20,24		
oo	20,24		
ou	20,24		
u	20,24		
/o͞o/			
ew	21,24	35	9
o	21,24	21,24	
oe		21,24	9
o-e		21,24	9
oo	21,24	21,24,35	9,12
ou	21,24		9,12
u	21,24	21,24,29	9,32
ue		21,24	9,12
u-e			9
ui	21,24	21,24	9,12
/ŭ/			
o	19,24	19,24	8,12
oe	16,18		
oo	19,24	19,24	8,12
ou	16,18	19,24	8,12
u	16,18	19,24	8,12
/û/			
e	31,36	26,30	26,30
ea	31,36	26,30	
i	31,36	26,30	26,30
o	31,36		26,30
u	31,36	26,30	26,30
/yo͞o/			
eau	21,24		9,12
u			9,12
u-e			9

Vowel Spellings (cont.)	Level 4	Level 5	Level 6
/ə/			
a	32,36	31,32,36	11,12,31,33, 36
ai			4,6
e	32,36	31,32,36	4,6,11,12,31, 33,36
i	32,36	31,36	31,36
o	32,36	31,36	4,6,31,36
ou			33,36
u		31,36	31,33,36
/ər/			
ar		33,36	32,36
er		33,36	32,36
or		33,36	32,36

Consonant Spellings

/b/			
bb	13	1	14
/ch/			
ch	1		1,14,25,26
t		22	2,11,17,26,27, 29,31
tch	3		
ti		3,29	
/d/			
d	2,10,20	2,9	14
dd	8	3	
/f/			
f		4,15,19	
ff		1	8,32,34
gh	16	1,9,19	1,8
ph		4,15,17	1,20,29,31
/g/			
g			1,14,34,35
gg			8,14
gue		19	3
/h/			
h		14	
/hw/			
wh	28,32	8,13	21
/j/			
d		34	35
dg	8,16	4,9,19	
g	8,28,31	1,4,10,22,27, 31,32	3,11,13,14,17, 29,31,33
j	16	22	31,33

Consonant Spellings (cont.)	Level 4	Level 5	Level 6
/k/			
c	1,7,8,13,14, 21,25,31,35	1,2,4,7,10,15, 17,20,21,25, 27,28,31,33, 34	3,5,13,14,16, 17,19,21,25, 31,34
cc		21	14
ch	3,19,27	16,33	3,15,21
ck	1,8,32	1,3,4,17,23, 32	
k	1,2,3	10,17,21,28	17
/ks/			
cc			1,7,23
x		9,10	35
/kw/			
qu	8,27	3,9,13,14,25, 31	13,16,19
/l/			
l			27
ll		4,20,21,34	8,13,16,22,23, 29
/m/			
mn	26		21
/n/			
kn	4,13,15,16,21	13,15	19
n	2		5
nn		22	
/ng/			
ng	7		29
/p/			
p		2,8	
pp			15,16,22,34
/r/			
rr		25,32	26,29
wr	8,10,26	4,9,32	22
/s/			
c	3,4,7,10,25, 31	3,4,9,13,16, 21,22,26,29, 31,33	1,2,5,7,8, 17,31,32
s	21	3,4,9,13,21, 26,29,31	1,7,14,23,29, 31,32
sc			11,15
ss	1,3	3,19	8,13,14,22
z		8	
zz	7	8	
/sh/			
c	14,32	31	
ci		4,17	
s	20	33	
sh		29	

Consonant Spellings (cont.)	Level 4	Level 5	Level 6
ss		23	
t		23	
/sk/			
sc		16,25	27
/skw/			
squ		27	
/t/			
ed	20		
t	21		
tt			34,35
z	7	8	
/th/			
th			22,23,29
th			7,23,32
/w/			
o	19		
w	13,32		
/y/			
i			4
/z/			
s	3,4,10,14,16, 20,21,25,26, 28	4,7,8,9,10, 13,15,21,22, 27,32	7,8,13,15,16, 19,23,25,26, 31,32
ss			13,23
x		32	
z	4,10,15	7,8,15	7,15
zz		32	
/zh/			
s		3,17	3,16

Vocabulary

Comparisons and Analogies	1,2,3,4,7,8,9, 10,11,13,14, 15,16,17,19, 20,21,22,23, 25,26,27,28, 29,31,32,33, 35	1,2,3,4,5,7,8, 9,11,13,14,15, 17,19,20,21, 23,25,26,31, 32,34,35	1,2,3,7,8,9, 10,11,13,14, 15,17,20,25, 26,27,31,32, 33,35
Antonyms	1,2,3,4,7,8,9, 10,11,13,14, 15,16,17,19, 20,21,22,23, 25,26,27,28, 29,31,32,33	1,2,3,4,7,8, 9,13,14,15, 16,19,20,21, 22,23,25,26, 27,31,32,33, 35	1,2,3,4,7,8, 9,11,13,14, 15,16,20,21, 23,25,26,27, 28,31,32,33, 34,35
Compound Words	33	28	22
Etymologies and Word Facts	1,2,3,4,5,7, 8,9,10,11,13, 14,15,16,17, 19,20,21,22, 23,25,26,27, 28,29,31,32, 33,34,35	1,2,3,4,5,7, 8,9,10,11,13, 14,15,16,19, 20,21,22,23, 25,26,27,28, 29,31,32,33, 34,35	1,2,3,4,5,7,8, 9,10,11,13,14, 15,16,17,19, 20,21,22,23, 25,26,27,28, 29,31,32,33, 34,35

Vocabulary (cont.)

	Level 4	Level 5	Level 6
Homographs and Homophones	21	19,35	25
Rhymes and Word Plays	1,2,3,4,5,7,9, 11,13,14,15, 16,20,21,22, 26,27,28,31, 33		1,3,4,8,9,11, 22,35
Context	1,3,4,5,7,8, 10,11,13,14, 15,16,17,19, 20,21,22,23, 25,26,27,28, 29,31,32,33, 34,35	1,2,3,4,5,7, 8,9,10,11,13, 14,15,16,17, 19,20,21,22, 23,25,26,27, 28,29,31,32, 33,34,35	1,2,3,4,5,7,8, 9,10,11,13, 14,15,16,17, 19,20,21,22, 23,25,26,27, 28,29,31,32, 33,34,35
Special Vocabularies	5,34,35	17,23,29	5,16,17,29
Synonyms	1,2,3,4,7,8,9, 10,11,13,14, 15,16,19,20, 21,22,23,25, 26,28,29,31, 32,33,35	1,2,4,7,8,9, 10,11,13,14, 15,16,17,19, 20,22,25,26, 29,31,32,33, 34,35	1,2,3,4,7,8, 9,11,13,14,15, 16,17,19,20, 21,22,23,25, 26,27,28,31, 32,33,34
Suffixes	23	33,34,36	28,30,34,35,36
Definitions	1,2,3,4,5,7,8, 9,10,13,14,15, 16,17,19,20, 21,22,23,25, 26,27,28,29, 32,33,35	1,2,3,4,5,7,8, 9,10,11,13,14, 15,16,17,19, 20,21,22,23, 25,26,27,28, 29,31,32,33, 34,35	1,2,3,4,7,8,9, 10,11,13,14, 15,16,17,19, 20,21,22,23, 25,26,27,28, 29,31,32,33, 34,35

Dictionary Skills

	Level 4	Level 5	Level 6
Accent Marks	19,32	22	7
Comparing Dictionaries		29	35
Entry Words	8,9,25	7,29	20,26,34
Guide Words	3	3	1
Multiple Meanings	9	7	7,11,16,21,27
Mutiple Spellings		25	19
Phonetic Spelling (Sound spelling)	16,19,28,32	21,22	7,9
Syllables	8	22	14

Proofreading

	Level 4	Level 5	Level 6
Proofreading	1,2,3,4,5,7,8, 9,10,11,13,14, 15,16,17,19, 20,21,22,23, 25,26,27,28, 29,31,32,33, 34,35	1,2,3,4,5,7,8, 9,10,11,13,14, 15,16,17,19, 20,21,22,23, 25,26,27,28, 29,31,32,33, 34,35	1,2,3,4,5,7,8, 9,10,11,13,14, 15,16,17,19, 20,21,22,23, 25,26,27,28, 29,31,32,33, 34,35

Mechanics

	Level 4	Level 5	Level 6
Abbreviations	34		22
Alphabetizing	1,13,16,31	1,3,7,9,29	1,26
Apostrophes	29	20	31
Capitals	5,14,20,26,33	2,5,16,17,27, 31	2,5,16,21,27, 29
Colons	35	34	3,13
Commas	7,27	10,23	3,23,27
Contractions	17	20	31
Exclamation Points	2	2	2
Periods	2	2	2
Question Marks	2	2	2
Quotation Marks	15,22	13	17
Titles	5		10

Grammar and Usage

	Level 4	Level 5	Level 6
Adjectives		26	28
Adverbs		32	33
Compound Sentences			23
Idioms	28	33	34
Inflected Forms (adding ed, ing, er) (plurals)	11,23,29,31	11	10
Nouns	10	4	4,5
Parts of Speech	13,25	9	
Past Tense	23,31		
Predicates	23	15	32
Recognition of Verbs	4,23	8	15
Subject of a Sentence	11	14	8

Process Writing

	Level 4	Level 5	Level 6
Personal Narrative	6	6	6
Narrative	12	12	12
Friendly Letter	18		
Business Letter		18	
Description	24,36	24	18
Explanation	30	30	24
Evaluation			30
Persuasive Letter		36	36

WORD LISTS

The following pages list the words for this grade level, as well as the words from the levels immediately above and below. The number after each word indicates the lesson in which the word appears. Words in bold type are the words from the Challenge Yourself activities on the Words at Work pages—they are not list words.

If you wish to keep a record of each student's mastery of words, reproduce a copy of the level word list for each student and cross off the words as the student learns them.

Level 4

A

above (19)
absence (1)
accuse (21)
acknowledge (8)
acquaint (2)
acquire (10)
acrobat (1)
address (32)
adorn (27)
afraid (2)
afternoon (33)
again (3)
against (3)
air (28)
airborne (28)
alarm (28)
almost (14)
alone (15)
already (26)
among (19)
angry (7)
animal (32)
another (19)
answer (1)
anything (33)
apart (28)
applaud (26)
appoint (25)
appropriate (14)
apricot (13)
April (5)
aren't (17)
ask (1)
asked (23)
attorney (7)
auction (26)
audio (26)
August (5)
aunt (1)
author (26)
automobile (32)
autumn (26)
Ave. (34)
avoid (25)
awake (2)
awesome (27)
awhile (10)
axle (1)

B

babies (11)
balloon (21)
banana (1)
banish (8)
barrier (7)
basketball (33)
beach (4)
beacon (4)
beautiful (21)
because (26)
become (19)
before (27)
began (1)
begin (8)
beginning (23)
behind (10)
below (15)
beside (10)
betray (2)
between (4)
beyond (13)
binoculars (32)
birth (31)
birthday (33)
blind (10)
blizzard (32)
blood (19)
blouse (22)
Blvd. (34)
body (7)
bookstore (20)
boost (21)
bottom (13)
bought (26)
bouquet (15)
boxes (11)
branch (1)
branches (11)
bread (3)
break (2)
breakfast (3)
bridge (8)
bright (9)
broke (15)
brook (20)
brother (19)
brothers (11)
brought (26)
brush (16)
brushes (11)
building (8)
burglar (32)
buses (11)
bush (20)
busy (7)
button (16)
buy (10)

C

C (34)
c. (34)
calendar (32)
Canada (32)
careful (28)
carrying (23)
cartoon (21)
caught (26)
cause (26)
caused (23)
changed (23)
chapter (32)
chase (2)
cheer (31)
cheeseburger (33)
chicken (8)
child (10)
child's (29)
children (29)
children's (29)
choice (25)
choose (21)
chorus (27)
chose (15)
circle (31)
circus (31)
cities (11)
city (7)
classes (11)
cleanse (3)
clear (31)
climb (10)
close (15)
closing (23)
clothes (14)
cloud (22)
cloud's (29)
cm (34)
coach (14)
coast (14)
coffee (26)
coin (25)
collage (28)
collide (10)
comb (14)
comet (35)
conceal (4)
constellation (35)
construct (16)
contest (13)
contribute (21)
convert (31)
cooked (20)
copied (23)
copy (7)
cotton (13)
cougar (21)
could (20)
couldn't (17)
counselor (22)
countdown (33)
counter (22)
country (16)
countryside (16)
couple (16)
coupon (21)
courtesy (31)
cover (19)
crack (1)
crawl (27)
cried (23)
crossroads (33)
crowd (22)
crowded (22)
crown (22)
curve (31)
customary (16)

D

daughter (26)
dawn (27)
deafen (3)
dear (31)
December (5)
defiant (10)
deliver (8)
deny (9)
desert (3)
destroy (25)
dewdrops (33)
didn't (17)
die (9)
different (8)
dignify (9)
dinosaur (32)
dirty (31)
discover (19)
dishes (11)
dishwasher (33)
dismal (8)
dispose (15)
doctor (13)
does (16)
doesn't (17)
dollar (13)
don't (17)
done (19)
double (16)
downtown (33)
Dr. (5)
draperies (11)
dried (23)
drowsy (22)
drugstore (33)
dry (9)
during (20)
dwindle (32)

E

early (31)
earn (31)
Earth (35)
easy (7)
echo (3)
edge (3)
eight (2)
elbow (15)
employ (25)
employer (25)
enclosure (14)
encounter (22)
energy (3)
enjoy (25)
enough (16)
erupt (16)
evening (7)
ever (3)
every (7)
everybody (33)
everywhere (33)
exotic (13)
explode (15)
explore (27)
eyesight (9)

F

fair (28)
families (11)
family (7)
fare (28)
farmland (33)
fatigue (7)
February (5)
feet (29)
fence (3)
festivities (11)
fight (9)
flight (9)
foe (14)
forever (33)
forgot (13)
fortified (23)
foxes (11)
freeze (4)
Friday (5)
friend (3)
front (19)
froze (15)
fruit (21)
ft (34)
fudge (16)
full (20)

G

g (34)
gal. (34)
galaxy (35)
geese (29)
germ (31)
giant (10)
glad (1)
gloves (11)
goes (14)
gone (26)
good-by (20)
goose (21)
Gov. (5)
grass (1)
gravity (35)
grew (21)
group (21)
growl (22)
guess (3)
guitar (8)
gym (8)
gypsy (8)

H

hadn't (17)
half (1)
happen (1)
haven't (17)
health (3)
hear (31)
heard (31)
heart (28)
heavy (3)
here (31)
high (9)
highway (9)
hikes (11)
hoard (27)
hobby (13)
hollow (15)
hoping (23)
hospital (13)
host (14)
hotel (14)
hours (22)
hover (19)
hundred (16)
hungry (7)
hunt (16)
hustled (23)

I

I'm (17)
important (27)
importing (23)
in (34)
inch (8)
inches (11)
inside (33)

Level 5

journalism (17)
judge (19)
juice (21)
July (5)
June (5)
jungle (19)
Jupiter (5)

K

kangaroo (21)
kitchen (10)
knife (13)
known (15)
knuckle (19)

L

landslide (1)
laughter (1)
lawnmower (20)
learning (26)
length (4)
liberty (7)
library (13)
light-year (29)
loathe (16)
lobster (14)
location (34)
loose (21)
lose (21)
loyal (22)
loyalty (22)
lunar (29)
lyrics (10)

M

magic (1)
magnet (1)
male (2)
marbles (27)
March (5)
margin (27)
maroon (21)
master (33)
masthead (17)
May (5)
meager (8)
measure (3)
meddle (3)
member (33)
Memorial Day (5)
memory (31)
mention (34)
merry (7)
message (10)
metal (4)
meteors (29)
metric (4)
microscope (15)
mild (13)
moisture (22)
Monday (5)
monkey (19)
mosquito (31)
motion (29)
muscular (33)
musical (32)
musician (17)
mutual (21)
mystery (10)

N

nation (34)
natural (32)
nautical (20)
needle (8)
neighbor (2)
neighbors (11)
network (17)
newspaper (17)
newsstand (17)
nickel (32)
nightmare (28)
ninth (13)
noise (22)
nomad (16)
North Pole (5)
notebook (28)
notice (16)
November (5)

O

oak (16)
object (14)
ocean (31)
October (5)
often (20)
Olympics (23)
omen (31)
onion (19)
orbit (29)
orchard (25)
owe (15)
oyster (22)

P

package (10)
paid (2)
parade (2)
parties (11)
peace (8)
pearl (26)
pecan (27)
pedestal (32)
penalties (11)
penalty (7)
pendulum (4)
pension (34)
perfect (26)
perform (25)
perfume (26)
perhaps (31)
periodical (17)
permit (26)
personal (26)
petal (4)
piano (8)
pickles (32)
picnic (10)
pinnacle (9)
pirate (13)
pitch (10)
pivot (32)
pizza (8)
plain (35)
plane (35)
planet (1)
plastic (1)
pleasure (3)
pledge (4)
poem (16)
polar (33)
polite (13)
pollution (34)
population (34)
pore (25)
precarious (27)
prepare (27)
presume (21)
pretty (7)
prime time (17)
prior (13)
problem (14)
producer (17)
professional (23)
program (1)
promise (14)
proof (21)
prove (21)
pumpkin (19)
purpose (26)
puzzle (32)

Q

qualify (31)
quantity (14)
quarrel (25)
questions (3)
quickly (9)
quit (9)
quite (13)
quizzical (9)

R

rabbit (1)
raccoon (21)
raise (2)
random (31)
rapid (1)
rather (33)
raw (20)
razor (33)
reason (8)
recede (7)
recorder (17)
recycle (13)
referee (23)
relax (9)
remain (2)
remember (4)
remind (13)
resourceful (25)
review (9)
revise (13)
revolution (29)
reward (25)
riddle (9)
right (35)
rightful (13)
road (35)
roar (25)
roast (16)
rode (35)
rookie (23)
roommate (28)
rooster (21)
rotation (29)
rough (19)
royal (22)
rummage (10)

S

safari (8)
sailboat (28)
salad (1)
sample (32)
sandwich (1)
sandwiches (11)
satellite (29)
Saturday (5)
sawdust (28)
scale (2)
scarves (11)
science (13)
scold (16)
score (25)
scoreboard (23)
season (31)
section (34)
selection (34)
self (3)
selfish (4)
sentence (3)
September (5)
service (26)
sew (15)
shady (7)
shampoo (21)
share (27)
sheet (8)
shock (14)
shoe (21)
shore (25)
shuttle (29)
siege (7)
signal (32)
silver (33)
similar (33)
simple (32)
since (9)
sixth (10)
skating (23)
ski (8)
skiing (23)
skill (10)
skin diving (23)
skirt (26)
skis (11)
smolder (16)
snack (1)
snake (2)
soccer (23)
solar (29)
solid (14)
solitude (14)
spaniel (32)
sparse (27)
special (4)
speech (8)
speeches (11)
square (27)
St. (5)
stare (27)
starve (27)
station (34)
steep (8)
stomachache (19)
stories (11)
stowaway (15)
straw (20)
strawberry (28)
studio (17)
sugar (33)
suitcase (28)
Sunday (5)
suppose (15)
surprise (31)
surveyor (2)
swallow (15)
sweater (3)
sweatshirt (28)
swimming (23)
symptom (10)
system (10)

T

tablespoon (28)
tape deck (17)
tardy (7)
taught (20)
teacher (33)
telephone (15)
telescope (29)
television (17)
tennis (23)
their (35)
theme (7)
there (35)
they're (35)
third (26)
thirteen (26)
though (16)
thought (20)
thread (3)
threw (35)
throat (16)
through (35)
throw (15)
thunderstorm (28)
Thursday (5)
timid (10)
to (35)
toaster (33)
token (16)
tomorrow (15)
tongue (19)
too (35)
tore (25)
tornado (16)
touch (19)
toward (25)
track (23)
traffic (1)
transportation (34)
trapeze (7)
treasure (3)
tremble (32)
tried (13)
trouble (32)
truth (21)
Tuesday (5)
tumble (32)
tutor (33)
tweed (8)
two (35)
tyrant (31)

U

ugly (7)
ultimate (31)
umpire (23)
universe (29)
uproar (28)
upset (28)
utility (7)

V

vacation (34)
vegetable (4)
vegetables (11)
velocity (29)
village (10)
virtual (26)
vocal (32)
voice (22)
void (22)
volleyball (23)
vote (15)
voyage (22)

W

waist (35)
wallow (15)
wander (14)
warn (25)
waste (35)
watch (14)
weak (8)
wealth (3)
weather (3)
Wednesday (5)
weekend (28)
weigh (2)
weight (2)
weightless (2)
wheat (8)
whether (33)
whistle (32)
whole (35)
whom (21)
whose (21)
wishes (11)
wives (11)
wonderful (19)
wore (25)
wreck (4)
wrinkle (32)

wrist (9)
write (35)
wrong (20)

Y

yolk (16)

Z

zone (15)

Level 6

A

absent (34)
accent (1)
accept (23)
acceptance (34)
accurate (14)
adapted (17)
advantage (14)
advertise (15)
Africa (5)
against (3)
agent (2)
agriculture (35)
albatross (33)
all ready (23)
all right (22)
allergic (26)
allot (19)
allowance (25)
alphabet (1)
Alps (5)
already (23)
although (20)
Amazon River (5)
among (8)
amount (31)
ancient (33)
Andes (5)
anonymous (33)
answer (32)
Antarctica (5)
anthropologist (17)
apartment (27)
Appalachian Mountains (5)
apparent (34)
appear (16)
appendage (14)
appetite (15)
applesauce (22)
apply (15)
approach (20)
arch (27)
archaeologist (17)
argument (27)
armor (27)
artifacts (17)
ascertain (2)
Asia (5)
assign (15)
assignment (34)
assistant (34)
astonish (19)
Atlantic Ocean (5)
atlas (31)
atmosphere (29)
attendance (34)
attention (35)
attract (1)
audible (21)
audience (21)
auditorium (21)
Australia (5)
autumn (21)
available (28)
average (14)
awful (21)

B

background (16)
backpack (22)
bakeries (10)
balance (1)
balcony (31)
balk (21)
balloon (31)
barber (27)
barometer (29)
barter (27)
bathrobe (22)
beautiful (9)
behavior (17)
Bering Sea (5)
beverage (14)
bicycle (11)
blouse (25)
blown (20)
bother (32)
bountiful (25)
boutique (9)
brand-new (22)
brawn (21)
breakable (28)
breakfast (3)
breath (23)
breathe (23)
breathing (7)
breeze (7)
brief (7)
brilliant (13)
bureau (20)
business (13)

C

cabbage (14)
cabinet (31)
calculator (32)
calendar (32)
calorie (7)
camera (1)
canoe (9)
canoes (10)
captain (4)
careen (7)
Caribbean Sea (5)
caricature (35)
carnival (11)
carpenter (27)
cartilage (14)
carve (27)
castle (11)
catalog (1)
ceiling (7)
celebrate (31)
cellar (32)
Celsius (29)
Central America (5)
ceremonies (17)
chalk (21)
cheeseburger (32)
chessboard (22)
chocolate (14)
choir (15)
choose (23)
chorus (21)
chose (23)
circus (31)
cirrus (29)
climate (17)
clockwise (16)
closet (19)
clothes (23)
cloths (23)
cloudy (25)
clue (9)
coarse (21)
collection (35)
colonize (17)
comfortable (28)
comic (19)
command (1)
commercial (33)
compass (8)
complain (2)
complete (7)
computer (32)
concentrate (16)
congratulate (2)
conscious (33)
constant (34)
constantly (16)
consumer (32)
continue (16)
conversation (35)
convertible (28)
correction (35)
couch (25)
countries (10)
coupon (9)
courage (14)
courageous (33)
course (21)
cousin (8)
coward (25)
crawl (21)
cross-country (22)
crowded (25)
crucial (33)
cruel (9)
crumb (8)
crystallized (13)
culture (17)
cumulus (29)
curious (33)
curly (26)
current (26)
curtains (26)
custom (4)
customer (32)

D

dairy (23)
dangerous (33)
darken (4)
daughter (21)
definite (13)
degrees (7)
delicious (33)
demolish (19)
density (23)
deny (15)
departure (27)
describe (15)
desert (23)
design (15)
desperate (14)
dessert (23)
destiny (23)
detective (13)
diary (23)
difference (34)
different (34)
difficult (8)
diligent (33)
direction (35)
director (32)
disagreeable (28)
disconnect (4)
discover (32)
discuss (8)
disdain (2)
disobey (2)
distance (34)
distant (34)
distort (16)
disturb (26)
divisible (28)
double (8)
doubt (25)
drowsiness (25)

E

echo (3)
echoes (10)
ecology (19)
education (35)
efficient (33)
effort (32)
elation (35)
election (35)
electric (13)
eligible (28)
emergency (26)
enamel (11)
energy (3)
engine (31)
enjoyable (28)
enough (8)
entertain (2)
entrance (34)
envelope (3)
environment (17)
equal (16)
equality (19)
equipment (13)
escape (2)
Europe (5)
evaporation (29)
evidence (17)
example (11)
excavation (17)
excellent (3)
except (23)
exhilarating (31)
experience (34)
experiment (13)
explain (2)
extremely (7)
eyebrow (25)

F

factories (10)
Fahrenheit (29)
farewell (22)
fasten (4)
favorite (32)
feature (35)
ferocity (19)
fever (32)
fisheries (10)
fixture (35)
flabbergasted (1)
flammable (28)
flashlight (22)
flexible (28)
flood (8)
flurries (29)
focus (31)
forecast (29)
foreground (16)
forfeit (13)
forgotten (19)
formal (21)
fortunate (14)
fortune (31)
forward (21)
fraction (35)
fracture (35)
fragile (17)
frostbite (29)
furniture (26)
fusion (4)
future (35)

G

Ganges River (5)
gasoline (7)
general (11)
generous (33)
genius (33)
geometric (16)
gloat (20)
glue (9)
good night (22)
government (8)
governor (32)
graph (1)
gravity (1)
groan (20)
growled (25)
grown (20)
grumble (11)
guard (27)
guessed (3)
guest (3)
guitar (27)
gymnastic (13)

H

halves (10)
hamburger (32)
handbook (22)
hangar (32)
harbor (27)
harmonica (27)
harmony (27)
headache (3)
heroes (10)
hesitate (2)
Himalayas (5)
history (31)
holidays (10)
honesty (19)
honor (19)
honorable (28)
hospital (11)
howl (25)
human (9)
humidity (29)
humor (9)
husband (31)
hypnotize (15)

I

identify (17)
ignorance (34)
illusion (16)
image (14)
imagine (1)
immaculate (1)
immediate (14)
immortality (13)
imperative (3)
implication (2)
imply (15)
impossible (19)
improvement (9)
impulsive (8)
inaccurate (31)
inadequate (14)
incident (34)
incorporate (2)
incorrect (16)
increase (7)
indelibly (3)
Indian Ocean (5)
indicator (32)
industries (10)
inevitable (28)
influence (17)
information (35)
injury (31)
innocence (34)
insects (3)

ANNOTATED STUDENT PAGES for Lessons 1-36

LESSON 1

Objectives

- To hear and say words with /ă/.
- To write words with /ă/ with attention to letter sequence and sound/symbol relationships.
- To write each spelling word at least once.
- To recognize that /ă/ may be spelled a and au.

Sample Sentences

1. The boats made rapid progress down the river.
2. There is a traffic jam on Third Street.
3. I'll pick up the nails with a magnet.
4. If we all act together, we can succeed.
5. The magician did many magic tricks.
6. Did you read the last chapter of this book?
7. Then the magician pulled a rabbit out of a hat.
8. Dave ate a snack of fruit and milk.
9. Many raincoats are made of plastic.
10. This cup has a crack in it.
11. I like to watch that educational program on television.
12. The earth is the third planet from the sun.
13. The lamp fell with a crash.
14. Ron cooked the dessert, and Manuel made the salad.
15. Cars are made in that factory.
16. What kind of bread do you use to make a sandwich?
17. I ate half the cherry pie.
18. Our cow had a calf last week.
19. My uncle and my aunt are coming to the party.
20. Her funny jokes made us all collapse with laughter.

Note

○ The sample sentences may be used for pretesting.

○ The first page of every lesson highlights the letter order of each spelling word and the special sound/symbol relationships. Words in this lesson are grouped according to spellings of /ă/:
a
au

Lesson 1 Words with /ă/

Listen for /ă/ in each word.

rapid
traffic
magnet
act
magic
chapter
rabbit
snack
plastic
crack
program
planet
crash
salad
factory
sandwich
half
calf

aunt
laughter

1. Write the two words that begin with a vowel. act aunt
2. Write the three words that begin with the letter p. plastic program planet
3. Which word begins and ends like market? magnet
4. Which word begins and ends like funny? factory
5. Write one word that begins with the letters ch and one that ends with ch. chapter sandwich
6. Which word ends with the letters sh? crash
7. Write the two words that end with the letter d. rapid salad
8. Which five words end with /k/? Circle the letters that spell /k/. traffic magic snack plastic crack
9. Which two words have /f/ in the middle? Circle the letters that spell /f/. traffic laughter
10. In which word is /b/ spelled bb? rabbit
11. Write the two words in which you see the letter l but don't hear /l/. half calf
12. Which two words have the same spelling of /ă/ as laugh? aunt laughter
13. Write the word in which you hear /j/ but don't see the letter j. magic

4

Preparation Have students read aloud the title of the lesson on page 4. Remind them that symbols inside the brackets stand for speech sounds, not letters. Write /ă/ on the board. Tell students this is the vowel sound they hear in pat. Read each spelling word aloud. Have students repeat and then spell each word aloud.

Note these special sound/symbol relationships: sandwich contains a d, which most people do not pronounce; aunt is pronounced /ănt/ or /änt/ but is always spelled aunt. Note that in the first 18 words, /ă/ is spelled a, and in the last two, au. (See **Note**.)

Read the sample sentences. Have students point to each spelling word as you read the sentence for it.

The Page Guide students through the exercises on page 4. Have volunteers write the answers on the board and have students correct their own work. For exercise 8, note that /k/ means the sound and not the letter. Remind students that /k/ may be spelled k, ck, or c.

Follow-Up Have students head columns on a sheet of paper with the following letters: a, c, f, h, l, m, p, r, s, t. Then have them write the spelling word or words that begin with each letter. Have volunteers write the answers on the board and have students correct their own work.

Checkpoint

Write a spelling word for each clue.
Then use the Checkpoint Study Plan on page 224.

1. Moving cars and trucks are ___.
2. One of two equal parts is a ___.
3. Another word for hare is ___.
4. The opposite of crying is ___.
5. Every play has a last ___.
6. A narrow opening or break is a ___.
7. In a house is a room, in a book is a ___.
8. A list of events is a ___.
9. Elroy is his uncle, Gertrude is his ___.
10. Workers make things in a ___.
11. A small meal is a ___.
12. The magician's trick seemed to be ___.
13. The opposite of slow is ___.
14. A mixture of uncooked vegetables is a ___.
15. A car accident may be called a ___.
16. A horse has a colt, a cow has a ___.
17. Many toys are made of ___.
18. The earth is a ___.
19. Something that attracts metal is a ___.

traffic
half
rabbit
laughter
act
crack
chapter
program
aunt
factory
snack
magic
rapid
salad
crash
calf
plastic
planet
magnet

20. This mystery word comes from the title of an English earl of the 18th century. The Earl was fond of games, especially cards. He loved games so much that he didn't allow meals to interrupt them. While he played, he had his servants bring him a slice of meat between two pieces of bread. This food soon became popular. Today we call two slices of bread with some filling by the title of this earl. His title was the Fourth Earl of ___.

Sandwich

5

Objectives

- To write spelling words in response to clues: definitions, synonyms, antonyms, analogies, and context.
- To develop the critical thinking skills of making inferences, comparing, and contrasting.
- To understand that some words in the English language have developed from people's names.

Spelling Strategy

If students have difficulty remembering the spelling of unaccented vowel sounds in words such as planet, salad, and rapid, it may be helpful to have them write each word several times, exaggerating the size of the problem letter.

Note

The **Checkpoint** page serves a dual purpose. In addition to the first set of objectives, it also provides a test/study strategy: the **Checkpoint Study Plan**. This study plan provides a self-test and a method of ongoing independent study for the students. Directions for the **Checkpoint Study Plan** are on page 224 of each student book.

Before students use the **Checkpoint Study Plan**, help them check their pages for correct responses to clues and for spelling accuracy.

Preparation The clues on this page are like crossword puzzle clues. Explain to students that the response to each clue is a spelling word. Use the following examples to illustrate the types of clues used:

Definition	A list of events is a (*program*).
Synonym	Another word for hare is (*rabbit*).
Antonym	The opposite of crying is (*laughter*).
Analogy	In a house is a room, in a book is a (*chapter*).
Context	Many toys are made of (*plastic*).

The final clue explains how sandwich came into the English language.

The Page Have students complete page 5 using the words on page 4. When students have finished, have them read each clue and spell the answer aloud. Check each response twice: once for the correct answer and a second time for spelling accuracy.

Follow-Up Guide pupils in using the **Checkpoint Study Plan** on page 224 to take a self-test. Then have them use the plan for independent study. (See **Note**.)

Objectives

- To write words with /ă/ in continuous text.
- To write each spelling word once.
- To integrate reading with spelling.

Note

- Point out the use of the word <u>program</u> in the story to mean a show on television. Ask students for other meanings of <u>program</u>.
- Point out the use of the word <u>crack</u> to describe a sound, rather than its more common meaning of a small space.
- Point out the use of the word <u>calf</u> to mean the fleshy back of the leg below the knee. Ask for another meaning of <u>calf</u>.

Use each list word once.

How Not to Buy Skis

George Ira Pshaw handed the driver the bus fare and jumped aboard. Even with all the ___traffic___, the bus was able to make ___rapid___ progress to the airport. If the bus arrived early, George would have time for lunch. He thought about what he would eat.

"Maybe I'll have a peanut butter ___sandwich___, or a lettuce and tomato ___salad___," he thought. "I want to eat a light ___snack___."

When George checked his luggage at the airport, a tall stranger spoke to him. "Skiing the North Slope tomorrow?"

George was flattered to be taken for an experienced skier. The North Slope was hard.

"Allow me to introduce myself," the stranger said. "My name is Yul B. Sawrey. Here's my card."

"Oh, you sell ski equipment," said George.

Preparation Have students turn to pages 6 and 7. Let them look at the story and the picture. Call their attention to the word list. Have the students say the words. Then explain that each spelling word belongs in one of the blanks in the story.

Write the title "How Not to Buy Skis" on the board. Ask students what is unusual about the title. (*Usually, we are taught <u>how to</u> do things. This story tells how <u>not</u> to do something.*)

Tell the students that puns are one way of making a story humorous. Explain that a pun is a word used in place of a similar-sounding word that has a different meaning. Ask the students to watch for the puns in the story.

The Pages Have students complete pages 6 and 7 independently by silently reading the story and writing the missing spelling words. Or you may read the story aloud, supplying the missing words as students follow along in their texts; then have the students complete the pages on their own.

When students have finished, you may wish to discuss the story. Ask a volunteer to tell the plot of the story. Have a student explain the title. (*George made a mistake buying skis he thought were magic.*) Ask students to identify the name in the story that is a pun. (*Yul B. Sawrey*)

"That's right. Maybe you've seen my skis advertised on your local TV program," Yul said. "My skis are the only ones on the planet Earth that won't break. They are so good that they are crash-proof."

"That sounds too good to be true. It's almost like magic," George said.

"Almost," said Sawrey slyly. "My skis are made in my own factory from a new, light plastic. They push you away from anything into which you might crash. They act like a reverse magnet."

"I'll buy a pair!" George shouted. "A beginner can certainly use magic skis."

At the ski slope the next day, George decided he didn't need skiing lessons. With his new skis, he could take on the hardest run. He didn't even finish reading the first chapter in his book, How to Ski. He began down the North Slope as fast as a rabbit. CRASH! He hit a rock. His new skis broke in half with a loud crack. The next thing he knew, he was in the hospital wearing a cast from his calf to his hip.

George's aunt came to see him in the hospital. She felt sorry for George. He told his aunt, "I should have known better than to buy skis from a man named 'Yul B. Sawrey.'"

His aunt answered, "Well, now we can call you 'G. I. Pshaw Was!'"

George's laughter could be heard down the hall.

7

rapid
traffic
magnet
act
magic
chapter
rabbit
snack
plastic
crack
program
planet
crash
salad
factory
sandwich
half
calf
aunt
laughter

Have a volunteer read each paragraph in the story, supplying each missing spelling word and spelling it aloud. Alternative answers from the spelling list may occasionally make sense, but suggest the word given as the preferred answer. Have other volunteers write the answers on the board and have students correct their own work. Check students' responses for the accurate spelling of each answer.

Follow-Up

Have students use each of the spelling words they missed in an original sentence that relates to the story.

As an additional follow-up activity, you may wish to have the students work in small groups with a cassette recorder to make "How Not to Buy Skis" into a "radio drama" with special sound effects. Have students select the roles of George and Yul. Students may use sound-effect records or create their own special sound effects.

Enrichment

Assign the blackline activity masters for Lesson 1 at this time if you wish to use the activity masters for enrichment and additional practice.

Maintenance and Review

If you wish to use the blackline activity masters for maintenance and review, wait until students have finished pages 12 and 13 before assigning the activities for Lesson 1.

Objectives

- To relate spelling words to a dictionary skill.
- To alphabetize words by the first, second, third, and fourth letters in a word.
- To write spelling words in alphabetical order.
- To use the **Spelling Dictionary**.

Note

Introduce the students to the **Spelling Dictionary** beginning on page 196. Discuss briefly the pronunciation key and how to use it.

Alphabetical Order

Words are listed in alphabetical order in a dictionary. Words that begin with a come first, then words that begin with b, and so on. It is simple to find a word in a dictionary if you know about alphabetical order. To put words in alphabetical order, look at the first letter of each word.

about
build

When words begin with the same letter, look at the second letter to put the words in alphabetical order.

about
around

When the first two letters are the same, look at the third letter.

able
about

When the first three letters are the same, look at the fourth letter.

aboard
about

★ Write the words in each group in alphabetical order.

1. traffic factory half snack

factory
half
snack
traffic

2. calf aunt chapter act

act
aunt
calf
chapter

3. sandwich rabbit rapid salad

rabbit
rapid
salad
sandwich

4. crack magnet magic crash

crack
crash
magic
magnet

8

Preparation

Have students read aloud the title of page 8. Have a volunteer explain what alphabetical order means. Write these words on the board:

plastic program planet laughter

Review with students that when the first letters are the same, we alphabetize by the first different letter. Have a volunteer rewrite the words on the board in alphabetical order (*laughter*, *planet*, *plastic*, *program*). Then have another volunteer underline the letter in each word that shows where to put it in alphabetical order.

The Page

Read the introduction on page 8 with the students and do the first exercise together. Have students complete the page on their own. Then ask volunteers to write the answers on the board and to spell the words aloud for immediate reinforcement of correct spelling.

Follow-Up

Tell students to write the spelling words on cards (or small pieces of paper) and alphabetize them. Students may check their work by looking up each word in the **Spelling Dictionary**.

WORDS AT WORK

Challenge Yourself

candid **landslide** **javelin** **jabber**

Write what you think each underlined Challenge Word means. Check your Spelling Dictionary to see if you were right. Then write sentences showing that you understand the meaning of each Challenge Word.

1. Having nothing to hide, the girl gave candid answers to the questions her teacher asked.
2. Heavy rains on the steep mountainside resulted in a landslide.
3. The athlete threw the javelin so that the point landed first.
4. Sometimes when I'm nervous, I jabber on with nobody listening.

Write to the Point

Did you ever make a mistake that seems funny now when you think about it? Maybe you took some bad advice, forgot to do something important, or tried to do something that was too hard for you. Write a story about what happened. Use spelling words from this lesson in your story.

Challenge Use one or more of the Challenge Words in your story.

Proofreading

Use the proofreading marks to show the errors in the paragraph below. Write the five misspelled words correctly in the blanks.

(oval)	word is misspelled
(circled dot)	period is missing
≡	letter should be capitalized

Skiing along at a rapud speed, kim suddenly landed with a krash. Nothing was hurt but the egg salad samwitch she had brought as a snak. it was squashed flat in its plastic wrapping Kim burst into laugter at the sight

1. rapid
2. crash
3. sandwich
4. snack
5. laughter

9

Objectives

- To extend the vowel spellings presented in Lesson 1 to the Challenge Words.
- To use context and the **Spelling Dictionary** to enlarge students' vocabulary.
- To apply the vowel spellings presented in Lesson 1 in a writing activity.
- To practice proofreading for spelling, punctuation, and capitalization.

Dictation Sentences

1. There was a lot of laughter during the magic act.
2. We had a snack after the program.
3. I ate a salad and a sandwich.
4. Mary read half a chapter in her book.
5. My aunt has a rabbit and a calf.
6. The factory makes plastic toys.
7. The traffic was rapid last night.
8. Can you attract a planet with a magnet?
9. There is a crack in the cup.
10. Stop, or we're going to crash!

Challenge Yourself Answers

Possible definitions:

1. honest
2. movement of land; falling earth and rock
3. lightweight spear used in track and field events
4. talk quickly about nothing

Students' sentences will vary.

Test Review these two ways to spell /ă/: a as in planet; au as in laughter. Test words with /ă/. Use one of these testing methods: (1) Say the word; read the sample sentence from page 4; say the word; have students write it. (2) Read each dictation sentence above; have students write the sentence. Correct the test with students.

Challenge Yourself The optional Challenge Words may be assigned to the entire class or limited to those students who do well on the test. Have students note the vowel spelling in the Challenge Words. Responses to this activity should be completed on separate paper. Answers to the questions are provided above.

Write to the Point Help students recall the selection "How Not to Buy Skis" on pages 6 and 7; then assign the story. Suggest to students that they write about their experience as if they were sharing it with a good friend. This activity should be completed on separate paper.

Proofreading The proofreading practice includes misspellings of words from this lesson as well as punctuation and capitalization errors.

LESSON 2

Objectives

- To hear and say words with /ā/.
- To write words with /ā/ with attention to letter sequence and sound/symbol relationships.
- To write each spelling word at least once.
- To recognize that /ā/ may be spelled ai, a–e, ei, ay, ea, and a.

Sample Sentences

1. Use your brain to figure things out.
2. Can you explain this story to me?
3. Jody can go, but we will remain here.
4. Please raise your hand if you know the answer.
5. We began to complain when the bus broke.
6. Please buy a container of milk at the store.
7. You will get paid as soon as I get enough money.
8. Each student stepped on the scale.
9. The male cat was licking his paw.
10. The town came out to watch the parade.
11. How did the mouse escape from its cage?
12. A milk snake is not poisonous.
13. My dog just had three female puppies.
14. How much does an elephant weigh?
15. The doctor says Jane should gain some weight.
16. My neighbor is a good friend of mine.
17. We will celebrate the holiday by having a picnic.
18. Because of the delay, the train was late.
19. If you drop this cup, it will break.
20. The smell of fresh bread is coming from the bakery.

Note

- The sample sentences may be used for pretesting.
- Words are grouped according to spellings of /ā/:

ai	ay
a_e	ea
ei	a

Lesson 2 Words with /ā/

Listen for /ā/ in each word.

brain
explain
remain
raise
complain
container
paid

scale
male
parade
escape
snake
female

weigh
weight
neighbor

holiday
delay

break

bakery

1. Which word begins with the letters ex? explain
2. Write the two words that begin with the letters br. brain break
3. Which word begins with the letters re? remain
4. Write the two words that begin with /k/. complain container
5. Which word begins and ends with a vowel? escape
6. Which two words begin with /p/ and end with /d/? paid parade
7. Which word begins and ends like rake? raise
8. Which word begins and ends like fence? female
9. Which word begins and ends like mile? male
10. Write the two words that begin with the letter s and end with the letter e. scale snake
11. Write the three words that have three syllables. container holiday bakery
12. Which word has the same spelling of /ā/ as steak? break
13. Which three words have the same spelling of /ā/ as eight? weigh weight neighbor
14. Which two words have the same spelling of /ā/ as ray? holiday delay

Preparation Have students read aloud the title of the lesson on page 10. Write /ā/ on the board. Tell pupils this is the vowel sound they hear in pay. Read each spelling word aloud. Have students repeat and spell each word aloud.

Many people mispronounce escape and say "excape". Ask students to identify the first two letters in this word and say escape. Note the letters eigh in weigh, weight, and neighbor. Point out the schwa in parade: /pə rād'/. Ask what letter spells /ə/ in parade. (a). Point out the /ə/ in bakery: /bā' kə rē/. What letter spells /ə/ in bakery? (e). (Although the schwa is not formally taught until Lesson 31, students should realize that it may be spelled with any vowel letter.) Then ask students to tell why the words are grouped as they are. Point out that in all the words in the first group, /ā/ is spelled ai. (See **Note**.)

Read the sample sentences. Have students point to each spelling word as you read the sentence for it.

The Page Guide students through the exercises on page 10. Have volunteers write the answers on the board and have students correct their own work.

Follow-Up Suggest that students work at home with family members or a friend and spell each word aloud.

Checkpoint

Write a spelling word for each clue.
Then use the Checkpoint Study Plan on page 224.

1. To measure in pounds or kilograms is to ___.
2. Another word for the mind is ___.
3. When the money was given, the bill was ___.
4. The person who lives next door is your ___.
5. To describe means to ___.
6. You run in a race, you march in a ___.
7. Another word for woman is ___.
8. To find fault is to ___.
9. One kind of reptile is a ___.
10. The opposite of fix is ___.
11. Weight can be measured on a ___.
12. The opposite of to leave is to ___.
13. Pounds or kilograms are a measure of ___.
14. A jar is a kind of ___.
15. Bread, cake, and pastry are sold in a ___.
16. The opposite of to lower is to ___.
17. Another word for man is ___.
18. Labor Day is a September ___.
19. To put off doing something is to ___.

20. This mystery word comes from two Latin words, *ex* and *cappa*. *Ex* meant out of. *Cappa* meant cape. Ancient Romans wore capes. When one Roman citizen wanted to arrest another, he grabbed the other by the cape. To get free, the arrested man would slip out of his cape and run away. The mystery word, which means to get free, comes from *ex cappa*. Can you guess the mystery word? Be sure to notice how the spelling of this word has changed. ___

11

weigh
brain
paid
neighbor
explain
parade
female
complain
snake
break
scale
remain
weight
container
bakery
raise
male
holiday
delay

escape

Objectives

- To write spelling words in response to clues: definitions, synonyms, antonyms, analogies, and context.
- To develop the critical thinking skills of making inferences, classifying, and drawing conclusions.
- To learn one of the many ways in which words have entered the English language.

Spelling Strategy

Some of the words in this lesson may be misspelled because students confuse them with their homophones. The words <u>weigh</u>, <u>break</u>, <u>weight</u>, and <u>male</u> all have familiar homophones. You may want to write the homophone pairs on the board and have students write sentences using each word correctly.

Preparation The clues on this page are like crossword puzzle clues. Explain to students that the response to each clue is a spelling word. Use the following examples to illustrate the types of clues used:

Definition	The person who lives next door is your (*neighbor*).
Synonym	Another word for woman is (*female*).
Antonym	The opposite of to leave is to (*remain*).
Analogy	You run in a race, you march in a (*parade*).
Context	Weight can be measured on a (*scale*).

The final clue explains the Latin origin of <u>escape</u>.

The Page Have students complete page 11 using the words on page 10. When students have finished, have them read each clue and spell the answer aloud. Check each response twice: once for the correct answer and a second time for spelling accuracy.

Follow-Up Guide pupils in using the **Checkpoint Study Plan** on page 224 to take a self-test. Then have them use the plan for independent study.

Objectives

- To write words with /ā/ in continuous text.
- To write each spelling word once.
- To integrate reading with spelling.

Use each list word once.

THE PARADE THAT ALMOST WASN'T

The trouble started with the escape of the pet snake from the apartment upstairs. Our next-door neighbor, who owns the snake, was away on a holiday. The snake got out through a break in its cage. Then it crawled under the door, down the hall, and into the freight elevator. When the elevator stopped, the snake crawled into our bakery.

There were two customers in the bakery, one male and one female. The woman had just paid for her cake. The man was watching the clerk weigh his pound of cookies on the scale. Outside, a big, noisy parade was passing. As the man reached for his money, he looked down and saw the snake on his shoe. The man screamed and ran out the door. He ran right into the tuba player, who dropped his tuba and fell down. The man from the bakery fell on top of him. Then the French horn player tripped over the tuba and fell on top of them. The parade stopped.

Note

Point out the use of the word holiday in the story as a synonym for vacation, as in "away on vacation."

Preparation Have students turn to pages 12 and 13. Let them look at the story and the picture. Call their attention to the word list. Have the students say the words. Then explain that each spelling word belongs in one of the blanks in the story.

Write the title "The Parade That Almost Wasn't" on the board. Then tell the students that this story is about a marching band that is frightened and confused by a snake. Help students identify the French horn in the picture.

Ask if any students have been in a parade. If so, have them describe what they did, whether things went smoothly, and so on. Ask students what they would do if they suddenly saw a snake while they were marching in a parade. (*Answers will vary.*) Ask what the drum majorette in the picture is doing. (*picking up the snake*) Ask students if this is a good idea. Point out that no one should ever handle a snake unless certain that the snake is not dangerous or poisonous.

While this was happening, the other customer in the bakery had dropped her cake and grabbed what she thought was an empty bucket. But it was a large container full of sugar. The heavy weight of the full bucket was too much. She dropped it, spilling all the sugar. Then she tried to catch the snake in the empty bucket. But she slipped on the sugar and fell to the floor. The snake crawled out the door and into the parade.

The drummer was the first to see the snake. He began to yell so loudly that a vein stood out on his forehead. Finally the drum majorette saw the snake. She used her brain. She shouted and told everyone to remain in line. Then she picked up the snake.

"Let's not delay the parade any longer," she said. "Start marching when I raise my baton." Holding the snake high in the air with her left hand, she raised her baton and began to march.

The French horn player got up and picked up her French horn. The man from the bakery left and got lost in the crowd. The tuba player got up slowly and began to complain about an ache in his back. The parade began to move.

The next day, a picture of the drum majorette holding the snake was in all the papers. Everyone said how brave she was.

She said, "Let me explain. When I was little, three snakes lived in a hole next to my house. Nothing can erase my memory of those snakes, and no silly old milk snake will ever scare me!"

13

brain
explain
remain
raise
complain
container
paid
scale
male
parade
escape
snake
female
weigh
weight
neighbor
holiday
delay
break
bakery

Enrichment

If you want to use the blackline activity masters for enrichment and additional practice, assign Lesson 2 activities at this time.

Maintenance and Review

OBJECTIVE

- To review words with /ă/ spelled: a, au.

ACTIVITIES

If you want to use the blackline activity masters for maintenance and review, assign Lesson 1 activities at this time.

You can also use the activity below to review Lesson 1 with students.

Write the following words on the board. Have students refer to the word list in Lesson 1 and write the word or words that rhyme with each word. (Answers are in parentheses.)

pack	(*snack, crack*)
staff	(*half, calf*)
tragic	(*magic*)
plant	(*aunt*)
after	(*laughter*)
habit	(*rabbit*)
dash	(*crash*)
packed	(*act*)

The Pages Have students complete pages 12 and 13 independently by silently reading the story and writing the missing spelling words. Or you may read the story aloud, supplying the missing words as students follow along in their texts; then have the students complete the pages on their own.

When students have finished, you may wish to discuss the story. Ask a volunteer to summarize the story. Ask why it was all right for the drum majorette to pick up the snake. (*She knew it was harmless.*) Tell students that milk snakes are about three feet long and grayish-brown. They are related to a family of snakes called king snakes and are very useful animals.

Have a volunteer read each paragraph in the story, supplying each missing spelling word and spelling it aloud. Have other volunteers write the answers on the board and have students correct their own work. Check students' responses for the accurate spelling of each answer.

Follow-Up Have students use each of the spelling words they missed in an original sentence that relates to the story.

As an additional follow-up activity, you may wish to have students illustrate their favorite scene in the story. Tell them to copy the sentence from the story that best describes the action in their picture.

Objectives

- To relate spelling to another language skill.
- To review the use of a capital letter to begin a sentence.
- To review the use of periods, question marks, and exclamation points.
- To write spelling words with attention to capitalization and punctuation.

Capitals and Punctuation

A sentence begins with a capital letter.

A sentence that tells something ends with a period.

I like chicken soup.

A sentence that asks something ends with a question mark.

Do you like chicken soup?

A sentence that shows strong feeling or surprise ends with an exclamation point.

This chicken soup tastes terrible!

★ From the story below, write the words that should be capitalized. Then find the words that should be followed by a period, a question mark, or an exclamation point. Write the words with the correct punctuation.

during the school year, our class decided to take a break from our studies we took a holiday trip to the mountains our leader, Mr. Peterson, explained to us the purpose of the trip we were to scale a mountain six thousand feet high after hearing this, most of the males and females in the group decided to remain at home how could Mr. Peterson expect us to do this and not complain

however, Mr. Peterson finally persuaded us to go we looked like a parade climbing up the mountain we hiked for a long time and finally reached the mountain top after a brief rest, we began our trip down at this rate we surely would lose weight

suddenly, we heard a scream we looked just in time to see a snake escape from the area by slithering away that was a close one

Capitals Needed		Words Before Punctuation	
During	We	studies.	mountains.
Our	We	trip.	high.
After	How	home.	complain?
However	We	go.	mountain.
We	After	top.	down.
At	Suddenly	weight. or!	scream.
We	That	away.	one!

14

Preparation

Have students read aloud the title of page 14. Then write the following sentences on the board:

i can explain   will you let me explain   please, let me explain

Ask students to explain what is wrong with these sentences. (*no capital letter at the beginning; no end punctuation*) Review these rules: A sentence always begins with a capital letter; a sentence that tells something ends with a period; a sentence that asks something ends with a question mark; a sentence that shows strong emotion ends with an exclamation point. Have volunteers correct the sentences. (*I can explain. Will you let me explain? Please, let me explain!*)

The Page

Read the instructions on page 14 with the students and do the first example together. Have students complete the page on their own. Then have students write the answers on the board for immediate reinforcement of correct spelling.

Follow-Up

Have students write their own story about a parade or a mountain-climbing trip using at least 10 spelling words. Remind them to use capitals, periods, question marks, and exclamation points correctly.

WORDS AT WORK

Challenge Yourself

ailment surveyor fray weightless

Decide which Challenge Word fits each clue. Check your Spelling Dictionary to see if you were right. Then write sentences showing that you understand the meaning of each Challenge Word.

1. Astronauts can do flips in their ships because people and objects are this in outer space.
2. People hire this person to measure their land.
3. The ends of the shoelaces on your tennis shoes may do this when they are old and worn out.
4. When you have one, you don't feel very well.

Write to the Point

There are many ways a person can be brave. Some people are brave in an emergency. Shy people are brave if they speak in front of a large group. Write a paragraph about the bravest thing you ever did. Tell what you did, how you felt before you did it, and how you felt afterward. Use spelling words from this lesson in your paragraph.

Challenge Use one or more of the Challenge Words in your paragraph.

Proofreading

Use the proofreading marks to show the errors in the paragraph below. Write the five misspelled words correctly in the blanks.

⬭	word is misspelled
⊙	period is missing
≡	letter should be capitalized

Our nayber pete has a pet snake named Toby. I don't really know if Toby is mail or femail. I like Toby, but I hope he or she will remane at Pete's house Toby, please don't excape and decide to visit my house!

1. neighbor
2. male
3. female
4. remain
5. escape

15

Objectives

- To extend the vowel spellings presented in Lesson 2 to the Challenge Words.
- To use clues and the **Spelling Dictionary** to enlarge students' vocabulary.
- To apply the vowel spellings presented in Lesson 2 in a writing activity.
- To practice proofreading for spelling, punctuation, and capitalization.

Dictation Sentences

1. I paid for the container of milk.
2. My neighbor works at the bakery.
3. She will weigh the puppy on the scale.
4. What is the weight of that snake?
5. I complain when they raise prices.
6. You use your brain to think.
7. Are you going to the holiday parade?
8. The female goat helped the male goat to escape.
9. Can you explain the delay?
10. I need a break!
11. Please remain seated.

Challenge Yourself Answers

1. weightless
2. surveyor
3. fray
4. ailment

Students' sentences will vary.

Test Review these six ways to spell /ā/: ai as in paid; a_e as in scale; ei as in weigh; ay as in delay; ea as in break; a as in bakery. Test words with /ā/. Use one of these testing methods: (1) Say the word; read the sample sentence from page 10; say the word; have students write it. (2) Read each dictation sentence above; have students write the sentence. Correct the test with students.

Challenge Yourself The optional Challenge Words may be assigned to the entire class or limited to those students who do well on the test. Have students note the vowel spellings in the Challenge Words, especially the following new spelling: ey as in surveyor. You may wish to have students work in pairs. Responses to this activity should be completed on separate paper. Answers to the questions are provided above.

Write to the Point Help students recall the selection "The Parade That Almost Wasn't" on pages 12 and 13; then assign the paragraph. This activity should be completed on separate paper.

Proofreading The proofreading practice includes misspellings of words from this lesson as well as a capitalization error and a punctuation error.

LESSON 3

Objectives

- To hear and say words with /ĕ/.
- To write words with /ĕ/ with attention to letter sequence and sound/symbol relationships.
- To write each spelling word once.
- To recognize that /ĕ/ may be spelled ea, e, and ie.

Sample Sentences

1. Frances was sick, but now she is healthy.
2. Jake uses a needle and thread to sew.
3. The millionaire left all her wealth to the museum.
4. After this storm passes, the weather will clear up.
5. Do you want to go, or will you wait here instead?
6. Jody began to measure the flour.
7. Some people find great pleasure in writing stories.
8. Jill ran so fast that she was soon out of breath.
9. Maria Elena put on her sweater.
10. The pirates buried the treasure.
11. Sam and Dave sat on a park bench.
12. We intend to stay here until we get an answer.
13. Juan likes to invent machines.
14. How many words are there in this sentence?
15. Fred is not his usual cheerful self today.
16. If you have any questions, ask them now.
17. Write your address on this paper.
18. Would you rather play chess or checkers?
19. The water reaches a depth of 30 feet.
20. Jan's cat is quite friendly.

Note

- The sample sentences may be used for pretesting.
- Words are grouped according to spellings of /ĕ/:
  ea
  e
  ie

Lesson 3 Words with /ĕ/

Listen for /ĕ/ in each word.

healthy
thread
wealth
weather
instead
measure
pleasure
breath
sweater
treasure

bench
intend
invent
sentence
self
questions
address
checkers
depth

friendly

1. Write the three words that begin with the letters in.
   instead intend
   invent
2. Which word begins with /kw/? questions
3. Which word begins and ends like cheers? Circle the letters that spell /k/. checkers
4. Which word begins and ends like family and has two syllables? friendly
5. Which word begins and ends like swagger?
   sweater
6. Which word ends with the letters ch? bench
7. Which word ends with the letters lf? self
8. Write the three words that end with the letters th.
   wealth breath
   depth
9. Write the three other words that contain the letters th.
   healthy thread
   weather
10. Which three words have /zh/ in the middle?
    measure pleasure
    treasure
11. In which word is /d/ spelled dd and /s/ spelled ss?
    address
12. Which word has two spellings for /s/? sentence
13. Write the word in which /ĕ/ is spelled ie.
    friendly
14. Write the word in which /ch/ is spelled ti.
    questions

16

Preparation Have students read aloud the title of the lesson on page 16. Write /ĕ/ on the board. Have students say /ĕ/ as in pet. Read each spelling word aloud. Have students repeat and then spell each word aloud.

Point out that address has two sets of double consonants, dd and ss, and can be pronounced two ways. Also note that friendly ends with the suffix ly. Then ask students to look at the way the words are grouped. Ask volunteers to identify the words in which /ĕ/ is spelled ea, e, and ie. (See **Note**.)

Read the sample sentences. Have students point to each spelling word as you read the sentence for it.

The Page Have students complete page 16 independently or as a class. Have volunteers write the answers on the board and have students correct their own work. For exercise 10, note the pronunciation of /zh/. For exercise 12, remind students that /s/ is different from /ch/, /sh/, /z/, and /zh/.

Follow-Up Suggest that students write each letter of a word in a different color. Double letters should be written in the same color.

Checkpoint

Write a spelling word for each clue.
Then use the Checkpoint Study Plan on page 224.

1. To think of and make for the first time is to ___.
2. A seat in the park for two or more persons is a ___.
3. Your street number and town name are your ___.
4. The new boy hopes his classmates will be ___.
5. Hidden gold may be a ___.
6. Wide is to width as deep is to ___.
7. You sew with a needle and ___.
8. When you're sick, you don't feel like your normal ___.
9. Take a deep ___ of clean air.
10. Great riches means great ___.
11. A feeling of enjoyment is ___.
12. The opposite of answers is ___.
13. To have in mind is to ___.
14. If you feel chilly, you may need a ___.
15. In place of or rather than means ___.
16. Parcheesi, chess, and ___ are games.
17. To be free of disease is to be ___.
18. If it's raining, it is wet ___.
19. To find the size of something is to ___.
20. We often see this mystery word in our grammar books. It is defined as a group of words that expresses a complete thought. Did you know that it comes from a word that meant thought? The mystery word comes from the Latin word *sententia*. *Sententia* meant a thought, opinion, or idea. Can you guess the mystery word? ___

invent
bench
address
friendly
treasure
depth
thread
self
breath
wealth
pleasure
questions
intend
sweater
instead
checkers
healthy
weather
measure

sentence

Objectives

- To write spelling words in response to clues: definitions, antonyms, classifications, analogies, and context.
- To develop the critical thinking skills of classifying, making inferences, and drawing conclusions.
- To understand that words have come into the English language from other languages.

Spelling Strategy

If students forget to double the d in address, suggest that they use the following mnemonic device: "An address is what you add to an envelope." Encourage students to make up mnemonic devices for other common errors, such as forgetting the i in friendly or confusing weather and whether.

Preparation The clues on this page are like crossword puzzle clues. Explain to students that the response to each clue is a spelling word. Use the following examples to illustrate the types of clues used:

Definition	A feeling of enjoyment is (*pleasure*).
Antonym	The opposite of answers is (*questions*).
Classification	Parcheesi, chess, and (*checkers*) are games.
Analogy	Wide is to width as deep is to (*depth*).
Context	Hidden gold may be a (*treasure*).

The final clue explains the Latin origin of sentence.

The Page Have students complete page 17 using the words on page 16. When students have finished, have them read each clue and spell the answer aloud. Check each response twice: once for the correct answer and a second time for spelling accuracy.

Follow-Up Guide pupils in using the **Checkpoint Study Plan** on page 224 to take a self-test. Then have them use the plan for independent study.

Objectives

- To write words with /ĕ/ in continuous text.
- To write each spelling word once.
- To integrate reading with spelling.

Use each list word once.

THE CHESS GAME

"How about a game of checkers or chess?" Freda asked. Dr. Wilson sat down beside her on the park bench.

"A game of chess would be a pleasure, Freda. We haven't played chess since I moved to my new address on Clinton Street," Dr. Wilson said. He looked down at the thread tied around his finger. He wondered why he had tied it there.

"Isn't this beautiful fall weather?" Freda took a deep breath of air. "It makes you feel so strong and healthy."

"My mother always called it sweater weather because it's too warm for a coat." Dr. Wilson paused after his sentence, as if in the depth of thought.

"What is it, Doctor?" Freda asked.

"I was just wondering about this thread. It's to remind me of something. But what? Well, never mind. I'll remember sooner or later. But now, a surprise."

Note

Point out that the height of the robot in the story is given in centimeters. If your class uses English measures, tell them that 5 centimeters is approximately 2 inches.

Preparation Have students turn to pages 18 and 19. Let them look at the story and the picture. Call their attention to the word list. Have the students say the words. Then explain that each spelling word belongs in one of the blanks in the story.

Write the title "The Chess Game" on the board. Ask if any students know how to play chess. If so, have them explain the game briefly. If not, tell students that chess is played on a checkerboard with 16 pieces for each player. The pieces—king, queen, castles, bishops, knights, and pawns—move and capture other pieces in different ways. The object of the game is to trap the other player's king so that it cannot move without being caught. The player who does this calls, "Checkmate," and then the game is over. Chess is a difficult game that takes a great deal of concentration and planning. One game can easily take an hour to play.

The Pages Have students complete pages 18 and 19 independently by silently reading the story and writing the missing spelling words. Or you may read the story aloud, supplying the missing words as students follow along in their texts; then have the students complete the pages on their own.

"You're always making things in your laboratory. Did you ___invent___ something new?" asked Freda.

"And you're still your usual curious ___self___, always asking ___questions___," laughed Dr. Wilson. Then he carefully pulled something from his pocket. He held it as if it were a valuable ___treasure___ that would bring him great ___wealth___.

"You wanted to play a game of chess with me. Why not play with my mini-robot ___instead___? I call it I-1."

"What a great idea!" Freda cried. "It's so tiny. Did you ever ___measure___ just how tall your robot is?"

"I-1 is five centimeters tall," Dr. Wilson answered.

"Trying to beat a robot is going to be quite difficult. But I ___intend___ to do it," Freda said.

"Pawn to Knight 4," said I-1.

"Pawn to Queen 3," countered Freda.

"About this thread . . ." wondered Dr. Wilson.

An hour later, Freda yelled, "Checkmate. I won!"

FIZZ! FIM!! FOOSH!!!

I-1 threw a fit, and sparks flew everywhere.

"I-1 won! I-1 won!" it screamed.

"I-1 certainly isn't very ___friendly___, Dr. Wilson," said Freda.

Dr. Wilson yelled, "I remember now! I-1 must always be allowed to win."

FIZZ! FIM!! FOOSH!!!

19

healthy
thread
wealth
weather
instead
measure
pleasure
breath
sweater
treasure
bench
intend
invent
sentence
self
questions
address
checkers
depth
friendly

When students have finished, you may wish to discuss the story. Ask students what parts of the story could take place and what parts are impossible. (*Computers can be programmed to play chess with people, and miniaturization of computer components has proceeded to a point where a small chess-playing robot is a possibility. However, it is not possible for a computer to throw a tantrum.*)

Have a volunteer read each paragraph in the story, supplying each missing spelling word and spelling it aloud. Have other volunteers write the answers on the board and have students correct their own work. Check students' responses for the accurate spelling of each answer.

Follow-Up

Have students use each of the spelling words they missed in an original sentence that relates to the story.

As an additional follow-up activity, you may wish to have three students act out "The Chess Game" for the class—one child reading Freda's part, one reading Dr. Wilson's part, and one reading I-1's part. When each student comes to a spelling word, have him or her spell the word aloud and then continue reading.

Enrichment

If you want to use the blackline activity masters for enrichment and additional practice, assign Lesson 3 activities at this time.

Maintenance and Review

OBJECTIVE

- To review words with /ā/ spelled: ai, a_e, ei, ay, ea, a.

ACTIVITIES

If you want to use the blackline activity masters for maintenance and review, assign Lesson 2 activities at this time.

You can also use the activity below to review Lesson 2 with students:

Write the following words on the board. Have students write the words from Lesson 2 that contain these smaller words. (Answers are in parentheses.)

day	(*holiday*)
eight	(*weight*)
lay	(*delay*)
ale	(*scale, male, female*)
plain	(*explain, complain*)
bake	(*bakery*)
aid	(*paid*)

Objectives

- To relate spelling words to a dictionary skill.
- To review the purpose of guide words.
- To write spelling words in alphabetical order.
- To write the guide words for given spelling words.
- To use the **Spelling Dictionary**.

Guide Words

Guide words are the two words in heavy type at the top of each dictionary page. Guide words make it easy to locate a word in a dictionary because the first guide word is the first word on the page, and the second guide word is the last word on the page. The other words come between in alphabetical order. When searching for a word in a dictionary, always check the guide words first to see if a word is on a particular page.

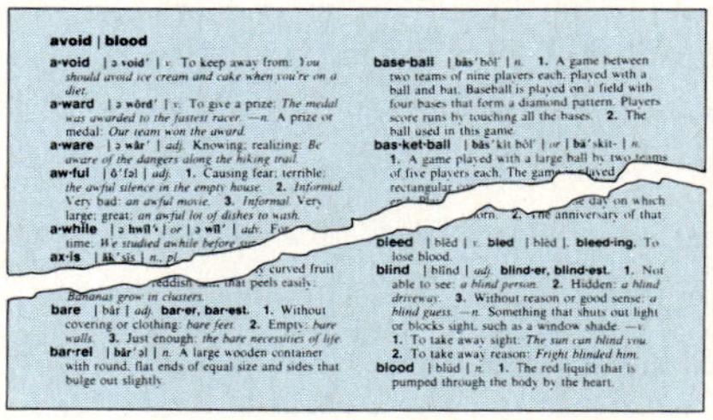
avoid | blood

a·void | ə void' | *v.* To keep away from: *You should avoid ice cream and cake when you're on a diet.*
a·ward | ə wôrd' | *v.* To give a prize: *The medal was awarded to the fastest racer.* —*n.* A prize or medal: *Our team won the award.*
a·ware | ə wâr' | *adj.* Knowing; realizing: *Be aware of the dangers along the hiking trail.*
aw·ful | ô'fəl | *adj.* **1.** Causing fear; terrible: *the awful silence in the empty house.* **2.** *Informal.* Very bad: *an awful movie.* **3.** *Informal.* Very large; great: *an awful lot of dishes to wash.*
a·while | ə hwīl' | *or* | ə wīl' | *adv.* For ... time: *We studied awhile before ...*
ax·is | ăk'sĭs | *n., pl.* ...
... curved fruit ... reddish ... that peels easily: *Bananas grow in clusters.*
bare | bâr | *adj.* **bar·er, bar·est.** **1.** Without covering or clothing: *bare feet.* **2.** Empty: *bare walls.* **3.** Just enough: *the bare necessities of life.*
bar·rel | băr'əl | *n.* A large wooden container with round, flat ends of equal size and sides that bulge out slightly.
base·ball | bās'bôl' | *n.* **1.** A game between two teams of nine players each, played with a ball and bat. Baseball is played on a field with four bases that form a diamond pattern. Players score runs by touching all the bases. **2.** The ball used in this game.
bas·ket·ball | băs'kĭt bôl' | *or* | bä'skĭt- | *n.* **1.** A game played with a large ball by two teams of five players each. The game ... played ... rectangular ...
... day on which ... born. **2.** The anniversary of that ...
bleed | blēd | *v.* **bled** | blĕd |, **bleed·ing.** To lose blood.
blind | blīnd | *adj.* **blind·er, blind·est.** **1.** Not able to see: *a blind person.* **2.** Hidden: *a blind driveway.* **3.** Without reason or good sense: *a blind guess.* —*n.* Something that shuts out light or blocks sight, such as a window shade. —*v.* **1.** To take away sight: *The sun can blind you.* **2.** To take away reason: *Fright blinded him.*
blood | blŭd | *n.* **1.** The red liquid that is pumped through the body by the heart.

★ Write the following words in alphabetical order. Then look them up in the Spelling Dictionary and write the guide words for each word.

bench	**address**	**depth**	**healthy**	**measure**	**pleasure**
breath	**sentence**	**instead**	**checkers**	**wealth**	**friendly**

	Word	Guide Words	
1.	address	absurd	alone
2.	bench	autumn	blunt
3.	breath	Blvd.	bring
4.	checkers	champion	comfort
5.	depth	court	discuss
6.	friendly	float	grasshopper
7.	healthy	greet	husband
8.	instead	idea	June
9.	measure	margin	mosquito
10.	pleasure	periodical	problem
11.	sentence	season	skin diving
12.	wealth	village	weekend

20

Preparation Have students read the title of page 20 and ask them what guide words are. If necessary, have a student read aloud the first sentence at the top of the page. Ask what the first guide word is on a dictionary page. (*the first entry on the page*) Ask what the second guide word is. (*the last entry on the page*) Review with students that the other words on the page are arranged alphabetically between the guide words. Ask why we use guide words. (*to make it easy to locate words in a dictionary*)

The Page Read the introduction on page 20 with the students and do the first exercise together. Have students complete the page on their own. Then have students write the answers on the board and review them aloud for immediate reinforcement.

Follow-Up Have students number their papers from 1 to 12, copy the guide words they wrote for each exercise, and write the other Lesson 3 words, if any, that appear on the **Spelling Dictionary** page between each pair of guide words. Have students check their work by looking up their answers.

WORDS AT WORK

Challenge Yourself

endeavor concept identical meddle

Write what you think each underlined Challenge Word means. Check your Spelling Dictionary to see if you were right. Then write sentences showing that you understand the meaning of each Challenge Word.

1. Because of the team's endeavor to improve, they now have a trophy.
2. The government of the United States is based on the concept that all people are equal.
3. People often called Anita by her sister's name because the girls were identical twins.
4. I'd give her advice, but I don't want to meddle.

Write to the Point

Imagine that you have a friend visiting you at your house. Your friend wants to learn how to play a new game. Think of a game you know that is fun to play but simple enough to explain in a few sentences. Then write instructions telling how to play it. Be sure to explain each part of the game clearly and in the correct order. Use spelling words from this lesson in your instructions.

Challenge Use one or more of the Challenge Words in your instructions.

Proofreading

Use the proofreading marks to show the errors in the paragraph below. Write the five misspelled words correctly in the blanks.

(oval)	word is misspelled
≡	letter should be capitalized
^	word is missing

The whether was bad, so i decided ^to invent a new indoor game insted of playing cheakers. First, i hid a tresure. Then my little sister asked ten qestions about what it was and where to find. ^it

1. weather
2. instead
3. checkers
4. treasure
5. questions

21

Objectives

- To extend the vowel spellings presented in Lesson 3 to the Challenge Words.
- To use context and the **Spelling Dictionary** to enlarge students' vocabulary.
- To apply the vowel spellings presented in Lesson 3 in a writing activity.
- To practice proofreading for spelling, capitalization, and missing words.

Dictation Sentences

1. They play checkers on a park bench when the weather is good.
2. I need thread to mend a hole in my sweater.
3. She went to the movies instead of the beach.
4. He was out of breath after the race.
5. There is a wealth of jewels in the treasure chest.
6. I intend to give you my new address.
7. What a pleasure it is to have such a friendly neighbor!
8. She is very healthy because she gets plenty of rest.
9. Answer these questions in one sentence.
10. How would you invent a machine to measure the depth of the sea?
11. I do not feel like my old self today.

Challenge Yourself Answers

Possible definitions:

1. attempt
2. idea
3. exactly the same
4. interfere

Students' sentences will vary.

Test Review these three ways to spell /ĕ/: ea as in weather; e as in depth; ie as in friendly. Test words with /ĕ/. Use one of these testing methods: (1) Say the word; read the sample sentence from page 16; say the word; have students write it. (2) Read each dictation sentence above; have students write the sentence. Correct the test with students.

Challenge Yourself The optional Challenge Words may be assigned to the entire class or limited to those students who do well on the test. Have students note the vowel spellings in the Challenge Words. Responses to this activity should be completed on separate paper. Answers to the questions are provided above.

Write to the Point Help students recall the selection "The Chess Game" on pages 18 and 19; then assign the game instructions. Tell students that using order words such as first, before, then, next, and after can help their readers understand the sequence of events in the game. This activity should be completed on separate paper.

Proofreading The proofreading practice includes misspellings of words from this lesson as well as capitalization errors and missing words.

LESSON 4

Objectives

- To hear and say words with /ĕ/.
- To write words with /ĕ/ with attention to letter sequence and sound/symbol relationships.
- To write each spelling word at least once.
- To recognize that /ĕ/ may be spelled e.

Sample Sentences

1. We said the pledge of allegiance.
2. I wish I could remember her name.
3. The circus rider balanced on the back of an elephant.
4. A gentle breeze ruffled the leaves.
5. Some desks are made of metal.
6. The roses began to bloom as each petal unfolded.
7. We'd better go now, or else we'll be late.
8. Mavis rides her horse each day to give it exercise.
9. You need lots of energy to climb a mountain.
10. This coat would look fine if it were the right length.
11. We brought extra food to share with you.
12. There is not much water in the desert.
13. After the pillow fight, my room was a wreck.
14. Ms. Pauling is an expert in spiders.
15. Today is a very special day.
16. The last year of this century is 2000.
17. Meters and kilometers are metric measures.
18. Steven's work is good, and Judy's is excellent.
19. Robert is selfish because he won't share his apple.
20. Kate planted peas in her vegetable garden.

Note

The sample sentences may be used for pretesting.

Lesson 4 Words with /ĕ/

Listen for /ĕ/ in each word.

pledge
remember
elephant
gentle
metal
petal
else
exercise
energy
length
extra
desert
wreck
expert
special
century
metric
excellent
selfish
vegetable

1. Which four words begin with the letters ex? exercise, extra, expert, excellent
2. Which three words begin with /s/? special, century, selfish
3. Which four words begin and end with a vowel? else, exercise, energy, extra
4. Which two words are spelled the same except for the first letter? metal, petal
5. Which word begins and ends like racer? remember
6. Which word ends with the letters th? length
7. Write the word that ends with the letters sh. selfish
8. Write the word in which /sh/ is spelled ci. special
9. Which two words end with /k/? Circle the letters that spell /k/. wreck, metric
10. Write the four words in which you hear /j/ but don't see the letter j. pledge, gentle, energy, vegetable
11. Which word has /z/ in the middle? desert
12. Which two words have /f/ in the middle? Circle the letters that spell /f/. elephant, selfish
13. Write the word in which you see the letter w but don't hear /w/. wreck
14. In which word is /l/ spelled ll? excellent

22

Preparation

Have students read aloud the title of the lesson on page 22. Write /ĕ/ on the board. Have students say /ĕ/ as in pet. Read each spelling word aloud. Have students repeat and spell each word aloud.

Point out these special sound/symbol relationships: In the word special, /sh/ is spelled ci. Selfish ends with the suffix ish. Ask students to find the word that contains three e's. (*vegetable*) Point out that desert is spelled with one s and does not mean sweet food that you eat after a meal. Then ask students to identify the letter that spells /ĕ/ in the words in this lesson.

Read the sample sentences. Have students point to each spelling word as you read the sentence for it.

The Page

Have students complete page 22 independently or as a class. Have volunteers give the answers and have students correct their own work. For exercise 3, tell students to count y as a vowel. For exercise 11, note that /z/ can be spelled with s.

Follow-Up

Suggest that students write the spelling words on cards or small pieces of paper. Then have them use these cards to study the words independently or with a spelling partner.

Checkpoint

Write a spelling word for each clue.
Then use the Checkpoint Study Plan on page 224.

1. One hundred years is a ___.
2. A dry place with sand and rocks is a ___.
3. Part of a flower is a ___.
4. Something not ordinary or usual is ___.
5. Another word for promise is ___.
6. The opposite of forget is ___.
7. Someone who knows a lot about a thing is an ___.
8. It is not here, but somewhere ___.
9. Sun, wind, water, and coal are sources of ___.
10. Our system of measurement may change to ___.
11. Broccoli is a ___.
12. Wide is to width as long is to ___.
13. Generous is the opposite of ___.
14. Another word for destroy is ___.
15. The opposite of harsh is ___.
16. Silver and iron are kinds of ___.
17. For good health, get enough ___.
18. Something over and above is ___.
19. Something very good is ___.

century
desert
petal
special
pledge
remember
expert
else
energy
metric
vegetable
length
selfish
wreck
gentle
metal
exercise
extra
excellent

20. This mystery word is the name of an animal. Like some other names for animals, it originally described something about the animal. Squirrel, for example, meant shadow tail in Greek. Spider meant spinner in Old English. The mystery word comes from the Greek word for ivory, *elephas*. It names an animal with ivory tusks. Can you guess the mystery word? ___

elephant

Objectives

- To write spelling words in response to clues: definitions, synonyms, antonyms, analogies, and context.
- To develop the critical thinking skills of making inferences, classifying, and drawing conclusions.
- To understand that some animal names in English come from words that describe a characteristic of the animal.

Spelling Strategy

Some students may misspell vegetable because they do not pronounce the second vowel. Tell students that, although that pronunciation is correct, it is also correct to pronounce the second vowel. Have students practice saying the word with four syllables to reinforce the correct spelling.

If students write z instead of s in exercise, suggest that they think of a word beginning with s that they associate with exercising, such as strong, sweaty, or sneakers.

Preparation The clues on this page are like crossword puzzle clues. Explain to students that the response to each clue is a spelling word. Use the following examples to illustrate the types of clues used:

Definition	A dry place with sand and rocks is a (*desert*).
Synonym	Another word for promise is (*pledge*).
Antonym	The opposite of harsh is (*gentle*).
Analogy	Wide is to width as long is to (*length*).
Context	Our system of measurement may change to (*metric*).

The final clue explains the Greek origin of elephant.

The Page Have students complete page 23 using the words on page 22. When students have finished, have them read each clue and spell the answer aloud. Check each response twice: once for the correct answer and a second time for spelling accuracy.

Follow-Up Guide pupils in using the **Checkpoint Study Plan** on page 224 to take a self-test. Then have them use the plan for independent study.

Objectives

- To write words with /ĕ/ in continuous text.
- To write each spelling word once.
- To integrate reading with spelling.

Use each list word once.

THE CIRCUS TRAIN

Carlo's whole family had been with the circus for more than a century. They all loved the circus. Carlo's mother was an expert animal trainer. Carlo's job was to feed the animals and walk them around to give them their exercise. But Carlo wanted something else. He made a pledge that soon he would show everyone he was ready to learn to train animals himself.

One night, the circus train was speeding across the desert. It was on its way to Los Angeles. The train was making excellent time. If things went smoothly, the circus would arrive in Los Angeles by dawn. But things did not go smoothly. The train hit something on the track, and tons of metal screeched to a halt. The train shook along its entire length. In the car where the animals were, a door flew open. A frightened elephant headed quickly through this exit. She ran across a bare stretch of desert and disappeared.

Now this was no ordinary elephant. Flower, as she was called, was very special. She liked to work. She always had plenty of energy for raising the

Note

Tell students that a metric ton is a few pounds heavier than a ton. A ton is 2,000 pounds.

Preparation

Have students turn to pages 24 and 25. Let them look at the story and the picture. Call their attention to the word list. Have the students say the words. Then explain that each spelling word belongs in one of the blanks in the story.

Write the title "The Circus Train" on the board. Ask if any students have been to a circus. If they have, ask them to describe it. If not, explain that a circus offers many types of entertainment including jugglers, clowns, acrobats, lions, tigers, and elephants.

The Pages

Have students complete pages 24 and 25 independently by silently reading the story and writing the missing spelling words. Or you may read the story aloud, supplying the missing words as students follow along in their texts; then have students complete the pages on their own.

When students have finished, you may wish to discuss the story. Ask students if, like Carlo, they have a strong ambition to do some particular kind of work. Discuss what training is necessary to realize these ambitions; ask what kind of personality traits are best for certain jobs. (*Answers will vary.*) Ask how Carlo showed that he was ready to become an animal trainer. (*He went off on his own to look for Flower and he found her and took charge of her.*) Ask students how they might show that they are ready to achieve their ambitions. (*Answers will vary.*)

huge circus tent. And she wasn't selfish. She would gladly share her food.

Carlo and Flower were good friends. Carlo would always remember to give Flower extra water and food. And even though Flower weighed three metric tons, she was very gentle with Carlo and would sometimes tickle him with her trunk.

When Carlo saw that Flower was gone, he started to worry. He went to the ledge at the back of the train to look for her. He saw only a trail of large footprints leading off into the darkness. Carlo got one of the tumbler's motorcycles. He pointed it in the direction of the footprints and stepped on the gas pedal.

He drove across the desert looking for Flower. He followed her footprints until he came to a little town. He saw Flower sitting in a vegetable garden, quietly eating some carrots. The rest of the garden was already a wreck. Flower had even destroyed all the roses on the edge of the garden. A bright red rose petal was still stuck to her trunk. Just then the police arrived, and Carlo explained what had happened. The police helped Carlo get Flower out of the garden and watched him as he led Flower back to the train.

When they got back, everyone was cheering. With Carlo's encouragement, Flower led all the other elephants in pulling the train back onto the tracks.

As the train was starting again, Carlo overheard his mother tell the circus manager that her son was ready to learn to be an animal trainer.

25

pledge
remember
elephant
gentle
metal
petal
else
exercise
energy
length
extra
desert
wreck
expert
special
century
metric
excellent
selfish
vegetable

Have a volunteer read each paragraph in the story, supplying each missing spelling word and spelling it aloud. Have other volunteers write the answers on the board and have students correct their own work. Check students' responses for the accurate spelling of each answer.

Follow-Up Have students use each of the spelling words they missed in an original sentence that relates to the story.

As an additional follow-up activity, you may wish to have one student read the story aloud to the class, pausing before each spelling word. The other students will say the spelling word at each appropriate time.

Enrichment

If you want to use the blackline activity masters for enrichment and additional practice, assign Lesson 4 activities at this time.

Maintenance and Review

OBJECTIVE

- To review words with /ĕ/ spelled: ea, e, ie.

ACTIVITIES

If you want to use the blackline activity masters for maintenance and review, assign Lesson 3 activities at this time.

You can also use the activity below to review Lesson 3 with students.

Write the following words on the board. Have students refer to the Lesson 3 word list and write the word or words that are synonyms for each word below. (Answers are in parentheses.)

make	(*invent*)
enjoyment	(*pleasure*)
mean	(*intend*)
riches	(*wealth, treasure*)
seat	(*bench*)
inquiries	(*questions*)
nice, kind	(*friendly*)
well	(*healthy*)
speech	(*address*)

Objectives

- To relate spelling to another language skill.
- To review and classify nouns.
- To write spelling words that are nouns in context.

Nouns

A noun is a word that names a person, place, thing, or idea.

woman	park	pumpkin	happiness
child	zoo	apple	beauty
man	city	pear	peace

★Find the noun in each group of words. Then write the noun.

1. metal remember until — metal

2. across complain energy — energy

3. paid elephant invent — elephant

4. erase century about — century

5. was petal excellent — petal

6. vegetable weigh remain — vegetable

★Unscramble and write each sentence. Then underline the nouns.

7. drove desert week We the last through

We drove through the desert last week.

8. The down swam wreck the to divers

The divers swam down to the wreck.

9. exercise likes of get Jill lots to

Jill likes to get lots of exercise.

10. class said of Allegiance Pledge Our the

Our class said the Pledge of Allegiance.

11. ran field length Andy the of the

Andy ran the length of the field.

26

Preparation Have students read the title of page 26. Review that a noun is a word that names a person, place, thing, or idea. Have students look at the word list on page 25 and name the nouns in the word list. Have them tell if each noun names a person, place, thing, or idea. Note that some words, such as pledge, can be nouns or verbs.

The Page Have students do page 26. Then have volunteers write the answers on the board and review them aloud for immediate reinforcement.

Follow-Up Have students write sentences containing the words in exercises 1–6.

WORDS AT WORK

Challenge Yourself

compel **condemn** **dedication** **pendulum**

Use your Spelling Dictionary to answer these questions. Then write sentences showing that you understand the meaning of each Challenge Word.

1. Do school rules compel you to walk backwards and wear gloves on your feet?
2. Should laws condemn cruel actions against people and animals?
3. Does a person who naps during a job show great dedication to his or her work?
4. Is a pendulum a part on some clocks?

Write to the Point

Imagine you are a newspaper reporter in Carlo's town. Your boss has sent you to cover the circus train story. Write a brief news article telling what happened to the circus train. Start with the headline "Elephant Escapes from Circus Train!" Remember to include the most important details. Use spelling words from this lesson in your article.

Challenge Use one or more of the Challenge Words in your article.

Proofreading

Use the proofreading marks to show the errors in the paragraph below. Write the five misspelled words correctly in the blanks.

⬭	word is misspelled
⊙	period is missing
⤳	take out word

To become an expurt circus acrobat like Ms. Chung, rember to practice every day and get the right kind of of exerize Get plenty of rest, too, or else you won't have the enerjy to give a an excellant performance.

1. expert
2. remember
3. exercise
4. energy
5. excellent

Objectives

- To extend the vowel spellings presented in Lesson 4 to the Challenge Words.
- To use context and the **Spelling Dictionary** to enlarge students' vocabulary.
- To apply the vowel spellings presented in Lesson 4 in a writing activity.
- To practice proofreading for spelling, punctuation, and extra words.

Dictation Sentences

1. He is an expert at fixing metal things.
2. Don't be selfish.
3. You must take a pledge or else you cannot join the club.
4. Save energy or we might run out before the end of the century.
5. What is the length of this line in the metric system?
6. The elephant is a gentle animal.
7. The exercise program at the school is excellent.
8. The wreck of the plane was found in the desert.
9. I would like extra butter for my vegetable.
10. Do you remember how to make a special rose petal jam?

Challenge Yourself Answers

1. no
2. yes
3. no
4. yes

Students' sentences will vary.

Test Review this way to spell /ĕ/: e as in century. Test words with /ĕ/. Use one of these testing methods: (1) Say the word; read the sample sentence from page 22; say the word; have students write it. (2) Read each dictation sentence above; have students write the sentence. Correct the test with students.

Challenge Yourself The optional Challenge Words may be assigned to the entire class or limited to those students who do well on the test. Have students note the vowel spelling in the Challenge Words. Responses to this activity should be completed on separate paper. Answers to the questions are provided above.

Write to the Point Help students recall the selection "The Circus Train" on pages 24 and 25; then assign the news article. You may want to read students a brief news article and point out how it answers the questions Who? What? Where? When? and Why? This activity should be completed on separate paper.

Proofreading The proofreading practice includes misspellings of words from this lesson as well as a punctuation error and extra words.

LESSON 5

Objectives

- To hear and say days, months, and an abbreviation.
- To write words that are days, months, and an abbreviation with attention to letter sequence and sound/symbol relationships.
- To write each spelling word once.

Sample Sentences

1. Sally's sister sang songs on Sunday.
2. Mara married Morris on Monday.
3. Ted traveled to Toronto on Tuesday.
4. Wilma will walk with Woody on Wednesday.
5. Theodore thanked Thurber on Thursday.
6. Frieda's friend fried fritters on Friday.
7. Sam saw seven seagulls on Saturday.
8. Janice jumps joyfully in January.
9. Fay found a fantastic fortune in February.
10. Molly motored merrily to Mississippi in March.
11. Ada argued angrily in April.
12. Mike met Maybelline in May.
13. Jill joins Judy jogging in June.
14. Jules jars jams in July.
15. Amos asked about astronauts in August.
16. Sandy sold seventy sodas in September.
17. Otto obtained an octopus in October.
18. Nora needs neither nets nor notes in November.
19. David dreams of dazzling daisies in December.
20. The abbreviation for Street is St.

Note

The sample sentences may be used for pretesting.

Lesson 5 Words with Capitals

Say each word.

Sunday
Monday
Tuesday
Wednesday
Thursday
Friday
Saturday

January
February
March
April
May
June
July
August
September
October
November
December

St.

1. Which three words begin with the letter m?
   Monday March
   May
2. Write the three words that begin with a vowel.
   April August
   October
3. Write the two words that begin with the letter t.
   Tuesday Thursday
4. Which two days and one month begin with the letter s?
   Sunday Saturday
   September
5. Which three words begin with the letter j? Circle the word that has one syllable. January
   (June) July
6. Which two words begin with the letter f? Circle the word that has four syllables.
   Friday (February)
7. Write the three words that end with the same five letters. September November
   December
8. Write the day of the week that has three syllables.
   Saturday
9. Write the word in which you see the letter d but don't hear /d/. Wednesday
10. Write the word in which the letter r appears twice.
    February
11. What is the abbreviation of the word Street?
    St.

28

Preparation Have students read aloud the title of the lesson on page 28. Read each spelling word aloud. Have students repeat and then spell each word aloud.

Ask students what kind of letter begins each word. (*a capital*) Ask them to identify the common ending for the names of the days. (*day*) Also note the schwa in Saturday: /săt′ ər dē/. Then note that St. can stand for Street or Saint. (*Johnson St.; St. Louis, Missouri*)

Read the sample sentences. Have students point to each spelling word as you read the sentence for it.

The Page Have students complete page 28 independently or as a class. Check the answers by having volunteers write the answers on the board and have students correct their own work.

Follow-Up Suggest that students write each syllable of each lesson word in a different color. Refer them to the **Spelling Dictionary** if they need help.

Checkpoint

Write a spelling word for each clue.
Then use the Checkpoint Study Plan on page 224.

1. The day after Saturday is ____. Sunday
2. The third month of the year is ____. March
3. Avenue is to Ave. as Street is to ____. St.
4. The calendar year begins on the first of ____. January
5. When the school week begins it is ____. Monday
6. The last month of the year is ____. December
7. Sunday is before Monday, Monday is before ____. Tuesday
8. The day after Tuesday is ____. Wednesday
9. Thanksgiving falls on the last Thursday in ____. November
10. The month that has only three letters is ____. May
11. School usually starts in the month of ____. September
12. Summer begins in the month of ____. June
13. The last school day in the week is ____. Friday
14. The day before Friday is ____. Thursday
15. The fourth month of the year is ____. April
16. The month after September is ____. October
17. The day named for Saturn is ____. Saturday
18. The shortest month is ____. February

19. These two mystery words are names for months. Both come from the names of great Romans. In one of these months, the great Roman general Julius Caesar was born. *Julius* Caesar had the Roman people name this month for him. Can you guess this month's name? ____ July
20. The other month was named for Julius Caesar's nephew. When the nephew became emperor, he was called Caesar Augustus. *Augustus* meant the great man. Can you guess which month was named for him? ____ August

29

Objectives

- To write spelling words in response to clues: definitions, analogies, and context.
- To develop the critical thinking skills of making inferences, sequencing, and drawing conclusions.
- To understand that some words in the English language have developed from people's names.

Spelling Strategy

Some students may misspell February because they do not pronounce the first r. Write February on the board, separating the syllables and circling the first r. Have students say the word aloud several times, pronouncing each consonant distinctly. Tell students that although February may be correctly pronounced with or without the first r, they must remember to include the first r when they write the word.

Wednesday is often misspelled because the first d and second e are not pronounced. Tell students that Wednesday comes from Woden's day, and explain that Woden was a god of ancient Norse mythology. Have students say Woden's day aloud and then *mis*pronounce Wednesday as /wĕd-nĕs-dā/ to hear the similarity between the modern word and its word of origin.

Preparation The clues on this page are like crossword puzzle clues. Explain to students that the response to each clue is a spelling word. Use the following examples to illustrate the types of clues used:

Definition	The fourth month of the year is (*April*).
Analogy	Avenue is to Ave. as Street is to (*St.*).
Context	The day named for Saturn is (*Saturday*).

The final clue explains how the names of the months July and August came from the names of two famous Romans.

The Page Have students complete page 29 using the words on page 28. When students have finished, have them read each clue and spell the answer aloud. Check each response twice: once for the correct answer and a second time for spelling accuracy.

Follow-Up Guide pupils in using the **Checkpoint Study Plan** on page 224 to take a self-test. Then have them use the plan for independent study.

Objectives

- To write the names of the months, days, and an abbreviation.
- To write each spelling word once.
- To integrate reading with spelling.

Use each list word once.

TIMELY PUZZLES

Write the name of a month in each blank.

Cuckoo, Cuckoo!
What do you do?
In April
I open my bill.
In __May__
I sing night and day.
In __June__
I change my tune.
In __July__
Away I fly.
In __August__
Away I must.

Some people think it is dangerous to eat fresh oysters in certain months. They say the oysters are not good during these months and can make a person very sick. They suggest following their rule for eating fresh oysters. Their rule is: EAT FRESH OYSTERS ONLY IN MONTHS WITH THE LETTER R IN THEIR NAMES.

Write the names of the months in which you can eat fresh oysters safely.

January	September
February	October
March	November
April	December

30

Preparation

Have students turn to pages 30 and 31. Let them look at the text and the pictures. Call their attention to the word list. Have the students say the words. Then explain that each spelling word belongs in one of the blanks.

Write the title "Timely Puzzles" on the board. Then ask how this part of the lesson is different from other lessons. (*There is no story; instead there is a poem and several exercises.*) Explain that students will do each part of the pages and then check the answers before going on to the next part.

The Pages

Have students complete pages 30 and 31 independently by silently reading the pages and writing the missing spelling words. Or you may read the pages aloud, supplying the missing words as students follow along in their texts; then have the students complete the pages on their own.

When students have finished, you may wish to discuss the exercises. Ask students why the title of this part of the lesson is "Timely Puzzles." (*Most of the spelling words have to do with time.*) Ask what an oyster is. (*an edible shellfish something like a clam*)

Have a volunteer read each exercise on the pages, supplying each missing spelling word and spelling it aloud. Have other volunteers write the answers on the board and have students correct their own work. Check students' responses for the accurate spelling of each answer.

Write the name of the day that matches each meaning.

Thursday	This day takes its name from the same word as thunder.
Monday	This day's name comes from a word meaning moon.
Sunday	This day was named for the sun.
Friday	This day was named for the Norse goddess Fria, the goddess of beauty and love.
Tuesday	This day's name comes from Tiw, a Norse god of war.
Saturday	This day was named for the Roman god of agriculture, Saturn.
Wednesday	The chief Norse god Woden, ruler of the sky, gave his name to this day.

Write the abbreviation that corresponds to this sign. St.

31

Monday
Tuesday
Wednesday
Thursday
Friday
Saturday
Sunday
January
February
March
April
May
June
July
August
September
October
November
December
St.

Enrichment

If you want to use the blackline activity masters for enrichment and additional practice, assign Lesson 5 activities at this time.

Maintenance and Review

OBJECTIVE

- To review words with /ĕ/ spelled: e.

ACTIVITIES

If you want to use the blackline activity masters for maintenance and review, assign Lesson 4 activities at this time.

You can also use the activity below to review Lesson 4 with students:

Write the Lesson 4 word list on the board or have students turn to it in their books. Ask students to write all the words that end in the silent letter e. (*pledge, gentle, else, exercise, vegetable*)

Follow-Up

Have students use each of the spelling words they missed in an original sentence that relates to the text.

As an additional follow-up activity, you may wish to remind students that they have seen that names of days are from the names of Roman and Norse gods. Explain that the names of some months come from the names of Roman emperors. If you wish, assign some students the task of researching the etymologies of day and month names and reporting their findings to the class.

Objectives

- To relate spelling to another language skill.
- To review capitalization of the names of days and months.
- To write spelling words in context.

Capitals

Use a capital letter to begin names of the days and months.

Sally was born on a Friday in December.

★ Unscramble the sentences below. Capitalize the names of the days and months. Remember to put a period at the end of each sentence.

1. is april balmy In the weather

In April the weather is balmy.

2. my birthday in is Don't forget february that

Don't forget that my birthday is in February.

3. field is in class trip november Our

Our class field trip is in November.

4. School in september begins

School begins in September.

5. on august We vacation in go july and

We go on vacation in July and August.

★ Roy made a list of the things he has to do. He made mistakes in spelling and capitalizing the days of the week. Write the seven words correctly.

Days		Things to Do
sonday	Sunday	visit grandparents
munday	Monday	brush dog
teusday	Tuesday	return library book
wenesday	Wednesday	go to baseball practice
thrusday	Thursday	study for test
fryday	Friday	take spelling test
saterday	Saturday	go to baseball game

Preparation Have students read aloud the title of page 32. Review with students that the names of days and months always begin with a capital letter.

Have volunteers come to the board to write the following: today's day and date; the day and date of the first day of next week; the day and date of their next birthday; the day and date of the next holiday. Be sure students begin each word with a capital letter and spell each word correctly.

The Page Have students do page 32. Then have volunteers write the answers on the board for immediate reinforcement.

Follow-Up Have students head columns on a sheet of paper with the following letters:

A D F J M N O S T W

Then have them write the names of the days and months that begin with each letter.

WORDS AT WORK

Challenge Yourself

Blvd. **Jupiter** **North Pole** **Memorial Day**

Decide which Challenge Word fits each clue. Check your Spelling Dictionary to see if you were right. Then write sentences showing that you understand the meaning of each Challenge Word.

1. This is when you might see a parade and remember those who died for their country.
2. It isn't a street, avenue, lane, or highway, but cars travel on it.
3. Because of its size, this place was named after the ancient Roman ruler of the gods.
4. You'll need your warmest clothes if you travel there.

Write to the Point

An itinerary lists places you will visit on a trip and the dates when you will arrive. Here is an example:

Monday, January 5—Disney World

Friday, February 11—Grand Canyon

Imagine you can take a yearlong trip. Plan one stop for each month. Write an itinerary for your trip. Use spelling words from this lesson.

Challenge Use one or more of the Challenge Words in your itinerary.

Proofreading

Use the proofreading marks to show the errors in the paragraph below. Write the five misspelled words correctly in the blanks.

(circle)	word is misspelled
≡	letter should be capitalized
! ^	exclamation point is missing

This may I started studying piano. Every (Wenesday) I go to my teacher's house on forest st. On (Munday), (Jully) 31, I give my first recital. How glad I'll be on (Teusday), (Awgust) 1, to wake up and know that the recital is over!

1. Wednesday
2. Monday
3. July
4. Tuesday
5. August

33

Objectives

- To extend the words with capitals presented in Lesson 5 to the Challenge Words.
- To use clues and the **Spelling Dictionary** to enlarge students' vocabulary.
- To apply the words with capitals presented in Lesson 5 in a writing activity.
- To practice proofreading for spelling, punctuation, and capitalization.

Dictation Sentences

1. I am leaving on Monday and will return next Wednesday.
2. The shop will be closed from March to June.
3. The park is open from May to September.
4. My club meets on Tuesday, Thursday, and Friday.
5. I can't wait until Saturday!
6. I was born in February.
7. Can you come for dinner on Sunday?
8. October and November are fall months.
9. I will leave for my trip in April and stay until August.
10. December and January are very cold months.
11. She lives on Main St.
12. We can go to the pool in July.

Challenge Yourself Answers

1. Memorial Day
2. Blvd.
3. Jupiter
4. North Pole

Students' sentences will vary.

Test Review and test the words from Lesson 5. Use one of these testing methods: (1) Say the word; read the sample sentence from page 28; say the word; have students write it. (2) Read each dictation sentence above; have students write the sentence. Correct the test with students.

Challenge Yourself The optional Challenge Words may be assigned to the entire class or limited to those students who do well on the test. You may wish to have students work in pairs. Responses to this activity should be completed on separate paper. Answers to the questions are provided above.

Write to the Point Help students recall the selection "Timely Puzzles" on pages 30 and 31; then assign the itinerary. Remind students to include both the day of the week and the month in their date. This activity should be completed on separate paper.

Proofreading The proofreading practice includes misspellings of words from this lesson as well as capitalization errors and a punctuation error.

LESSON 6

Objectives

- To review and reinforce vowel spellings for /ă/, /ā/, and /ĕ/.
- To hear, say, spell, and write representative spelling words from Lessons 1–4.
- To write a personal narrative using the five steps in the writing process.
- To use a prewriting activity to plan the sequence of events in a personal narrative.

Dictation Sentences

1. Our neighbor is friendly.
2. The factory was closed for the holiday.
3. I ate a sandwich and a vegetable salad.
4. That elephant will break the scale.
5. I will measure the length of this line with a metric ruler.
6. We got this special cake from the bakery.
7. It will take a lot of energy to escape from this trap.
8. She gave away half her wealth.
9. The gift of laughter is a great treasure.
10. Do you complain about doing work?

Note

A review test blackline master in standardized format and an answer sheet have been provided on pages T35 and T41 of this Teacher's Edition. The answers to the review test are given below.

1–A	11–C
2–D	12–A
3–B	13–D
4–B	14–B
5–C	15–C
6–D	16–D
7–B	17–B
8–A	18–A
9–C	19–C
10–A	20–D

If words misspelled were from:	have students complete activities:
List A	1, 3, 6
List B	2, 3, 6
List C	4, 6, 7

Lesson 6 Words in Review

A. factory, half, laughter, sandwich

B. neighbor, break, bakery, escape, holiday, complain, scale

C. friendly, measure, metric, length, wealth, energy, vegetable, treasure, special

★ You will need a piece of paper for these review activities.

1. In Lesson 1 you studied two different ways to spell /ă/: **a, au.** Write the words in list A.
   factory, half, laughter, sandwich
2. In Lesson 2 you studied six different ways to spell /ā/: **ai, a_e, ei, ay, ea, a.** Write the words in list B.
   neighbor, break, bakery, escape, holiday, complain, scale
3. ★ Use each review word from lists A and B in a sentence.
4. In Lessons 3 and 4 you studied three different ways to spell /ĕ/: **ea, e, ie.** Write the words in list C.
   friendly, measure, metric, length, wealth, energy, vegetable, treasure, special
5. ★ Look up each review word from list C in the Spelling Dictionary. Write the guide words.
6. ★ Write all 20 review words in alphabetical order.

Your teacher may give you a test. Answer these questions when you have finished.

7. Did you spell all the words correctly? Yes or No
8. Did you leave out a letter? Yes or No
9. Did you write the wrong letter? Yes or No
10. Did you miss the spelling of a vowel sound? Yes or No

34

Test Pretest the review words on page 34 to determine which students need reinforcement. Use one of these testing methods: (1) Read the words and the dictation sentences; have students write only the spelling words. (2) Read the dictation sentences and have students write the entire sentences. (3) Have students complete the review test blackline master. (See **Note**.) Correct the pretest with students.

The Pages Assign pages 34 and 35 according to students' needs.

- Students who have mastered all of the review words may go on to the **Writer's Workshop** on page 35.
- Students who have not mastered all of the review words should complete the activities on page 34 and take a post-test administered with one of the pretesting methods. After the post-test students can then go on to the **Writer's Workshop** on page 35. For students who have misspelled only a few of the review words, you may wish to use the list at left to determine the activities they should complete on page 34.

For students who have misspelled several of the review words, you may wish to assign all of the activities on page 34.

Writer's Workshop

A Personal Narrative

In a personal narrative, a writer tells a true story about his or her own life. The story captures a memory that is special to the writer because of something good, bad, funny, or important that happened. The writer uses first-person words such as I and me because he or she is the person telling the story. Here is part of Michiko's personal narrative about the time her cat disappeared.

The Search for Star

When my cat Star didn't show up for dinner on Friday, I wasn't too worried. Star likes to wander, and I knew he would be home by morning. But when he didn't show up for breakfast or lunch the next day, I began to worry.

I walked all over the neighborhood calling him. I looked on the playground and behind the corner store where the trash cans are. Since Star had gotten stuck in a tree three times, I checked out all the tall trees. By evening I had nearly lost hope.

To write her personal narrative, Michiko followed the steps in the writing process. She used a chain of events chart as a **Prewriting** activity. The chart helped her to remember what happened. It also helped her to put the events in the order in which they happened. Part of Michiko's chain of events chart is shown here. Study what Michiko did.

1	2	3
Star didn't show up for meals.	**I walked in the neighborhood calling him.**	**I looked in the tall trees.**

Get ready to write your own personal narrative. Choose a special memory that you would enjoy sharing. After you have decided what to write about, make a chain of events chart. Then follow the other steps in the writing process—**Writing, Revising, Proofreading,** and **Publishing.**

Note

If students have difficulty deciding on a topic, you may wish to suggest one of the following:

- A birthday I'll never forget
- The joke was on me
- My proudest moment

Writer's Workshop Explain that in personal narratives writers tell a true story about their own life. Usually they tell about something especially happy, sad, funny, or important that happened to them. Read with students the beginning of the personal narrative "The Search for Star" and point out how this story opening shows not only what happened but also how the writer felt about it.

Allow students to study the portion of the chain of events chart shown on the pupil's page and guide students to see how this graphic organizer helped Michiko prepare to write her personal narrative.

It's Your Turn Review the steps in the writing process with students. If students are not satisfied with the result of their prewriting, allow them to revise it as often as necessary or to choose another topic and repeat the prewriting activity.

Process Writing Blackline Masters

- Chain of Events Chart, page T46
- Steps in the Writing Process, page T44
- Proofreading Symbols/Checklist, page T45

LESSON 7

Objectives

- To hear and say words with /ē/.
- To write words with /ē/ with attention to letter sequence and sound/symbol relationships.
- To write each spelling word once.
- To recognize that /ē/ may be spelled y, e_e, and ie.

Sample Sentences

1. The letter carrier makes a delivery once a day.
2. My hobby is collecting stamps.
3. If you break that bowl, Jill will be angry.
4. I didn't mean to be late, but the storm made me tardy.
5. This is a fancy card.
6. We all had a merry time at Andrea's party.
7. The hills and the river look very pretty.
8. The Red team loses a turn as the penalty for fighting.
9. The garbage in the river is quite ugly.
10. All the guests are at liberty to go wherever they want.
11. The classroom looks strange when it is quiet and empty.
12. Let's sit in that shady place.
13. Can you play now, or are you busy?
14. Danny read a complete book in three hours!
15. The theme of today's lesson is energy.
16. The best athlete won the contest.
17. He swung upside down on the trapeze.
18. Our party will begin at seven o'clock this evening.
19. The two teams will compete for the prize.
20. You won't believe what just happened!

Note

- The sample sentences may be used for pretesting.
- Words are grouped according to spellings of /ē/:
  y
  e_e
  ie

Lesson 7 Words with /ē/

Listen for /ē/ in each word.

delivery
hobby
angry
tardy
fancy
merry
pretty
penalty
ugly
liberty
empty
shady
busy

complete
theme
athlete
trapeze
evening
compete

believe

1. Write the two words that begin with /k/.
   complete ____ compete
2. Which three words begin with the letter t? Circle the word that has one syllable. tardy
   (theme) ____ trapeze
3. Which word begins with the letters sh?
   shady
4. Which word begins and ends like factory?
   fancy
5. Which four words begin and end with a vowel?
   angry ____ ugly
   empty ____ athlete
6. Which word begins with a vowel and ends with a consonant? evening
7. Which word has the same spelling of /ē/ as relieve?
   believe
8. Which two words contain the /z/ sound?
   busy ____ trapeze
9. Write the two words that have three syllables.
   penalty ____ liberty
10. Write the word that has four syllables.
    delivery
11. Write the three words in which a double consonant letter spells one sound.
    bb hobby ____ rr merry
    tt pretty
12. Which two words contain the letters th?
    theme ____ athlete

36

Preparation Have students read aloud the title of the lesson on page 36. Write /ē/ on the board. Have students say /ē/ as in be. Read each spelling word aloud. Have students repeat and then spell each word aloud.

Note that penalty and liberty each have three syllables. Ask students to find the word that has four syllables. (*delivery*) Point out the schwa in letter: /lĕt′ ər/ and in delivery: /dĭ lĭv′ ə rē/. Ask students which letter spells /ə/ in letter and delivery. (*e*) Although the /ə/ is not formally taught until Lesson 31, students should realize that it may be spelled with any vowel letter.

Then ask students to identify how /ē/ is spelled in the first two groups of words. (*y*, *e_e*) Point out that /ē/ can also be spelled ie as in the last word believe. (See **Note**.)

Read the sample sentences. Have students point to each word as you read the sentence for it.

The Page Have students complete page 36 independently or as a class. Have volunteers write the answers on the board and have students correct their own work.

Follow-Up Have students fold a piece of paper into thirds and write words with the y spelling of /ē/ in the first column, words with the e_e spelling in the second column, and the word with the ie spelling in the third column.

Checkpoint

Write a spelling word for each clue.
Then use the Checkpoint Study Plan on page 224.

1. If he is mad, he is ____.
2. If your day is filled with activity, you are ____.
3. Discover is to discovery as deliver is to ____.
4. After sundown, it is ____.
5. The opposite of full is ____.
6. Jolly, happy, and ____ go together.
7. A subject or topic may be called a ____.
8. Another word for late is ____.
9. The opposite of plain is ____.
10. Under the trees we found a ____ spot.
11. If I break a rule, I must pay a ____.
12. Collecting stamps is a ____.
13. She is ____ enough to win a beauty contest.
14. Something with no part left out is ____.
15. An acrobat might do stunts on a ____.
16. The opposite of beautiful is ____.
17. If you are free, you have ____.
18. To pretend is to make ____.
19. To take part in a contest is to ____.

angry
busy
delivery
evening
empty
merry
theme
tardy
fancy
shady
penalty
hobby
pretty
complete
trapeze
ugly
liberty
believe
compete

20. The ancient Greeks were enthusiastic sports fans. They held many contests in running, boxing, and wrestling. The winner of these contests was given a prize. The prize was called the *athlon* in Greek. The contest for the prize was called the *athlos*. The name for a person who competed for the prize comes from these words. We use the word today to describe someone who participates in sports. Can you guess it? ____

athlete

37

Objectives

- To write spelling words in response to clues: definitions, synonyms, antonyms, classifications, analogies, and context.
- To develop the critical thinking skills of classifying, making inferences, and drawing conclusions.
- To understand that words have come into the English language from other languages.

Spelling Strategy

Some students may misspell athlete because they add an extra syllable when they pronounce it /ăth-ə-lēt/. It may be helpful to write athlete on the board, separating the syllables, and to point out that the word has only two syllables. Have students practice pronouncing athlete without adding an extra vowel sound between the syllables.

Preparation The clues on this page are like crossword puzzle clues. Explain to students that the response to each clue is a spelling word. Use the following examples to illustrate the types of clues used:

Definition	A subject or topic may be called a (*theme*).
Synonym	Another word for late is (*tardy*).
Antonym	The opposite of plain is (*fancy*).
Classification	Jolly, happy, and (*merry*) go together.
Analogy	Discover is to discovery as deliver is to (*delivery*).
Context	An acrobat might do stunts on a (*trapeze*).

The final clue explains the Greek origin of athlete.

The Page Have students complete page 37 using the words on page 36. When students have finished, have them read each clue and spell the answer aloud. Check each response twice: once for the correct answer and a second time for spelling accuracy.

Follow-Up Guide pupils in using the **Checkpoint Study Plan** on page 224 to take a self-test. Then have them use the plan for independent study.

Objectives

- To write words with /ē/ in continuous text.
- To write each spelling word once.
- To integrate reading with spelling.

Note

Point out that the word <u>liberty</u> in the phrase "at liberty to" <u>means</u> free to.

Use each list word once.

The Ambassadors

Samantha waited for the ambassadors from the planet Ixod to arrive. It was a hot day, so she waited on the ___shady___ side of the landing pad. Samantha had made sure she was on time to greet the visitors. The Ixodians did not like anyone to be ___tardy___.

What a sight the Ixodians were as they left their ship. They were tall and rainbow-colored. Each Ixodian uniform came ___complete___ with a red helmet. Samantha thought the ambassadors looked very ___pretty___.

"Welcome," Samantha said. "I have planned lots of fun for you. I hope you will have a very ___merry___ time. I thought you would like to rest while you wait for the ___delivery___ of your things. Then this ___evening___ we will go to a magic show."

Xio, the Ixodian leader said, "Samantha, please feel at ___liberty___ to show us what you think we will like." However, the Ixodians were very quiet during the show. They never seemed surprised by the magic.

"Circus clowns" was the ___theme___ for the next day's entertainment. Samantha took her guests to a store that sold clown puppets. There were puppets with sad faces and puppets with mean, ___ugly___ faces. There were clown dolls with colorful, ___fancy___ costumes. The Ixodians seemed to have seen the puppets before. Later, at the circus,

Preparation

Have students turn to pages 38 and 39. Let them look at the story and the picture. Call their attention to the word list. Have the students say the words. Then explain that each spelling word belongs in one of the blanks in the story.

Write the title "The Ambassadors" on the board. Then have a student read the title aloud. Ask what an ambassador is. (*a person representing a government in a different country*) Ask where the ambassadors in this story probably come from. (*another planet*)

The Pages

Have students complete pages 38 and 39 independently by silently reading the story and writing the missing spelling words. Or you may read the story aloud, supplying the missing words as students follow along in their texts; then have the students complete the pages on their own.

When students have finished, you may wish to discuss the story. Ask students what the Ixodians learned from Samantha. (*Life is much more interesting when you don't always know what lies ahead.*) Ask students if they agree or not, and why. Ask if they have seen the same television program or movie the ambassadors didn't bat an eyelash at the funny clown on the tightrope. Even the man on the flying __trapeze__ didn't excite the Ixodians.

Samantha did not want to be upset or __angry__. She decided to ask Xio what the problem was. She found him watching TV.

"Xio! What are you doing?" she asked.

"I'm watching a football game," he explained. "I have always been an __athlete__, and football has long been a __hobby__ of mine. I love it so much I don't even wear my future-predicting helmet while I watch the game."

Samantha could not __believe__ her ears. "Do you mean your helmet tells you everything that is going to happen before it happens? That's why your people seem so lifeless and __empty__. Now I know how to make your people enjoy their visit more."

Xio listened. Then Xio and Samantha gathered the Ixodians together.

"Today," Samantha said, "you are going to learn to play football. But first, please remove your red helmets and put on these football helmets instead."

The Ixodians did as asked. They learned how to make a goal and how not to cause a __penalty__. They were kept __busy__ cheering each other on.

When it was time to go, Xio said to Samantha, "Someday Ixod may __compete__ against Earth in an intergalactic football game. But for now, you have taught my people that life is much more interesting when you don't always know what lies ahead."

39

delivery
hobby
angry
tardy
fancy
merry
pretty
penalty
ugly
liberty
empty
shady
busy
complete
theme
athlete
trapeze
evening
compete
believe

more than once. Did they like it the second time as much as the first time? Were they bored? Did they appreciate the show more, or less? (*Answers will vary.*) Ask when it might be important to know what will happen in the future. (*for example, when a storm is coming, or when a plane you're meeting is going to be late*)

Have a volunteer read each paragraph in the story, supplying each missing spelling word and spelling it aloud. Have other volunteers write the answers on the board and have students correct their own work. Check students' responses for the accurate spelling of each answer.

Follow-Up

Have students use each of the spelling words they missed in an original sentence that relates to the story.

As an additional follow-up activity, you may wish to have the students work in small groups with a cassette recorder to make "The Ambassadors" into a "radio drama" with special sound effects. Have students select the roles of Samantha, Xio, and the other Ixodians. Students may use sound-effect records or create their own special sound effects.

Enrichment

If you want to use the blackline activity masters for enrichment and additional practice, assign Lesson 7 activities at this time.

Maintenance and Review

OBJECTIVE

- To review the names of days and months.

ACTIVITIES

If you want to use the blackline activity masters for maintenance and review, assign Lesson 5 activities at this time.

You can also use the activity below to review Lesson 5 with students.

Write the following words on the board. Have students write the names of the days or months that come just before and after each. (Answers are in parentheses.)

Thursday	(*Wednesday, Friday*)
Sunday	(*Saturday, Monday*)
Wednesday	(*Tuesday, Thursday*)
May	(*April, June*)
October	(*September, November*)
January	(*December, February*)

Objectives

- To relate spelling words to a dictionary skill.
- To analyze the parts of a dictionary entry.
- To locate spelling words in the **Spelling Dictionary**.
- To write spelling words in alphabetical order.
- To recognize the multiple meanings of some spelling words.
- To use the **Spelling Dictionary**.

Parts of a Dictionary Entry

The words that are listed in alphabetical order under the guide words in a dictionary are called entry words. They are printed in dark type with a dot between the syllables. A dictionary entry includes the entry word, the sound spelling, the part of speech, the definition or meaning of the word, and anything else important about the word.

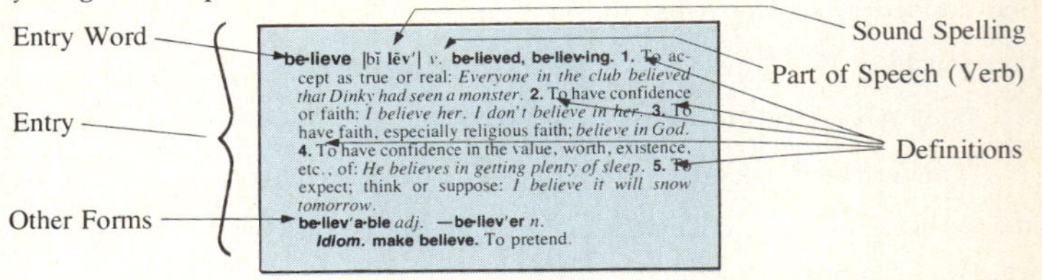

Many words have more than one meaning. To decide how a word is used in a sentence, a dictionary and context clues must be used.

★ Read the above entry and answer these questions.

1. What is the entry word in the above entry? believe

2. How many meanings does the dictionary show for this entry word? 5

★ Write the number of the definition used in each of these sentences.

3. Our teacher believes in homework. 4

4. I believe everything Grandma tells me. 2

5. Ted believes the rain will stop before the game. 5

★ Write the following words in alphabetical order. Then look them up in the Spelling Dictionary. Write the number of meanings each word has.

shady **angry** **trapeze** **complete** **fancy**

	Word	Number of Meanings
6.	angry	3
7.	complete	3
8.	fancy	2, 2
9.	shady	2
10.	trapeze	1

Preparation Have students read aloud the title of page 40. Tell students to read the first paragraph and study the entry. Ask what each label means. Then ask where they would look to find the answers to these questions: How many syllables does believe have? (*Look at the entry word.*) How is believe pronounced? (*Look at the sound spelling just after the entry word.*) How are other forms of the word spelled? (*Look at the bottom of the entry.*) What part of speech is believe? (*Look at the abbreviation after the sound spelling.*)

The Page Have students do page 40. Then have volunteers write the answers on the board and review them orally for immediate reinforcement.

Follow-Up Have students write the last meaning given for each word in exercises 6–10. Then have them write a sentence using this meaning of each word.

WORDS AT WORK

Challenge Yourself

canopy **recede** **utility** **siege**

Write what you think each underlined Challenge Word means. Check your Spelling Dictionary to see if you were right. Then write sentences showing that you understand the meaning of each Challenge Word.

1. Marta's bed has a white lace canopy over it.
2. If we have a drought, the water in the river will recede.
3. We get utility bills for water, telephone, and electricity.
4. The enemy held the town under siege, so no one was allowed to leave.

Write to the Point

Imagine that you are directing a movie about aliens from outer space who have landed on Earth. Write a paragraph describing these beings. Create a name for these unusual beings and their home planet. What do the aliens look like? How do they move? How do they communicate? Use spelling words from this lesson in your description.

Challenge Use one or more of the Challenge Words in your description.

Proofreading

Use the proofreading marks to show the errors in the paragraph below. Write the five misspelled words correctly in the blanks.

⬭	word is misspelled
? ^	question mark is missing
^	word is missing

Can you believe it^? Friday (evning) I was in the library, (buzy) reading about life ^on other planets. Suddenly, to my (compleet) surprise, a Martian sat down in the (emty) seat beside me. He ^was pretty (uggly) but seemed quite nice.

1. evening
2. busy
3. complete
4. empty
5. ugly

41

Objectives

- To extend the vowel spellings presented in Lesson 7 to the Challenge Words.
- To use context and the **Spelling Dictionary** to enlarge students' vocabulary.
- To apply the vowel spellings presented in Lesson 7 in a writing activity.
- To practice proofreading for spelling, punctuation, and missing words.

Dictation Sentences

1. A good athlete can compete in many sports.
2. I was tardy with my paper delivery this week.
3. I work on my hobby each evening.
4. I wear my pretty red shoes with my fancy white dress.
5. The theme of my paper is liberty for all.
6. I can't believe the trapeze artist did a flip without a net!
7. Are you too busy to empty the trash can right now?
8. I am angry because I did not complete the test.
9. I have to pay a penalty.
10. We had a merry time talking under the shady trees.
11. The gray sky looks dark and ugly.

Challenge Yourself Answers

Possible definitions:

1. cloth covering over a bed
2. to move back
3. company that provides a service
4. blockade

Students' sentences will vary.

Test Review these three ways to spell /ē/: y as in busy; e_e as in theme; ie as in believe. Test words with /ē/. Use one of these testing methods: (1) Say the word; read the sample sentence from page 36; say the word; have students write it. (2) Read each dictation sentence above; have students write the sentence. Correct the test with students.

Challenge Yourself The optional Challenge Words may be assigned to the entire class or limited to those students who do well on the test. Have students note the vowel spellings in the Challenge Words. Responses to this activity should be completed on separate paper. Answers to the questions are provided above.

Write to the Point Help students recall the selection "The Ambassador" on pages 38 and 39; then assign the description. Encourage students to choose vivid words that will help their readers visualize the extraterrestrials. This activity should be completed on separate paper.

Proofreading The proofreading practice includes misspellings of words from this lesson as well as a punctuation error and missing words.

LESSON 8

Objectives

- To hear and say words with /ē/.
- To write words with /ē/ with attention to letter sequence and sound/symbol relationships.
- To write each spelling word once.
- To recognize that /ē/ may be spelled ee, ea, ea_e, and i.

Sample Sentences

1. The family was there to greet May.
2. Doris will make a speech to the class.
3. Sidney fell asleep in his chair.
4. I lost the thread and dropped the needle.
5. We can't ride up that steep hill on our bikes.
6. Mark woke up to find himself tangled in the sheet.
7. It's silly to argue when we really agree about this.
8. The temperature dropped one more degree.
9. Wear your mittens, or your hands may freeze.
10. Max felt too weak to climb the rest of the mountain.
11. We can defeat their team.
12. Do you have a good reason for being late?
13. We drove past fields of corn and wheat.
14. We found four kittens beneath the porch.
15. After the party I enjoyed the peace and quiet.
16. We will increase the number of plants in the garden.
17. I could hardly breathe the smoky air.
18. Rita is going to the mountains to ski.
19. Fran will play her new song on the piano.
20. Let's have a big pizza with sausage.

Note

- The sample sentences may be used for pretesting.
- Words are grouped according to spellings of /ē/:
  ee
  ea
  ea_e
  i

Lesson 8 Words with /ē/

Listen for /ē/ in each word.

greet
speech
asleep
needle
steep
sheet
agree
degree
freeze

weak
defeat
reason
wheat
beneath
peace
increase

breathe

ski
piano
pizza

1. Write the two words that begin with the letter b. beneath breathe
2. Write the two words that begin with the letter w. weak wheat
3. Which two words begin with the letters de? degree defeat
4. Write the four words that begin with the letter s. speech steep sheet ski
5. Write the three words that begin with a vowel. asleep agree increase
6. Which three words begin with /p/? Write the word with one syllable first. Then write the word with two syllables. Write the word with three syllables last. peace pizza piano
7. Which word ends with /z/? freeze
8. In which word does the same letter spell both /t/ and /s/? pizza
9. Write the other two words that have the same spelling of /ē/ as pizza. ski piano
10. Which word begins and ends like great? greet
11. Which word begins and ends like noodle? needle
12. Which word begins and ends like raisin? reason
13. Write the word in which you hear /hw/. wheat

42

Preparation Have students read aloud the title of the lesson on page 42. Write /ē/ on the board. Have students say /ē/ as in be. Read each spelling word. Ask students to repeat and then spell each word aloud.

Note that wheat begins with wh, that breathe ends with a silent e, and that pizza contains two z's and no t's. Have a volunteer identify the letters that spell /ē/ in the first group of words. (ee) Ask students to identify the letter or letters in the other groups in the list that spell /ē/. (See **Note**.)

Read the sample sentences. Have students point to each spelling word as you read the sentence for it.

The Page Have students complete page 42 independently or as a class. Help them pronounce /hw/ in exercise 13. Then ask volunteers to write the answers on the board and have students correct their own work.

Follow-Up Suggest that students write each word three times and then spell it aloud.

Checkpoint

Write a spelling word for each clue.
Then use the Checkpoint Study Plan on page 224.

1. A large musical instrument with a keyboard is a ____. — piano
2. Powerless means ____. — weak
3. To have the same opinion is to ____. — agree
4. It was so cold, I thought I would ____. — freeze
5. The opposite of war is ____. — peace
6. A piece of paper may be called a ____. — sheet
7. Another word for under is ____. — beneath
8. You use your nose to ____. — breathe
9. In water you swim, on snow you ____. — ski
10. The opposite of decrease is ____. — increase
11. The opposite of awake is ____. — asleep
12. A unit of temperature is a ____. — degree
13. How you talk makes up your ____. — speech
14. The opposite of victory is ____. — defeat
15. On a farm you may grow ____. — wheat
16. To sew, you need a sharp ____. — needle
17. A hill with a sharp slope is ____. — steep
18. Why you did something is the ____. — reason
19. To welcome is to ____. — greet

20. The origin of this mystery word is uncertain. But we know it came to English from Italian. It may have come from the Italian word *pizzicare*. *Pizzicare* means to pluck or pinch something. When dough is kneaded and patted, it is plucked and pinched. So the word came to be used for something made out of dough. That is what we use it for today. Can you guess the word? ____ — pizza

43

Objectives

- To write spelling words in response to clues: definitions, synonyms, antonyms, analogies, and context.
- To develop the critical thinking skills of making inferences and contrasting.
- To understand that words have come into the English language from other languages.

Spelling Strategy

Some students may forget to include the final e when they write breathe. Write breathe and breath on the board and use each word in a sentence, explaining that breathe is a verb and breath is a noun. Ask students to write sentences for each word, leaving a blank line in place of breathe or breath. Have them exchange papers with a partner and complete each other's sentences with the appropriate word.

Preparation

The clues on this page are like crossword puzzle clues. Explain to students that the response to each clue is a spelling word. Use the following examples to illustrate the types of clues used:

Definition	To have the same opinion is to (*agree*).
Synonym	Another word for under is (*beneath*).
Antonym	The opposite of decrease is (*increase*).
Analogy	In water you swim, on snow you (*ski*).
Context	On a farm you may grow (*wheat*).

The final clue explains how pizza might have come into the English language.

The Page

Have students complete page 43 using the words on page 42. When students have finished, have them read each clue and spell the answer aloud. Check each response twice: once for the correct answer and a second time for spelling accuracy.

Follow-Up

Guide pupils in using the **Checkpoint Study Plan** on page 224 to take a self-test. Then have them use the plan for independent study.

Objectives

- To write words with /ē/ in continuous text.
- To write each spelling word once.
- To integrate reading with spelling.

Note

- Point out the use of the word degree as the measure of an angle in the story. A 45-degree angle is halfway between the vertical and the horizontal.
- Point out that Beethoven was a composer of classical music who lived about 200 years ago. The "Moonlight Sonata" is beautiful but very difficult to play.

Use each list word once.

The Homework Assignment

Here I sit staring at this piece of paper. Mr. Costa has given everyone in class a writing assignment for tomorrow. He wants us to write a story about what we would like to be doing ten years from now. I can never think of anything. I start daydreaming right away. . . .

I am on a ___steep___ *ski slope. The hill must be at least a forty-five-* ___degree___ *angle. The snow on the hill is covered with a thin sheet of ice because there was a big* ___freeze___ *last night. I know the hill is dangerous, but I'm not afraid. I can* ___ski___ *better than anyone I know. I take a deep breath, forcing myself to* ___breathe___ *slowly and evenly. I concentrate on the* ___peace___ *and quiet here on the mountain. I count down very slowly and push off. The ice feels slippery* ___beneath___ *my skis. I am flying down the hill, faster, faster, faster . . .*

My best friend wrote her story this afternoon. She invited me to share a ___pizza___ with her for supper this evening, but Mom says I can't go anywhere until I finish my homework. . . .

I am sitting at the grand ___piano___. *I have just finished playing Beethoven's "Moonlight Sonata." The crowd is going wild. I take one bow, two bows, three bows. They are still clapping. Finally I* ___agree___ *to play one more piece. The crowd is quiet as I raise my hands to begin . . .*

44

Preparation Have students turn to pages 44 and 45. Let them look at the story and the pictures. Call their attention to the word list. Have the students say the words. Then explain that each spelling word belongs in one of the blanks in the story.

Write the title "The Homework Assignment" on the board. Ask students if they can tell anything about this story. Explain that it is about a girl who is daydreaming instead of writing her homework assignment. Note that the paragraphs that are daydreams are set in italics, a different kind of type from the usual.

Ask students if they ever daydream about being very good at doing something, or about being famous. Point out that most people do have such daydreams, but it is only by doing that we can ever fulfill our dreams. Tell students to look for ways that the narrator of the story could do something with her daydreams.

Maybe I'll just sneak into the kitchen for a slice of Mom's freshly baked whole ___wheat___ bread. All this homework sure makes me hungry! . . .

As I enter the auditorium, the President smiles and stands up to ___greet___ me. I begin to give my ___speech___. Several people in the back of the hall begin to scream because they disagree with my opinions. I see that I will have to give them a good ___reason___ to vote for me or else they will ___defeat___ me in this election. . . .

Yawn! I'm getting tired. I think I'll take a little nap. I may even get a good idea from a dream while I'm ___asleep___. I can't think of what to write about yet. . . .

I am in the operating room. The patient is covered with a ___sheet___. He was very ___weak___ when they brought him in, and he is getting weaker every minute. The nurse put a bandage on his arm so that his wound wouldn't bleed. There is only one way to ___increase___ his chances of living. I ask the nurse for the ___needle___ and give him the injection that will put him to sleep. I am the best doctor in the country. If anyone can save him, I can. . . .

I've wasted an hour. And I still don't have an idea for that story! I guess I just don't have a good imagination.

greet
speech
asleep
needle
steep
sheet
agree
degree
freeze
weak
defeat
reason
wheat
beneath
peace
increase
breathe
ski
piano
pizza

The Pages

Have students complete pages 44 and 45 independently by silently reading the story and writing the missing spelling words. Or you may read the story aloud, supplying the missing words as students follow along in their texts; then have the students complete the pages on their own.

When students have finished, you may wish to discuss the story. Ask what the story's narrator could have done with her daydreams. (*She could have written about them as her homework assignment.*) Ask if students think her dreams were silly or if they were things that could take place. Ask what the narrator could do to make each dream come true. (*learn to ski, practice the piano, work as a volunteer in politics, study to become a doctor*)

Have a volunteer read each paragraph in the story, supplying each missing spelling word and spelling it aloud. Have other volunteers write the answers on the board and have students correct their own work. Check students' responses for the accurate spelling of each answer.

Follow-Up

Have students use each of the spelling words they missed in an original sentence that relates to the story.

As an additional follow-up activity, you may wish to have pairs of students take turns reading the story aloud to each other, pausing before each spelling word. The other student will supply the missing word by spelling it aloud at the appropriate time.

Enrichment

If you want to use the blackline activity masters for enrichment and additional practice, assign Lesson 8 activities at this time.

Maintenance and Review

OBJECTIVE

- To review words with /ē/ spelled: y, e_e, ie.

ACTIVITIES

If you want to use the blackline activity masters for maintenance and review, assign Lesson 7 activities at this time. You can also use the activity below to review Lesson 7 with students:

Write the following words on the board. Have students write the word from Lesson 7 that is a synonym for each word. (Answers are in parentheses.)

freedom	(*liberty*)
mad	(*angry*)
vacant	(*empty*)
happy	(*merry*)
late	(*tardy*)
finished	(*complete*)
pastime	(*hobby*)
occupied	(*busy*)

Objectives

- To relate spelling to another language skill.
- To review and identify verbs.
- To write spelling words.
- To use the **Spelling Dictionary**.

Verbs

A verb is a word that describes action.

Alex <u>walked</u> to the fair with me.

★ Complete each sentence below with one of these verbs.

greet **agree** **freeze** **needle** **defeat**
reason **breathe** **increase** **ski**

1. That team is difficult to defeat.
2. Mother said that Mrs. Hatch will greet us at the door.
3. Robert likes to tease the dog and needle his little brother.
4. We need oxygen in order to breathe.
5. At what temperature does milk freeze?
6. We all agree that Merin is the most talented piano player.
7. Gloria will ski from the snowy mountain's summit.
8. Jay's family fed him six times a day to increase his weight.
9. Alice can reason with even the most unreasonable people.

★ Unscramble and write each sentence. Then underline the verbs. Don't forget to put the correct punctuation at the end of each sentence.

10. climbed We steep hill the
    We <u>climbed</u> the steep hill.
11. and ate Tom the pizza all Mary
    Tom and Mary <u>ate</u> all the pizza.
12. gave speech her yesterday She
    She <u>gave</u> her speech yesterday.
13. Jones wheat Farmer raises
    Farmer Jones <u>raises</u> wheat.
14. the beneath crushed feet I my grass
    I <u>crushed</u> the grass beneath my feet.

46

Preparation Have students read the title of page 46. Review that a verb is a word that expresses action. Have students look at the word list on page 45 and have them name the words that are verbs. Then have students look at the list of words for the first set of exercises on page 46. Note that although <u>needle</u> is usually used as a noun, it is also a verb meaning to annoy, and that <u>reason</u> is also a verb meaning to think or to try to persuade.

The Page Have students do page 46. Then have volunteers write the answers on the board and review them orally.

Follow-Up Have students write the words for the first set of exercises on page 46, look them up in the **Spelling Dictionary**, and write one verb meaning of each word.

WORDS AT WORK

Challenge Yourself

easel **tweed** **meager** **safari**

Decide which Challenge Word fits each clue. Check your Spelling Dictionary to see if you were right. Then write sentences showing that you understand the meaning of each Challenge Word.

1. Clothing made of this would help keep you warm in winter.
2. If painters don't have one, they won't have anything to stand their latest work on.
3. If you like wild animals but don't like zoos, try going on this with a camera.
4. This might describe a serving of food that leaves you hungry.

Write to the Point

What kind of career would you like to have someday? Perhaps it's one you read about in "The Homework Assignment." Write a paragraph about your dream career. Describe the kind of work you would do. Explain why you would find this work exciting or satisfying. Use spelling words from this lesson in your paragraph.

Challenge Use one or more of the Challenge Words in your paragraph.

Proofreading

Use the proofreading marks to show the errors in the paragraph below. Write the five misspelled words correctly in the blanks.

⬭	word is misspelled
≡	letter should be capitalized
⸺୨	take out word

When i enter ~~to~~ Uncle Al's bakery and (breath) in, lovely odors greet me. That is one (reazon) why I ~~am~~ want to be a baker. I also like to help Uncle Al toss the (wheet) dough for (pitza) or roll it into a (sheat) for cookies. A baker's life is the life for me!

1. breathe
2. reason
3. wheat
4. pizza
5. sheet

Objectives

- To extend the vowel spellings presented in Lesson 8 to the Challenge Words.
- To use clues and the **Spelling Dictionary** to enlarge students' vocabulary.
- To apply the vowel spellings presented in Lesson 8 in a writing activity.
- To practice proofreading for spelling, capitalization, and extra words.

Dictation Sentences

1. I used whole wheat flour to make the pizza crust.
2. After his defeat, he came out to greet the press.
3. What is the reason for the increase in prices?
4. I cannot ski down the steep hill because I have a weak stomach.
5. I fell asleep during the piano concert.
6. She dropped her needle beneath the chair.
7. On a sheet of paper, write a short theme on how fish breathe.
8. I agree with you.
9. She gave a speech about peace.
10. The pond will freeze if the temperature drops another degree.

Challenge Yourself Answers

1. tweed
2. easel
3. safari
4. meager

Students' sentences will vary.

Test Review these four ways to spell /ē/: ee as in agree; ea as in weak; ea_e as in breathe; i as in ski. Test words with /ē/. Use one of these testing methods: (1) Say the word; read the sample sentence from page 42; say the word; have students write it. (2) Read each dictation sentence above; have students write the sentence. Correct the test with students.

Challenge Yourself The optional Challenge Words may be assigned to the entire class or limited to those students who do well on the test. Have students note the vowel spellings in the Challenge Words. You may wish to have students work in pairs. Responses to this activity should be completed on separate paper. Answers to the questions are provided above.

Write to the Point Help students recall the selection "The Homework Assignment" on pages 44 and 45; then assign the paragraph. Encourage students to provide specific details or examples when explaining what they would enjoy about their dream career. This activity should be completed on separate paper.

Proofreading The proofreading practice includes misspellings of words from this lesson as well a capitalization error and extra words.

LESSON 9

Objectives

- To hear and say words with /ĭ/.
- To write words with /ĭ/ with attention to letter sequence and sound/symbol relationships.
- To write each spelling word once.
- To recognize that /ĭ/ may be spelled i, e, and ui.

Sample Sentences

1. Jim hasn't been to school since Tuesday.
2. Do you know a good joke or a riddle?
3. The workers are building a bridge.
4. Jan's disease was cured by the medicine.
5. Your hand joins your arm at the wrist.
6. Strips of grass divide the highway into two parts.
7. We'll talk later; I can't discuss it now.
8. Bobby looks quite different than his brother looks.
9. The players ran quickly down the field.
10. The game was over, and it was time to quit.
11. We saw the smoke coming out of the chimney.
12. Everyone is here except Rupert, who is sick.
13. Put the bats with the other playing equipment.
14. At the end of a hard day, it's nice to relax.
15. Let's review what we've learned so far.
16. Do you think 10 bottles of juice are enough?
17. We expect 25 people to come to the party.
18. Sammy built a house entirely out of cards.
19. When I broke my dad's bike, I felt guilty.
20. Jeff plays the guitar in our band.

Note

○ The sample sentences may be used for pretesting.

○ Words are grouped according to spellings of /ĭ/:
i
e
ui

Lesson 9 Words with /ĭ/

Listen for /ĭ/ in each word.

since
riddle
bridge
disease
wrist
divide
discuss
different
quickly
quit
chimney

except
equipment
relax
review
enough
expect

built
guilty
guitar

1. Which two words begin with the letters ex? except expect
2. Write the two words that begin with the letters re. relax review
3. Which three words have /kw/ in them? quickly quit equipment
4. Which word begins and ends with /s/? since
5. Which word begins and ends with /d/? divide
6. Which word begins with the letters ch? chimney
7. Which word ends with /j/? bridge
8. Which word ends with /f/? Circle the letters that spell /f/. enough
9. Which word ends with /ks/? Circle the letter that spells /ks/. relax
10. Which word ends with /z/? disease
11. Which three words have the same spelling of /ĭ/ as building? (Remember, qu spells /kw/.) built guilty guitar
12. Write the word in which you see the letter w at the beginning but don't hear /w/. wrist
13. Write the words in which a double consonant spells one sound.
dd riddle ff different
ss discuss

48

Preparation Ask students to read aloud the title of the lesson on page 48. Write /ĭ/ on the board. Have students say /ĭ/ as in pit. Read each spelling word aloud. Have students repeat and then spell each word aloud.

Note the suffix ment at the end of equipment. Ask what suffix is at the end of quickly. (*ly*) Have students identify how /ĭ/ is spelled in the other groups in the list. (See **Note**.)

Read the sample sentences. Have students point to each spelling word as you read the sentence for it.

The Page Have students complete page 48 independently or as a group. Have volunteers write the answers on the board. You may wish to have the volunteers circle the letters that spell the sound /kw/ in exercise 3. Have students correct their own work.

Follow-Up Suggest that students practice spelling the words with a partner. One student says a word and the partner spells it aloud or writes it. Then they alternate.

Checkpoint

Write a spelling word for each clue.
Then use the Checkpoint Study Plan on page 224.

1. He stopped working when he ___ his job.	quit
2. The musician played the ___.	guitar
3. Today I build, yesterday I ___.	built
4. To separate into parts is to ___.	divide
5. She wears a watch on her ___.	wrist
6. The opposite of innocent is ___.	guilty
7. Smoke goes up a ___.	chimney
8. The opposite of the same is ___.	different
9. Something hard to answer or understand is a ___.	riddle
10. As much as you need is ___.	enough
11. You may go over a river by walking on a ___.	bridge
12. Another word for sickness is ___.	disease
13. To go over or to see again is to ___.	review
14. The opposite of stiffen up is ___.	relax
15. To look forward to means to ___.	expect
16. A word for apart from is ___.	except
17. Tents and sleeping bags are camping ___.	equipment
18. It has rained steadily ___ early morning.	since
19. The opposite of slowly is ___.	quickly
20. When we speak, we do more than move our lips and make sounds. We also use our minds. Before words are said, the mind has separated out the ideas it wants to express. The origin of the mystery word reflects this process. The word means to speak. But its base word has nothing to do with speaking. Its base is the Latin word *discutio,* meaning to shake apart. Because we shake apart or separate our thoughts when we speak, the word came to mean speak. Can you guess it? ___	discuss

Objectives

- To write spelling words in response to clues: definitions, synonyms, antonyms, analogies, and context.
- To develop the critical thinking skills of making inferences and contrasting.
- To understand that word meanings often change over time.

Spelling Strategy

Some students may misspell different because they don't pronounce the second vowel. Tell them that different may be pronounced either with or without the second vowel sound but that they must remember to include the e that spells that sound when they write the word. Have students practice saying different with three syllables to reinforce the correct spelling.

Preparation The clues on this page are like crossword puzzle clues. Explain to students that the response to each clue is a spelling word. Use the following examples to illustrate the types of clues used:

Definition	To separate into parts is to (*divide*).
Synonym	Another word for sickness is (*disease*).
Antonym	The opposite of slowly is (*quickly*).
Analogy	Today I build, yesterday I (*built*).
Context	You may go over a river by walking on a (*bridge*).

The final clue explains the Latin origin of discuss.

The Page Have students complete page 49 using the words on page 48. When students have finished, have them read each clue and spell the answer aloud. Check each response twice: once for the correct answer and a second time for spelling accuracy.

Follow-Up Guide pupils in using the **Checkpoint Study Plan** on page 224 to take a self-test. Then have them use the plan for independent study.

Objectives

- To write words with /ī/ in continuous text.
- To write each spelling word once.
- To integrate reading with spelling.

Use words from the first half of the list to do this page.

THE GARDEN

There used to be a cabin here.
There's the fireplace
And the brick chimney.
And here's where we'll plant
our garden.
It's where one used to grow
Years ago.

A spider built a web,
A silken bridge across
a puddle.
Across it she can
quickly scurry.
So
WATCH OUT!
If you're a fly in a hurry.

I didn't expect it
to happen
So fast.
But the seed I planted took root,
And now it's a shoot.

Twist the wrist,
Bend the knee.
Did all these weeds
Grow just for me?

In our tool shed
Are all the
different
things
You need to make a
Garden grow,
Rakes and shovels,
Trowels and hoes.
All the equipment
To dig out a furrow
And build up a ridge
Where seedlings can grow.
In our tool shed
Are all the
different
things
You need to make a
Garden grow—
Except sun and earth
and water.

Look at this squash.
Long neck,
Fat, tan body,
Like a guitar
without strings.

50

Note

- Point out the use of the word squash to mean a vegetable in the poem. Ask students for another meaning of squash.
- Point out that spuds is a slang term for potatoes.

Preparation Have students turn to pages 50 and 51. Let them look at the poems and the pictures. Call their attention to the word list. Have the students say the words. Then explain that each spelling word belongs in one of the blanks in the poems.

Write the title "The Garden" on the board. Ask students what kind of selection they see on these pages. (*poems*) Ask what the poems are about. (*a garden*) Ask if any students have planted a garden. If so, have them describe the processes of preparing the soil and planting the seeds. If not, explain that a gardener must break up the ground and dig furrows, which are shallow trenches, for the seeds. Gardeners use trowels, which are something like small shovels, and hoes, which are something like rakes, to prepare the soil. Ask what problems a gardener might have to deal with. (*weeds, bad weather, plant diseases*) Point out that making a garden grow is hard work.

The Pages Have students complete pages 50 and 51 independently by silently reading the poems and writing the missing spelling words. Or you may read the poems aloud, supplying the missing words as students follow along in their texts; then have the students complete the pages on their own.

Use words from the second half of the list to do this page.

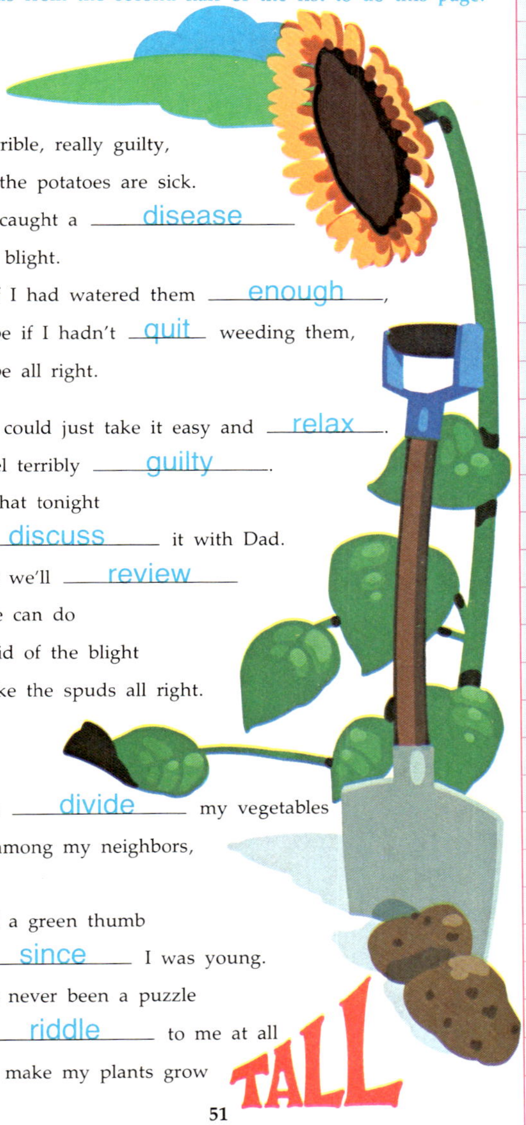

I feel terrible, really guilty,
Because the potatoes are sick.
They've caught a disease
Called a blight.
Maybe if I had watered them enough,
Or maybe if I hadn't quit weeding them,
They'd be all right.

I wish I could just take it easy and relax.
But I feel terribly guilty.
I think that tonight
I'll discuss it with Dad.
Together we'll review
What we can do
To get rid of the blight
And make the spuds all right.

I always divide my vegetables
Evenly among my neighbors,
Because
I've had a green thumb
Ever since I was young.
And it's never been a puzzle
Or a riddle to me at all
How to make my plants grow TALL

51

quickly
equipment
wrist
built
different
guitar
except
expect
chimney
bridge

since
riddle
disease
divide
discuss
quit
relax
review
enough
guilty

When students have finished, you may wish to discuss the poems. Ask students to tell what happens in the poems. Ask what kind of person wrote the poems. (*a young boy or girl who is a good gardener, takes a lot of responsibility, and feels bad when things go wrong*) Ask students who have planted a garden how they felt when things did not go exactly right. (*Answers will vary.*)

Have a volunteer read each poem, supplying each spelling word and spelling it aloud. Have other volunteers write the answers on the board and have students correct their own work. Check students' responses for the accurate spelling of each answer.

Follow-Up

Have students use each of the spelling words they missed in an original sentence that relates to the poems.

As an additional follow-up activity, you may wish to have one student read the poems aloud to the class, pausing before each spelling word. The other students will say the spelling word at the appropriate time.

Enrichment

If you want to use the blackline activity masters for enrichment and additional practice, assign Lesson 9 activities at this time.

Maintenance and Review

OBJECTIVE

- To review words with /ē/ spelled: ee, ea, ea_e, i.

ACTIVITIES

If you want to use the blackline activity masters for maintenance and review, assign Lesson 8 activities at this time.

You can also use the activity below to review Lesson 8 with students.

Write the following on the board. Have students refer to the Lesson 8 word list and write the word that is an antonym of each word. (Answers are in parentheses.)

melt	(*freeze*)
disagree	(*agree*)
awake	(*asleep*)
decrease	(*increase*)
war	(*peace*)
strong	(*weak*)
level	(*steep*)
above	(*beneath*)

Objectives

- To relate spelling words to a dictionary skill.
- To review parts of speech.
- To write spelling words in alphabetical order.
- To identify the parts of speech of spelling words.
- To use the **Spelling Dictionary**.

Parts of Speech

A dictionary lists the part of speech for each entry word. The part of speech tells if a word is one of the following:

noun *n.*	adjective *adj.*	pronoun *pron.*	conjunction *conj.*
verb *v.*	adverb *adv.*	preposition *prep.*	interjection *interj.*

★ Write the following words in alphabetical order. Then look up each word in the Spelling Dictionary and write its part of speech.

wrist disease divide expect

	Word	Part of Speech
1.	disease	noun
2.	divide	verb
3.	expect	verb
4.	wrist	noun

★ Some words are used as more than one part of speech. A dictionary lists the most commonly used part of speech first. Then the other parts of speech and definitions follow.

e·nough |ĭ nŭf'| *adj.* Sufficient to meet a need or satisfy a desire: *There is enough food for everybody. Will $10 be enough to pay for the tickets?* —*n.* An adequate quantity: *He ate enough for two.* —*adv.* **1.** To a satisfactory amount or degree; sufficiently: *Are you warm enough?* **2.** Very; fully; quite: *We were glad enough to leave.* **3.** Tolerably; rather: *She sang well enough, but the show was a failure.*

adjective
noun
adverb

5. What is the entry word of the above entry? enough
6. How many parts of speech are listed? three
7. What are they? adjective, noun, adverb

★ What part of speech is enough used as in each of these sentences?

8. We ate enough to last us a week! noun
9. There are enough tickets for everyone in the class. adjective
10. Is this table big enough for our art project? adverb

52

Preparation Have students read the title of page 52. Review the parts of speech listed at the top of the page. Note that the parts of speech are abbreviated in dictionary entries. Have students tell what a noun is and what a verb is. Remind students that adjectives describe nouns and pronouns; adverbs tell about verbs, adjectives, and other adverbs; pronouns are words such as he and she that take the place of nouns; prepositions are words such as under and over that show relationships; conjunctions are connecting words such as and and or; interjections are words such as ha and wow that stand alone and show emotion.

The Page Have students do page 52. Then have volunteers write the answers on the board and review the answers orally.

Follow-Up Write these words on the board: **guilty, review, bridge, except, since,** and **quickly**. Have students write each word, look it up in the **Spelling Dictionary**, and write its part or parts of speech.

WORDS AT WORK

Challenge Yourself

quizzical bliss commit pinnacle

Use your Spelling Dictionary to answer these questions. Then write sentences showing that you understand the meaning of each Challenge Word.

1. When people are puzzled, do their faces sometimes show a quizzical look?
2. Do most people feel bliss if they do badly on a test?
3. Is it a detective's job to catch people who commit crimes?
4. If you were climbing a steep mountain, would you start at the pinnacle?

Write to the Point

Think of something you know how to make, grow, fix, or clean. Then write a paragraph or two explaining how you do it. Describe each step in the process from start to finish, and be sure to present the steps in their correct order. Use spelling words from this lesson in your explanation.

Challenge Use one or more of the Challenge Words in your explanation.

Proofreading

Use the proofreading marks to show the errors in the paragraph below. Write the five misspelled words correctly in the blanks.

(oval)	word is misspelled
⊙	period is missing
!^	exclamation point is missing

Mr. Hertz's tomatoes had grown (quikly) since last month⊙ All (exept) a few of them were ripe (enugh) to eat, so he gave me some. Wow!^ I didn't (expeck) them to be so good and so (diffrent) from the ones at the store⊙

1. quickly
2. except
3. enough
4. expect
5. different

53

Objectives

- To extend the vowel spellings presented in Lesson 9 to the Challenge Words.
- To use context and the **Spelling Dictionary** to enlarge students' vocabulary.
- To apply the vowel spellings presented in Lesson 9 in a writing activity.
- To practice proofreading for spelling and punctuation.

Dictation Sentences

1. We will review the chapter quickly before the test.
2. He has not been able to play since he hurt his wrist.
3. The town built a bridge with new equipment.
4. Do not feel guilty if you want to quit the team.
5. When I want to relax, I play the guitar.
6. The children gave different answers to the riddle.
7. I will divide the pie so that there is enough for everyone.
8. Do the doctors expect to find a cure for the disease?
9. I have cleaned the house except for the chimney.
10. I want to discuss plans for the party with you.

Challenge Yourself Answers

1. yes
2. no
3. yes
4. no

Students' sentences will vary.

Test Review these three ways to spell /ĭ/: i as in bridge; e as in relax; ui as in built. Test words with /i/. Use one of these testing methods: (1) Say the word; read the sample sentence from page 48; say the word; have students write it. (2) Read each dictation sentence above; have students write the sentence. Correct the test with students.

Challenge Yourself The optional Challenge Words may be assigned to the entire class or limited to those students who do well on the test. Have students note the vowel spelling in the Challenge Words. Responses to this activity should be completed on separate paper. Answers to the questions are provided above.

Write to the Point Help students recall the selection "The Garden" on pages 50 and 51; then assign the explanation. Suggest to students that they picture themselves going through the process as they write about it. This activity should be completed on separate paper.

Proofreading The proofreading practice includes misspellings of words from this lesson as well as punctuation errors.

LESSON 10

Objectives

- To hear and say words with /ĭ/.
- To spell words with /ĭ/ with attention to letter sequence and sound/symbol relationships.
- To write each spelling word once.
- To recognize that /ĭ/ may be spelled i, a, y, and u.

Sample Sentences

1. Joanna bought film for her new camera.
2. A good pilot has the skill to fly any plane.
3. We're having fried chicken for dinner.
4. Joe is good at arithmetic.
5. Don't be too timid to speak out for what you want.
6. I must insist that you listen to my complaint.
7. An insect crawled up Maria's arm and tickled her.
8. Rosa will pitch in this game.
9. The sixth grade is putting on a play today.
10. Rod put the groceries on the kitchen table.
11. The picnic will be held in Croton Park.
12. The hurricane caused a lot of damage.
13. Six hundred people live in this village.
14. Wrap up your garbage before you dump it.
15. The cottage has three rooms and a porch.
16. If I'm not home, leave a message with my brother.
17. This package is too heavy for me to carry.
18. Do you like to read mystery stories?
19. Our school has a new system for taking attendance.
20. My mother runs a radio repair business.

Note

- The sample sentences may be used for pretesting.
- Words are grouped according to spellings of /ĭ/:
  i y
  a u

Lesson 10 Words with /ĭ/

Listen for /ĭ/ in each word.

film
skill
chicken
arithmetic
timid
insist
insect
pitch
sixth
kitchen
picnic

damage
village
garbage
cottage
message
package

mystery
system

business

1. Which two words begin with /k/? Circle the letter that spells /k/. kitchen cottage
2. Which two words end with /k/? Circle the letter that spells the final /k/. arithmetic picnic
3. Which two words begin with the letter i and end with the letter t? insist insect
4. Which word begins and ends like farm? film
5. Which word begins and ends like tied? timid
6. Write one word that begins with the letters ch, one that ends with ch, and one that has ch in the middle. chicken pitch kitchen
7. Write the six words in which you hear /j/ but don't see the letter j. damage village garbage cottage message package
8. Which two words have y as the second letter? mystery system
9. Which word has /ks/ in the middle? Circle the letter that spells /ks/. sixth
10. Which word has /z/ in the middle? business
11. Write the words in which a double consonant spells one sound.
    ll skill ll village
    ss message ss business
    tt cottage

54

Preparation

Have students read aloud the title of the lesson on page 54. Write /ĭ/ on the board. Have students say /ĭ/ as in pit. Read each spelling word aloud. Have students repeat and then spell each word aloud.

Ask what suffix is at the end of sixth. (*th*) Ask what letters are at the end of each syllable in picnic. (*ic*) Then ask which letter in business is written but not pronounced. (*i*) Note the schwa in the last syllable of kitchen: /kĭch′ ən/ and chicken: /chĭk′ ən/. Ask the students to identify the letter that spells /ĭ/ in each group of words in the list. (See **Note**.)

Read the sample sentences. Have students point to each spelling word as you read the sentence for it.

The Page

Have the students complete page 54 independently or as a group. For exercise 9, tell students that /ks/ is often spelled x. Have volunteers write the answers on the board and have students correct their own work.

Follow-Up

Suggest that students write all the list words in alphabetical order.

Checkpoint

Write a spelling word for each clue.
Then use the Checkpoint Study Plan on page 224.

1. To throw a ball to the batter in baseball is to ____. pitch
2. Mind your own ____. business
3. A community smaller than a town is a ____. village
4. Another word for shy is ____. timid
5. A small house is a ____. cottage
6. We add, subtract, multiply, and divide in ____ class. arithmetic
7. The ability to do something well is a ____. skill
8. Spoken or written words make up a ____. message
9. A bee is a type of ____. insect
10. An orderly way is a ____. system
11. Another word for parcel is ____. package
12. Another word for movie is ____. film
13. Let's eat outdoors and have a ____. picnic
14. After fifth comes ____. sixth
15. At the dump there is a lot of ____. garbage
16. A kind of fowl is a ____. chicken
17. To hurt or harm is to ____. damage
18. The place to cook is in the ____. kitchen
19. To take a strong stand is to ____. insist

20. This word comes from the Greek word *mystes*. *Mystes* meant close-mouthed or silent. The Romans borrowed the word and changed it to *mysterium*. Today we use the word to mean something people don't know and therefore don't talk about. Can you guess what it is? ____ mystery

55

Objectives

- To write spelling words in response to clues: definitions, synonyms, and context.
- To develop the critical thinking skills of making inferences, classifying, and sequencing.
- To understand that cultures adopt words from other languages, sometimes changing the spelling and meaning.

Spelling Strategy

If students have difficulty remembering that /ĭ/ is spelled y in system and mystery, they might benefit from focusing on the shape of the words. Have them write each word in pencil and outline it in pen. Then have them erase the penciled letters, observe the shape of the ink outline, and fill the letters back in.

Preparation The clues on this page are like crossword puzzle clues. Explain to students that the response to each clue is a spelling word. Use the following examples to illustrate the types of clues used:

Definition	An orderly way is a (*system*).
Synonym	Another word for movie is (*film*).
Context	Let's eat outdoors and have a (*picnic*).

The final clue explains how mystery came into the English language.

The Page Have students complete page 55 using the words on page 54. When students have finished, have them read each clue and spell the answer aloud. Check each response twice: once for the correct answer and a second time for spelling accuracy.

Follow-Up Guide pupils in using the **Checkpoint Study Plan** on page 224 to take a self-test. Then have them use the plan for independent study.

Objectives

- To write words with /ĭ/ in continuous text.
- To write each spelling word once.
- To integrate reading with spelling.

Note

Point out the use of the word film as a verb in the story. Ask students for other meanings of film.

Use each list word once.

A Pitch in Time

Everyone in the village where I live was ready for the big baseball game, especially my family. They had been waiting all summer to see me pitch for my team. My parents had made a picnic lunch of cold chicken, apple juice, and cabbage salad. And they had brought a movie camera so they could film the whole event.

The game started. My team did well, but the other team did better. Through the first five innings, the other team made five runs. My team made two runs. Then came the sixth inning — and my turn to pitch. The team was depending on my pitching skill. I thought I could manage to win. I have my own system of pitching, though I won't ever tell anybody what it is. I just say that it isn't anyone's business but my own.

Soon I had two strikes on the hitter. I wound up for the next pitch. Just then an insect flew into my eye. The ball flew from my hand, out of control. It flew over the fence and crashed through the kitchen window of the cottage across the street.

Preparation Have students turn to pages 56 and 57. Let them look at the story and the picture. Call their attention to the word list. Have the students say the words. Then explain that each spelling word belongs in one of the blanks in the story.

Write the title "A Pitch in Time Stops Crime" on the board. Ask students what the pitcher in a baseball game does. (*throws balls to the batter, trying to strike out the batter*) Ask what a "ball" is. (*a pitch that is too high, too low, too close, or too far away from the batter*) If any of your students have pitched, ask them what it is like.

The Pages Have students complete pages 56 and 57 independently by silently reading the story and writing the missing spelling words. Or you may read the story aloud, supplying the missing words as students follow along in their texts; then have the students complete the pages on their own.

When students have finished, you may wish to discuss the story. Ask a volunteer to summarize the plot of the story. Then ask if students have ever been embarrassed when they did something wrong. Ask how the boy in the story makes himself feel better. (*He stands up to the police officer.*) Point out that we cannot always correct an embarrassing situation, but we can sometimes do something else to help us (and others) forget the embarrassment.

Stops Crime

I was so embarrassed I wanted to hide. All the players ran across the street. The door of the cottage was open, so we went in to see how much ___damage___ had been done. The window was broken, of course, and the ball had knocked over the ___garbage___ can. As I was picking up the garbage, I came across a ___message___ written in big print. It said:

> Sept. 20
> Pick up the ___package___ in two days.
> Meet me behind the store at the regular time.
> S.C.

I was always good at adding, so I did some quick ___arithmetic___ in my head and realized that the note meant today. I figured that the police could solve this ___mystery___, so I took the note to them.

The man at the desk made me feel ___timid___ and unsure of myself. He tried to dismiss me; he didn't even want to listen to me. I had already been embarrassed once that day. I wasn't going to let it happen again. I found the courage to ___insist___ he look at the note. And then I left.

Well, we lost the game. But several days later, the police chief called to congratulate me. The police had arrested several people in a robbery ring. I was a hero after all!

57

film
skill
chicken
arithmetic
timid
insist
insect
pitch
sixth
kitchen
picnic
damage
village
garbage
cottage
message
package
mystery
system
business

Have a volunteer read each paragraph in the story, supplying each missing spelling word and spelling it aloud. Have other volunteers write the answers on the board and have students correct their own work. Check students' responses for the accurate spelling of each answer.

Follow-Up Have the students use each of the spelling words they missed in an original sentence that relates to the story.

As an additional follow-up activity, you may wish to have students make a mural illustrating the story. Attach a large piece of paper to the wall, and have several students plan and draw the mural.

Enrichment

If you want to use the blackline activity masters for enrichment and additional practice, assign Lesson 10 activities at this time.

Maintenance and Review

OBJECTIVE

- To review words with /ĭ/ spelled: i, e, ui.

ACTIVITIES

If you want to use the blackline activity masters for maintenance and review, assign Lesson 9 activities at this time.

You can also use the activity below to review Lesson 9 with students.

Write the following words on the board. Have students refer to the Lesson 9 word list and write the word that is a synonym for each word below. (Answers are in parentheses.)

talk	(*discuss*)
sickness	(*disease*)
erected	(*built*)
gear	(*equipment*)
but	(*except*)
stop	(*quit*)
hope	(*expect*)
fast	(*quickly*)

Objectives

- To relate spelling to another language skill.
- To review the use of commas in a series.
- To write spelling words in the context of sentences.
- To practice proofreading.

Commas

Use a comma to separate a series of words or word groups in a sentence.

Bill had a sandwich, a piece of pie, and a glass of milk.
Then he gathered up his baseball glove, bat, and ball.

★ Write the sentences below, adding commas where they are needed. Correct the misspelled word in each sentence.

1. I need a pencil eraser and paper to do my arithmatick.
I need a pencil, eraser, and paper to do my arithmetic.

2. Chicen can be fried broiled or baked.
Chicken can be fried, broiled, or baked.

3. I can't decide whether spiders ants or beetles are my favorite insecks.
I can't decide whether spiders, ants, or beetles are my favorite insects.

4. We brought ham eggs chicken and brownies for our piknik.
We brought ham, eggs, chicken, and brownies for our picnic.

5. The timmid elephant was afraid of mice snakes and his own shadow!
The timid elephant was afraid of mice, snakes, and his own shadow!

6. In the vilaje were a bakery a post office and a town hall.
In the village were a bakery, a post office, and a town hall.

7. The kitchin was a mess with pots pans and dishes everywhere.
The kitchen was a mess with pots, pans, and dishes everywhere.

8. Lynn wanted to study bizness teaching and medicine.
Lynn wanted to study business, teaching, and medicine.

58

Preparation Have students read the title of page 58. Ask what a series is. (*a group or a list of related things*) Write on the board the two sample sentences at the top of page 58, leaving out the commas. Have volunteers add the commas in the correct places. Remind students that without the commas, these sentences would be hard to understand.

The Page Have students do page 58. Then have volunteers write the answers on the board and review the answers orally.

Follow-Up Write the following sentence fragments on the board. Have students copy the sentence fragments and complete them by writing a series of words or word groups. (Remind them to use commas where necessary.)

1. This business sells . . .
2. This kitchen has . . .
3. In arithmetic we study . . .
4. In this film you'll see . . .
5. This chicken can . . .
6. In the garage we found . . .

WORDS AT WORK

Challenge Yourself

rummage symptom abyss lyrics

Decide which Challenge Word fits each clue. Check your Spelling Dictionary to see if you were right. Then write sentences showing that you understand the meaning of each Challenge Word.

1. You might hum a song because you can't remember these.
2. When someone is getting a cold, the first one might be a sore throat, sneezing, or a cough.
3. You might have to do this to find a pencil or eraser in a messy desk drawer.
4. If you drop something into this, you will probably never see it again.

Write to the Point

Think of a time when you made an embarrassing mistake. What did you learn from your mistake? Did the lesson you learned help you later? Write a paragraph about your embarrassing mistake and the lesson you learned. Use spelling words from this lesson in your paragraph.

Challenge Use one or more of the Challenge Words in your paragraph.

Proofreading

Use the proofreading marks to show the errors in the paragraph below. Write the five misspelled words correctly in the blanks.

⬭	word is misspelled
^	word is missing
≡	letter should be capitalized

At our family picnic, we all ensist on playing baseball by our own sistum. Mom likes to pich with ^her eyes closed. once Aunt Rita let the sixt strike go by before she called me out. And it's ^a mistery who wins, because my brother forgets to keep score.

1. insist
2. system
3. pitch
4. sixth
5. mystery

Objectives

- To extend the vowel spellings presented in Lesson 10 to the Challenge Words.
- To use clues and the **Spelling Dictionary** to enlarge students' vocabulary.
- To apply the vowel spellings presented in Lesson 10 in a writing activity.
- To practice proofreading for spelling, capitalization, and missing words.

Dictation Sentences

1. If you want to go to business school, you must do well in arithmetic.
2. Take this package to the sixth floor!
3. I left the message in the kitchen.
4. The ant is one insect you always find at a picnic.
5. Did you make a film of the damage done by the storm?
6. Her mystery story is about a cottage in a tiny village.
7. I like to pitch paper into the garbage can.
8. I insist that an alarm system be installed.
9. It takes a lot of skill to make this chicken dish.
10. My cat is timid.

Challenge Yourself Answers

1. lyrics
2. symptom
3. rummage
4. abyss

Students' sentences will vary.

Test Review these four ways to spell /ĭ/: i as in film; a as in cottage; y as in system; u as in business. Test words with /ĭ/. Use one of these testing methods: (1) Say the word; read the sample sentence from page 54; say the word; have students write it. (2) Read each dictation sentence above; have students write the sentence. Correct the test with students.

Challenge Yourself The optional Challenge Words may be assigned to the entire class or limited to those students who do well on the test. Have students note the vowel spellings in the Challenge Words. You may wish to have students work in pairs. Responses to this activity should be completed on separate paper. Answers to the questions are provided above.

Write to the Point Help students recall the selection "A Pitch in Time Stops Crime" on pages 56 and 57; then assign the paragraph. You might suggest that students begin by writing a topic sentence that concisely states the lesson that was learned. This activity should be completed on separate paper.

Proofreading The proofreading practice includes misspellings of words from this lesson as well as a capitalization error and missing words.

LESSON 11

Objectives

- To hear and say plurals.
- To write plurals with attention to letter sequence and sound/symbol relationships.
- To write each spelling word at least once.
- To recognize that plurals may be formed by adding s or es, by changing y to i and adding es, and by changing f to v and adding es or s.

Sample Sentences

1. Some people sat on benches in the park.
2. We brought fruit and sandwiches for lunch.
3. Some birds build nests in the branches of trees.
4. The candidates made speeches.
5. The play began with crashes of cymbals.
6. She saw three stars and made three wishes.
7. All the businesses in town helped pay for a parade.
8. That store sells skis and sleds.
9. It also sells other equipment for athletes.
10. Our neighbors are friendly.
11. I planted vegetables in my garden.
12. We do exercises in gym class.
13. It was 90 degrees one day last summer.
14. Mr. Hyde told us stories about his childhood.
15. She went to three parties last weekend.
16. My parents work for different companies.
17. Do you have any hobbies?
18. I don't like games with penalties.
19. The cows and their calves looked over the fence.
20. All the husbands and wives were invited to the picnic.

Note

The sample sentences may be used for pretesting.

Lesson 11 Plurals

Say each word.

benches
sandwiches
branches
speeches
crashes
wishes
businesses

skis
athletes
neighbors
vegetables
exercises
degrees

stories
parties
companies
hobbies
penalties

calves

wives

Solve these plural puzzles.

cartwheel + s = cartwheels

1. ski + s = skis
2. vegetable + s = vegetables
3. athlete + s = athletes
4. degree + s = degrees
5. exercise + s = exercises
6. neighbor + s = neighbors

peach + es = peaches

7. bench + es = benches
8. crash + es = crashes
9. branch + es = branches
10. sandwich + es = sandwiches
11. speech + es = speeches
12. wish + es = wishes
13. business + es = businesses

body − y + i + es = bodies

14. story − y + i + es = stories
15. hobby − y + i + es = hobbies
16. company − y + i + es = companies
17. penalty − y + i + es = penalties
18. party − y + i + es = parties

wolf − f + v + es = wolves

19. calf − f + v + es = calves

Find the word that forms its plural the way life does.

life ⟶ lives

20. wife ⟶ wives

60

Preparation

Have students read aloud the title of the lesson on page 60. Ask students to define plurals. (*words that name more than one*) Read each spelling word aloud. Tell students to repeat and then spell each word aloud.

Note that the singular forms of many of the words were studied in previous lessons. Ask the students how the plurals are formed in the first three groups. (*The first group adds es; the second group adds s; the third group changes y to i and adds es.*) How are the plurals of calf and wife formed in the last groups? (*The f in the singular form is changed to v before es or s is added.*)

Read the sample sentences. Have students point to each spelling word as you read the sentence for it.

The Page

Have the students complete page 60 independently or as a group. Have volunteers write the answers on the board and have students correct their own work.

Follow-Up

Suggest that students write the base words with a blue pen or pencil and the plural endings with a red pen or pencil.

Checkpoint

Write a spelling word for each clue.
Then use the Checkpoint Study Plan on page 224.

1. The plural form of wife is ____. wives
2. Another word for tales is ____. stories
3. Cows give birth to ____. calves
4. Activities for fun may be ____. hobbies
5. If I go to work out, then I want to do my ____. exercises
6. Formal talks in front of an audience are ____. speeches
7. In a factory are workers, on a ball field are ____. athletes
8. Fruits and ____ are part of a good diet. vegetables
9. You need bread to make ____. sandwiches
10. A tree has a trunk and many ____. branches
11. Hopes and dreams are like ____. wishes
12. Race-cars may have ____. crashes
13. Long seats in parks are called ____. benches
14. Social gatherings are ____. parties
15. Ice is for skates, snow is for ____. skis
16. The people who live nearby are your ____. neighbors
17. Another word for fines is ____. penalties
18. Water freezes at 32 ____. degrees
19. More than one company is ____. companies

20. This word comes from the word busy. It originally meant the state of being engaged in any activity that made one busy. Later it came to mean an activity of a serious and important kind. Today when we use this word by itself, we usually mean someone's job or occupation. Can you make this word plural and guess the word? ____ businesses

61

Objectives

- To write spelling words in response to clues: definitions, synonyms, analogies, and context.
- To develop the critical thinking skills of making inferences and analyzing.
- To understand that new words may develop from older ones and to recognize that word meanings may change over time.

Spelling Strategy

If students have difficulty remembering that words such as branches and wishes end with es rather than s, point out that the e is included to make the word easier to pronounce. Demonstrate by writing branchs and wishs on the board and asking students to try to pronounce the words without adding a vowel sound to the ending.

Preparation The clues on this page are like crossword puzzle clues. Explain to students that the response to each clue is a spelling word. Use the following examples to illustrate the types of clues used:

Definition	Long seats in parks are called (*benches*).
Synonym	Another word for fines is (*penalties*).
Analogy	Ice is for skates, snow is for (*skis*).
Context	A tree has a trunk and many (*branches*).

The final clue explains how businesses developed from the word busy.

The Page Have students complete page 61 using the words on page 60. When students have finished, have them read each clue and spell the answer aloud. Check each response twice: once for the correct answer and a second time for spelling accuracy.

Follow-Up Guide pupils in using the **Checkpoint Study Plan** on page 224 to take a self-test. Then have them use the plan for independent study.

Objectives

- To write plurals in continuous text.
- To write each spelling word once.
- To integrate reading with spelling.

Use each list word once.

THE FAIR

My great-grandfather is from Japan. He settled on a farm in California in 1904. He tells me lots of stories about the "good old days." Our family still farms in the northern Sacramento Valley. Many of our neighbors are Japanese also.

Every year there is a fair in our area. All the farmers show the best things they have grown. Blue-and-white striped tents hold big yellow squashes and plump green avocadoes. Juicy red tomatoes and purple beets stand out amid the zucchinis and lettuce. I'm always amazed how colorful vegetables are. The cut branches of trees also lend color to the decorations.

One of my father's cows won a blue ribbon last year for best cow in the show. Her two baby calves won the judges' hearts, I think. The judges never marked any penalties against Flossie for poor teeth, dull coat, or anything else. Winning a prize at the fair is a happy event in our family. We usually have several parties to celebrate.

Note

- Point out the use of the word calves to mean baby cows in the story. In Lesson 1, calf was used to mean a part of the leg.
- Point out the use of the word degrees to mean a measure of temperature. Ask students for other definitions of degrees.

Preparation Have students turn to pages 62 and 63. Let them look at the story and the picture. Call their attention to the word list. Have the students say the words. Then explain that each spelling word belongs in one of the blanks in the story. Write the title "The Fair" on the board. Tell the students that this story is about an annual fair and is told by a boy or girl who lives and works on a farm.

The Pages Have students complete pages 62 and 63 independently by silently reading the story and writing the missing spelling words. Or you may read the story aloud, supplying the missing words as students follow along in their texts; then have the students complete the pages on their own.

Ask students about the kinds of fairs they have attended. Ask a volunteer to describe the sights and sounds he or she noticed. (*Answers will vary.*)

Have volunteers take turns reading each paragraph in the story, supplying each missing spelling word and spelling it aloud. Have other volunteers write the answers on the board and have students correct their own work. Check students' responses for the accurate spelling of each answer.

The Chamber of Commerce always has a tent at the fair. Local businesses show people what they sell. Small businesses and big companies all participate. There is also a tent for crafts. People show the beautiful things they make in their spare time. Their hobbies range from woodcarving to rugmaking.

This year there is going to be a sports tent. High school athletes will show people how to do exercises. Equipment dealers are going to display everything from fishing poles to skis.

Children get lost and look for parents. Husbands look for wives, and wives look for husbands. Friends look for friends. Amid the confusion, politicians give speeches and people lounge on wooden benches to listen to folk musicians play their banjos. Children throw pennies into the goldfish pond and make wishes. You can hear laughter and shouts as one bumper car crashes into another. You can smell the aroma of spicy meatball sandwiches.

The fair is my favorite week of the year. It doesn't matter whether it rains or shines, and I never care if it's freezing or 90 degrees. It makes me feel good to be part of farming and the fair.

63

benches
sandwiches
branches
speeches
crashes
wishes
businesses
skis
athletes
neighbors
vegetables
exercises
degrees
stories
parties
companies
hobbies
penalties
calves
wives

Follow-Up

Have the students use each of the spelling words they missed in an original sentence that relates to the story.

As an additional follow-up activity, you may wish to have the students write one or two paragraphs describing a place or event they enjoy, using at least two of the spelling words in this lesson.

Enrichment

If you want to use the blackline activity masters for enrichment and additional practice, assign Lesson 11 activities at this time.

Maintenance and Review

OBJECTIVE

- To review /ĭ/ spelled i, a, y, u.

ACTIVITIES

If you want to use the blackline activity masters for maintenance and review, assign Lesson 10 activities at this time. You can also use the activity below to review Lesson 10 with students.

Write the following words on the board. Have students refer to the Lesson 10 word list and change one letter in each word below to make a word from the Lesson 10 list. (Answers are in parentheses.)

patch (*pitch*)
skull (*skill*)
fill (*film*)
mastery (*mystery*)
timed (*timid*)
insert (*insect*)
massage (*message*)

Objectives

- To relate spelling words to a dictionary skill.
- To write spelling words and their plural forms.
- To write spelling words in alphabetical order.
- To use the **Spelling Dictionary** to locate plurals.

Plurals

A dictionary lists the plural form of a noun when the plural is formed in a special way. Some dictionaries list plural forms of all nouns.

bench | bĕnch | *n., pl.* **bench·es. 1.** A long seat: *park bench.* **2.** A heavy work table: *the carpenter's bench.* **3.** The seat for judges in a court of law. —*v.* To take a player out of a game: *The referee benched the player for bad conduct.*

half | hăf | *or* | häf | *n., pl.* **halves** | hăvz | *or* | hävz |. **1.** One of two equal parts. **2.** One of two equal periods of time in certain games: *the first half of the football game.* ***Idioms.*** **in half.** Into two equal parts. **not half bad.** Good.

de·gree | dĭ grē′ | *n., pl.* **de·grees. 1.** A unit used in measuring temperature. **2.** A unit used in measuring angles: *a 90-degree angle.* **3.** A title given by a college or university. **4.** Amount, extent: *a high degree of skill.*

par·ty | pär′tē | *n., pl.* **par·ties. 1.** An entertainment or social gathering: *a birthday party.* **2.** A group of people acting together: *A search party was sent out to find the missing child.* **3.** A political organization: *In an election, each party has a candidate.*

★ Read the entries above and answer these questions.

1. What is the plural of the noun bench? benches
   How is the plural of bench formed? add es
2. What is the plural of the noun degree? degrees
   How is the plural of degree formed? add s
3. What is the plural of the noun half? halves
   How is the plural of half formed? change f to v and add es
4. What is the plural of the noun party? parties
   How is the plural of party formed? change y to i and add es

★ Write the following nouns in alphabetical order. Then write the plural form next to each word. Check your answers in the Spelling Dictionary.

ski wife sandwich business company

	Word	Plural
5.	business	businesses
6.	company	companies
7.	sandwich	sandwiches
8.	ski	skis
9.	wife	wives

64

Preparation Have students read aloud the title of page 64. Note that all the plural spelling words are nouns. Ask where they should look in a dictionary to find each of the plural nouns in the spelling list. (*under the entry of the singular form of the word*) Remind students that most dictionaries list the plural form of a word only if the plural is made in a special way.

The Page Have students do page 64. Then have volunteers write the answers on the board and review them orally.

Follow-Up Have students write the singular form of each spelling word. Then have them look up the word in the **Spelling Dictionary**, put a check by the word if the plural is given, and write the plural form of the word.

WORDS AT WORK

Challenge Yourself

cosmetics scarves apologies actresses

Decide which Challenge Word fits each clue. Check your Spelling Dictionary to see if you were right. Then write sentences showing that you understand the meaning of each Challenge Word.

1. They can be long or square, plain or fancy, woolly or silky.
2. You will never see them in the sky at night, but some of them are well-known stars.
3. They can change what you see when you look in the mirror.
4. When you have made a serious mistake, sometimes you need to make these, too.

Write to the Point

Is there a special event that you look forward to every year? It might be a holiday, a festival, a sports event, or even your birthday. At what time of the year does the event happen? Write a paragraph telling what happens on the occasion and why you enjoy it. Use spelling words from this lesson in your paragraph.

Challenge Use one or more of the Challenge Words in your paragraph.

Proofreading

Use the proofreading marks to show the errors in the paragraph below. Write the five misspelled words correctly in the blanks.

⬭	word is misspelled
/	letter should be lower case
≡	letter should be capitalized

In july my neighbores hold a Summer street party. everyone enjoys these partys. The kids play or sit on picnic benchs and eat sandwichs. The adults share funny storys or talk about their businesses. Some show off their hobbies.

1. neighbors
2. parties
3. benches
4. sandwiches
5. stories

Objectives

- To extend the plural endings presented in Lesson 11 to the Challenge Words.
- To use clues and the **Spelling Dictionary** to enlarge students' vocabulary.
- To apply the plural endings presented in Lesson 11 in a writing activity.
- To practice proofreading for spelling and capitalization.

Dictation Sentences

1. Are you bringing sandwiches or vegetables to the picnic?
2. Her hobbies are writing ghost stories and taking care of calves.
3. There are penalties for people who skip practice.
4. The exercises are hard at first, but they get easier by degrees.
5. Many businesses and companies have parties for the people who work for them.
6. They cut the branches off the trees to make new park benches.
7. The neighbors said they heard two loud crashes last night.
8. My two wishes are for skis and skates.
9. The wives of three athletes gave speeches.

Challenge Yourself Answers

1. scarves
2. actresses
3. cosmetics
4. apologies

Students' sentences will vary.

Test Review and test plurals. Use one of these testing methods: (1) Say the word; read the sample sentence from page 60; say the word; have students write it. (2) Read each dictation sentence above; have students write the sentence. Correct the test with students.

Challenge Yourself The optional Challenge Words may be assigned to the entire class or limited to those students who do well on the test. Have students note these plural endings in the Challenge Words. You may wish to have students work in pairs. Responses to this activity should be completed on separate paper. Answers to the questions are provided above.

Write to the Point Help students recall the selection "The Fair" on pages 62 and 63; then assign the paragraph. Encourage students to provide details that will help the reader understand why they enjoy the occasion. This activity should be completed on separate paper.

Proofreading The proofreading practice includes misspellings of words from this lesson as well as capitalization errors.

LESSON 12

Objectives

- To review and reinforce vowel spellings for /ē/ and /ĭ/.
- To hear, say, spell, and write representative spelling words from Lessons 7–10.
- To write a narrative using the five steps in the writing process.
- To use a prewriting activity to plot a narrative.

Dictation Sentences

1. He plays the piano in the evening.
2. Is there any business to discuss?
3. I insist that you read this message.
4. She wrote a review of this mystery book.
5. Will we damage this bottle if we freeze it?
6. I believe in liberty for all.
7. All the jars are empty except this one.
8. He must complete his speech soon.
9. I have no reason to feel guilty.
10. We must breathe to stay alive.
11. We go to different schools.

Note

A review test blackline master in standardized format and an answer sheet have been provided on pages T36 and T41 of this Teacher's Edition. The answers to the review test are given below.

1–D	11–D
2–B	12–B
3–B	13–A
4–A	14–A
5–C	15–B
6–A	16–A
7–C	17–C
8–C	18–B
9–A	19–D
10–B	20–C

If words misspelled were from:	have students complete activities:
List A	1, 2, 5
List B	3, 4, 5

Lesson 12 Words in Review

A. piano
complete
speech
believe
empty
evening
reason
liberty
breathe
freeze

B. damage
mystery
except
insist
business
discuss
message
different
guilty
review

★ You will need a piece of paper for these review activities.

1. In Lessons 7 and 8 you studied seven different ways to spell /ē/: **y, e_e, ie, ee, ea, ea_e, i.** Write the words in list A.

piano	complete	speech
believe	empty	evening
reason	liberty	breathe
freeze		

★ 2. Look up each review word from list A in the Spelling Dictionary. Write the first definition of each word.

3. In Lessons 9 and 10 you studied six different ways to spell /ĭ/: **i, e, ui, a, y, u.** Write the words in list B.

damage	mystery	except
insist	business	discuss
message	different	guilty
review		

★ 4. Use each review word from list B in a sentence.

★ 5. Write all 20 review words in alphabetical order.

Your teacher may give you a test. Answer these questions when you have finished.

6. Did you spell all the words correctly? Yes or No
7. Did you leave out a letter? Yes or No
8. Did you write the wrong letter? Yes or No
9. Did you miss the spelling of a vowel sound? Yes or No

66

Test

Pretest the review words on page 66 to determine which students need reinforcement. Use one of these testing methods: (1) Read the words and the dictation sentences; have students write only the spelling words. (2) Read the dictation sentences and have students write the entire sentences. (3) Have students complete the review test blackline master. (See **Note.**) Correct the pretest with students.

The Pages

Assign pages 66 and 67 according to students' needs.

- Students who have mastered all of the review words may go on to the **Writer's Workshop** on page 67.
- Students who have not mastered all of the review words should complete the activities on page 66 and take a post-test administered with one of the pretesting methods. After the post-test students can then go on to the **Writer's Workshop** on page 67. For students who have misspelled only a few of the review words, you may wish to use the list at left to determine the activities they should complete on page 66.

For students who have misspelled several of the review words, you may wish to assign all of the activities on page 66.

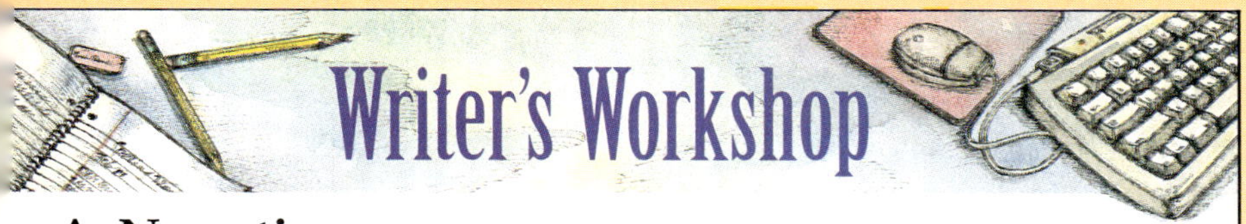

Writer's Workshop

A Narrative

A narrative is a story. Every good story has a beginning, a middle, and an end. In the beginning the main character and the problem that the main character must solve are introduced. In the middle of the story, the main character tries to solve the problem. The end of the story tells how the problem is solved. Notice how Diego introduces the main character and the problem in the beginning of his story "The Hardest Race."

The Hardest Race

Luke knew he should be training for the big race next week, but he didn't feel like it. Usually he loved to race. He spent all his free time getting into shape. This time it was different, though, because Luke would be racing against his best friend, Carlos. Luke knew how much Carlos wanted to win. After all, Luke had helped Carlos practice for a whole year. Winning against Carlos wouldn't be any fun, but losing might feel even worse.

To write his story, Diego followed the steps in the writing process. First he decided what kind of story he wanted to write and who the main character would be. Then he used a story map as a **Prewriting** activity. The map helped Diego plan the three main ingredients of the plot of his story—the beginning, the middle, and the end. The map also helped him put the events of his story in an order that made sense. Diego's story map is shown here. Study what Diego did.

Beginning
Luke must race against his best friend, Carlos.

Middle
Luke wins the race.

End
Carlos is a good sport.

Get ready to write your own story. You can write a realistic story like Diego's, a mystery, a fairy tale, or any kind of story you wish. After you have decided what to write about, make a story map. Then follow the other steps in the writing process—**Writing, Revising, Proofreading,** and **Publishing.**

67

Note

If students have difficulty deciding on a topic, you may wish to suggest one of the following:

Trapped in a tree house

The candy store mystery

How the turtle got its shell

Writer's Workshop Explain to students that a narrative is a story. Point out that in the beginning of a good story, the writer introduces the main character and the problem. The middle of the story includes a series of events that build up to the most exciting point. In the end the writer tells how the problem is solved, and the story draws to a close. Read with students the beginning of the narrative "The Hardest Race" and help them identify the main character's problem.

Allow students to study the sample story map shown on the pupil's page and guide students to see how this graphic organizer helped Diego prepare to write his story.

It's Your Turn Review the steps in the writing process with students. If students are not satisfied with the result of their prewriting, allow them to revise it as often as necessary or to choose another topic and repeat the prewriting activity.

Process Writing Blackline Masters
- Story Map, page T47
- Steps in the Writing Process, page T44
- Proofreading Symbols/Checklist, page T45

LESSON 13

Objectives

- To hear and say words with /ī/.
- To write words with /ī/ with attention to letter sequence and sound/symbol relationships.
- To write each spelling word once.
- To recognize that /ī/ may be spelled i, i_e, and ui_e.

Sample Sentences

1. That sauce is spicy, but this one is mild.
2. I like to grind nutmeg for pumpkin pie.
3. Pat can climb to the highest branches of that tree.
4. I felt blind in the pitch-dark room.
5. This is the ninth time I've read this book.
6. Marty tried to open the locked door.
7. Please remind me to take my umbrella.
8. We're learning how to do experiments in science class.
9. I have an idea — let's go to the beach!
10. Anyone can borrow films and records from the library.
11. The pirate sailed away with our treasures.
12. We'll have to take a boat to get to the island.
13. It is quite unusual to see snow in April.
14. Stan put a knife beside each plate.
15. How many people are you going to invite to the party?
16. Let's sit here awhile and talk.
17. It's polite to say please and thank you.
18. I can't decide which movie to see tonight.
19. Flora will revise the report she wrote.
20. A guide took us to the interesting parts of the park.

Note

- The sample sentences may be used for pretesting.
- Words are grouped according to spellings of /ī/:
  i
  i_e
  ui_e

Lesson 13 Words with /ī/

Listen for /ī/ in each word.

mild
grind
climb
blind
ninth
tried
remind
science
idea
library
pirate
island

quite
knife
invite
awhile
polite
decide
revise

guide

1. Which word begins with /kw/? Circle the letters that spell /kw/. quite
2. Write the word in which you see the letter k but don't hear /k/. knife
3. Write the three words that begin and end with a vowel. idea invite awhile
4. Write the two words that begin with the letter g. grind guide
5. Write the two words that begin with the letter p. pirate polite
6. Which word begins and ends with /s/? science
7. Which six words end with the letter d? mild grind blind tried remind island
8. Which word ends with /z/? revise
9. Which word ends with the letters th? ninth
10. Write the word in which you see the letter s but don't hear /s/ or /z/. island
11. Write the word in which you see the letter b but don't hear /b/. climb
12. Write the word in which the letter r appears twice. library
13. Which word has /s/ in the middle? decide
14. Write the word in which /hw/ is spelled wh. awhile

68

Preparation

Have students read aloud the title of the lesson on Page 68. Write /ī/ on the board. Have students say /ī/ as in pie. Read each spelling word aloud. Have students repeat and then spell each word aloud.

Note that tried is a past tense form; ask what the present tense form is. (*try*) Point out the i spelling of the vowel sound in tried. Also note the proper pronunciation of library: /lī' brĕr' ē/. Point out the schwa in the first syllable of polite: /pə līt'/. Have students identify another word with a schwa in the first syllable. (*awhile:* / ə *hwīl'*/) Ask what letter spells /ə/ in polite. (*o*) In awhile? (*a*) Then ask students to identify the letter or letters that spell /ī/ in each group of words in the list. (See **Note**.)

Read the sample sentences. Have students point to each spelling word as you read the sentence for it.

The Page

Have students complete page 68 independently or as a group. Correct the page by having volunteers write the answers on the board. Have students correct their own work.

Follow-Up

Suggest that students write each letter of a word in a different color.

Checkpoint

Write a spelling word for each clue.
Then use the Checkpoint Study Plan on page 224.

1. Another word for gentle is ___. mild
2. After seventh and eighth comes ___. ninth
3. Another word for sightless is ___. blind
4. Today I try, yesterday I ___. tried
5. To crush into fine particles is to ___. grind
6. To lead means to ___. guide
7. Spoon, fork, and ___ go together. knife
8. To change something is to ___. revise
9. Land surrounded by water is an ___. island
10. A public place for books and magazines is a ___. library
11. To ask someone to come or go to a place is to ___. invite
12. A sea thief is a ___. pirate
13. Another word for very is ___. quite
14. Biology is one kind of ___. science
15. To reach a decision means to ___. decide
16. For a short time is the same as ___. awhile
17. The opposite of cause to forget is ___. remind
18. To go up a tree is to ___. climb
19. Another word for a thought is an ___. idea

20. Very often two languages have similar expressions. In English, if we say that a person is polished, we usually mean well-mannered. The Romans had a similar expression. In Latin, the word *politus* means polished. Like the English word polished, it was used to refer to someone with good manners. The mystery word comes from the Latin word *politus*. It means well-mannered. Can you guess it? ___ polite

69

Objectives

- To write spelling words in response to clues: definitions, synonyms, antonyms, analogies, classifications, and context.
- To develop the critical thinking skills of classifying, making inferences, and sequencing.
- To understand that different languages may have similar words with the same meaning.

Spelling Strategy

If students have trouble remembering the silent s in island, it may be helpful to write the following sentence on the board and have students use it as a mnemonic device: "An island is land surrounded by water." Encourage students to invent mnemonic devices for other tricky spellings, such as the silent k in knife and the silent b in climb.

Preparation The clues on this page are like crossword puzzle clues. Explain to students that the response to each clue is a spelling word. Use the following examples to illustrate the types of clues used:

Definition	To crush into fine particles is to (*grind*).
Synonym	Another word for sightless is (*blind*).
Antonym	The opposite of cause to forget is (*remind*).
Analogy	Today I try, yesterday I (*tried*).
Classification	Spoon, fork, and (*knife*) go together.
Context	Biology is one kind of (*science*).

The final clue explains the origin of polite.

The Page Have students complete page 69 using the words on page 68. When students have finished, have them read each clue and spell the answer aloud. Check each response twice: once for the correct answer and a second time for spelling accuracy.

Follow-Up Guide pupils in using the **Checkpoint Study Plan** on page 224 to take a self-test. Then have them use the plan for independent study.

Objectives

- To write words with /ī/ in continuous text.
- To write each spelling word once.
- To integrate reading with spelling.

Use each list word once.

Lost at Sea

June 6, 1843

I have always wanted to be a sailor. When I had a chance to sign on board the ship <u>*Fairweather,*</u> *I did!*

We have been at sea for eight months, and all that time the weather has been pleasant and ____mild____. *Once, we were almost attacked by a* ____pirate____ *ship. But we got away. The rest of our trip has been peaceful.*

I like my life as a sailor. Each day, after I finish my work, I ____climb____ *to the top of the main mast and watch the sea. I am* ____quite____ *happy.*

July 1, 1843

This is the first day of the ____ninth____ *month of our voyage, and the weather has changed. The sky is growing very dark and a great wind is blowing. The waves are getting bigger. . . .*

July 3, 1843

The storm got worse and worse. A huge wave crashed over the deck and threw me into the sea. I grabbed an empty barrel. Then I watched in horror as the ship sailed on without me.

Preparation Have students turn to pages 70 and 71. Have them look at the story and the picture. Call their attention to the word list. Have the students say the words. Then explain that each spelling word belongs in one of the blanks in the story.

Write the title "Lost at Sea" on the board. Ask students what kind of selection this is. (*entries from an old diary*) Tell students that many sailors keep daily accounts of their lives at sea.

The Pages Have students complete pages 70 and 71 independently by silently reading the diary entries and writing the missing spelling words. Or you may read the entries aloud, supplying the missing words as students follow along in their texts; then have students complete the pages on their own.

This morning I found myself washed up on the shore of an island. All I had were the clothes I was wearing and the diary that I had put in my pocket. I tried to discover where I was. But without a compass or a map, I had no idea. I could not decide what to do. Then I saw a boy about my own age walking toward me. I wanted to be polite, so I bowed to him. He bowed back and offered to guide me through the forest to his family's hut. Although we didn't speak the same language, we were able to understand each other by using a kind of sign language.

When we got to the hut, he introduced me to his family. I signaled that I was hungry. They pointed to a cooking pot, and I understood that they wanted to invite me to eat with them. They used a stone to grind some spices into a fine powder. Then they sliced some vegetables with a knife. They fried all this in some oil and added rice. It was the most delicious meal I have ever eaten. Whenever I taste a certain rare spice in the future, it will remind me of that meal.

May 10, 1844

Today a ship sailed into the bay. I can't believe I'm going home. My island friends have asked me to stay awhile longer. But I explained that I have to return to my family.

I have had plenty of time to revise my opinion of a sailor's life. How could I have been so blind to the dangers of a life at sea? When I reach home, perhaps I will study science and spend my life in a laboratory. Or perhaps I'll just read about the sea in a quiet library. I will definitely not be a sailor.

71

mild
grind
climb
blind
ninth
tried
remind
science
idea
library
pirate
island
quite
knife
invite
awhile
polite
decide
revise
guide

When students have finished, you may wish to discuss the diary entries. Ask if any students have ever been on a boat for many days at a time and if they were at all frightened. Ask if there are many wrecks at sea in this day and age. (*very few on large ships*) Ask students how they would communicate with someone who did not know how to speak English. (*sign language is probably the most common way*) Ask students how they would tell someone they were in a shipwreck. (*Answers will vary.*)

Follow-Up Have students use each of the spelling words they missed in an original sentence that relates to the diary entries.

As an additional follow-up activity, you may wish to have students write a diary entry for each day of the week, using the spelling words from the story.

Enrichment

If you want to use the blackline activity masters for enrichment and additional practice, assign Lesson 13 activities at this time.

Maintenance and Review

OBJECTIVE

- To review plurals.

ACTIVITIES

If you want to use the blackline activity masters for maintenance and review, assign Lesson 11 activities at this time.

You can also use the activity below to review Lesson 11 with students.

Write the following singular forms on the board. Have students write the plural form of each word. (Answers are in parentheses.)

sandwich	(*sandwiches*)
story	(*stories*)
wife	(*wives*)
hobby	(*hobbies*)
company	(*companies*)
athlete	(*athletes*)
speech	(*speeches*)
ski	(*skis*)
calf	(*calves*)
branch	(*branches*)

Objectives

- To relate spelling to another language skill.
- To use correct punctuation in direct quotations.
- To write spelling words in the context of sentences.

Punctuation

Put quotation marks around the exact words of a speaker. Notice the position of the quotation marks and commas in the following:

Lisa asked, "Will you come to the parade with us?"
Bob said, "I would love to go with you."

A comma follows the word that introduces a quotation. The first word in a direct quotation begins with a capital letter. The end punctuation comes inside the final quotation marks.

★ Write the following sentences. Add quotation marks, commas, and other punctuation where needed.

1. Mr. Perry said My job is getting to be a grind
Mr. Perry said, "My job is getting to be a grind."

2. Mrs. Perry asked Why don't you decide to take a vacation
Mrs. Perry asked, "Why don't you decide to take a vacation?"

3. Mr. Perry answered We could go to a deserted island
Mr. Perry answered, "We could go to a deserted island."

Sometimes a speaker's exact words are at the beginning of a sentence. Notice the position of the quotation marks and punctuation marks now.

"Will you come to the parade with us?" Lisa asked.
"I would love to go with you," said Bob.

★ Write the following sentences. Add quotation marks, commas, and other punctuation where needed.

4. Don't you think it would be fun to climb a mountain asked Mrs. Perry
"Don't you think it would be fun to climb a mountain?" asked Mrs. Perry.

5. We should take a guide so we won't get lost added Mr. Perry
"We should take a guide so we won't get lost," added Mr. Perry.

72

Preparation Have students read aloud the title of page 72. Then write the following sentence on the board: **Hal said, "Dinner is ready."**

Ask students what punctuation mark comes after the word said. (*a comma*) What punctuation mark comes before the word Dinner? (*a quotation mark*) What two punctuation marks end the sentence? (*a period and a quotation mark*) Review with students that a speaker's exact words begin with a capital letter and that quotation marks are used to set them off. Then write the following sentence on the board: **"Where should I sit?" asked Marnie.**

Explain that when the exact words of the speaker are at the beginning of the sentence, punctuation marks must be used after the speaker's words and at the end of the sentence.

The Page Have students do page 72. Then have volunteers write the answers on the board.

Follow-Up Have students reread the last part of the story "Lost at Sea" on page 71. Then have them rewrite the part of the story where the narrator tells his friends that he must leave, using direct quotes for the characters' words. Remind students to use correct punctuation.

WORDS AT WORK

Challenge Yourself

rightful **recycle** **prior** **exile**

Use your Spelling Dictionary to answer these questions. Then write sentences showing that you understand the meaning of each Challenge Word.

1. Does a person who buys a new or used car become the car's rightful owner?
2. Does it hurt the environment to recycle old newspapers or glass bottles?
3. Were you in fourth grade prior to being in fifth grade?
4. Could a person in exile go back home to see friends?

Write to the Point

Write an adventure story in the form of a diary. Imagine you're in a dangerous situation, and write three diary entries telling what happens. Begin each entry with a date so that the reader will know how much time has passed. Use spelling words from this lesson in your diary.

Challenge Use one or more of the Challenge Words in your diary.

Proofreading

Use the proofreading marks to show the errors in the paragraph below. Write the five misspelled words correctly in the blanks.

(circle)	word is misspelled
? (caret)	question mark is missing
(delete mark)	take out word

The stars were the sailor's (giude,) but the night had a grown quite foggy. The sailor had no (iddea) where he was, and he couldn't (deside) what to do. Should he drop the boat's anchor and wait for (awile,) or would the that just invite a (pyrate) attack?

1. guide
2. idea
3. decide
4. awhile
5. pirate

73

Objectives

- To extend the vowel spellings presented in Lesson 13 to the Challenge Words.
- To use context and the **Spelling Dictionary** to enlarge students' vocabulary.
- To apply the vowel spellings presented in Lesson 13 in a writing activity.
- To practice proofreading for spelling, punctuation, and extra words.

Dictation Sentences

1. A guide helped us climb the mountains on the island.
2. That is a great idea for a science project!
3. I cannot decide whom to invite to my party.
4. I tried to remind her to bring her books to the library.
5. I will grind the wheat.
6. The pirate was blind in one eye.
7. She is quite nice and very polite.
8. I'll stay in the library awhile to revise this report.
9. I was the ninth person in line.
10. The weather was mild.
11. Where is the butter knife?

Challenge Yourself Answers

1. yes
2. no
3. yes
4. no

Students' sentences will vary.

Test Review these three ways to spell /ī/: i as in idea; i_e as in decide; ui_e as in guide. Test words with /ī/. Use one of these testing methods: (1) Say the word; read the sample sentence from page 68; say the word; have students write it. (2) Read each dictation sentence above; have students write the sentence. Correct the test with students.

Challenge Yourself The optional Challenge Words may be assigned to the entire class or limited to those students who do well on the test. Have students note the vowel spellings in the Challenge Words, especially the following new spelling: y as in recycle. Responses to this activity should be completed on separate paper. Answers to the questions are provided above.

Write to the Point Help students recall the selection "Lost at Sea" on pages 70 and 71; then assign the diary. Remind students that a story written in the form of a diary should be told in the first person, using pronouns such as I and me. This activity should be completed on separate paper.

Proofreading The proofreading practice includes misspellings of words from this lesson as well as a punctuation error and extra words.

LESSON 14

Objectives

- To hear and say words with /ŏ/.
- To write words with /ŏ/ with attention to letter sequence and sound/symbol relationships.
- To write each spelling word once.
- To recognize that /ŏ/ may be spelled o and a.

Sample Sentences

1. If you touch that wire, you'll get a shock.
2. This pot is made of copper.
3. Dennis found a dime in the bottom of his drawer.
4. Don't forget to put a comma between the city and state.
5. The lake was frozen solid.
6. Roberta works as a nurse in the hospital.
7. Storms are quite common in summer.
8. Thelma talked about her problem.
9. Do you like to eat lobster?
10. Tom kept his promise to his brother.
11. Please don't bother me when I'm reading.
12. Seth put a collar on his puppy.
13. Carlos earns more than a dollar an hour by baby-sitting.
14. Hang your hat and coat in the closet.
15. This object looks like a pillow, but it's really a chair.
16. I've told you the truth, on my honor.
17. Please give an honest answer to my question.
18. The sheep are free to wander over the hills.
19. We'll need a large quantity of rice to feed us all.
20. Frank has to watch the baby.

Note

- The sample sentences may be used for pretesting.
- Words are grouped according to spellings of /ŏ/:
  - o
  - a

Lesson 14 Words with /ŏ/

Listen for /ŏ/ in each word.

shock
copper
bottom
comma
solid
hospital
common
problem
lobster
promise
bother
collar
dollar
closet
object
honor
honest

wander
quantity
watch

1. Write the two words that begin with the letter p.
   problem promise
2. Which word begins with the letters sh?
   shock
3. Which word begins with /kw/? Circle the letters that spell /kw/. quantity
4. Write the two words in which you see the letter h at the beginning of the word but don't hear /h/.
   honor honest
5. Which other word begins with the letter h that is pronounced /h/? hospital
6. Which word begins and ends like sand? solid
7. Which word begins and ends like later? lobster
8. Write the three words that end with the letter t.
   closet object
   honest
9. Write the two words that end with the letters ar.
   collar dollar
10. Which three words have the same spelling of /ŏ/ as quality? wander quantity
    watch
11. Write the word that has the letters th in the middle.
    bother
12. Write the words in which a double consonant spells one sound.

ll	collar	ll	dollar
mm	comma	mm	common
pp	copper	tt	bottom

74

Preparation Have students read aloud the title of the lesson on page 74. Write /ŏ/ on the board. Have students say /ŏ/ as in pot. Read each spelling word aloud. Have students repeat and then spell each word aloud.

Note that although object can be pronounced /ŏb′ jĭkt/ or /əb jĕkt′/, it is always spelled the same. Point out the /ə/ in the last syllables of comma and common. Ask students to identify the letter that spells /ə/ in each. (a, o) Then have students identify the two spellings for /ŏ/ in this lesson. (See **Note**.) Read the sample sentences. Have students point to each spelling word as you read the sentence for it.

The Page Have students complete page 74 independently or as a group. Correct the page by having volunteers write the answers on the board. Have students correct their own work.

Follow-Up Suggest that students fold a piece of paper in half. Then have them write words with the o spelling of /ŏ/ in one column and words with the a spelling of /ŏ/ in the other.

Checkpoint

Write a spelling word for each clue.
Then use the Checkpoint Study Plan on page 224.

1. The opposite of top is ___. — bottom
2. Ten dimes make one ___. — dollar
3. Another word for vow is ___. — promise
4. Water is a liquid, ice is a ___. — solid
5. Another word for look at or be careful is ___. — watch
6. If frightened suddenly, you may feel a ___. — shock
7. Foods go in the refrigerator, clothes go in the ___. — closet
8. To roam means to ___. — wander
9. Another word for amount is ___. — quantity
10. A sea animal with claws is a ___. — lobster
11. A thing that has shape and can be seen is an ___. — object
12. One kind of metal is ___. — copper
13. A word for medical center is ___. — hospital
14. The opposite of rare is ___. — common
15. Another word for tease is ___. — bother
16. If you tell the truth, you are ___. — honest
17. Something you try to solve is a ___. — problem
18. A part of your shirt is the ___. — collar
19. To show respect is to ___. — honor

20. The words period and colon are names of punctuation marks. They come from ancient Greek words. This is odd because the ancient Greeks did not use punctuation marks in their writing. In ancient Greek, these words did not name marks. They were grammar terms that named certain groups of words. This mystery word comes from the Greek word *komma,* which meant clause. Now the mystery word names the punctuation mark that often follows a clause. Can you guess it? ___ — comma

75

Objectives

- To write spelling words in response to clues: definitions, synonyms, antonyms, analogies, and context.
- To develop the critical thinking skills of making inferences, comparing, and contrasting.
- To understand that the spelling and meaning of words in the English language often change over time.

Spelling Strategy

Some students may misspell quantity because they do not pronounce the first t. It may be helpful to write the word on the board, exaggerating the size of both t's. Point out to students that quantity has two t's and tell them that both should be pronounced. Have students practice pronouncing the word correctly.

Preparation

The clues on this page are like crossword puzzle clues. Explain to students that the response to each clue is a spelling word. Use the following examples to illustrate the types of clues used:

Definition	A sea animal with claws is a (*lobster*).
Synonym	Another word for amount is (*quantity*).
Antonym	The opposite of top is (*bottom*).
Analogy	Foods go in the refrigerator, clothes go in the (*closet*).
Context	If you tell the truth, you are (*honest*).

The final clue explains the Greek origin of comma.

The Page

Have students complete page 75 using the words on page 74. When students have finished, have them read each clue and spell the answer aloud. Check each response twice: once for the correct answer and a second time for spelling accuracy.

Follow-Up

Guide pupils in using the **Checkpoint Study Plan** on page 224 to take a self-test. Then have them use the plan for independent study.

Objectives

- To write words with /ŏ/ in continuous text.
- To write each spelling word once.
- To integrate reading with spelling.

Note

- Point out the use of the word <u>honor</u> in the selection to mean to accept as payment. The more common meaning is a sense of what is right.
- Point out the use of the word <u>choicest</u> to mean of the best quality.
- Point out that shock absorbers are parts in a car or truck that make the ride smooth.

Use each list word once.

THE QUARK GIFT BOOK

Greetings, people from Earth!

Welcome to this light-year's new and better Quark Gift Book. We __promise__ that you will never have to __wander__ around trying to find a gift for that important person or thing on your holiday shopping list. Now you can order gifts in the __quantity__ you need without any trouble or __bother__. We __honor__ all major space cards.

Down in the dumps? Wear a Liftoff rocket __collar__ around your neck and things will be looking up. It comes in the choicest Earth tones, __lobster__ red, and sky blue. Small or Large.

750 Bloteems

The last word in getting rid of garbage! Just throw an unwanted __object__ into the Black Hole and POOF! You can __watch__ it disappear. And it won't harm the ecology either!

120,000 Bloteems

We must be __honest__ with you. This does not come gift wrapped.

76

Preparation

Have students turn to pages 76 and 77. Let them look at the catalog and the pictures. Call their attention to the word list. Have the students say the words. Then explain that each spelling word belongs in one of the blanks in the catalog.

Write the title "The Quark Gift Book" on the board. Ask students what kind of selection this is. (*sections of a catalog*) Ask what kinds of items are listed in the catalog. (*items from outer space*) Ask whether the mood of the selection is funny or sad. (*It is funny.*)

The Pages

Have students complete pages 76 and 77 independently by silently reading the catalog and writing the missing spelling words. Or you may read the catalog aloud, supplying the missing words as students follow along in their texts; then have the students complete the pages on their own.

When students have finished, you may wish to discuss the catalog. Ask students which items they would like to order and why. Ask if any of these items are made now. (*no*) Ask which, if any, they think might be made in the future. (*Answers will vary.*)

Have a volunteer read each paragraph in the catalog and supply each spelling word and spelling it aloud. Have other volunteers write the answers on the board and have students correct their own work. Check students' responses for the accurate spelling of each answer.

Do you have a sick friend in the ___hospital___? Finding the right gift for a shut-in is not an unusual problem. In fact, it's very ___common___. But don't worry. Give the Intergalactic Environmental Unit. By setting the buttons, you can feel as if you have ___solid___ earth under your feet. Or, if you like, it can make you feel like you are living at the ___bottom___ of the ocean. No more dusty feelers! No more sticky bimnuls! And the IEV is easy to store in a ___closet___. It comes in a silver or ___copper___ case.

7000 Bloteems

Tired of bumping around while flying through space? Try our new ___shock___ absorbers. They will get rid of that awful ___problem___.

Set of 4, only 150 Bloteems

To order a gift from this book, please use your space card number. And don't forget the ___comma___ between the planet and galaxy in your address. Remember, three Bloteems equal one ___dollar___ ($1.00).

77

shock
copper
bottom
comma
solid
hospital
common
problem
lobster
promise
bother
collar
dollar
closet
object
honor
honest
wander
quantity
watch

Enrichment

If you want to use the blackline activity masters for enrichment and additional practice, assign Lesson 14 activities at this time.

Maintenance and Review

- To review words with /ī/ spelled: i, i_e, ui_e.

ACTIVITIES

If you want to use the blackline activity masters for maintenance and review, assign Lesson 13 activities at this time.

You can also use the activity below to review Lesson 13 with students.

Write the following word pairs on the board. Have students write a sentence containing each word pair.

climb–ninth
pirate–knife
science–library
decide–idea
island–guide

Follow-Up

Have students use each of the spelling words they missed in an original sentence that relates to the catalog.

As an additional follow-up activity, you may wish to have pairs of students take turns reading aloud to each other the items in the catalog pausing before each spelling word. The other student will supply the missing word by spelling it aloud at the appropriate time.

Objectives

- To relate spelling to another language skill.
- To identify and review subjects of sentences.
- To write spelling words in context.

Subject of a Sentence

The subject of a sentence tells who or what is doing the action or is being talked about. A subject can be more than one word.

That little boy won the race.
Judy is best at hopscotch.

★ Read the sentences above and answer these questions.

1. What is the action verb in the first sentence? won

2. Who or what won something? That little boy

That little boy is the subject of the first sentence.

3. Who is being talked about in the second sentence? Judy

Judy is the subject of the second sentence.

★ Write the subject of each sentence below.

4. The hospital was a busy place on Saturday. The hospital

5. Lobster is a tasty treat. Lobster

6. The dog collar was lying in the mud. The dog collar

7. A comma is a punctuation mark. A comma

8. Debbie saw the deer through the trees. Debbie

9. Our cat can jump very high. Our cat

10. A dollar doesn't buy very much. A dollar

11. Susan wandered aimlessly around the house. Susan

12. The problem can be solved easily. The problem

13. The object of the game is simple. The object of the game

14. Jack saw the sunset. Jack

15. My watch can't be fixed. My watch

16. That closet is a mess. That closet

17. The woman waiting for the bus looked dismayed. The woman waiting for the bus

78

Preparation Have students read aloud the title of page 78. Review that a sentence is a complete thought, and it contains a subject and a predicate. The subject tells who or what is doing the action or is being talked about. Have students give examples of sentences and have them identify each subject. You may wish to start them off with this sentence, in which the subject is underlined:

Our class is going on a trip.

The Page Have students do page 78. Then have volunteers write the answers on the board and review the answers orally.

Follow-Up Have students rewrite the sentences in exercises 4–17, supplying their own subject for each sentence. Students should use spelling words wherever possible. Encourage students to use their imagination, but remind them that each sentence must make sense.

WORDS AT WORK

Challenge Yourself

solitude **jot** **jostled** **dislodge**

Write what you think each underlined Challenge Word means. Check your Spelling Dictionary to see if you were right. Then write sentences that show the meaning of each Challenge Word.

1. The author needed solitude to write her book, so she spent hours alone, working in her room.
2. You had better jot this address down in case you forget it.
3. The people jostled one another as they tried to get off the crowded bus.
4. I shook the piggy bank to dislodge the coin that was stuck in the slot.

Write to the Point

Think of an idea for a fantastic new product that you would like to invent. Then write an advertisement for the product. Explain what it does and why it would make an excellent gift. Give the price, too. Use spelling words from this lesson in your advertisement.

Challenge Use one or more of the Challenge Words in your advertisement.

Proofreading

Use the proofreading marks to show the errors in the paragraph below. Write the five misspelled words correctly in the blanks.

⬭	word is misspelled
!‸	exclamation point is missing
≡	letter should be capitalized

Help! Does the catalog promis to return my money if I can't use an objikt I bought? i don't want my dog to wandur when I walk him on Mars, so I ordered a coller and leash to fix the problum. But I didn't bother to check if they make space suits in his size.

1. promise
2. object
3. wander
4. collar
5. problem

79

Objectives

- To extend the vowel spellings presented in Lesson 14 to the Challenge Words.
- To use context and the **Spelling Dictionary** to enlarge students' vocabulary.
- To apply the vowel spellings presented in Lesson 14 in a writing activity.
- To practice proofreading for spelling, punctuation, and capitalization.

Dictation Sentences

1. My ring was on the bottom shelf of the closet.
2. It is an honor to be named head of the new hospital.
3. A watch is a common object.
4. I promise to take you for a lobster dinner.
5. I got a copper ring for a dollar.
6. There is a problem with the stove.
7. Do not bother me if I decide to wander along the beach.
8. Her honest answers may shock you.
9. The dog collar is made of solid metal.
10. What quantity should we order?
11. Use a comma when you write the date.

Challenge Yourself Answers

Possible definitions:

1. aloneness; isolation
2. write
3. pushed
4. move; unstick

Students' sentences will vary.

Test Review these two ways to spell /ŏ/: o as in copper; a as in watch. Test words with /ŏ/. Use one of these testing methods: (1) Say the word; read the sample sentence from page 74; say the word; have students write it. (2) Read each dictation sentence above; have students write the sentence. Correct the test with students.

Challenge Yourself The optional Challenge Words may be assigned to the entire class or limited to those students who do well on the test. Have students note the vowel spelling in the Challenge Words. Responses to this activity should be completed on separate paper. Answers to the questions are provided above.

Write to the Point Help students recall the selection "The Quark Gift Book" on pages 76 and 77; then assign the advertisement. Remind students to include words and details that will make their product sound attractive to the reader. This activity should be completed on separate paper.

Proofreading The proofreading practice includes misspellings of words from this lesson as well as a capitalization error and a punctuation error.

LESSON 15

Objectives

- To hear and say words with /ō/.
- To write words with /ō/ with attention to letter sequence and sound/symbol relationships.
- To write each spelling word once.
- To recognize that /ō/ may be spelled ow, o_e, ew, and owe.

Sample Sentences

1. If I had known you were here, I'd have told everyone.
2. How far can you throw a ball?
3. Donna put the cherries into a big bowl.
4. If you follow the path, you won't get lost.
5. A sign with an arrow pointed the way.
6. I hurt my elbow playing baseball.
7. My plant has grown eight inches.
8. You may borrow this record.
9. It's hard to swallow a big mouthful of food.
10. We'll be in New York tomorrow.
11. The safety zone is behind this line.
12. Our club will vote for a new president.
13. Jan's family got a new push-button telephone.
14. Harry broke the secret code.
15. Everyone else turned back, so Ben went on alone.
16. You can see very tiny animals through a microscope.
17. Bob will have a good reason for being late, I suppose.
18. Buddy chose the blue cup.
19. Ralph will sew a button on his shirt.
20. I'll pay you the money I owe you next week.

Note

- The sample sentences may be used for pretesting.
- Words are grouped according to spellings of /ō/:
  - ow
  - o_e
  - ew
  - owe

Lesson 15 Words with /ō/

Listen for /ō/ in each word.

known
throw
bowl
follow
arrow
elbow
grown
borrow
swallow
tomorrow

zone
vote
telephone
code
alone
microscope
suppose
chose

sew

owe

1. Which word begins with the letters th? throw
2. Write the four words that begin with a vowel. arrow, elbow, alone, owe
3. Which word begins with /k/? code
4. Write one word that begins with /z/ and two that end with /z/. zone, suppose, chose
5. Which word begins with the letter v? vote
6. Which word begins and ends like boil? bowl
7. Which word begins and ends like given? grown
8. Which word begins and ends like male? microscope
9. In which word is /ō/ spelled ew? sew
10. Write the word whose pronunciation is made up of one vowel sound. owe
11. Write the word in which you see the letter k but don't hear /k/. known
12. In which two words do you hear /f/? Circle the letters that spell /f/. follow, telephone
13. Write the words in which a double consonant spells one sound.

ll	follow	ll	swallow
pp	suppose	rr	arrow
rr	borrow	rr	tomorrow

80

Preparation Have students read aloud the title of the lesson on page 80. Write /ō/ on the board. Have students say /ō/ as in go. Read each spelling word aloud. Have students repeat and then spell each word aloud.

Ask which letter in known is silent. (*k*) Point out the schwa in the first syllable of alone: /ə lōn′/, and suppose: /sə pōz′/. Then ask students what letters spell /ō/ in the first group of words (*ow*); in the second group (*o_e*). Note the unusual spellings of /ō/ in sew and owe. (See **Note**.)

Read the sample sentences. Have students point to each spelling word as you read the sentence for it.

The Page Have students complete page 80 independently or as a group. Then have volunteers write the answers on the board. Have students correct their own work.

Follow-Up Suggest that students draw 10 triangles, 8 rectangles, and 2 circles. Then have them write the words with the ow spelling of /ō/ on the triangles, the words with the o_e spelling of /ō/ on the rectangles, and the other two words on the circles.

Checkpoint

Write a spelling word for each clue.
Then use the Checkpoint Study Plan on page 224.

1. A needle and thread are used to ___.	sew
2. Today I grow, before that I had ___.	grown
3. Another word for toss is ___.	throw
4. The opposite of to lead is to ___.	follow
5. In an election you cast your ___.	vote
6. The day following today will be ___.	tomorrow
7. To be with no one else is to be ___.	alone
8. If you're in debt, you ___ a bill.	owe
9. A secret message may be in ___.	code
10. Hit the target by using a bow and ___.	arrow
11. I know, I knew, I had ___.	known
12. Another word for guess is ___.	suppose
13. The opposite of lend is ___.	borrow
14. A certain area is a ___.	zone
15. After you chew, you ___.	swallow
16. As dinner is to plate, soup is to ___.	bowl
17. Picked out or selected means ___.	chose
18. As knee is to leg, ___ is to arm.	elbow

19. When scientists invent things, they like to give them Greek names. The two mystery words name scientific inventions. The first word names an instrument that allows us to see small things. It comes from the Greek words for small (*micros*) and for see (*skŏpeō*). Can you guess this word? ___

microscope

20. The second mystery word names something that allows you to make sounds that can be heard far away. It comes from two Greek words. *Telos* meant far away. *Phoneo* meant to make a sound. What is this word? ___

telephone

Objectives

- To write spelling words in response to clues: definitions, synonyms, antonyms, analogies, and context.
- To develop the critical thinking skills of making inferences and sequencing.
- To understand that many English words come from the Greek language, and that words may be combined to form new words.

Spelling Strategy

To help students remember which consonant to double in tomorrow, explain that morrow is an old-fashioned word for "morning" or "the next day" and that tomorrow was created by adding to onto morrow.

Preparation The clues on this page are like crossword puzzle clues. Explain to students that the response to each clue is a spelling word. Use the following examples to illustrate the types of clues used:

Definition	To be with no one else is to be (*alone*).
Synonym	Another word for toss is (*throw*).
Antonym	The opposite of to lead is to (*follow*).
Analogy	As dinner is to plate, soup is to (*bowl*).
Context	A needle and thread are used to (*sew*).

The final clue names the Greek words that were combined to make the words microscope and telephone.

The Page Have students complete page 81 using the words on page 80. When students have finished, have them read each clue and spell the answer aloud. Check each response twice: once for the correct answer and a second time for spelling accuracy.

Follow-Up Guide pupils in using the **Checkpoint Study Plan** on page 224 to take a self-test. Then have them use the plan for independent study.

Objectives

- To write words with /ō/ in continuous text.
- To write each spelling word once.
- To integrate reading with spelling.

Note

Point out that South Bend is in Indiana. Show students its location on a map of the United States.

Use each list word once.

Letter from the Science Fair

Dear Susie,

Every year one student from the seventh grade is chosen to go to the science fair in South Bend. This year, they ___chose___ me! The whole seventh grade took a ___vote___, and I won!

You know I've always wanted to be a scientist. I ___suppose___ it all started when I found out that a caterpillar turns into a butterfly. Ever since then, I've wanted to know everything about nature.

I'm going to look really great at the science fair. I asked Mom to ___sew___ a new skirt for me. And my best friend, Jean, said I could ___borrow___ her red sweater.

This morning I got on the train for South Bend. Mom walked down the narrow aisle to my seat with me. She asked the conductor to help me get a taxi to the university when the train arrived in South Bend. Then she kissed me good-by and got off the train.

It's the first time I've ever traveled ___alone___. I felt all ___grown___ up. I also felt a little bit lonely. I wish now that I had ___known___ someone else on the train. I sat with my ___elbow___ on the arm rest and my chin in my hand, looking out the window.

Preparation Have students turn to pages 82 and 83. Let them look at the letter and the picture. Call their attention to the word list. Have the students say the words. Then explain that each spelling word belongs in one of the blanks in the letter.

Write the title "Letter from the Science Fair" on the board. Ask what form this selection takes. (*a letter*) Ask students if they are familiar with science fairs and if so, what they are like. Explain that junior high and high schools sometimes put on exhibits of students' science projects. This story is about a science fair at a university. The participants come from many different schools, and some travel long distances to get there.

The Pages Have students complete pages 82 and 83 independently by silently reading the letter and writing the missing spelling words. Or you may read the letter aloud, supplying the missing words as students follow along in their texts; then have the students complete the pages on their own.

When students have finished, you may wish to discuss the letter. Ask if any students have taken a trip by themselves, like the one Anne took. If so, have

When we got to the train station in South Bend, the conductor told me to follow him to a taxi. Then he folded my wheelchair and put it in the taxi for me. The taxi took me to the main building of the university. Just inside the front door I saw an arrow pointing to a large room. A sign read TO THE SCIENCE FAIR. I wheeled right into the room.

A woman met me at the door, gave me a name tag, and pointed to where my table was. She explained that the room was divided into several zones. My table is in the special zone reserved for seventh graders. I began to unpack my exhibit immediately. I was especially worried about the microscope and slides, but they were fine. I set up the microscope and looked at one of my slides. Then I set up the rest of my exhibit.

When I was finished with my exhibit, I found a telephone and called home. I dialed my area code and the number. Mom answered. She and Dad were glad to hear I had arrived safely.

I bought a sandwich on the train, but I was so excited that I could hardly swallow a bite. Now I'm hungry. When I finish this letter, I think I'll just throw on my coat and join some of the other kids in the cafeteria for a bowl of chili.

Well, tomorrow is the big day! I feel so great to be at the science fair on my own. I guess I really owe it all to that caterpillar!

Your friend,
Anne

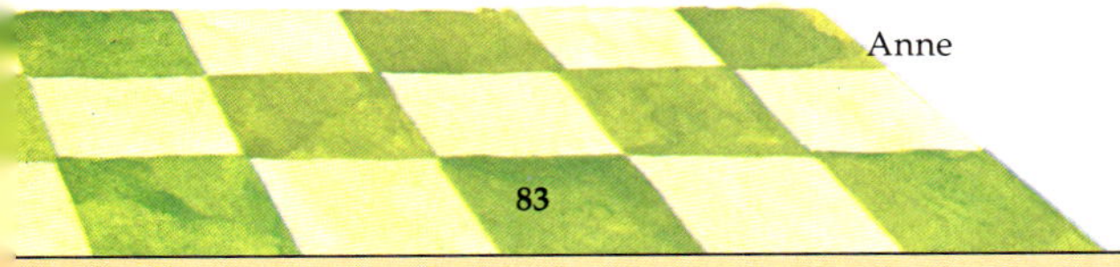

known
throw
bowl
follow
arrow
elbow
grown
borrow
swallow
tomorrow
zone
vote
telephone
code
alone
microscope
suppose
chose
sew
owe

83

them compare their experiences and feelings with Anne's. Were they lonely? Afraid? So excited they couldn't eat? Ask how Anne's experience was different because she was in a wheelchair. (*A train conductor helped her put her wheelchair in a taxi; otherwise, no special help was needed.*) Ask what Anne's attitude was toward being in a wheelchair. (*She was not upset or embarrassed by it, but carried on quite normally.*) Point out that Anne did not let her handicap stop her from following her interests and goals.

Have a volunteer read each paragraph in the letter, supplying each missing spelling word and spelling it aloud. Have other volunteers write the answers on the board and have students correct their own work. Check students' responses for the accurate spelling of each answer.

Follow-Up Have students use each of the spelling words they missed in an original sentence that relates to the letter.

As an additional follow-up activity, you may wish to have one student read the letter aloud to the class, pausing before each spelling word. The other students will say the spelling word at the appropriate time.

Enrichment

If you want to use the blackline activity masters for enrichment and additional practice, assign Lesson 14 activities at this time.

Maintenance and Review

OBJECTIVE

- To review words with /ō/ spelled: o, a.

ACTIVITIES

If you want to use the blackline activity masters for maintenance and review, assign Lesson 13 activities at this time.

You can also use the activity below to review Lesson 13 with students.

Write the following groups of letters on the board. Have students refer to the Lesson 14 word list and unscramble each group below to make a word from Lesson 14. (Answers are in parentheses.)

toslec	(*closet*)
nerwad	(*wander*)
lipstaoh	(*hospital*)
natiquyt	(*quantity*)
thober	(*bother*)
lardol	(*dollar*)
storelb	(*lobster*)
ropcep	(*copper*)
rohon	(*honor*)
tobcje	(*object*)

Objectives

- To relate spelling to another language skill.
- To identify and review predicates of sentences.
- To write spelling words in the context of sentences.
- To practice proofreading.

Predicate

The predicate is the part of a sentence that tells what the subject does or did, or what the subject is or was. In these sentences Jason is the subject.

Jason jogs to school every day.
Jason is a very good athlete.

Read the sentences above and answer these questions.

1. What words tell what Jason does or did in the first sentence?

jogs to school every day

2. What words tell what Jason is or was in the second sentence?

is a very good athlete

★ Write each sentence below, correcting the misspelled words. Then underline the complete predicate.

3. Becky will telefone you after school.

Becky will telephone you after school.

4. Jack wants to borow my bike.

Jack wants to borrow my bike.

5. You ow me a dime.

You owe me a dime.

6. I like to so my own clothes.

I like to sew my own clothes.

7. Kim and Evan arrive tommorow.

Kim and Evan arrive tomorrow.

8. Anne has groan an inch this year.

Anne has grown an inch this year.

9. Jesse couldn't swalow when he was sick.

Jesse couldn't swallow when he was sick.

10. I suppoze I should study now.

I suppose I should study now.

84

Preparation Have students read aloud the title of page 84. Review that the predicate of a sentence is the part that tells what the subject does or did, or what the subject is or was. Have students make up sentences, write them on the board, and underline the predicate of each. You may wish to start with this sentence, in which the predicate is underlined:

We will visit my sister tomorrow.

The Page Have students do page 84. Then have volunteers write the answers on the board.

Follow-Up Have students rewrite exercises 3–10, supplying their own predicate for each sentence. Students should use a spelling word in each sentence. Encourage students to use their imagination, but remind them that each sentence must make sense.

WORDS AT WORK

Challenge Yourself

disclose wallow stowaway brooch

Decide which Challenge Word fits each clue. Check your Spelling Dictionary to see if you were right. Then write sentences showing that you understand the meaning of each Challenge Word.

1. This person might hide in a car trunk or on a ship in the hope of getting a free ride.
2. You do this to a secret when you tell it to someone.
3. You could pin one on the collar of a blouse or jacket to dress it up.
4. Pigs do this in mud to cool themselves off.

Write to the Point

Do you have a friend or relative whom you haven't seen in a while? Write a letter telling that person some of the news in your life that you would like to share. If you wish, share some of your thoughts and feelings, too. Use spelling words from this lesson in your letter.

Challenge Use one or more of the Challenge Words in your letter.

Proofreading

Use the proofreading marks to show the errors in the paragraph below. Write the five misspelled words correctly in the blanks.

⬭	word is misspelled
≡	letter should be capitalized
^	word is missing

Tommorrow I will give my report called "The Amazing microscope." I choze this topic because ^I have grone very interested in studying nature. I have already learned quite a lot about nature, but I suppoze there ^is much more to be knoan.

1. Tomorrow
2. chose
3. grown
4. suppose
5. known

Objectives

- To extend the vowel spellings presented in Lesson 15 to the Challenge Words.
- To use clues and the **Spelling Dictionary** to enlarge students' vocabulary.
- To apply the vowel spellings presented in Lesson 15 in a writing activity.
- To practice proofreading for spelling, capitalization, and missing words.

Dictation Sentences

1. I am going to vote tomorrow.
2. I have to sew the hole in the elbow of my shirt.
3. I owe ten dollars for the telephone bill.
4. What is the area code in this zone?
5. This arrow is very old.
6. I need to borrow a microscope.
7. I must follow the directions and swallow two pills every six hours.
8. I suppose I will go the movies alone.
9. He chose to throw the ball instead of running with it.
10. I have known him all my life.
11. The bowl is on the table.
12. I have grown two inches!

Challenge Yourself Answers

1. stowaway
2. disclose
3. brooch
4. wallow

Students' sentences will vary.

Test Review these four ways to spell /ō/: ow as in elbow; o_e as in code; ew as in sew; owe as in owe. Test words with /ō/. Use one of these testing methods: (1) Say the word; read the sample sentence from page 80; say the word; have students write it. (2) Read each dictation sentence above; have students write the sentence. Correct the test with students.

Challenge Yourself The optional Challenge Words may be assigned to the entire class or limited to those students who do well on the test. Have students note the vowel spellings in the Challenge Words, especially the following new spelling: oo as in brooch. You may wish to have students work in pairs. Responses to this activity should be completed on separate paper. Answers to the questions are provided above.

Write to the Point Help students recall the selection "Letter from the Science Fair" on pages 82 and 83; then assign the letter. Remind students that the first word in the greeting and closing of a letter should begin with a capital letter and that people's names and titles are always capitalized. This activity should be completed on separate paper.

Proofreading The proofreading practice includes misspellings of words from this lesson as well as a capitalization error and missing words.

LESSON 16

Objectives

- To hear and say words with /ō/.
- To write words with /ō/ with attention to letter sequence and sound/symbol relationships.
- To write each spelling word once.
- To recognize that /ō/ may be spelled o, oa, and ou.

Sample Sentences

1. Danny waved at Janice, but she didn't notice him.
2. Several houses were ruined by the tornado.
3. We'll stay in a big hotel in Paris.
4. They'll scold us for sneaking in.
5. In this tunnel, you hear an echo when you shout.
6. Sam is the hero of the story.
7. The astronauts control the ship.
8. They wear clothing that protects them from the cold.
9. Judy wrote a poem about her puppy.
10. First, separate the egg white from the yolk.
11. We watched the leaves float on the water.
12. Jamie has a cold and a sore throat.
13. We will see the coast first and then travel inland.
14. These are oak trees.
15. The coach talked about the game.
16. Fred began to groan when he woke up.
17. Rick started to boast that he could eat three pizzas.
18. Should we fry the chicken or roast it?
19. They are coming, though I don't know when.
20. Mix the cookie dough and then bake it.

Note

- The sample sentences may be used for pretesting.
- Words are grouped according to spelling of /ō/:
  o
  oa
  ou

Lesson 16 Words with /ō/

Listen for /ō/ in each word.

notice
tornado
hotel
scold
echo
hero
control
clothing
poem
yolk

float
throat
coast
oak
coach
groan
boast
roast

though
dough

1. Which word begins with /sk/? Circle the letters that spell /sk/. scold
2. Write the two words that begin with the letters th. throat though
3. Which word has the letters th in the middle? clothing
4. Which word begins and ends like flat? float
5. Which word begins and ends like coal? control
6. Which word begins and ends like hospital? hotel
7. Which word begins with the letter p? poem
8. Write the three words that end with the letter o. tornado echo hero
9. Which word ends with the letters ch? coach
10. Write the two words that end with the letter k. yolk oak
11. Write the three words that end with the letters st. coast boast roast
12. Which word ends with /s/? notice
13. Which two words have the same spelling of /ō/ as thorough? though dough
14. In which word do the letters ch spell /k/? echo
15. Which word sounds exactly like grown? groan

86

Preparation

Have students read aloud the title of the lesson on page 86. Write /ō/ on the board. Have students say /ō/ as in go. Read each spelling word aloud. Have students repeat and then spell each word aloud.

Note that poem ends with the letters em. Ask which letter is not pronounced in the word yolk. (*l*) Ask which two consonants are not pronounced in though and dough. (*gh*) Then ask what letter spells /ō/ in the first group of words. (*o*) Have students identify the letters that spell /ō/ in the other groups of words in the list. (See **Note**.)

Read the sample sentences. Have students point to each spelling word as you read the sentence for it.

The Page

Have students complete page 86, independently or as a group. Ask volunteers to write the answers on the board and have students correct their own work.

Follow-Up

Suggest that students write each word. Then have them trace over each word with a finger while they spell the word aloud.

Checkpoint

Write a spelling word for each clue.
Then use the Checkpoint Study Plan on page 224.

Clue	Answer
1. To cook with dry heat in an oven is to ___.	roast
2. A repeated sound is an ___.	echo
3. Another word for see or pay attention to is ___.	notice
4. The opposite of to sink is to ___.	float
5. A kind of trainer is a ___.	coach
6. At the edge of the sea is the ___.	coast
7. Socks, pants, and shirts are ___.	clothing
8. To talk to harshly is to ___.	scold
9. To have power over is to ___.	control
10. Someone who likes to brag likes to ___.	boast
11. Part of an egg is the ___.	yolk
12. Another word for however is ___.	though
13. The opposite of coward is ___.	hero
14. An acorn grows into an ___.	oak
15. The front part of the neck is the ___.	throat
16. A sound of dismay or pain is a ___.	groan
17. A baker makes bread from ___.	dough
18. Another word for inn is ___.	hotel
19. A piece of writing that rhymes is a ___.	poem

20. This mystery word names a violent wind. The wind takes on a funnel shape and whirls about. It spins at up to 300 miles per hour. This wind can cause much damage. It takes its name from the Spanish word *tronada*. *Tronada* means thunderstorm. It probably got this name because thunder often comes with funnel-shaped winds. Can you guess the mystery word? ___ tornado

Objectives

- To write spelling words in response to clues: definitions, synonyms, antonyms, and context.
- To develop the critical thinking skills of making inferences and classifying.
- To learn one of the many ways in which words have entered the English language.

Spelling Strategy

If students have difficulty remembering to include the unpronounced consonants g and h in though and dough, they might benefit by focusing on the shape of the words. Have them write each word in pencil and outline it in pen. Then have them erase the penciled letters, observe the shape of the ink outline, and rewrite the letters in the outline.

Preparation The clues on this page are like crossword puzzle clues. Explain to students that the response to each clue is a spelling word. Use the following examples to illustrate the types of clues used:

Definition	A repeated sound is an (*echo*).
Synonym	Another word for see or pay attention to is (*notice*).
Antonym	The opposite of to sink is to (*float*).
Context	A baker makes bread from (*dough*).

The final clue explains the Spanish origin of tornado.

The Page Have students complete page 87 using the words on page 86. When students have finished, have them read each clue and spell the answer aloud. Check each response twice: once for the correct answer and a second time for spelling accuracy.

Follow-Up Guide pupils in using the **Checkpoint Study Plan** on page 224 to take a self-test. Then have them use the plan for independent study.

Objectives

- To write words with /ō/ in continuous text.
- To write each spelling word once.
- To integrate reading with spelling.

Note

- Point out that Casa Grande means big house in Spanish.
- Point out the use of the word notice as a noun meaning a written announcement. Ask students for another meaning of notice.

Use each list word once.

HURRICANE

Marie's father was the head cook at Casa Grande, the most famous seaside hotel on the western coast of the island. Marie often helped in the kitchen. Today was no different. While her father kneaded dough for bread and put a roast in the oven, she broke an egg and stirred the yolk into the cake batter.

When she was finished, she changed from her work clothing to her swimsuit. It had been hot in the kitchen. Now she was ready to float on the gentle waves of the sea. On her way down to the beach, she saw Juan, the hotel manager. He was posting a notice on the bulletin board. It was a storm warning. She ran to alert the hotel guests.

One guest, a softball trainer and coach, didn't seem afraid. In fact, she began to boast. "No hurricane or tornado can scare me," she bragged.

A second guest began to moan and groan when he heard the news. "I'm not brave. I'm no hero," he said.

Just then, Juan announced over a loudspeaker that everyone should take shelter in the hotel. They listened to his voice echo up and down the beach for a long moment. Then Marie led them to the hotel's kitchen, which was in the basement. They would be safe there.

88

Preparation Have students turn to pages 88 and 89. Let them look at the story and the pictures. Call their attention to the word list. Have the students say the words. Then explain that each spelling word belongs in one of the blanks in the story.

Write the title "Hurricane" on the board. Ask if any students have experienced a hurricane or another type of major storm. If so, have them tell what it was like. Explain that a hurricane is a severe storm with rain and very high winds. A hurricane is dangerous to people who are not inside a strong shelter. Hurricanes often last for many hours.

The Pages Have students complete pages 88 and 89 independently by silently reading the story and writing the missing spelling words. Or you may read the story aloud, supplying the missing words as students follow along in their texts; then have the students complete the pages on their own.

When students have finished, you may wish to discuss the story. Ask what students think of Marie's attempt to make the hotel guests feel better. (*It was successful because it got their minds off the storm.*) Ask what kind of per-

Even in the basement, they could hear the wind roaring and the huge waves crashing over the beach. The guests tried hard to control their rising fears. Even the brave coach felt her throat become so tight that she couldn't swallow. She began to scold herself for being so afraid.

Marie decided she had to do something to take their minds off the storm. She grabbed some paper and pencils. "May I have your attention?" she shouted above the noise of the storm. "Even though we're stuck in the kitchen until the storm blows over, there's no reason we can't have a good time. Let's all sit around the big oak table and make believe that we are poets. There will be a prize for the best poem about the storm." Everyone scrambled for seats and began to write.

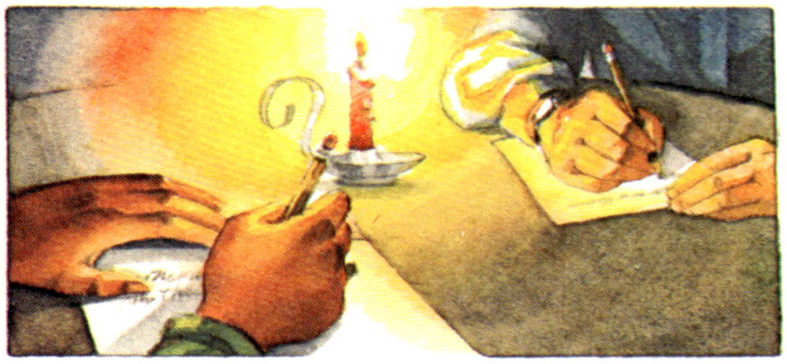

Marie breathed a deep sigh as she heard the storm die down. Everyone was safe. Juan announced that the prize for the writing contest would be a free dinner. Then he thanked Marie for entertaining the guests and keeping them busy during the storm.

Marie often helped in the kitchen. Today had been no different from any other.

89

notice
tornado
hotel
scold
echo
hero
control
clothing
poem
yolk
float
throat
coast
oak
coach
groan
boast
roast
though
dough

son Marie is. (*responsible, imaginative, caring*) Ask how the softball coach handled her fears. (*First she denied having any; then she scolded herself for being afraid.*) Ask how the other guest mentioned in the story handled his fears. (*He moaned and groaned and admitted he was afraid.*) Ask students whom they might act like, the softball coach or the other guest. (*Answers will vary.*)

Have a volunteer read each paragraph in the story, supplying each missing spelling word and spelling it aloud. Have other volunteers write the answers on the board and have students correct their own work. Check students' responses for the accurate spelling of each answer.

Follow-Up

Have students use each of the spelling words they missed in an original sentence that relates to the story.

As an additional follow-up activity, you may wish to have students make a mural illustrating the story. Attach a large piece of paper to the wall and have several students plan and draw the mural.

Enrichment

If you want to use the blackline activity masters for enrichment and additional practice, assign lesson 16 activities at this time.

Maintenance and Review

OBJECTIVE

To review words with /ō/ spelled: ow, o_e, ew, owe.

ACTIVITIES

If you want to use the blackline activity masters for maintenance and review, assign Lesson 15 activities at this time.

You can also use the activity below to review Lesson 15 with students:

Write the following words on the board. Have students write the word or words from Lesson 15 that rhyme with each word. (Answers are in parentheses.)

hollow	(*swallow, follow*)
phone	(*known, grown, zone*)
sorrow	(*borrow, tomorrow*)
hose	(*chose*)
sparrow	(*arrow*)
go	(*sew, owe*)

Objectives

- To relate spelling to another language skill.
- To review capitalization of people's names, titles, and the word I.
- To write spelling words in the context of sentences.
- To practice proofreading.

Capitals

Use a capital letter to begin a person's first or last name. Also, use a capital letter to begin a title that goes with someone's name. Always capitalize the word I.

My neighbor, Mrs. Allison, and I enjoy each other's company.
Her son, Tom, is very friendly, too.

★ Write the sentences below. Correct the misspelled words and capitalize where necessary.

1. I'll never forget our class trip to the cost with mr. and mrs. lane.
   I'll never forget our class trip to the coast with Mr. and Mrs. Lane.
2. Adam and i packed our clotheing, and justin packed the food.
   Adam and I packed our clothing, and Justin packed the food.
3. We knew mr. lane would never skold us for packing too much.
   We knew Mr. Lane would never scold us for packing too much.
4. Our track coch, mr. wallace, came to see us off.
   Our track coach, Mr. Wallace, came to see us off.
5. Coach wallace is everyone's hiro.
   Coach Wallace is everyone's hero.
6. He cleared his troat and said good-by to us and good luck to mr. and mrs. lane.
   He cleared his throat and said good-bye to us and good luck to Mr. and Mrs. Lane.
7. After driving most of the day, mrs. lane asked us to notise signs for a place to stay.
   After driving most of the day, Mrs. Lane asked us to notice signs for a place to stay.
8. With a cheer, justin, scott, and i spotted a sign for a hotell.
   With a cheer, Justin, Scott, and I spotted a sign for a hotel.

90

Preparation Have students read aloud the title of page 90. Write your name, including the title, on the board, without capitalizing the first letters. Ask volunteers to correct the spelling.

Next, write a student's first and last names without capitalizing them. Ask that student to correct the spelling.

Write this phrase on the board: **you and i**. Have a volunteer capitalize the word i. Review with students the rules to capitalize the first letter of people's names, titles, and the word I.

The Page Have students do page 90. Then have volunteers write the answers on the board.

Follow-Up Have students write each spelling word in a sentence. Have them also use either a name or the word I in each.

WORDS AT WORK

Challenge Yourself

loathe nomad token smolder

Use your Spelling Dictionary to answer these questions. Then write sentences showing that you understand the meaning of each Challenge Word.

1. Would the coals from a fire smolder if you didn't put the fire out completely?
2. Would someone who is a nomad stay in one place all her life?
3. Could a flower or a photograph be a token of a special day?
4. If you care for someone very much, do you loathe that person?

Write to the Point

Some emergencies, like hurricanes, can't be prevented. Others, such as accidents, can often be prevented. Write a list of rules telling what to do in a certain kind of emergency or how to prevent such an emergency from happening. Use spelling words from this lesson in your rules.

Challenge Use one or more of the Challenge Words in your rules.

Proofreading

Use the proofreading marks to show the errors in the paragraph below. Write the five misspelled words correctly in the blanks.

(oval)	word is misspelled
(circled dot)	period is missing
/	letter should be lower case

We stayed in our hotell during the storm and listened to the wind grown. Along the coste the wind made waves crash on the Beach We saw a boat come untied and flote away. The wind seemed out of controll. We weren't afraid, though We were very careful.

1. hotel
2. groan
3. coast
4. float
5. control

Objectives

- To extend the vowel spellings presented in Lesson 16 to the Challenge Words.
- To use clues and the **Spelling Dictionary** to enlarge students' vocabulary.
- To apply the vowel spellings presented in Lesson 16 in a writing activity.
- To practice proofreading for spelling, punctuation, and capitalization.

Dictation Sentences

1. We stayed at a hotel along the coast.
2. The hero let out a groan.
3. The coach will notice if we are late.
4. We will roast the nuts and bake them in the pie dough.
5. The oak tree in our yard was blown over by the tornado.
6. She likes to boast that she is the best athlete, even though it is not true.
7. My teacher will scold me if I do not rest my throat before the show.
8. The egg yolk seemed to float in the pan until it was cooked.
9. The control on the left makes an echo sound.
10. Do you like my poem?
11. Wear warm clothing in the winter.

Challenge Yourself Answers

1. yes
2. no
3. yes
4. no

Students' sentences will vary.

Test Review these three ways to spell /ō/: o as in echo; oa as in oak; ou as in dough. Test words with /ō/. Use one of these testing methods: (1) Say the word; read the sample sentence from page 86; say the word; have students write it. (2) Read each dictation sentence above; have students write the sentence. Correct the test with students.

Challenge Yourself The optional Challenge Words may be assigned to the entire class or limited to those students who do well on the test. Have students note the vowel spellings in the Challenge Words, especially the following new spelling: oa_e as in loathe. You may wish to have students work in pairs. Responses to this activity should be completed on separate paper. Answers to the questions are provided above.

Write to the Point Help students recall the selection "Hurricane" on pages 88 and 89; then assign the list of rules. Remind students to state their rules briefly and clearly, so that their reader will be able to remember them. This activity should be completed on separate paper.

Proofreading The proofreading practice includes misspellings of words from this lesson as well as capitalization errors and a punctuation error.

LESSON 17

Objectives

- To hear and say media words.
- To write media words with attention to letter sequence and sound/symbol relationships.
- To write each spelling word at least once.

Sample Sentences

1. The new movie will be shot in this studio.
2. The director will tell the actors where to stand.
3. The producer hired the writer.
4. Do you like that commercial?
5. The film will be shown on television.
6. The show will be broadcast Tuesday.
7. The story is about a famous musician.
8. I'm glad it will be shown during prime time.
9. Many television stations are part of a network.
10. Put a new roll of film into the camera.
11. We can tape this program on the video recorder.
12. It looks like a big cassette tape recorder.
13. It's something like the tape deck in my car.
14. Listen to this song with the earphones.
15. Ron reads the newspaper every day.
16. His favorite columnist writes a funny article every day.
17. Editors' names are listed on the masthead.
18. The writer's name appears in the by-line under the title.
19. Editors express their opinions on the editorial page.
20. The headline read: City to Get Funds.

Note

Point out that a compound word, which combines two or more words to form a single unit with its own meaning, may be written without a space, as everybody, or with a hyphen, as self-defense, or as separate words that have one special meaning, as ice cream.

Lesson 17 Media Words

Say each word.

studio
director
producer
commercial
television
broadcast
musician
prime time
network
camera
recorder
cassette
tape deck
earphones
newspaper
columnist
masthead
by-line
editorial
headline

1. Which word begins with the letter h? headline
2. Which word begins and ends like cafeteria? camera
3. Write one word that begins with the letters st and two words that end with st. studio broadcast columnist
4. Which word has the letters st in the middle? masthead
5. Write the word in which you hear /zh/. television
6. Which two words end with /k/? Circle the letters that spell /k/. network tape deck
7. Which three words have /k/ in the middle? director broadcast recorder
8. Write the three words that end with the letters er. producer recorder newspaper
9. Which word ends with the letters or? director
10. Which word has /f/ in the middle? Circle the letters that spell /f/. earphones
11. Which word has a hyphen? by-line
12. In which two words do you hear /sh/ but don't see the letters sh? commercial musician
13. Which word has two pairs of double consonants? cassette
14. Which word has five syllables? editorial
15. Which word is made up of two words that rhyme? prime time

92

Preparation Have students read aloud the title of the lesson on page 92. Ask students what the communication media are. (*newspapers, magazines, radio, and television*) Read each word aloud. Have students repeat and spell each word aloud.

Ask students to identify the base word in director (*direct*), producer (*produce*), recorder (*record*), columnist (*column*), and editorial (*edit*). Have them identify the two words in each compound word. (*broad, cast; prime, time; net, work; tape, deck; ear, phones; news, paper; mast, head; by, line; head, line*)

Write the sample sentences on the board, or have students write them as you dictate. Tell students to underline the spelling words and save their papers for use with Checkpoint and Story activities.

If you write the sentences on the board, leave them until students have completed their work on lesson 17.

The Page Have students complete page 92 independently or as a group. Ask volunteers to write the answers on the board. Have students correct their own work.

Follow-Up Suggest that students write each word in two colors, using the same color for every other letter. Double letters should be in the same color.

Checkpoint

Write a spelling word for each clue.
Then use the Checkpoint Study Plan on page 224.

1. A listing of people who work on a newspaper is a ____. masthead
2. An advertisement on radio or television is a ____. commercial
3. You can play a cassette on a ____. tape deck
4. The time when the most people watch TV is ____. prime time
5. To put on the air is to ____. broadcast
6. Many TV stations belong to a ____. network
7. Pictures are taken with a ____. camera
8. Stereo is to album as tape deck is to ____. cassette
9. The one who manages the show is the ____. producer
10. Someone who writes or plays music is a ____. musician
11. The writer of a newspaper column is a ____. columnist
12. I record songs on my tape ____. recorder
13. The line giving an author's name is a ____. by-line
14. Daily or weekly news is found in the ____. newspaper
15. Many shows are taped in a ____. studio
16. The one who guides the show is a ____. director
17. The title of a news article is a ____. headline
18. A journalist writes his or her opinion in an ____. editorial
19. Another name for headsets is ____. earphones

20. New inventions are usually given Greek or Latin names. Sometimes an invention gets an odd name that is half Greek and half Latin. This mystery word has such a name. The mystery word names an electronic device that turns radio waves into sight and sound. It comes from two words, *telos* and *video*. *Telos* is Greek. It means far away. *Video* comes from Latin and means see. The mystery word names a device that lets us see things that happen far away. Can you guess the word? ____ television

Objectives

- To write media words in response to clues: definitions, synonyms, analogies, and context.
- To develop the critical thinking skills of making inferences and comparing.
- To understand that many English words come from Greek and Latin and that words may be combined to form new words.

Spelling Strategy

If students have difficulty remembering which compound words are written with a space or a hyphen between their word parts, have them practice spelling tape deck, prime time, and by-line aloud using a special sound to represent the space or the hyphen. For example, they might make a hissing sound to represent a space and snap their fingers or clap their hands to represent a hyphen.

Preparation The clues on this page are like crossword puzzle clues. Explain to students that the response to each clue is a spelling word. Use the following examples to illustrate the types of clues used:

Definition	to put on the air is to (*broadcast*).
Synonym	Another name for headset is (*earphones*).
Analogy	Stereo is to album as tape deck is to (*cassette*).
Context	Many shows are taped in a (*studio*).

The final clue names the Greek and Latin words that were combined to make the English word television.

The Page Have students complete page 93 using the words on page 92. When students have finished, have them read each clue and spell the answer aloud. Check each response twice: once for the correct answer and a second time for spelling accuracy.

Follow-Up Guide pupils in using the **Checkpoint Study Plan** on page 224 to take a self-test. Then have them use the plan for independent study.

Objectives

- To write media words in continuous text.
- To write each spelling word once.
- To integrate reading with spelling.

Note

Remind students that many of these media words are compound words. The reason for this is that, as technology has advanced, people have had to invent new terms for their work, often by combining two words to make the new term.

Use words from the first part of the list to do this page.

MULTIMEDIA

My mother works for a television network. She is a producer. As a producer, she plans each show. She gets to choose all the people who work on it. One of the most important people she chooses is the director. He directs people in the show.

Mother's show is broadcast at nine every Wednesday evening, during prime time. Every weekday evening from eight o'clock to eleven is called prime time.

Every morning at eight, my mother goes to the studio where the show is filmed. Yesterday, I went with her. First she met with the director and the musician who is in charge of the music. The music for each show is recorded on a cassette tape. This is done in a studio where they have the best tape recorder. I had thought that the musician would just put his earphones on his ears, put the tape into the tape deck, and push "PLAY." It wasn't that simple.

The musician, the director, and Mother went over the script for the show. Together they decided which camera would be used to film each scene. They also had to decide where they would break for a commercial.

I stayed at work with Mother until nine that night. I was surprised to find out how much work it takes to put together one half-hour television show.

94

Preparation

Have students turn to pages 94 and 95. Let them look at the story and the pictures. Call their attention to the word list. Have the students say the words. Then explain that each spelling word belongs in one of the blanks in the story.

Write the title "Multimedia" on the board. Then ask if any students have seen a television show being taped. If so, have them describe what it was like. Explain that there are many steps involved in making a show, both before and after the taping takes place.

Ask if any students have been to a newspaper office. Have them describe what it was like. Explain that a newspaper office is a noisy, busy place where many people work to put together a newspaper in a few hours.

The Pages

Have students refer to the sample sentences you wrote on the board or had students write and have them complete pages 94 and 95 independently by silently reading the story and writing the missing spelling words. Or you may read the story aloud, supplying the missing words as students follow along in their texts; then have the students complete the pages on their own.

Use words from the second part of the list to do this page.

My father works at the Daily Times. Dad writes a daily column about television. He is a ___columnist___. His name appears after his column. This is called his ___by-line___. Dad's name also appears on the masthead followed by his title, Television Editor. Dad's boss is also listed on the ___masthead___ of the paper. His boss is the Managing Editor.

Last week I visited my father at his office. He showed me a copy of the ___newspaper___ from the day he started work there. Then we watched the program that he was going to write about in his column. We watched it on a video cassette recorder. The show was about a woman who was lost in the desert for five days. After Dad wrote his column, I helped him write the ___headline___ for it. We finally decided on "One Woman's Fight for Life."

Then we went out to a coffee shop for lunch. Dad's best friend, Morty, went with us. Morty works on the ___editorial___ page where all of the editorials and letters to the editor appear.

I really enjoyed the day with Dad. I felt important because I had helped to write the headline. The next day, when I saw Dad's by-line, I was proud.

studio
director
producer
commercial
television
broadcast
musician
prime time
network
camera
recorder
cassette
tape deck
earphones

newspaper
columnist
masthead
by-line
editorial
headline

When students have finished, you may wish to discuss the story. Ask students which place they would rather visit, the television studio or the newspaper office, and why. Some television stations and newspapers give tours to groups. If possible, you may want to arrange such a tour for your class.

Have a volunteer read each paragraph in the story, supplying each missing spelling word and spelling it aloud. Have other volunteers write the answers on the board and have students correct their own work. Check students' responses for the accurate spelling of each answer.

Follow-Up

Have students use each of the spelling words they missed in an original sentence that relates to the story.

As an additional follow-up activity, you may wish to have students make a scrapbook on the media using the information provided in "Multimedia." Ask students to illustrate the scrapbook and use sentences from the story as captions.

Enrichment

If you want to use the blackline activity masters for enrichment and additional practice, assign Lesson 17 activities at this time.

Maintenance and Review

OBJECTIVE

- To review words with /ō/ spelled: o, oa, ou.

ACTIVITIES

If you want to use the blackline activity masters for maintenance and review, assign Lesson 16 activities at this time.

You can also use the activity below to review Lesson 16 with students.

Write the following CHAINWORDS on the board. Have students refer to the Lesson 16 word list and have them find the two list words hidden in each chainword below. (Answers are in parentheses.)

tornadough	(*tornado, dough*)
echoak	(*echo, oak*)
heroast	(*hero, roast*)
thoughotel	(*though, hotel*)
clothingroan	(*clothing, groan*)

Objectives

- To relate spelling to another language skill.
- To capitalize the names of places.
- To put sentences in correct word order.
- To write spelling words in the context of sentences.

Capitals

Names of places such as cities, states, countries, bodies of water, mountains, and streets are capitalized.

Larry visited San Francisco, California, last summer.
He saw the Pacific Ocean.

★ Unscramble and write each sentence below. Capitalize where necessary.

1. was broadcast The new york from
   The broadcast was from New York.
2. team camera to johnson street rushed A
   A camera team rushed to Johnson Street.
3. the was commercial rocky mountains The filmed in
   The commercial was filmed in the Rocky Mountains.
4. a hollywood We studio visited
   We visited a Hollywood studio.
5. said newspaper miami, florida The was held in concert the
   The newspaper said the concert was held in Miami, Florida.
6. lives director paris in The of that film
   The director of that film lives in Paris.
7. often the is washington, d.c. headlines in
   Washington, D.C., is often in the headlines.
8. music of and georgia We played a tennessee cassette about the tape
   We played a cassette tape about the music of Tennessee and Georgia.
9. The show atlantic ocean television was about the
   The television show was about the Atlantic Ocean.
10. editorial london The about was
    The editorial was about London.

96

Preparation Have students read aloud the title of page 96. Tell them that the names of places begin with a capital letter. Have volunteers write on the board the names of your school, street address, town, state, and country. Then tell students that the names of bridges, mountains, rivers, and other bodies of water are also capitalized and discuss examples.

The Page Have students do page 96. Then have volunteers write the answers on the board.

Follow-Up Have students rewrite exercises 1–10, supplying their own place names. Remind them to use capitals correctly.

WORDS AT WORK

Challenge Yourself

journalism **periodical** **front-page** **newsstand**

Use your Spelling Dictionary to answer these questions. Then write sentences showing that you understand the meaning of each Challenge Word.

1. Would a person who likes writing about people and events enjoy a job in journalism?
2. Is a magazine an example of a periodical?
3. In a newspaper, is front-page news usually important?
4. Is a newsstand a place where newspapers are printed?

Write to the Point

Some people think young people watch too much TV. What do you think? Write a paragraph giving your opinion of television. What is good about it? What is bad? Give reasons and examples to support your opinions. Use spelling words from this lesson in your paragraph.

Challenge Use one or more of the Challenge Words in your paragraph.

Proofreading

Use the proofreading marks to show the errors in the paragraph below. Write the five misspelled words correctly in the blanks.

(oval)	word is misspelled
≡	letter should be capitalized
(delete mark)	take out word

At primetime my grandfather he does more than just watch telavision. he sometimes pops a casette into the tape deck. Then he puts on on the earfones and settles in his favorite chair. Then he opens the newspapper in his lap to the front page and starts to read.

1. prime time
2. television
3. cassette
4. earphones
5. newspaper

Objectives

- To extend students' knowledge of media words through the Challenge Words.
- To use clues and the **Spelling Dictionary** to enlarge students' vocabulary.
- To apply the media words presented in Lesson 17 in a writing activity.
- To practice proofreading for spelling, capitalization, and extra words.

Dictation Sentences

1. Was the newspaper editorial in favor of the new highway?
2. The head of the network is also the producer of several prime time shows.
3. We have a new musician playing with the band in the studio.
4. I like to watch the television news broadcast.
5. I got a new cassette for the tape deck in my car.
6. The director of the play used a tape recorder for special effects.
7. The headline says that we must save energy.
8. I bought a new camera and a pair of earphones.
9. The name of the columnist who wrote the story is in the by-line.
10. My name is first on the masthead.
11. The song in that commercial is great!

Challenge Yourself Answers

1. yes
2. yes
3. yes
4. no

Students' sentences will vary.

Test Review and test media words. Use one of these testing methods: (1) Say the word; read the sample sentence from page 92; say the word; have students write it. (2) Read each dictation sentence above; have students write the sentence. Correct the test with students.

Challenge Yourself The optional Challenge Words may be assigned to the entire class or limited to those students who do well on the test. You may wish to have students work in pairs. Responses to this activity should be completed on separate paper. Answers to the questions are provided above.

Write to the Point Help students recall the selection "Multimedia" on pages 94 and 95; then assign the paragraph. Remind students to give supporting reasons and examples for their opinions. This activity should be completed on separate paper.

Proofreading The proofreading practice includes misspellings of words from this lesson as well as a capitalization error and extra words.

LESSON 18

Objectives

- To review and reinforce vowel spellings for /ī/, /ŏ/, and /ō/.
- To hear, say, spell, and write representative spelling words from Lessons 13–16.
- To write a business letter using the five steps in the writing process.
- To use a prewriting activity to plan information to include in a business letter.

Dictation Sentences

1. I promise to call you on the telephone.
2. Let me be your guide around the island.
3. There is a library in the hospital.
4. We heard a groan come from his throat.
5. I will be honest and pay what I owe you.
6. She must sew a longer skirt because she has grown taller.
7. We learned about the yolk of an egg in science.
8. Who will decide what quantity to order?
9. Can we control the echo in here?
10. That sport is not common here, though some people like it.

Note

A review test blackline master in standardized format and an answer sheet have been provided on pages T37 and T41 of this Teacher's Edition. The answers to the review test are given below.

1–C	11–D
2–D	12–B
3–C	13–C
4–A	14–A
5–C	15–C
6–A	16–A
7–B	17–D
8–D	18–A
9–C	19–C
10–B	20–C

If words misspelled were from:	have students complete activities:
List A	1, 3, 6
List B	2, 3, 6
List C	4, 5, 6

Lesson 18 Words in Review

A. decide
guide
science
island
library

B. quantity
common
hospital
promise
honest

C. control
sew
throat
echo
though
yolk
owe
grown
groan
telephone

★ You will need a piece of paper for these review activities.

1. In Lesson 13 you studied three different ways to spell /ī/: **i, i_e, ui_e.** Write the words in list A.
   decide guide science island library
2. In Lesson 14 you studied two different ways to spell /ŏ/: **o, a.** Write the words in list B.
   quantity common hospital promise honest
3. ★ Use each review word from lists A and B in a sentence.
4. In Lessons 15 and 16 you studied seven different ways to spell /ō/: **ow, o_e, ew, owe, o, oa, ou.** Write the words in list C.
   control sew throat echo though yolk owe grown groan telephone
5. ★ Look up each review word from list C in the Spelling Dictionary. Write the part of speech for each word. (Hint: Some words may be more than one part of speech.)
6. ★ Write all 20 review words in alphabetical order.

Your teacher may give you a test. Answer these questions when you have finished.

7. Did you spell all the words correctly? Yes or No
8. Did you leave out a letter? Yes or No
9. Did you write the wrong letter? Yes or No
10. Did you miss the spelling of a vowel sound? Yes or N

98

Test Pretest the review words on page 98 to determine which students need reinforcement. Use one of these testing methods: (1) Read the words and the dictation sentences; have students write only the spelling words. (2) Read the dictation sentences and have students write the entire sentences. (3) Have students complete the review test blackline master. (See **Note**.) Correct the pretest with students.

The Pages Assign pages 98 and 99 according to students' needs.

- Students who have mastered all of the review words may go on to the **Writer's Workshop** on page 99.
- Students who have not mastered all of the review words should complete the activities on page 98 and take a post-test administered with one of the pretesting methods. After the post-test students can then go on to the **Writer's Workshop** on page 99. For students who have misspelled only a few of the review words, you may wish to use the list at left to determine the activities they should complete on page 98.

For students who have misspelled several of the review words, you may wish to assign all of the activities on page 98.

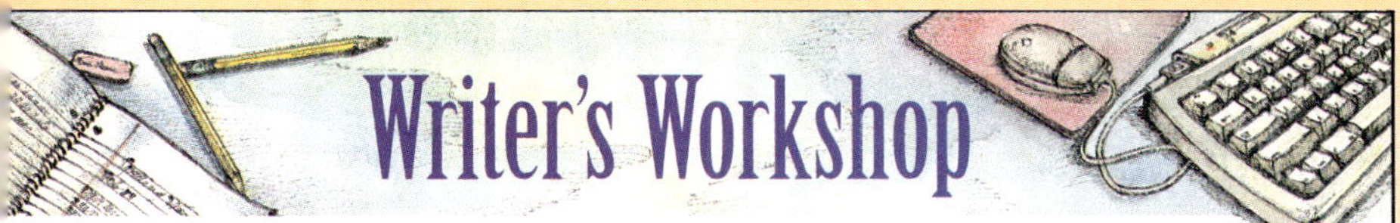

A Business Letter

Suppose that you read a great book and wanted to write a letter to the author to tell him or her how much you liked the book. You would need the author's address. One way to get the address is to write a business letter to the publisher of the book. Here is a business letter that Leah wrote to a publisher.

27 Palm Road
Jacksonville, FL 32216
April 3, 1996

Hall Publishing Company
157 Madison Avenue
New York, NY 10023

Dear Hall Publishing Company:

I really enjoyed the book South Pacific Adventure by Kate Rossini. Please send me Ms. Rossini's address so that I can tell her how much I liked the book. Thank you.

Sincerely,
Leah Yu
Leah Yu

To write her business letter, Leah followed the steps in the writing process. She used a list as a **Prewriting** activity. The list helped her make sure that she did not forget to include any important information in the letter. Leah's list is shown here. Study what Leah did.

My address
Address of publishing company
Name of book: South Pacific Adventure
Author: Kate Rossini

Get ready to write your own business letter. Choose a company that sells books or games through a catalog. Write a letter to the company, asking for a copy of the catalog. When you have decided what company to write to, make a list like Leah's. Then follow the other steps in the writing process—**Writing, Revising, Proofreading,** and **Publishing.**

99

Note

If students have difficulty in choosing a catalog company to write to, you may wish to suggest this fictitious company:

Comfy Clothing, Inc.
143 Seventh Street
Lakeside, OR 97034

Writer's Workshop Explain that one reason for writing a business letter is to request information. Read Leah's letter with students and point out the heading, inside address, colon after the greeting, and closing. Also point out the types of information Leah included in her letter.

Allow students to study the list shown on the pupil's page and guide students to see how this graphic organizer helped Leah prepare to write her letter.

It's Your Turn Review the steps in the writing process with students. If students are not satisfied with the result of their prewriting, allow them to revise it as often as necessary or to choose another topic and repeat the prewriting activity.

Process Writing Blackline Masters

- Steps in the Writing Process, page T44
- Proofreading Symbols/Checklist, page T45

LESSON 19

Objectives

- To hear and say words with /ŭ/.
- To write words with /ŭ/ with attention to letter sequence and sound/symbol relationships.
- To write each spelling word once.
- To recognize that /ŭ/ may be spelled u, o, ou, and oo.

Sample Sentences

1. The judge came into the courtroom.
2. Martha and her husband run a bicycle shop.
3. We'll use that pumpkin to make a jack-o'-lantern.
4. Be careful with the flowers or you'll crush them.
5. Seven hundred people came to see our play.
6. They cleared a path through the jungle.
7. Sara scraped the knuckle on her thumb.
8. The nurse will instruct us about first aid.
9. The doctor told me to stick out my tongue.
10. The tiny brown monkey hung by its tail.
11. I'll have a hamburger with a slice of onion.
12. Gloria dropped a dozen eggs and broke them all.
13. A compass needle always points north.
14. Marty was chosen the best among all the contestants.
15. Mary Anne wrote a wonderful story.
16. The road was so rough that we couldn't bike on it.
17. There are 50 states in this country.
18. Barbara likes to touch the cat's fur.
19. Steve didn't know he'd cut his hand till he saw blood.
20. The flood washed out the bridge.

Note

- The sample sentences may be used for pretesting.
- Words are grouped according to spellings of /ŭ/:
  - u
  - o
  - ou
  - oo

Lesson 19 Words with /ŭ/

Listen for /ŭ/ in each word.

judge
husband
pumpkin
crush
hundred
jungle
knuckle
instruct

tongue
monkey
onion
dozen
compass
among
wonderful

rough
country
touch

blood
flood

1. Write the three words that begin with a vowel. instruct onion among
2. Which word begins and ends like watchful? wonderful
3. Which word begins and ends like pin? pumpkin
4. Which two words begin and end like hurried? husband hundred
5. Which word begins with a letter k that you don't hear? knuckle
6. Write one word that begins with /f/ and one that ends with /f/. Circle the letters that spell /f/. flood rough
7. Which two words begin with the letter j? Circle the word that ends with /j/. judge jungle
8. Write the word that has the same spelling of /ŭ/ as flood. blood
9. Write the word that ends with the letters sh. crush
10. Which two words end with /ē/? monkey country
11. Which word ends with the letters ch? touch
12. In which word is /s/ spelled ss? compass
13. Which word contains the letter z? dozen
14. In which word do you see the letters gue but hear only /g/? tongue

100

Preparation Have students read aloud the title of the lesson on page 100. Write /ŭ/ on the board. Have students say /ŭ/ as in cut. Read each spelling word aloud. Have students repeat and then spell each word aloud.

Ask students how many p's there are in pumpkin. (*two*) Ask which two letters end jungle and knuckle. (*le*) Note the /ə/ in the le syllable of these words: /jŭng′ gəl/ and /nŭk′ əl/. Then ask what the base word of wonderful is. (*wonder*) Have students identify the letter that spells /ŭ/ in each group of words in the list. (See **Note.**)

Read the sample sentences. Have students point to each spelling word as you read the sentence for it.

The Page Have students complete page 100. Have volunteers write the answers on the board and have students correct their own work.

Follow-Up Suggest that students write the spelling words on cards (or small pieces of paper). Have them put the cards face down on a table. Then have them pick up one card at a time, read the word, spell it aloud, and repeat the process until they can spell all the words.

Checkpoint

Write a spelling word for each clue.
Then use the Checkpoint Study Plan on page 224.

1. Pipes are for water, veins are for ____. — blood
2. In a group of means ____. — among
3. The opposite of smooth is ____. — rough
4. To feel silk, use your sense of ____. — touch
5. A jack-o'-lantern is a carved ____. — pumpkin
6. North and south are points on a ____. — compass
7. A thick growth of trees and plants is a ____. — jungle
8. An overflow of water is a ____. — flood
9. I cry when I slice an ____. — onion
10. An animal that lives in the jungle is a ____. — monkey
11. A nation or state is a ____. — country
12. To teach is to ____. — instruct
13. Another word for marvelous is ____. — wonderful
14. To crumple is to ____. — crush
15. A joint on your finger is a ____. — knuckle
16. Twelve is one ____. — dozen
17. To decide right and wrong is to ____. — judge
18. The main organ of taste is the ____. — tongue
19. Ninety-nine plus one makes one ____. — hundred

20. This mystery word looks and sounds like its very old base word, *husbonda*. But the mystery word does not mean what *husbonda* meant. A *husbonda* was a man who lived in a house. Later *husbonda* came to mean farmer. The mystery word that comes from *husbonda* means a married man. Can you guess the mystery word? ____ — husband

101

Objectives

- To write spelling words in response to clues: definitions, synonyms, antonyms, analogies, and context.
- To develop the critical thinking skills of making inferences and sequencing.
- To recognize that word meanings often change over time.

Spelling Strategy

If students forget to include the first k in knuckle, write the following mnemonic device on the board, making the k's in knock and knuckles very large: "You knock with your knuckles." If students mastered the spelling of knock in an earlier grade, associating knuckle with knock may help them remember the silent k in knuckle. Encourage students to develop their own mnemonic devices for other tricky spellings, such as the silent ue in tongue or the silent d in judge.

Preparation The clues on this page are like crossword puzzle clues. Explain to students that the response to each clue is a spelling word. Use the following examples to illustrate the types of clues used:

Definition	In a group of means (*among*).
Synonym	Another word for marvelous is (*wonderful*).
Antonym	The opposite of smooth is (*rough*).
Analogy	Pipes are for water, veins are for (*blood*).
Context	North and south are points on a (*compass*).

The final clue explains how the meaning and spelling of husband have changed over time.

The Page Have students complete page 101 using the words on page 100. When students have finished, have them read each clue and spell the answer aloud. Check each response twice: once for the correct answer and a second time for spelling accuracy.

Follow-Up Guide pupils in using the **Checkpoint Study Plan** on page 224 to take a self-test. Then have them use the plan for independent study.

Objectives

- To write words with /ŭ/ in continuous text.
- To write each spelling word once.
- To integrate reading with spelling.

Note

Point out that monkey's uncle is part of the old-fashioned expression "I'll be a monkey's uncle" used to express surprise.

Use each list word once.

MAD ADS

INSTA-BOAT

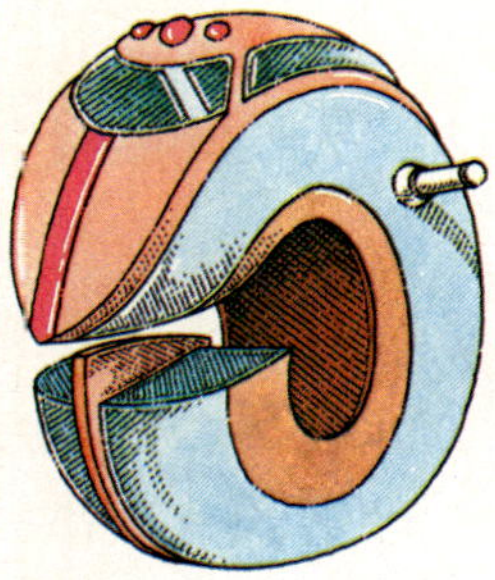

Live near a river? Do you worry about floods? Here's a great way to prepare for next spring's __flood__. Buy an Insta-Boat. It inflates with a __touch__ of your finger. Then __crush__ it up into a ball for easy storage between floods. It comes in one size that is large enough for the whole family: wife, __husband__, children, and grandparents.

Compass Ring

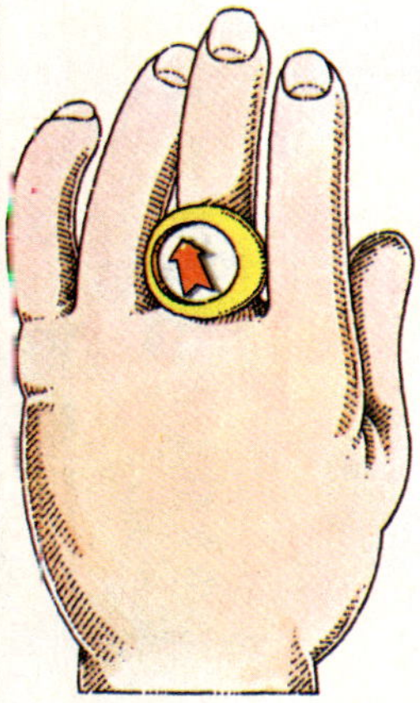

Going for a sail, a trip to another __country__, a hike through __rough__ and rocky country? The __compass__ ring is a must! You can change the size so that it fits over the largest __knuckle__. It always points home. You may not be able to get there, but you will always know which direction it's in! But don't take our word for it, __judge__ for yourself. (It makes a __wonderful__ gift for someone who owns an Insta-Boat.)

102

Preparation Have students turn to pages 102 and 103. Let them look at the ads and the pictures. Call their attention to the word list. Have the students say the words. Then explain that each spelling word belongs in one of the blanks in the ads.

Write the title "Mad Ads" on the board. Ask students what kind of selection this is. (*a series of humorous advertisements*) Ask if students ever make fun of popular ads by changing them to make them silly. Ask for examples of students' ideas.

The Pages Have students complete pages 102 and 103 independently by silently reading the ads and writing the missing spelling words. Or you may read the ads aloud, supplying the missing words as students follow along in their texts; then have the students complete the pages on their own.

When students have finished, you may wish to discuss the ads. Ask if any of these ads could be for real products. (*Perhaps the boat could be a real product; the others are imaginary.*) Ask which items students would like to order and why.

Have a volunteer read each ad, supplying each missing spelling word and spelling it aloud. Have other volunteers write the answers on the board and have students correct their own work. Check students' responses for the accurate spelling of each answer.

COWARD'S BANDAGES

Can't stand the sight of blood? Try Coward's Bandages. As soon as you cut yourself, simply place the bandages over your eyes and stop worrying. When the bleeding stops, remove bandages from the eyes and place them on the wound. Order a dozen (12) now.

A MONKEY'S UNCLE

You can be a monkey's uncle. That's right! Make reservations now to sail through the Amazon waterways. Go sightseeing in a tropical jungle. And choose your pet monkey from among the thousands you will see. Just sign the adoption papers, pay your hundred dollars, and you are a monkey's uncle! (You also get a set of monkey bars and 500 bananas.)

PUMPIONS

Try this taste treat and give your tongue a surprise. As its name hints, the pumpion is a cross between a pumpkin and an onion. It's sweet enough for dessert but snappy enough to add zest to any casserole. Send for our colorful, free idea book. It will instruct you in how to prepare such delicious delights as french-fried pumpion rings and homemade pumpion pie.

103

judge
husband
pumpkin
crush
hundred
jungle
knuckle
instruct
tongue
monkey
onion
dozen
compass
among
wonderful
rough
country
touch
blood
flood

Follow-Up

Have students use each of the spelling words they missed in an original sentence that relates to the ads.

As an additional follow-up activity, you may wish to have students illustrate their favorite ad. Tell them that they do not have to make their picture of the item look like the picture in the text. Have students label their finished pictures.

Enrichment

If you want to use the blackline activity masters for enrichment and additional practice, assign Lesson 19 activities at this time.

Maintenance and Review

OBJECTIVE

- To review media words.

ACTIVITIES

If you want to use the blackline activity masters for maintenance and review, assign Lesson 17 activities at this time.

You can also use the activity below to review Lesson 17 with students.

Write the following nonsense words on the board. Have students refer to the Lesson 17 word list and write the word from Lesson 17 that is suggested by each nonsense word. (Answers are in parentheses.)

ape deck	(*tape deck*)
headlion	(*headline*)
stewdio	(*studio*)
yearphones	(*earphones*)
oldpaper	(*newspaper*)
fly-line	(*by-line*)
narrowcast	(*broadcast*)
prime mime	(*prime time*)
misthead	(*masthead*)
telversion	(*television*)
netplay	(*network*)

Objectives

- To relate spelling words to a dictionary skill.
- To identify homographs.
- To write spelling words in the context of sentences.
- To use the **Spelling Dictionary**.

Homographs

Some words in our language are spelled exactly like other words. But they came into our language at different times and from different places. And they have different meanings. Such words are called homographs (*homo* means same, and *graph* means word). Homographs appear as separate entry words in dictionaries, and they are numbered.

des·ert[1] | dĕz′ərt | *n.* A dry, sandy region.
de·sert[2] | dĭ zûrt′ | *v.* To forsake; abandon: *She did not desert her friends when they needed her.*

★ Which entry defines the word desert used in each of these sentences?

1. Thelma left the hot desert and went to live in the jungle. desert[1]
2. Jim had to desert his car to get gas. desert[2]

★ Now use these homographs in the sentences below. Write each sentence. Then tell which entry you used.

bowl[1] | bōl | *n.* A round dish used to hold things.
bowl[2] | bōl | *v.* To play the game of bowling.
ob·ject[1] | ŏb′jĭkt | *or* | -jĕkt′ | *n.* A thing that has shape and can be touched and seen.
ob·ject[2] | əb jĕkt′ | *v.* To protest, to show disapproval.

3. I ____ to having onion in my salad. I object to having onion in my salad. object[2]
4. May I have a ____ of berries? May I have a bowl of berries? bowl[1]
5. I like to ____ with my team on Saturdays. I like to bowl with my team on Saturdays. bowl[2]
6. What is that strange ____ on the table? What is that strange object on the table? object[1]

104

Preparation Have students read aloud the title of page 104. Write this word on the board: **bridge**. Have volunteers give two meanings for bridge. (*Something built over a river or other obstacle so people can get across; a card game for four people*) Have students look up this word in the **Spelling Dictionary**. Ask how many times bridge occurs as an entry word. (*twice*) Tell students that a word that has two different unrelated meanings is called a homograph.

The Page Have students do page 104. Then have volunteers write the answers on the board and review the answers orally.

Follow-Up Have students use each homograph on page 104 in an original sentence. Each sentence should also contain a spelling word.

WORDS AT WORK

Challenge Yourself

blunt budget doubly stomachache

Write what you think each underlined Challenge Word means. Check your Spelling Dictionary to see if you were right. Then write sentences showing that you understand the meaning of each Challenge Word.

1. A pencil point starts out sharp but grows blunt as you write with it.
2. We wrote out a budget for the party so that we would know how much to spend on food and decorations.
3. To finish an hour's work in half an hour, you must work doubly fast.
4. Eating too much food can give you a stomachache.

Write to the Point

Satisfied customers often appear in television commercials. They tell what happened when they used the product and why they were pleased with it. Imagine that you tried one of the "Mad Ads" products. Write a commercial telling why you liked it. Use spelling words from this lesson in your commercial.

Challenge Use one or more of the Challenge Words in your commercial.

Proofreading

Use the proofreading marks to show the errors in the paragraph below. Write the five misspelled words correctly in the blanks.

(circle)	word is misspelled
? ^	question mark is missing
^	word is missing

Do you cry when ^you peel an (onium) ^? Just place two No-Cry pills on your (tung.) No store in the (countrie) sells them, so order a bottle now. In fact, order a (dozan.) Each bottle contains a hundred pills. They ^are (wonderfull!)

1. onion
2. tongue
3. country
4. dozen
5. wonderful

105

Objectives

- To extend the vowel spellings presented in Lesson 19 to the Challenge Words.
- To use context and the **Spelling Dictionary** to enlarge students' vocabulary.
- To apply the vowel spellings presented in Lesson 19 in a writing activity.
- To practice proofreading for spelling, punctuation, and missing words.

Dictation Sentences

1. Did you have a wonderful time in the country last weekend?
2. The monkey lives in the jungle.
3. A pumpkin is round and smooth to the touch.
4. The tongue of a cat feels rough.
5. I dropped my compass in the woods among the trees.
6. I will buy a dozen bags of ice to crush for the party.
7. Her husband is a judge.
8. I will instruct you on how to cut an onion so that you don't cry.
9. There was blood on her knuckle when she cut her hand.
10. A flood covered one hundred houses in the town.

Challenge Yourself Answers

Possible definitions:

1. thick; dull
2. money plan
3. twice as
4. pain in the stomach

Students' sentences will vary.

Test Review these four ways to spell /ŭ/: u as in hundred; o as in among; ou as in touch; oo as in flood. Test words with /ŭ/. Use one of these testing methods: (1) Say the word; read the sample sentence from page 100; say the word; have students write it. (2) Read each dictation sentence above; have students write the sentence. Correct the test with students.

Challenge Yourself The optional Challenge Words may be assigned to the entire class or limited to those students who do well on the test. Have students note the vowel spellings in the Challenge Words. Responses to this activity should be completed on separate paper. Answers to the questions are provided above.

Write to the Point Help students recall the selection "Mad Ads" on pages 102 and 103; then assign the commercial. To provide students with a model, remind them of the kinds of commercials they may have seen on TV, such as a parent recommending a cold medicine or a chef recommending a kitchen gadget. This activity should be completed on separate paper.

Proofreading The proofreading practice includes misspellings of words from this lesson as well as a punctuation error and missing words.

LESSON 20

Objectives

- To hear and say words with /ô/.
- To write words with /ô/ with attention to letter sequence and sound/symbol relationships.
- To write each spelling word at least once.
- To recognize that /ô/ may be spelled aw, au, ou, a, and o.

Sample Sentences

1. I like raw carrots.
2. Eddie watched a worm crawl over his foot.
3. I'd cut the grass, but the lawnmower is broken.
4. Please get me a straw for my juice.
5. If you get up early, you may see the dawn.
6. A peanut butter and prune sandwich would taste awful!
7. We go camping in autumn when it's not hot anymore.
8. It's not my fault that I was late.
9. Aunt Harriet likes to drive her new automobile.
10. My daughter Sylvie will meet us there.
11. On our trip Rita caught three fish and a cold.
12. Marie taught her younger brother to roller-skate.
13. I thought I told you not to disturb me.
14. Two ants fought over a bread crumb.
15. Jack bought a birthday present for David.
16. Jack brought the gift to the party.
17. I heard a noise; is everything all right?
18. Thanks, but we're not hungry; we ate already.
19. I was wrong to yell at you.
20. It rains often in the summer.

Note

- The sample sentences may be used for pretesting.
- Words are grouped according to spellings of /ô/:
  aw a
  au o
  ou

Lesson 20 Words with /ô/

Listen for /ô/ in each word.

raw
crawl
lawnmower
straw
dawn
awful

autumn
fault
automobile
daughter
caught
taught

thought
fought
bought
brought

all right
already

wrong
often

1. Which word begins with a letter w that you don't hear? wrong
2. Write the two words that begin with /k/. crawl caught
3. Which word begins and ends like den? dawn
4. Which word begins and ends like laughter and is a compound word? lawnmower
5. Which two words begin and end with vowels? automobile already
6. Write two words that begin with the letter f and two that have f in the middle. fault fought awful often
7. Write the word that ends with /ē/. Circle the letter that spells /ē/. already
8. Write the two words that end with the letters aw. raw straw
9. In which two words is /ô/ spelled a? all right already
10. In which two words is /ô/ spelled o? wrong often
11. In which word is /l/ spelled ll? all right
12. Write the word in which you see the letter n but don't hear /n/. autumn
13. Write the eight words in which you see the letters gh but don't hear /g/ or /f/ for those letters. daughter caught taught thought fought bought brought all right

106

Preparation Have students read aloud the title of the lesson on page 106. Write /ô/ on the board. Have students say /ô/ as in paw. Read each spelling word aloud. Tell students to repeat and then spell each word aloud.

Ask students to identify the two words in the compound word lawnmower. *(lawn, mower)* Ask them what suffix ends awful. *(ful)* What is the difference in spelling between bought and brought? *(an r)* What two letters end autumn? *(mn)* Note that the present tense form of caught is catch and the present tense form of taught is teach. Ask which letter may be silent in often. *(t)* Then identify the five spellings of /ô/ in this lesson. (See **Note**.)

Read the sample sentences. Have students point to each spelling word as you read the sentence for it.

The Page Have students complete page 106. Have volunteers write the answers on the board and have students correct their own work.

Follow-Up Suggest that students write all the words in the list in alphabetical order.

Checkpoint

Write a spelling word for each clue.
Then use the Checkpoint Study Plan on page 224.

1. To move slowly on the hands and knees is to ____.
2. If you make a mistake, it's your ____.
3. If it has been done before, then it has been done ____.
4. Today I buy, yesterday I ____.
5. Today I teach, yesterday I ____.
6. You can drink through a ____.
7. Frequently means ____.
8. I cut the grass with a ____.
9. The time of day when the sun rises is ____.
10. The past tense of fight is ____.
11. After summer comes ____.
12. The opposite of right or correct is ____.
13. Very bad or unpleasant is ____.
14. Today I bring, last week I ____.
15. Father is to son as mother is to ____.
16. The opposite of cooked is ____.
17. O.K. means ____.
18. The past tense of catch is ____.
19. Today I think, last month I ____.

20. Some words have both Greek and Latin roots. This mystery word is such a word. It is made up of two separate words. The first comes from the Greek word for self, *autos*. The second comes from the Latin word for moving, *mobilis*. When we put these words together, we get *automobilis* (self-moving). The mystery word names a means of transportation that runs by itself. Can you guess what it is? ____

107

crawl
fault
already
bought
taught
straw
often
lawnmower
dawn
fought
autumn
wrong
awful
brought
daughter
raw
all right
caught
thought

automobile

Objectives

- To write spelling words in response to clues: definitions, synonyms, antonyms, analogies, and context.
- To develop the critical thinking skills of sequencing, comparing, and contrasting.
- To understand that words can be combined to form new words.

Spelling Strategy

Some students may have difficulty remembering the silent gh that occurs in a number of the words in this lesson. Have them write ght eight times in a vertical list down the center of a sheet of paper. Then have them fill in the missing letters, using words from the lesson such as bought, taught, fought, brought, daughter, all right, caught, thought. For example:

bought
daughter
all right
ght
ght

If students confuse the spellings of already and all right (allready, alright), write both words on the board and have students help make a list of their similarities and differences. (Similarities: Both are made from the word all and a five-letter word beginning with r. Differences: In already, one l is dropped, and there is no space between the words.) You may want to tell students that although they may come across all right spelled alright in some published writing, this spelling is generally considered incorrect.

Preparation The clues on this page are like crossword puzzle clues. Explain to students that the response to each clue is a spelling word. Use the following examples to illustrate the types of clues used:

Definition	The time of day when the sun rises is (*dawn*).
Synonym	Frequently means (*often*).
Antonym	The opposite of cooked is (*raw*).
Analogy	Father is to son as mother is to (*daughter*).
Context	I cut the grass with a (*lawnmower*).

The final clue identifies the Greek and Latin words that make up automobile.

The Page Have students complete page 107 using the words on page 106. When students have finished, have them read each clue and spell the answer aloud. Check each response twice: once for the correct answer and a second time for spelling accuracy.

Follow-Up Guide pupils in using the **Checkpoint Study Plan** on page 224 to take a self-test. Then have them use the plan for independent study.

Objectives

- To write words with /ô/ in continuous text.
- To write each spelling word once.
- To integrate reading with spelling.

Note

Point out the use of the word straw in the letter to mean dried stems of grain. Ask students for another meaning of straw.

CAMP MAIL

Use each list word once.

Dear Mom and Dad,

I know it isn't your fault. Next time, though, I'll read between the lines in any camp ad that says, "GET READY TO LAUNCH INTO AN EXCITING SUMMER!" The only thing we launched was the canoe. Our counselors woke us up at dawn this morning and drove us several miles up river in their automobile. The canoe was on top of the car. When we stopped, guess who got to carry the canoe to the water. I thought that the counselors would help us. Ha!

When the canoe was packed, we all fought for the best seats. It took awhile to get in, because you can't stand up in a canoe. You must hold the sides with your hands and crawl to your seat. Finally we began the long journey back to camp.

We pulled up to the bank at noon for lunch. The counselors told us we would have to help cook. We cooked the stew while they made fruit salad. Our stew wasn't very good. In fact, it was awful. Some of the meat was still raw. The beans were as dry as straw. But luckily for us, the fruit salad tasted all right.

We got back to camp late this afternoon. The counselors got out their fishing poles and caught some fish for supper. Then they taught us how to clean fish. I guess they're not really so bad, after all. And I certainly hope that their fish will taste better than our stew.

Love,

Your daughter Jane

108

Preparation

Have students turn to pages 108 and 109. Let them look at the letters and the pictures. Call their attention to the word list. Have the students say the words. Then explain that each spelling word belongs in one of the blanks in the letters.

Write the title "Camp Mail" on the board. Then ask what form this selection takes. (*a letter from camp and a reply*) Ask if any students have been to a sleep-away camp. If so, have them describe the camp and tell what they liked and didn't like. Explain that most camps emphasize sports such as swimming, canoeing, and hiking, as well as team sports.

The Pages

Have students complete pages 108 and 109 independently by silently reading the letters and writing the missing spelling words. Or you may read the letters aloud, supplying the missing words as students follow along in their texts; then have the students complete the pages on their own.

When students have finished, you may wish to discuss the letters. Ask students if they think that Jane was justified in complaining about the camp or not. Ask if they thought Jane's mother gave a reasonable reply or not. (*Answers will vary.*) Point out that camps teach self-reliance—doing things for yourself—and that means many mistakes will be made before the necessary skills are learned. Mistakes are a natural part of the learning process.

Dear Jane,

Your letter was the nicest surprise the mail carrier brought us.

I must say, Jane, that I do not think the camp ad gave us the wrong impression. There wasn't an automatic guarantee that it was going to be easy right from the beginning. Being away from home always takes time to get used to. When autumn comes, you'll probably miss your summer friends and even the counselors more than you can imagine.

Our lawn doesn't look the same since you left. Your long-lost friend, the lawnmower, is always asking for you. I am sure, though, that is one friend you are happy to be away from.

By the way, Uncle Todd passed his exams to become a lawyer. To celebrate, we bought him a book by his favorite author. I don't suppose he'll have much time to read it, however.

It's noon already and just about time for the mail carrier to pick up the mail. I promise to write more soon. We think of you often.

Love,
Mom

raw
crawl
lawnmower
straw
dawn
awful
autumn
fault
automobile
daughter
caught
taught
thought
fought
bought
brought
all right
already
wrong
often

Have volunteers read each paragraph in the letters, supply each spelling word, and spell it aloud. Have other volunteers write the answers on the board and have students correct their own work. Check students' responses for the accurate spelling of each answer.

Follow-Up Have students use each of the spelling words they missed in an original sentence that relates to the letters.

As an additional follow-up activity, you may wish to have students make a mural illustrating the letters. Attach a large piece of paper to the wall and have several students plan and draw the mural.

Enrichment

If you want to use the blackline activity masters for enrichment and additional practice, assign Lesson 20 activities at this time.

Maintenance and Review

OBJECTIVE

- To review words with /ŭ/ spelled: u, o, ou, oo.

ACTIVITIES

If you want to use the blackline activity masters for maintenance and review, assign Lesson 19 activities at this time.

You can also use the activity below to review Lesson 19 with students.

Write the following words on the board. Have students refer to the Lesson 19 word list and have students change one letter in each word below to spell a word or words from Lesson 19. (Answers are in parentheses.)

jingle (*jungle*)
tough (*rough, touch*)
bloom (*blood*)
crash (*crush*)
union (*onion*)
along (*among*)
fudge (*judge*)
dozed (*dozen*)

Objectives

- To relate spelling to another language skill.
- To review the use of an apostrophe in a contraction and to form the possessive of singular and plural nouns.
- To write spelling words in the context of sentences.
- To practice proofreading.

Apostrophes

Use an apostrophe when writing a contraction. A contraction combines two words into one word by leaving out one or more letters. The apostrophe shows where the letters have been left out.

had not *hadn't*

Use an apostrophe to show ownership. Add 's to a singular noun to make it possessive.

Sally's hat *the dog's house*

To form the possessive of a plural noun that ends in s, add only an apostrophe.

the boys' bikes

If a plural noun does not end in s, add 's to form the possessive.

the cattle's pen

★ Write the following sentences. Use apostrophes where they are needed. Correct the spelling mistakes.

1. Mom: Ive brawt you a surprise.
   I've brought you a surprise.
2. Stu: I thawt youd forgotten my birthday.
   I thought you'd forgotten my birthday.
3. Mom: Youre rong, I remembered.
   You're wrong, I remembered.
4. Stu: I cant guess what you bawt me.
   I can't guess what you bought me.
5. Mom: Its a little like the Jones automobel.
   It's a little like the Jones' automobile.
6. Stu: Dont give me any more afful hints.
   Don't give me any more awful hints.
7. Mom: Alright, they both have wheels — its a bicycle!
   All right, they both have wheels—it's a bicycle!

Preparation Have students read aloud the title of page 110. Write the following contractions on the board: I've let's he'd we're

Ask students what a contraction is. (*two words combined to make one word by leaving out one or more letters*) Then ask what punctuation mark is used in place of the omitted letters. (*an apostrophe*) Have volunteers say each contraction and circle the apostrophe. Then write these on the board:

Jane's counselor's cities' husbands' children's

Review with students that to form the possessive of a singular noun, add 's. To form the possessive of a plural noun ending in s, add an apostrophe. If the plural doesn't end in s, add 's.

The Page Have students do page 110. Then have volunteers write the answers on the board.

Follow-Up Have students write a sentence using the possessive form of each of the following words: lawnmower dawn autumn automobile

Have students write sentences using contractions and these words:

craw awful taught fought already

WORDS AT WORK

Challenge Yourself

authentic nautical fraud awning

Decide which Challenge Word fits each clue. Check your Spelling Dictionary to see if you were right. Then write sentences showing that you understand the meaning of each Challenge Word.

1. This word could be used to describe all of the following items: an anchor, a sail, and a sailor's cap.
2. Putting the name of a famous artist on a painting by someone else would be an example of this.
3. This is the opposite of fake.
4. This is good to stand under if you're caught in the rain.

Write to the Point

Is there a summer that you remember especially well because of something unusual, exciting, or funny that happened? Write a true story about this incident. Tell how it began, what happened, and how it all came out. Use spelling words from this lesson in your story.

Challenge Use one or more of the Challenge Words in your story.

Proofreading

Use the proofreading marks to show the errors in the paragraph below. Write the five misspelled words correctly in the blanks.

(circle)	word is misspelled
≡	letter should be capitalized
! ^	exclamation point is missing

What an awfull mess I was in I was supposed to mow mrs. Hu's lawn each week this summer until she returned in the autum. She taught me how to use her lawn-mower, and I thougt I caught on. When i found out I was wrong, she was allready gone.

1. awful
2. autumn
3. lawnmower
4. thought
5. already

111

Objectives

- To extend the vowel spellings presented in Lesson 20 to the Challenge Words.
- To use clues and the **Spelling Dictionary** to enlarge students' vocabulary.
- To apply the vowel spellings presented in Lesson 20 in a writing activity.
- To practice proofreading for spelling, punctuation, and capitalization.

Dictation Sentences

1. Come see the new automobile I just bought!
2. I got up at dawn to give the animals fresh straw.
3. I taught his daughter how to swim.
4. What is wrong with the lawnmower?
5. The baby already knows how to crawl.
6. I thought it would be all right if I brought my guitar to the party.
7. The fish fought hard before being caught.
8. In the autumn we often go for long walks.
9. It is my fault that the cake tastes awful.
10. I like raw vegetables.

Challenge Yourself Answers

1. nautical
2. fraud
3. authentic
4. awning

Students' sentences will vary.

Test Review these five ways to spell /ô/: aw as in raw; au as in autumn; ou as in bought; a as in already; o as in often. Test words with /ô/. Use one of these testing methods: (1) Say the word; read the sample sentence from page 106; say the word; have students write it. (2) Read each dictation sentence above; have students write the sentence. Correct the test with students.

Challenge Yourself The optional Challenge Words may be assigned to the entire class or limited to those students who do well on the test. Have students note the vowel spellings in the Challenge Words. You may wish to have students work in pairs. Responses to this activity should be completed on separate paper. Answers to the questions are provided above.

Write to the Point Help students recall the selection "Camp Mail" on pages 108 and 109; then assign the story. Suggest that students use such transition words as first, next, then, and finally to keep the sequence of events clear in their stories. This activity should be completed on separate paper.

Proofreading The proofreading practice includes misspellings of words from this lesson as well as capitalization errors and a punctuation error.

LESSON 21

Objectives

- To hear and say words with /o͞o/.
- To write words with /o͞o/ with attention to letter sequence and sound/symbol relationships.
- To write each spelling word at least once.
- To recognize that /o͞o/ may be spelled oo, o_e, ue, ui, u, oe, and o.

Sample Sentences

1. This shirt doesn't fit because it's too loose.
2. The rooster began to crow at dawn.
3. If you blow up a balloon too much, it will pop.
4. Sal bought some shampoo to wash his hair.
5. A kangaroo hops using its strong hind legs.
6. I think the butler did it, but I have no proof.
7. Look over these books and choose the one you want.
8. The clown looked foolish in his costume.
9. When we went camping, a raccoon stole our food.
10. Katy put her key in her bag so she wouldn't lose it.
11. I hope to improve my grades by studying.
12. Maria can prove that she went straight home.
13. Does anyone know whose mittens these are?
14. We can't solve the mystery without a clue.
15. Paste the leaves to the paper with glue.
16. Do you want a piece of fruit?
17. Pedro drinks a glass of juice each morning.
18. Please tell me the truth about this.
19. Dennis needs a new heel on his right shoe.
20. To whom do I address this letter?

Note

- The sample sentences may be used for pretesting.
- Words are grouped according to spellings of /o͞o/:

oo	u
o_e	oe
ue	o
ui	

Lesson 21 Words with /o͞o/

Listen for /o͞o/ in each word.

loose
rooster
balloon
shampoo
kangaroo
proof
choose
foolish
raccoon

lose
improve
prove
whose

clue
glue

fruit
juice

truth

shoe

whom

1. Which two words begin with /k/? Circle the letter that spells /k/. kangaroo clue
2. Write the two words in which you see the letter w but don't hear /w/. whose whom
3. Which word begins with the letter g? glue
4. Which word begins and ends like front? fruit
5. Which word begins and ends with the letter r? rooster
6. Write the word that begins with the letters ch. choose
7. Write the word that begins with the letters im. improve
8. Write two words that begin with the letters sh and one that ends with sh. shampoo shoe foolish
9. Write two words that begin with the letters pr and one that has pr in the middle. proof prove improve
10. Which word ends with the letters th? truth
11. Write the three words that end with /z/. choose lose whose
12. Write the two words that end with /s/. loose juice
13. In which word is /l/ spelled ll? balloon
14. In which word is /k/ spelled cc? raccoon

112

Preparation Have students read aloud the title of the lesson on page 112. Write /o͞o/ on the board. Have students say /o͞o/ as in boot. Read each spelling word aloud. Tell students to repeat and then spell each word aloud.

Ask students to name the base word of foolish. (*fool*) Note that both whose and whom begin with the letters who. Point out the /ə/ in balloon: /bə lo͞on'/. Then have students identify the letters that spell /o͞o/ in the first group of words. (*oo*) Have them identify the spelling of /o͞o/ in the other groups of words in the list. (See **Note**.)

Read the sample sentences. Have students point to each spelling word as you read the sentence for it.

The Page Have students complete page 112. Have students correct their own work after volunteers write the answers on the board.

Follow-Up Suggest that students work with a partner, taking turns reading and spelling the words aloud.

Checkpoint

Write a spelling word for each clue.
Then use the Checkpoint Study Plan on page 224.

1. On a farm you wake up to the call of a ____.
2. On your foot you wear your ____.
3. Yesterday I chose, today I ____.
4. They stick to me like ____.
5. Evidence is part of ____.
6. The opposite of tight is ____.
7. An apple is a kind of ____.
8. To show to be true means to ____.
9. A masked animal is a ____.
10. Another word that sounds like who's is ____.
11. They crossed the Atlantic Ocean in a hot-air ____.
12. Soap for the hair is ____.
13. Yesterday I lost, today I ____.
14. The opposite of a lie is the ____.
15. A hint is a ____.
16. The opposite of wise is ____.
17. To make better means to ____.
18. Squeeze an orange to get ____.
19. We is to us as who is to ____.
20. The people who first settled in Australia are called Aborigines. The Aborigines have been living in Australia for 12,000 years. Two hundred years ago some new people went to live in Australia. They saw plants and animals there that they had never seen before. Since they didn't have names for these plants and animals, they used the Aborigine names. This mystery word names an Australian animal. It is from the Aborigine word *kanga,* which means jumper. Can you guess it? ____

rooster
shoe
choose
glue
proof
loose
fruit
prove
raccoon
whose
balloon
shampoo
lose
truth
clue
foolish
improve
juice
whom

kangaroo

Objectives

- To write spelling words in response to clues: definitions, antonyms, analogies, and context.
- To develop the critical thinking skills of making inferences and predicting outcomes.
- To learn one of the many ways in which words have entered the English language.

Spelling Strategy

Some students may confuse the spellings loose and lose or choose and chose. Help them to differentiate these words by pointing out the differences in meaning and pronunciation. Then have students write sentences using each pair of words, such as:

You will soon lose a loose tooth.

Will you choose the same outfit you chose yesterday?

Have students exchange sentences with a partner and check each other's spelling.

Preparation The clues on this page are like crossword puzzle clues. Explain to students that the response to each clue is a spelling word. Use the following examples to illustrate the types of clues used:

Definition	Soap for the hair is (*shampoo*).
Antonym	The opposite of a lie is the (*truth*).
Analogy	Yesterday I lost, today I (*lose*).
Context	On your foot you wear your (*shoe*).

The final clue explains the Australian Aborigine origin of kangaroo.

The Page Have students complete page 113 using the words on page 112. When students have finished, have them read each clue and spell the answer aloud. Check each response twice: once for the correct answer and a second time for spelling accuracy.

Follow-Up Guide pupils in using the **Checkpoint Study Plan** on page 224 to take a self-test. Then have them use the plan for independent study.

Objectives

- To write words with /o͞o/ in continuous text.
- To write each spelling word once.
- To integrate reading with spelling.

Note

Point out that Pry Vitigh is a play on private eye and should be pronounced in the same way.

Use each list word once.

THE CASE OF THE MISSING SHOE

I was sitting in my office, drinking a glass of orange juice, when the call came from the famous naturalist, Mrs. Annie Mall. Oh, by the way, I'm Pry Vitigh, private eye. I solve mysteries.

I went to Mrs. Mall's zoo and rang the bell. She answered it herself. Right away, I knew something was wrong. She was wearing two socks, but only one shoe.

"That's the mystery," she told me. "I took a little nap after lunch, and I took off my shoes. When I woke up, one shoe was gone. Now you can't lose one shoe. Somebody must have taken it."

I asked Mrs. Mall who she thought was guilty. This is whom she suspected:

The baboon is a real strong character who could easily walk off with a shoe.

The kangaroo, whose pocket could hide more than you think.

The rooster is a real loud character who is not to be trusted.

The raccoon, whose mask looked very suspicious.

Mrs. Mall said, "These are the ones that could have done it. But I can't prove anything."

114

Preparation Have students turn to pages 114 and 115. Let them look at the story and the pictures. Call their attention to the word list. Have the students say the words. Then explain that each spelling word belongs in one of the blanks in the story.

Write the title "The Case of the Missing Shoe" on the board. Tell students that this is a funny detective story. Remind students that in traditional detective stories, the detective is tough, mean, and smart. This story is a spoof of such a story. Tell students to look for puns as they read.

The Pages Have students complete pages 114 and 115 independently by silently reading the story and writing the missing spelling words. Or you may read the story aloud, supplying the missing words as students follow along in their texts; then have the students complete the pages on their own.

When students have finished, you may wish to discuss the story. Ask if this detective is tough. (*no*) Have students support this answer. (*He is afraid of the suspects.*) Ask what the solution to the mystery was. (*Mrs. Mall's son had*

"Don't worry," I told her. "We'll find out the truth, and I'll show you proof."

I had to admit it was a tough case. First I searched the house from the basement to the roof, and I couldn't find one single clue. But I did notice some loose tiles on the roof.

Then I went to see the baboon. He was in the kitchen eating a piece of fruit. When I tried to question him, he grabbed my arm so hard that I got a big bruise.

"That was a cruel thing to do," I said. And since I saw no sign of a shoe, I decided to go on to the next suspect.

I went to see the raccoon. She was a smart animal, even though she looked kind of foolish in that silly mask. When I tried to question her, she nipped me on the hand. I didn't choose to stick around.

I needed to improve my method of questioning suspects. I decided to go and get Mrs. Mall. After all, she was the one whose shoe was missing. Let her face the other two suspects with me.

When I got back to the living room, a boy came in the front door. In one hand, he held a long string with a balloon tied to it. In the other hand, he held a paper bag.

"Hi, Mom," the boy said. "I took your shoe to the repair shop. They'll glue on a new sole this afternoon. I bought some shampoo so you can wash your hair, just like you asked me."

Another case was solved.

115

loose
rooster
balloon
shampoo
kangaroo
proof
choose
foolish
raccoon
lose
improve
prove
whose
clue
glue
fruit
juice
truth
shoe
whom

Enrichment

If you want to use the blackline activity masters for enrichment and additional practice, assign Lesson 21 activities at this time.

Maintenance and Review

OBJECTIVE

- To review words with /ô/ spelled: aw, au, ou, a, o.

ACTIVITIES

If you want to use the blackline activity masters for maintenance and review, assign Lesson 20 activities at this time.

You can also use the activity below to review Lesson 20 with students.

Write the following words on the board. Have students refer to the Lesson 20 word list and write the word that is a synonym for each word below. (Answers are in parentheses.)

okay	(*all right*)
car	(*automobile*)
sunrise	(*dawn*)
creep	(*crawl*)
terrible	(*awful*)
incorrect	(*wrong*)
argued	(*fought*)
fall	(*autumn*)
uncooked	(*raw*)
defect	(*fault*)

taken the shoe to the repair shop; she had forgotten that she had told him to do this.) Ask if the detective solved the mystery. (*no*) Have students identify the puns in the story. (*Pry Vitigh is a play on the words private eye; Annie Mall is a play on the word animal.*)

Have a volunteer read each paragraph in the story, supplying each missing spelling word and spelling it aloud. Have other volunteers write the answers on the board and have students correct their own work. Check students' responses for the correct spelling of each answer.

Follow-Up Have students use each of the spelling words they missed in an original sentence that relates to the story.

As an additional follow-up activity, you may wish to have the students work in small groups with a cassette recorder to make "The Case of the Missing Shoe" into a mystery "radio drama" with special sound effects. Have students select the roles of Pry, Annie, her son, and the animals. Students may use sound-effect records or create their own special sound effects.

Objectives

- To relate spelling words to a dictionary skill.
- To review the use of the pronunciation key.
- To review the use of sound spellings.
- To write spelling words and their sound spellings.
- To use the **Spelling Dictionary**.

Pronunciation

A dictionary lists the pronunciation of each entry word. This pronunciation is written in special symbols. The symbols are a guide to the sounds of a word and are called the sound spelling.

im·prove | ĭm pro͞ov′ |

Sometimes a word may have more than one acceptable pronunciation. All possible pronunciations are listed after the entry word.

roof | ro͞of | *or* | ro͝of |

To know what sound each of the symbols has, you must refer to the pronunciation key. This key lists all the symbols and gives examples of words that have the sounds of the symbols. The key is usually printed on every other page in a dictionary.

/ă/	pat	/ĭ/	pit	/o͝o/	took	/zh/	vision
/ā/	pay	/ī/	pie, by	/o͞o/	boot	/ə/	about,
/â/	care	/î/	pier	/ou/	out		item,
/ä/	father	/ŏ/	pot	/th/	thin		edible,
/ĕ/	pet	/ō/	toe	/*th*/	this		gallop,
/ē/	bee	/ô/	paw, for	/ŭ/	cut		circus
/hw/	whoop	/oi/	noise	/û/	urge	/ər/	butter

★ Write the key words for these symbols:

/ĭ/ pit /o͞o/ boot

★ Write the word that goes with each sound spelling below. Check the answers in the Spelling Dictionary.

truth **balloon** **raccoon** **juice**

1. /ră **koon**′/ raccoon **2.** /jo͞os/ juice

3. /bə **loon**′/ balloon **4.** /tro͞oth/ truth

★ The words below are followed by two sound spellings. Only one is correct. Look up each word in the Spelling Dictionary and write the correct sound spelling.

5. choose /cho͞os/ /cho͞oz/ /cho͞oz/

6. whose /ho͞oz/ /hwo͞oz/ /ho͞oz/

7. proof /pro͞of/ /prŭf/ /pro͞of/

8. kangaroo /kăn găr **o͞o**′/ /kăng′ gə **ro͞o**′/ /kăng′ gə ro͞o′/

Preparation

Have students read aloud the title of page 116. Review that a dictionary entry shows how to pronounce the entry word. The pronunciation is shown using special symbols in brackets. This is called the sound spelling. Have a volunteer write the sound spelling for this lesson on the board: /o͞o/. Have all the students pronounce this sound.

Write these sound spellings on the board: /lo͞oz/ /lo͞os/. Have volunteers write the word each sound spelling represents and pronounce it. (*lose*, *loose*) Remind students of the importance of looking at every letter of the sound spelling to figure out the pronunciation of a word.

The Page

Have students do page 116. Then have volunteers write the answers on the board.

Follow-Up

Have students write the sound spellings for any six words not covered on the page. Then have them look up the words in the **Spelling Dictionary** to check their work.

WORDS AT WORK

Challenge Yourself

feud **mutual** **presume** **maroon**

Use your Spelling Dictionary to answer these questions. Then write sentences showing that you understand the meaning of each Challenge Word.

1. Would you expect a feud to start between best friends who always say kind words to each other?
2. If you and a friend both like to collect stamps, is stamp-collecting your mutual interest?
3. Would you presume that someone was happy if you saw him or her smile?
4. Would you call the color of a lemon maroon?

Write to the Point

Suppose Mrs. Mall's son had not taken the missing shoe in the detective story. How else might the shoe have disappeared? Imagine that you are the author of the story. Write a new ending for it. Tell what happened to the shoe and how Pry Vitigh solved the mystery. Use spelling words from this lesson in your new ending.

Challenge Use one or more of the Challenge Words in your ending.

Proofreading

Use the proofreading marks to show the errors in the paragraph below. Write the five misspelled words correctly in the blanks.

⬭	word is misspelled
/	letter should be lower case
⊙	period is missing

Who had stolen Bushy's fruite? A Rooster named Rudy B. Loud was the one whom the Raccoon suspected Her clew was a feather whoze color matched Rudy's, but how could she proove it had come lose from his tail?

1. fruit
2. clue
3. whose
4. prove
5. loose

Objectives

- To extend the vowel spellings presented in Lesson 21 to the Challenge Words.
- To use context and the **Spelling Dictionary** to enlarge students' vocabulary.
- To apply the vowel spellings presented in Lesson 21 in a writing activity.
- To practice proofreading for spelling, punctuation, and capitalization.

Dictation Sentences

1. Did you choose the shampoo with lemon juice in it?
2. Do you have proof that the raccoon ate the fruit?
3. He didn't leave a clue.
4. The heel on my shoe was loose, so I used some glue to fix it.
5. Do you want to improve your grades?
6. I know whose hat that is!
7. The truth is easy to prove.
8. The kangaroo had a foolish look on its face.
9. The rooster crows in the morning.
10. I do not know to whom this box belongs.
11. Do not lose that balloon.

Challenge Yourself Answers

1. no
2. yes
3. yes
4. no

Students' sentences will vary.

Test Review these seven ways to spell /o͞o/: oo as in choose; o_e as in prove; ue as in clue; ui as in fruit; u as in truth; oe as in shoe; o as in whom. Test words with /o͞o/. Use one of these testing methods: (1) Say the word; read the sample sentence from page 112; say the word; have students write it. (2) Read each dictation sentence above; have students write the sentence. Correct the test with students.

Challenge Yourself The optional Challenge Words may be assigned to the entire class or limited to those students who do well on the test. Have students note the vowel spellings in the Challenge Words, especially the following new spellings: eu as in feud; u_e as in presume. Responses to this activity should be completed on separate paper. Answers to the questions are provided above.

Write to the Point Help students recall the selection "The Missing Shoe" on pages 114 and 115; then assign the story ending. Encourage students to maintain the humorous tone of the story in their new endings. This activity should be completed on separate paper.

Proofreading The proofreading practice includes misspellings of words from this lesson as well as capitalization errors and a punctuation error.

LESSON 22

Objectives

- To hear and say words with /oi/.
- To write words with /oi/ with attention to letter sequence and sound/symbol relationships.
- To write each spelling word at least once.
- To recognize that /oi/ may be spelled oy and oi.

Sample Sentences

1. A bad storm will destroy those trees.
2. That pesky fly is beginning to annoy me.
3. The books I enjoy most are mysteries.
4. Mrs. Davis will employ Jan as a baby sitter.
5. The employment office will help you find a job.
6. Mike ate an oyster.
7. The team's fans see every game because they are loyal.
8. They continue to show their loyalty when we lose.
9. The voyage to the moon took three days.
10. The royal family visited Canada.
11. We have a choice between ham or beef.
12. Ms. Pagano will appoint helpers tomorrow.
13. Millie has an appointment with the doctor.
14. David shook drops of moisture off his wet coat.
15. The boiler in the basement heats the water.
16. Nancy has a very large coin collection.
17. You can avoid getting wet by wearing a raincoat.
18. The voice of the principal came over the loudspeaker.
19. The wind in the trees made a lovely noise.
20. We can fry this fish, or we can broil it.

Note

- The sample sentences may be used for pretesting.
- Words are grouped according to spellings of /oi/:
  - oy
  - oi

Lesson 22 Words with /oi/

Listen for /oi/ in each word.

destroy
annoy
enjoy
employ
employment
oyster
loyal
loyalty
voyage
royal

choice
appoint
appointment
moisture
boiler
coin
avoid
voice
noise
broil

1. Which word begins with the letters br? broil
2. Which word begins and ends like bother? boiler
3. Which word begins and ends like ahead? avoid
4. Which word begins and ends like complain? coin
5. Which word begins and ends like real? royal
6. Write the two words that end with /s/. choice voice
7. Which word ends with /z/? noise
8. Which three words have the letters st in the middle? destroy oyster moisture
9. Which word has /ch/ in the middle? moisture
10. Write the two words that contain the /j/ sound. enjoy voyage
11. Write the word in which /n/ is spelled nn. annoy
12. Three of the list words are base words for other words that are also on the list. Write all three pairs.
    employ loyal appoint
    employment loyalty appointment
13. Write the three words that have three syllables. employment loyalty appointment

118

Preparation Have students read aloud the title of the lesson on page 118. Write /oi/ on the board. Have students say /oi/ as in oil. Read each spelling word aloud. Have students repeat and then spell each word aloud.

Note the ure ending in moisture and the er ending in boiler. Then have students identify the two letters that spell /oi/ in each group of words in the list. (See **Note**.)

Read the sample sentences. Have students point to each spelling word as you read the sentence for it.

The Page Have students complete page 118. Have volunteers write the answers on the board. You may wish to have them circle the suffixes in the answers to exercise 12. Have students correct their own work.

Follow-Up Suggest that students fold a piece of paper in half. Then have them write words with the oy spelling of /oi/ in one column and words with the oi spelling of /oi/ in the other.

Checkpoint

Write a spelling word for each clue.
Then use the Checkpoint Study Plan on page 224.

1. To wreck is to ____. destroy
2. Faithful means ____. loyal
3. The opposite of silence is ____. noise
4. Of a king or queen means ____. royal
5. Take pleasure means to ____. enjoy
6. To keep away from is to ____. avoid
7. If you make a date, you have an ____. appointment
8. To name someone to a position means to ____. appoint
9. A long trip or journey is a ____. voyage
10. If you can go only one way, you have no ____. choice
11. To make sounds for singing you use your ____. voice
12. To hire for a job is to ____. employ
13. Wetness is ____. moisture
14. Faithfulness is ____. loyalty
15. To cook close to direct heat is to ____. broil
16. To bother or irritate is to ____. annoy
17. To make steam heat you need a ____. boiler
18. If you are working, then you have ____. employment
19. A pearl comes from an ____. oyster

20. This word was first used to describe a tool called a mold or die. This tool was used to make markings on silver and gold money. Later this same word was used to refer to the markings instead of the tool. Finally, it came to be used for the money itself. This word used to be spelled *coigne*. How is it spelled today? ____ coin

Objectives

- To write spelling words in response to clues: definitions, synonyms, antonyms, and context.
- To develop the critical thinking skills of making inferences, understanding cause and effect, and drawing conclusions.
- To understand that the spellings and meanings of words in the English language often change over time.

Spelling Strategy

If students have difficulty remembering which letter spells the unaccented vowel sound in words such as destroy, loyal, boiler, and voyage, it may help to have them write this letter larger than the other letters in the word or write it in a bright contrasting color. Then have them practice looking at the word, looking away to form a mental image of it, and spelling it from memory.

Preparation The clues on this page are like crossword puzzle clues. Explain to students that the response to each clue is a spelling word. Use the following examples to illustrate the types of clues used:

Definition	To hire for a job is to (*employ*).
Synonym	Wetness is (*moisture*).
Antonym	The opposite of silence is (*noise*).
Context	To make steam heat you need a (*boiler*).

The final clue explains how the spelling and meaning of coin have changed over time.

The Page Have students complete page 119 using the words on page 118. When students have finished, have them read each clue and spell the answer aloud. Check each response twice: once for the correct answer and a second time for spelling accuracy.

Follow-Up Guide pupils in using the **Checkpoint Study Plan** on page 224 to take a self-test. Then have them use the plan for independent study.

Objectives

- To write words with /oi/ in continuous text.
- To write each spelling word once.
- To integrate reading with spelling.

Use each list word once.

Do What You Like

What kind of job would you like to get when you finish school? It's hard to make a choice about a career. You'll be happiest, though, if you pick something you enjoy doing. If you have a coin collection, you might buy and sell coins as your job. If you like to sing, and you have a good voice, you might want to become a professional singer. Do you like to cook? Look for employment in a restaurant. Would you like to see other parts of the world? You can take a free ocean voyage if you get someone to appoint you to a ship's crew. Do you like to destroy things? Get a job with a wrecking company. Then you can knock down some old buildings.

Stay away from things you don't like. If animals annoy you, avoid jobs in pet stores. If you don't like lots of noise, don't ask a record store to employ you. You won't feel any loyalty to a job you hate. But you'll find that it's easy to be loyal and true to a job you like. It's more likely you'll be good at it, too.

120

Preparation Have students turn to pages 120 and 121. Let them look at the article and the pictures. Call their attention to the word list. Have students say the words. Then explain that each spelling word belongs in one of the blanks in the article.

Write the title "Do What You Like" on the board. Then ask students to tell what jobs they would like to have when they get older. Ask how many students know what kind of career they would like. Explain that most people find it hard to decide what career paths to take. Ask what idea the title of the selection expresses. (*Answers will vary.*)

The Pages Have students complete pages 120 and 121 independently by silently reading the article and writing the missing spelling words. Or you may read the article and related sentences aloud, supplying the missing words as students follow along in their texts; then have the students complete the pages on their own.

When students have finished, you may wish to discuss the pages. Ask students if they like to do any of the things mentioned in the article. Do they

If you want to ask someone for a job, you must make an ___appointment___ to see that person. As a chef, your specialty might be ___oyster___ stew. A chef must know when to ___broil___ foods in the broiler and when to use a double ___boiler___.

If you were a maid to a ___royal___ family, you might ask visitors to wait in the foyer.

A weather forecaster reports the ___moisture___ in the air as well as the temperature.

destroy
annoy
enjoy
employ
employment
oyster
loyal
loyalty
voyage
royal
choice
appoint
appointment
moisture
boiler
coin
avoid
voice
noise
broil

think they might want any of the jobs suggested? Ask if they can think of other jobs that go with these interests. (*For example, a person who likes to travel could try to become an airline pilot.*) Ask students to name other interests they have in sports, science, media, or other fields, and suggestions for related jobs.

Have a volunteer read each paragraph on the pages, supplying each missing spelling word and spelling it aloud. Have other volunteers write the answers on the board and have students correct their own work. Check students' responses for the accurate spelling of each answer.

Follow-Up

Have students use each of the spelling words they missed in an original sentence that relates to the article.

As an additional follow-up activity, you may wish to have pairs of students take turns reading the article aloud to each other, pausing before each spelling word. The other student will supply the missing word by spelling it aloud at the appropriate time.

Enrichment

If you want to use the blackline activity masters for enrichment and additional practice, assign Lesson 22 activities at this time.

Maintenance and Review

OBJECTIVE

- To review words with /o͞o/ spelled: oo, o_e, ue, ui, u, oe, o.

ACTIVITIES

If you want to use the blackline activity masters for maintenance and review, assign Lesson 21 activities at this time.

You can also use the activity below to review Lesson 21 with students.

Write the following word pairs on the board. Have students write a sentence containing each word pair.

loose–glue
choose–shampoo
clue–proof
whose–balloon
fruit–juice
kangaroo–raccoon

Objectives

- To relate spelling words to a dictionary skill.
- To write spelling words with attention to syllabication.
- To write sound spellings.
- To understand the placement of accent marks in a word.
- To use the **Spelling Dictionary**.

Syllables and Accent Marks

An entry word in a dictionary is divided into syllables. A syllable is a single sound that forms part of a word.

en·joy | ĕn joi′ |

★ Find each of the words below in the Spelling Dictionary. Write them in syllables, putting a dot between the syllables.

1. oyster oy·ster **2.** loyalty loy·al·ty

3. avoid a·void **4.** voyage voy·age

The sound spellings in a dictionary tell how to pronounce a word. An accent mark (′) is a part of this guide. It tells which syllable in a word is spoken with more stress or force.

loy·al | loi′əl | **an·noy** | ə noi′ |

★ Look at the sound spellings above. Then answer these questions.

5. Which word has the accent on the first syllable? loyal

6. Which word has the accent on the second syllable? annoy

★ Write the sound spelling of each word below.

7. destroy /dĭ stroi′/ **8.** royal /roi′ əl/

9. appoint /ə point′/ **10.** moisture /mois′ chər/

Some words of two or more syllables have two accented syllables. The stronger accent (′) is called the primary accent. The weaker accent (′) is called the secondary accent.

tin·foil | tĭn′foil′ |

★ Look at the sound spelling above. Then answer these questions.

11. Which syllable has the primary accent? first syllable

12. Which syllable has the secondary accent? second syllable

122

Preparation Have students read aloud the title of page 122. Ask them what a syllable is. (*a single sound that forms part of a word*) Write the following words on the board:

coin enjoy choice appointment boiler

Ask students how many syllables each word has. *(one; two; one; three; two)* Remind students that if a word has more than one syllable, we usually say one of the syllables with more emphasis than the others. Ask where the accent occurs in enjoy *(the second syllable)*, appointment *(second syllable)*, and boiler *(first syllable)*. Review with students that a dictionary divides the entry word into syllables. An accent mark is given in the sound spelling to show which syllable is spoken with more stress.

The Page Have students do page 122. Then have volunteers write the answers on the board and review the answers orally.

Follow-Up Have students write the multi-syllabic spelling words not covered on page 122. Then have them look up the words in the **Spelling Dictionary**, divide them into syllables, and put in the accent marks.

WORDS AT WORK

Challenge Yourself

boisterous void exploit employer

Write what you think each underlined Challenge Word means. Check your Spelling Dictionary to see if you were right. Then write sentences showing that you understand the meaning of each Challenge Word.

1. The class was usually quiet and well-behaved, but today the students were boisterous.
2. We tried to use the torn coupon, but the clerk said it was void.
3. He should exploit his cooking skill by becoming a chef.
4. The people who work for her are glad that she is their employer.

Write to the Point

You have seen adults doing many different jobs, such as teaching, working in stores and libraries, and constructing buildings. Choose a job that you have seen and write a paragraph telling what you would and would not like about this work. Use spelling words from this lesson in your paragraph.

Challenge Use one or more of the Challenge Words in your paragraph.

Proofreading

Use the proofreading marks to show the errors in the paragraph below. Write the five misspelled words correctly in the blanks.

- word is misspelled
- take out word
- letter should be capitalized

I can't decide which job I'd enjoie. Each day i seem to have a new choyce. I'd like to to avoid being a singer, because my voyce sounds more like noyze than music! Would someone employe me to ride horses?

1. enjoy
2. choice
3. voice
4. noise
5. employ

Objectives

- To extend the vowel spellings presented in Lesson 22 to the Challenge Words.
- To use context and the **Spelling Dictionary** to enlarge students' vocabulary.
- To apply the vowel spellings presented in Lesson 22 in a writing activity.
- To practice proofreading for spelling, capitalization, and extra words.

Dictation Sentences

1. I will enjoy the voyage.
2. The boiler made a funny noise when I turned it on.
3. I have an appointment at the employment office today.
4. To avoid dry skin, use a moisture cream.
5. Did you see the royal wedding on television?
6. My dog is loyal and comes when she hears my voice.
7. The coin rolled under the table.
8. I will broil the fish.
9. They will not appoint a captain who does not have loyalty to the team.
10. She is a good choice to employ.
11. He ate the last oyster.
12. The flood will destroy the town.
13. Don't annoy me!

Challenge Yourself Answers

Possible definitions:

1. noisy
2. not valid
3. use; take advantage of
4. person or company an employee works for

Students' sentences will vary.

Test Review these two ways to spell /oi/: oy as in enjoy; oi as in coin. Test words with /oi/. Use one of these testing methods: (1) Say the word; read the sample sentence from page 118; say the word; have students write it. (2) Read each dictation sentence above; have students write the sentence. Correct the test with students.

Challenge Yourself The optional Challenge Words may be assigned to the entire class or limited to those students who do well on the test. Have students note the vowel spellings in the Challenge Words. Responses to this activity should be completed on separate paper. Answers to the questions are provided above.

Write to the Point Help students recall the selection "Do What You Like" on pages 120 and 121; then assign the paragraph. Encourage students to give a specific example of what they would and would not like about the job and to explain why they feel this way. This activity should be completed on separate paper.

Proofreading The proofreading practice includes misspellings of words from this lesson as well as a capitalization error and an extra word.

LESSON 23

Objectives

- To hear and say sports words.
- To write sports words with attention to letter sequence and sound/symbol relationships.
- To write each spelling word at least once.

Sample Sentences

1. Janice often goes bowling with her friends.
2. Eileen is on our volleyball team.
3. Deana got a new tennis racquet.
4. Rhoda took her bike and went cycling.
5. Steve likes to go swimming in the lake.
6. He hopes to become a professional swimmer.
7. This contest is open to any amateur bowler.
8. Sam ran down the basketball court and scored two points.
9. These two teams are in competition for first place.
10. Keith wants to play on the football team.
11. A golf course usually has 18 holes.
12. Ice hockey is a fast, dangerous game.
13. You must take a course before you can go skin diving.
14. Linda won the 100-yard dash in the track meet.
15. Chris goes ice skating every weekend.
16. In soccer you can't touch the ball with your hands.
17. Our baseball team has never won the World Series.
18. Jane is the dancing champion of our school.
19. Arnold goes skiing in the mountains.
20. The Olympics are held every four years.

Note

The sample sentences may be used for pretesting.

Lesson 23 Sports Words

Say each word.

bowling
volleyball
tennis
cycling
swimming
professional
amateur
basketball
competition
football
golf
hockey
skin diving
track
skating
soccer
baseball
champion
skiing
Olympics

1. Which word begins with the letters ch? champion
2. Write the three words that begin with the letters sk. skiing, skin diving, skating
3. Which two words begin with a vowel? Circle the proper noun. amateur, (Olympics)
4. In which two words do you hear /sh/ but don't see the letters sh? professional, competition
5. Which word begins with a capital? Olympics
6. In which two words is /k/ spelled ck? hockey, track
7. Which word begins and ends like beginning? bowling
8. Which word begins and ends like gulf? golf
9. Which word ends with /ē/? hockey
10. Write the word in which the second letter is y. cycling
11. Which word has the letters ii? skiing
12. Write the word that is made of two separate words. skin diving
13. Which four words are compounds made with the word ball? volleyball, basketball, football, baseball
14. Write the three words that have these double consonants: cc soccer, mm swimming, nn tennis

124

Preparation Have students read aloud the title of the lesson on page 124. Read each spelling word aloud. Have students repeat and then spell each word aloud.

Ask students to name the base words in bowling (*bowl*) and skiing (*ski*). Note the two i's together in skiing. Ask students to name the base word in swimming (*swim*) and have them tell what spelling change was made when ing was added (*The m was doubled*). Ask students to name the base words in skating (*skate*) and cycling (*cycle*). Ask what spelling change was made when ing was added. (*The e was dropped.*)

Read the sample sentences. Have students point to each spelling word as you read the sentence for it.

The Page Have students complete page 124. Have volunteers write the answers on the board and have students correct their own work.

Follow-Up Suggest that students write each word three times without lifting their pencils from the paper.

Checkpoint

Write a spelling word for each clue.
Then use the Checkpoint Study Plan on page 224.

1. Riding a bicycle or motorcycle is ____. — cycling
2. Running, jumping, and pole-vaulting are events in ____. — track
3. You can hit a ball with your head in ____. — soccer
4. If the ball is pointed at both ends, it's a ____. — football
5. Playing for pay is done by a ____. — professional
6. Scoring a basket to win is done in ____. — basketball
7. An underwater sport is ____. — skin diving
8. Snowy slopes are good for ____. — skiing
9. The final winner is the ____. — champion
10. There are teams on either side of a high net in ____. — volleyball
11. Try to knock all the pins down when you're ____. — bowling
12. Water is for boating, ice is for ____. — skating
13. You say "fore" when you play ____. — golf
14. A home run is a score in ____. — baseball
15. The opposite of professional is ____. — amateur
16. The backstroke is used when ____. — swimming
17. A court sport with a low net is ____. — tennis
18. You need a puck to play ____. — hockey
19. If teams play to win, they are in ____. — competition

20. Long ago, foot races were held in the Olympian Valley in Greece. The races were part of a festival in honor of Zeus, the king of the Greek gods. Soon, all the Greek states began to take part in these sport festivals. Gradually, more events like jumping and wrestling were added. Now athletes from many nations get together every four years and compete in athletic events. The events are named after the old Greek festival. Do you know what they're called? ____ — Olympics

Objectives

- To write spelling words in response to clues: definitions, antonyms, analogies, and context.
- To develop the critical thinking skills of making inferences and classifying.
- To understand that words have come into the English language from other languages and that words may develop from the names of places.

Spelling Strategy

If students misspell the second vowel sound in competition, remind them that the word comes from compete. Point out to students that remembering the /ē/ in compete can help them remember that the corresponding vowel sound in competition is spelled e.

Preparation The clues on this page are like crossword puzzle clues. Explain to students that the response to each clue is a spelling word. Use the following examples to illustrate the types of clues used:

Definition	The final winner is the (*champion*).
Antonym	The opposite of professional is (*amateur*).
Analogy	Water is for boating, ice is for (*skating*).
Context	You say "fore" when you play (*golf*).

The final clue explains how Olympics came into the English language.

The Page Have students complete page 125 using the words on page 124. When students have finished, have them read each clue and spell the answer aloud. Check each response twice: once for the correct answer and a second time for spelling accuracy.

Follow-Up Guide pupils in using the **Checkpoint Study Plan** on page 224 to take a self-test. Then have them use the plan for independent study.

Objectives

- To write sports words in continuous text.
- To write each spelling word once.
- To integrate reading with spelling.

Use each list word once.
Identify the sport with which these things are associated.

THE NAME OF THE GAME

Preparation Have students turn to pages 126 and 127. Let them look at the pages and the pictures. Call their attention to the word list. Have the students say the words. Then explain that each spelling word belongs in one of the blanks on the pages.

Write the title "The Name of the Game" on the board. Tell the students that these pages are about sports.

The Pages Have students look at page 126. Tell them that they are going to compete to write the names of the sports that match the pictures. Divide the class into two teams. Each student must write the name of every sport, but the team members may confer with each other to decide on the correct answers. Some will be easy and others may be more difficult, such as track or golf. The first team to complete page 126 announces that it is finished. Check to see that every team member has written every answer. Then let volunteers from the winning team write the answers on the board in rows that correspond to the rows on the text page. Have students correct their own work.

Use the remaining words to complete the bulletin board.

Sign up for the Olympic team today!

There will be lots of competition for medals. Only one champion can be chosen in each event.

Remember, professional athletes, who earn money for their skill in a sport, are now eligible. Not only amateur athletes can compete in the Olympics.

See your gym coach for entry forms.

bowling
volleyball
tennis
skiing
swimming
professional
amateur
basketball
competition
football
golf
hockey
skin diving
track
skating
soccer
baseball
champion
cycling
Olympics

Then have students complete page 127 independently by silently reading the bulletin board and writing the missing spelling words. Or you may read the page aloud, supplying the missing words as students follow along in their texts; then have the students complete the page on their own.

Have a volunteer read the bulletin board, supplying each spelling word and spelling it aloud. Have other volunteers write the answers on the board and have students correct their own work. Check students' responses for the accurate spelling of each answer.

Follow-Up

Have students use each of the spelling words they missed in an original sentence that relates to the pages.

As an additional follow-up activity, you may wish to have students make a sports scrapbook on one or more of the sports mentioned in "The Name of the Game." Ask the students to illustrate the scrapbook and use spelling words as captions.

Enrichment

If you want to use the blackline activity masters for enrichment and additional practice, assign Lesson 23 activities at this time.

Maintenance and Review

OBJECTIVE

- To review words with /oi/ spelled: oi, oy.

ACTIVITIES

If you want to use the blackline activity masters for maintenance and review, assign Lesson 22 activities at this time.

You can also use the activity below to review Lesson 22 with students.

Write the following CHAINWORDS on the board. Have the students refer to the Lesson 22 word list and find the two list words hidden in each chainword below. (Answers are in parentheses.)

avoidestroy	(*avoid, destroy*)
oysteroyal	(*oyster, royal*)
broiloyalty	(*broil, loyalty*)
choicenjoy	(*choice, enjoy*)
coinoise	(*coin, noise*)
moisturemploy	(*moisture, employ*)

Objectives

- To relate spelling to another language skill.
- To review the use of commas in a letter.
- To write spelling words in letters.
- To practice proofreading.

Commas

Use commas in a friendly letter:

- to separate the day from the year in the heading,

February 4, 199__

- after the person's name in the greeting,

Dear Bob,

- after the last word in the closing.

Yours truly,

★ Rewrite the friendly letters below, adding commas to the date, greeting, and closing. Correct the misspelled words in each letter.

April 15, 199__

Dear Martha,

I am planning a trip to Boston soon. It has been so long since we got together, I thought this would be a good time to do so. What would be a good day? Will it be possible for us to play tenis or gulf during my visit?

Please drop a note or call. I look forward to seeing you!

Your friend,
Alicia

tennis golf

May 5, 199__

Dear Alicia,

I'm so pleased that you're coming to visit. How about the first weekend in June?

We can certainly plan lots of time for sports. As you know, swiming and skatting have always been my favorites. Oh, speaking of sports, you'll be interested to learn that my brother is going to become a profesional baskitball player.

See you soon, fellow amatuer athlete!

Sincerely,
Martha

swimming skating professional basketball amateur

128

Preparation Have students read aloud the title of page 128. Then write the following on the board:

April 1 1996 Dear Pat Sincerely yours

Review with students the places commas are used in a friendly letter. (*in the date, between the day and year; after the greeting; after the closing*) Have volunteers add the commas where they belong. (*April 1, 1996; Dear Pat,; Sincerely yours,*)

The Page Have students do page 128. Then have volunteers write the answers on the board and review them orally.

Follow-Up Have students write a friendly letter about one or more of the sports in the spelling list. Remind students to use commas correctly.

WORDS AT WORK

Challenge Yourself

referee umpire rookie scoreboard

Use your Spelling Dictionary to answer these questions. Then write sentences showing that you understand the meaning of each Challenge Word.

1. At a football game, what can you look at to find out the score?
2. Who makes sure that each team's baseball players follow the rules during a game?
3. Who makes sure that soccer and basketball players follow the rules during a game?
4. What is a nickname that is often given to a new player on a sports team?

Write to the Point

Choose two of the pairs of sports below. For each pair write a sentence or two about how the sports are similar and different. If you wish, you may create other pairs, such as golf/bowling or swimming/track. Use spelling words from this lesson in your comparisons.

tennis/volleyball baseball/basketball
ice-skating/skiing swimming/skin diving

Challenge Use one or more of the Challenge Words in your comparisons.

Proofreading

Use the proofreading marks to show the errors in the paragraph below. Write the five misspelled words correctly in the blanks.

⬭	word is misspelled
≡	letter should be capitalized
∧	word is missing

Everyone in my family is an amatuer athlete. Dad swims and plays gulf, and mom loves sking. I play basket ball, and my sister leona is the star of her trak team. Maybe someday one of us will be in the olympics! Maybe one of us will even become a professional some day!

1. amateur
2. golf
3. skiing
4. basketball
5. track

Objectives

- To extend students' knowledge of sports words through the Challenge Words.
- To use clues and the **Spelling Dictionary** to enlarge students' vocabulary.
- To apply the sports words presented in Lesson 23 in a writing activity.
- To practice proofreading for spelling, capitalization, and missing words.

Dictation Sentences

1. Both amateur and professional athletes take part in the Olympics.
2. I like to go skiing and ice skating in the winter.
3. Our school won the track meet and the cycling race.
4. The coach says competition is good in sports like baseball and basketball.
5. We went skin diving and played tennis on our vacation.
6. He is on his school's hockey and football teams.
7. Is this your first time to play volleyball?
8. I want to join the soccer and swimming teams.
9. I do not like to play golf, but I do like to go bowling.
10. She is a champion horse racer.

Challenge Yourself Answers

1. scoreboard
2. umpire
3. referee
4. rookie

Students' sentences will vary.

Test Review and test sports words. Use one of these testing methods: (1) Say the word; read the sample sentence from page 124; say the word; have students write it. (2) Read each dictation sentence above; have students write the sentence. Correct the test with students.

Challenge Yourself The optional Challenge Words may be assigned to the entire class or limited to those students who do well on the test. You may wish to have students work in pairs. Responses to this activity should be completed on separate paper. Answers to the questions are provided above.

Write to the Point Help students recall the selection "The Name of the Game" on pages 126 and 127; then assign the comparisons. Remind students that the words but, however, on the other hand, and whereas are useful when pointing out differences. This activity should be completed on separate paper.

Proofreading The proofreading practice includes misspellings of words from this lesson as well as capitalization errors and a missing word.

LESSON 24

Objectives

- To review and reinforce vowel spellings for /ŭ/, /ô/, /o͞o/, and /oi/.
- To hear, say, spell, and write representative spelling words from Lessons 19–22.
- To write a description using the five steps in the writing process.
- To use a prewriting activity to generate details for a description.

Dictation Sentences

1. The flood will destroy the crops.
2. This shoe is loose.
3. The judge told them to tell the truth.
4. We found a clue.
5. We have a choice of water or juice.
6. Try to avoid that rough road.
7. It would be awful to lose your compass on a hike.
8. We fought for clean air.
9. To whom did you send the letter?
10. Is it all right for your daughter to be in the play?
11. They don't often find fault with us.

Note

A review test blackline master in standardized format and an answer sheet have been provided on pages T38 and T41 of this Teacher's Edition. The answers to the review test are given below.

1–C	11–C
2–B	12–D
3–A	13–B
4–B	14–A
5–D	15–A
6–B	16–C
7–C	17–B
8–A	18–D
9–B	19–B
10–C	20–B

If words misspelled were from:	have students complete activities:
List A	1, 3
List B	2, 3
List C	4, 6
List D	5, 6

Lesson 24 Words in Review

A. compass
flood
rough
judge

B. fault
often
fought
all right
awful
daughter

C. clue
shoe
lose
loose
truth
whom
juice

D. avoid
choice
destroy

★ You will need a piece of paper for these review activities.

1. In Lesson 19 you studied four different ways to spell /ŭ/: **u, o, ou, oo.** Write the words in list A.

compass flood
rough judge

2. In Lesson 20 you studied five different ways to spell /ô/: **aw, au, ou, a, o.** Write the words in list B.

fault often fought
all right awful daughter

★ **3.** Look up each review word from lists A and B in the Spelling Dictionary. Divide each word into syllables.

4. In Lesson 21 you studied seven different ways to spell /o͞o/: **oo, o_e, ue, ui, u, oe, o.** Write the words in list C.

clue shoe lose
loose truth whom
juice

5. In Lesson 22 you studied two different ways to spell /oi/: **oy, oi.** Write the words in list D.

avoid choice destroy

★ **6.** Use each review word from lists C and D in a sentence.

Your teacher may give you a test. Answer these questions when you have finished.

7. Did you spell all the words correctly? Yes or No

8. Did you leave out a letter? Yes or No

9. Did you write the wrong letter? Yes or No

10. Did you miss the spelling of a vowel sound? Yes or No

130

Test Pretest the review words on page 130 to determine which students need reinforcement. Use one of these testing methods: (1) Read the words and the dictation sentences; have students write only the spelling words. (2) Read the dictation sentences and have students write the entire sentences. (3) Have students complete the review test blackline master. (See **Note**.) Correct the pretest with students.

The Pages Assign pages 130 and 131 according to students' needs.

- Students who have mastered all of the review words may go on to the **Writer's Workshop** on page 131.
- Students who have not mastered all of the review words should complete the activities on page 130 and take a post-test administered with one of the pretesting methods. After the post-test students can then go on to the **Writer's Workshop** on page 131. For students who have misspelled only a few of the review words, you may wish to use the list at left to determine the activities they should complete on page 130.

For students who have misspelled several of the review words, you may wish to assign all of the activities on page 130.

Writer's Workshop

A Description

When you write a description, you picture something in your mind and then use words to help your reader see or imagine the same thing. A description can do more than tell what something looks like. It can also tell how something sounds, feels, smells, or tastes. To appeal to readers' senses, writers choose the most vivid details of the thing they are describing and use words that describe those details as closely as possible. Here is Mark's description of the ocean.

The Ocean

The ocean was huge. It stretched as far as I could see. White gulls soared above it in the blue sky. The water was green and shining like glass, and the waves rolled and sparkled in the sun. They rumbled and roared as they crashed against the rocks. When the waves reached the shore, they slapped and splashed against the sand, bursting into white foam. Walking into the water, I felt the slippery seaweed and the rough pebbles under my feet. Little waves smacked gently against my legs. The icy water cooled me, and I breathed in its fishy scent. When I licked my lips, I tasted salt water.

To write his description, Mark followed the steps in the writing process. He used a senses web as a **Prewriting** activity. The web helped Mark think of words and phrases that describe the ocean. Once he had completed his web, he decided which details to use in his description. Part of Mark's senses web is shown here. Study what Mark did.

Ocean

Sound
waves
- rumbled
- roared
- crashed
- slapped

It's Your Turn

Get ready to write your own description. Choose an object or a place that is very familiar to you and that you would enjoy describing. After you have decided what to write about, make a senses web. Then follow the other steps in the writing process—**Writing, Revising, Proofreading,** and **Publishing.**

131

Note

If students have difficulty deciding on a topic, you may wish to suggest one of the following:

My pet (or an animal I know)

My favorite food

My own special place

Writer's Workshop Explain that in a description writers use words to help their readers picture or imagine something. They choose words and phrases that appeal to one or more of the five senses—sight, sound, touch, taste, and smell. Read with students the description "The Ocean" and point out the different sensory words and phrases that Mark used.

Allow students to study the portion of the senses web shown on the pupil's page and guide students to see how this graphic organizer helped Mark prepare to write his description.

It's Your Turn Review the steps in the writing process with students. If students are not satisfied with the result of their prewriting, allow them to revise it as often as necessary or to choose another topic and repeat the prewriting activity.

Process Writing Blackline Masters
- Senses Web, page T48
- Steps in the Writing Process, page T44
- Proofreading Symbols/Checklist, page T45

LESSON 25

Objectives

- To hear and say words with /ô/.
- To write words with /ô/ with attention to letter sequence and sound/symbol relationships.
- To write each spelling word at least once.
- To recognize that /ô/ may be spelled o, a, ou, and oa.

Sample Sentences

1. The kittens adore their mother and follow her around.
2. We went to the shore and swam in the ocean.
3. Come inside before it gets dark.
4. Karen wore her new shirt to the party.
5. Our team won by a score of 6 to 5.
6. The wind tore the leaves off the trees.
7. We export food to many other countries.
8. The actors will now perform their play.
9. Molly was fortunate to catch the train.
10. Let's go pick apples in the orchard.
11. That store will import shoes from Italy.
12. It's important to know your phone number.
13. Let's not quarrel over nothing.
14. The one who catches the thief will get a reward.
15. I must warn you not to touch that switch.
16. Skip ran toward the door as fast as he could.
17. The buildings form a square around a court.
18. This social studies course is about American history.
19. The lion let out a huge roar.
20. If we saw that board in half, it will just fit.

Note

- The sample sentences may be used for pretesting.
- Words are grouped according to spellings of /ô/:
  - o
  - a
  - ou
  - oa

Lesson 25 Words with /ô/

Listen for /ô/ in each word.

adore
shore
before
wore
score
tore
export
perform
fortunate
orchard
import
important

quarrel
reward
warn
toward

court
course

roar
board

1. Which word begins with the letters sh?
   shore
2. Write the five words that begin with a vowel.
   adore export
   orchard import
   important
3. Which two words begin with /k/? Circle the letter that spells /k/. court course
4. Which word begins with /sk/? Circle the letters that spell /sk/. score
5. Which word begins with /kw/? Circle the letters that spell /kw/. quarrel
6. Which three words have the same spelling of /ô/ as quarrel? reward warn
   toward
7. Which two words have the same spelling of /ô/ as soar?
   roar board
8. Which word begins with the letters per?
   perform
9. Which word begins and ends like believe?
   before
10. Which word begins and ends like telephone?
    tore
11. Which word begins with the letter f? fortunate
12. Which word is pronounced exactly like war?
    wore
13. Write the word in which /r/ is spelled rr.
    quarrel

132

Preparation Have students read aloud the title of the lesson on page 132. Write /ô/ on the board. Have students say /ô/ as in paw. Read each spelling word aloud. Tell students to repeat and then spell each word aloud.

Ask students what double consonant appears in quarrel (*rr*) and what two letters end it (*el*). Note the /ə/ in the last syllable of quarrel: /**kwôr**'əl/. Ask what letter stands for /ə/ in quarrel (*e*). Ask what two letters begin toward. (*to*) Then have students identify the ways /ô/ is spelled in this lesson. (See **Note**.) Read the sample sentences. Have students point to each spelling word as you read the sentence for it.

The Page Have students complete page 132. Have volunteers write the answers on the board and have students correct their own work.

Follow-Up Suggest that students write each word, starting with tiny letters that get larger until the last letter is very large.

Checkpoint

Write a spelling word for each clue.
Then use the Checkpoint Study Plan on page 224.

1. The opposite of after is ___.	before
2. A loud yell is a ___.	roar
3. The opposite of hate is ___.	adore
4. Another word for ripped is ___.	tore
5. The route taken or the path followed is the ___.	course
6. The winner is the one with the highest ___.	score
7. If you act in a play, then you ___.	perform
8. A river has a bank, a sea has a ___.	shore
9. Today I wear, last week I ___.	wore
10. The opposite of unlucky is ___.	fortunate
11. Tennis is played on a ___.	court
12. In the direction of means ___.	toward
13. If you find my lost cat, I'll give you a ___.	reward
14. These apples come from an ___.	orchard
15. An argument is a ___.	quarrel
16. A piece of wood is a ___.	board
17. Something really needed is something ___.	important
18. To alert to danger is to ___.	warn

19. Sometimes two words that have the same base word are antonyms. This is because they contain prefixes that have opposite meanings. Both mystery words have the base word *portare*. *Portare* meant carry in Latin. The first mystery word begins with the Latin prefix *im*. *Im* meant into. *Importare* meant to carry in. Can you guess this mystery word? ___	import
20. The other mystery word begins with the Latin prefix *ex*. *Ex* meant away from. *Exportare* meant to carry out. Can you guess this word? ___	export

133

Objectives

- To write spelling words in response to clues: definitions, synonyms, antonyms, analogies, and context.
- To develop the critical thinking skills of making inferences, comparing, and contrasting.
- To understand that words have come into the English language from other languages and that a prefix and a root word may be combined to form a new word.

Spelling Strategy

Some students may have difficulty remembering the spelling of toward because they pronounce it /tôrd/, with one syllable. Tell students that although this pronunciation is preferred, another correct pronunciation is /tə **wôrd'**/, with two syllables. Being aware of the second pronunciation can help students remember the w in toward.

Preparation The clues on this page are like crossword puzzle clues. Explain to students that the response to each clue is a spelling word. Use the following examples to illustrate the types of clues used:

Definition	A piece of wood is a (*board*).
Synonym	Another word for ripped is (*torn*).
Antonym	The opposite of after is (*before*).
Analogy	A river has a bank, a sea has a (*shore*).
Context	If you find my lost cat, I'll give you a (*reward*).

The final clues identify the prefixes and the root word in import and export.

The Page Have students complete page 133 using the words on page 132. When students have finished, have them read each clue and spell the answer aloud. Check each response twice: once for the correct answer and a second time for spelling accuracy.

Follow-Up Guide pupils in using the **Checkpoint Study Plan** on page 224 to take a self-test. Then have them use the plan for independent study.

Objectives

- To write words with /ô/ in continuous text.
- To write each spelling word once.
- To integrate reading with spelling.

Note

- Point out the use of the word course in the newspaper as part of the expression of course, meaning naturally. Ask students for another meaning of course.
- Point out the use of the word court to mean a place marked for a game. Ask students for other meanings of court.

Use each list word once.

The Daily Herald

SCIENTIST'S NEW DISCOVERY

Mr. Ivor Gott, who works for the Sigh Ents Company, has discovered a formula that improves the memory.

"With this pill," explained Mr. Gott, "you can remember just about anything."

Mr. Gott says he got the idea for his formula while looking at the ocean. "I was walking along the shore. I just adore the sea. I forget exactly when it was. I forget how I worked it out, but it's written in my notes somewhere. Or maybe I tore that page out."

Ms. Selma Gradey, President of the Sigh Ents Company, said, "We couldn't be more pleased with Mr. Gott's idea. For years, our major business has been to import toothpicks from other countries. Then we export them to other places. But now we'll be famous."

Can the formula do any harm? Mr. Gott told us, "We did lots of tests, but I forget what the results were."

FLEAS FLEE FLUE'S FLEA CIRCUS

Ten performing fleas escaped from Flue's Fabulous Flea Circus last night. "The fleas were just about ready to perform the most important part of their act. That's the part where they jump off a tiny diving board," Mr. Flue said. "Just before they began, a dog came into the hall. Before I knew it, my fleas were rushing toward the dog. That was the last time I saw them."

134

Preparation Have students turn to pages 134 and 135. Let them look at the newspaper and the pictures. Call their attention to the word list. Have the students say the words. Then explain that each spelling word belongs in one of the blanks in the newspaper.

Write the title "The Daily Herald" on the board. Then ask what kind of selection this is. (*a newspaper*) Ask students if they read newspapers, and if so, what parts. Ask them what kinds of information are on the front page of a newspaper. (*news articles of international, national, and local importance*) Ask what other kinds of information are published in a newspaper. (*other news, sports, feature articles, classified ads, weather, and other features such as comics or crossword puzzles*) Tell students to decide whether this selection contains real articles or fictional ones as they complete the pages.

The Pages Have students complete pages 134 and 135 independently by silently reading the newspaper and writing the missing spelling words. Or you may read the newspaper aloud, supplying the missing words as students follow along in their texts; then have the students complete the pages on their own.

When the fleas landed on it, the dog made a noise between a howl and a roar. Then the dog raced out of the room. It was last seen near the apple orchard on the Edgeware farm. No one seems to know the dog, even though it wore a collar. Mr. Flue is offering a $25 reward for the return of his fleas.

"Those fleas are very unusual," he explained. "They were brought here by an explorer. I was fortunate to get them. Of course, I'll organize a search party, but I fear the worst. I may have to find a new source of income."

SPORTS

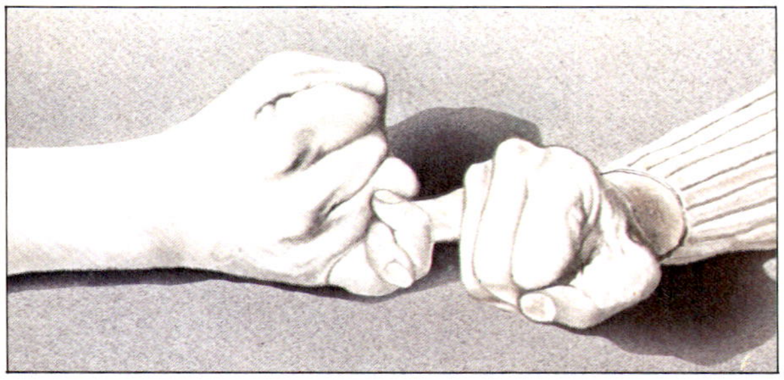

LOWE HIGH WINS TITLE

Lowe High School won the city pinky wrestling championship, but it was a rough match. The match was held on Lowe High's basketball court. It was attended by several noisy fans. During the match, an argument broke out. The referee had to warn the fans not to quarrel. The final score was tied, 1-1, but Lowe's rival decided to let Lowe have the title, so that its team could go home.

135

adore
shore
before
wore
score
tore
export
perform
fortunate
orchard
import
important
quarrel
reward
warn
toward
court
course
roar
board

When students have finished, you may wish to discuss the newspaper. Ask students if this is a real or fictional newspaper and why they think so. (*It is fictional; the events could not really happen.*) Ask what is funny or absurd about each article. (*The scientist who discovered the memory formula is forgetful; a flea circus is silly; there would not be a pinky wrestling contest.*) Have students identify the puns in the article about the scientist. (*Ivor Gott is a play on the words I forgot; Sigh Ents is a play on the word science.*)

Have a volunteer read each paragraph in the newspaper, supplying each spelling word and spelling it aloud. Have other volunteers write the answers on the board and have students correct their own work. Check students' responses for the accurate spelling of each answer.

Follow-Up Have students use each of the spelling words they missed in an original sentence that relates to the newspaper.

As an additional follow-up activity, you may wish to have one student read the story aloud to the class, pausing before each spelling word. The other students will say the spelling word at the appropriate time.

Enrichment

If you want to use the blackline activity masters for enrichment and additional practice, assign Lesson 25 activities at this time.

Maintenance and Review

OBJECTIVE

- To review sports words.

ACTIVITIES

If you want to use the blackline activity masters for maintenance and review, assign Lesson 23 activities at this time.

You can also use the activity below to review Lesson 23 with students.

Write the following words on the board. Have students refer to the Lesson 23 word list and write the word that rhymes with each word below. (Answers are in parentheses.)

jockey	(*hockey*)
waiting	(*skating*)
Dennis	(*tennis*)
slimming	(*swimming*)
fleeing	(*skiing*)
rocker	(*soccer*)
rolling	(*bowling*)
processional	(*professional*)
slack	(*track*)

Objectives

- To relate spelling words to a dictionary skill.
- To identify multiple spellings of words.
- To write spelling words in the context of sentences.
- To use the **Spelling Dictionary**.

Multiple Spellings

A dictionary is a good place to look for correct spellings of words. Some words have two acceptable spellings. The more common spelling is listed first.

ax or **axe** |ăks| *n., pl.* **ax·es** |ăk′sĭz|. A chopping or cutting tool consisting of a head with a sharp blade, mounted on a long handle.

light-year |līt′yîr′| *n.* Also **light year.** A measure of distance equal to the distance light travels through empty space in a year; about 5.878 trillion (5.878×10^{12}) miles.

★ In the sentences below, one or two of the words in parentheses are misspelled. Write each sentence with the more common spelling of the word in parentheses. If the word has another acceptable spelling in the parentheses, write the other spelling after the sentence. Check your choices in the Spelling Dictionary.

1. Joan likes to wash the dishes (befor, bifore, before) she watches her favorite television program. Joan likes to wash the dishes before she watches her favorite television program.
2. Michael will (perform, prefrom, purform) at the piano recital. Michael will perform at the piano recital.
3. The young reporter wrote such a good story that he got his first (byline, by line, by-line). The young reporter wrote such a good story that he got his first by-line. byline.
4. Ray is sorry that he had such a bad (quarel, quarrel, quarrle) with his sister. Ray is sorry that he had such a bad quarrel with his sister.
5. Davida wants to mow the lawn, but the (lawnmower, lawn mower, lawn-mower) is broken. Davida wants to mow the lawn, but the lawnmower is broken. lawn mower
6. We could finish building our tree house if we had just one more (bored, board, bord). We could finish building our tree house if we had just one more board.

136

Preparation Have students read the title of page 136. Then write these words on the board:

catalog catalogue

Have students read the words aloud. Tell students that some words can be spelled in two ways. These words are listed in the dictionary under the more common spelling, and the entry usually gives the other spelling as well.

The Page Have students do page 136. Then have volunteers write the answers on the board.

Follow-Up Write these words on the board:

mosquitos tornados zeros

Have students write each word, look it up in the **Spelling Dictionary**, write the other acceptable spelling for the word, and write a sentence using one of the acceptable spellings. Each sentence should also include a spelling word.

WORDS AT WORK

Challenge Yourself

pore furor resourceful distort

Write what you think each underlined Challenge Word means. Check your Spelling Dictionary to see if you were right. Then write sentences showing that you understand the meaning of each Challenge Word.

1. You sweat through the pores in your skin.
2. The crowd was in a furor because their favorite band never showed up for the concert.
3. A resourceful student uses library books to find and check facts.
4. A mirror that is bent or cracked can distort your image.

Write to the Point

Imagine you are a reporter for The Daily Herald. Write another funny news article like the ones you read on pages 134 and 135. Choose any subject that you might find in a real newspaper, such as sports, weather, science, and important events. Then have some fun with it. Use spelling words from this lesson in your news article.

Challenge Use one or more of the Challenge Words in your article.

Proofreading

Use the proofreading marks to show the errors in the paragraph below. Write the five misspelled words correctly in the blanks.

(oval)	word is misspelled
⊙	period is missing
/	letter should be lower case

The Newspaper said that Dr. G.Y. Nott made an importent Discovery He found that people who woar funny hats usually didn't kwarrel with each other Of coarse, this makes me feel fortunat. I adore funny hats!

1. important
2. wore
3. quarrel
4. course
5. fortunate

137

Objectives

- To extend the vowel spellings presented in Lesson 25 to the Challenge Words.
- To use context and the **Spelling Dictionary** to enlarge students' vocabulary.
- To apply the vowel spellings presented in Lesson 25 in a writing activity.
- To practice proofreading for spelling, punctuation, and capitalization.

Dictation Sentences

1. It is important to pick the apples in the orchard before winter.
2. I saw them walking toward the shore.
3. The soldiers wore green jackets.
4. There is a reward for any news about a missing gold ring.
5. The crowd began to roar when our team tied the score.
6. Wasn't it fortunate that Kim caught the dog before it tore up my homework?
7. What time will Tomás perform on the piano?
8. The buyers often quarrel over the prices of import and export goods.
9. We need a new board for the court in the gym.
10. I absolutely adore this course!
11. I must warn you to stay away from there.

Challenge Yourself Answers

Possible definitions:

1. tiny openings
2. an uproar
3. able to make good use of things
4. change

Students' sentences will vary.

Test Review these four ways to spell /ô/: o as in wore; a as in warn; ou as in court; oa as in roar. Test words with /ô/. Use one of these testing methods: (1) Say the word; read the sample sentence from page 132; say the word; have students write it. (2) Read each dictation sentence above; have students write the sentence. Correct the test with students.

Challenge Yourself The optional Challenge Words may be assigned to the entire class or limited to those students who do well on the test. Have students note the vowel spellings in the Challenge Words. Responses to this activity should be completed on separate paper. Answers to the questions are provided above.

Write to the Point Help students recall the selection "The Daily Herald" on pages 134 and 135; then assign the article. If students have trouble thinking of an idea, suggest that they base their article on a real event or discovery and then add a funny twist to it. This activity should be completed on separate paper.

Proofreading The proofreading practice includes misspellings of words from this lesson as well as capitalization and punctuation errors.

LESSON 26

Objectives

- To hear and say words with /û/.
- To write words with /û/ with attention to letter sequence and sound/symbol relationships.
- To write each spelling word at least once.
- To recognize that /û/ may be spelled e, i, ea, and u.

Sample Sentences

1. I think I can go, but I'm not certain.
2. The service is fast in this restaurant.
3. Jim got a perfect score on the test.
4. The teacher does not permit talking in class.
5. The magnolia flowers smelled like perfume.
6. You can store your personal items in the locker.
7. Peter got his hands dirty making mud pies.
8. Susan will be thirteen years old tomorrow.
9. If you speak in a firm voice, the dog will obey.
10. Judy wore a skirt that came down to her ankles.
11. Bill answered the phone on the third ring.
12. We can earn five dollars by mowing the lawn.
13. They ate an early lunch at 11:30.
14. Our class is learning the names of birds.
15. Have you heard that Monday is a holiday?
16. Mom let me wear her pearl necklace.
17. The purpose of this meeting is to settle the argument.
18. They will furnish the bedroom with pillows.
19. Lenny hurt his toe when he fell.
20. Donny bought a table at the furniture store.

Note

- The sample sentences may be used for pretesting.
- Words are grouped according to spellings of /û/:
  e
  i
  ea
  u

Lesson 26 Words with /û/

Listen for /û/ in each word.

certain
service
perfect
permit
perfume
personal

dirty
thirteen
firm
skirt
third

earn
early
learning
heard
pearl

purpose
furnish
hurt
furniture

1. Write the two words that begin with the letters th. thirteen third
2. Which word begins with a vowel and ends with a consonant? earn
3. Which three words begin with the letter f? First write the word that has one syllable. Then write the word that has two syllables. Write the word that has three syllables last. firm furnish furniture
4. Which word begins with /s/ but isn't spelled with the letter s? certain
5. Which word begins and ends like hard? heard
6. Which word begins and ends with /s/? service
7. Which two words begin with the letter p and end with the letter l? personal pearl
8. Which two words begin with the letter p and end with the letter e? perfume purpose
9. Which two words begin with the letter p and end with the letter t? perfect permit
10. Write the other two words that end with the letter t. skirt hurt
11. Which word ends with ing? learning
12. Which two words end with /ē/? Circle the letter that spells /ē/. dirty early
13. Write the word that ends with the letters sh. furnish

138

Preparation Have students read aloud the title of the lesson on page 138. Write /û/ on the board. Have students say /û/ as in fur. Read each spelling word aloud. Tell students to repeat and then spell each word aloud.

Note that although perfect and permit are pronounced either with the accent on the first or the second syllable, their spelling remains the same. Ask students to name the base words in personal (*person*); in dirty (*dirt*); in learning (*learn*). Then have students identify the letter or letters that spell /û/ in each group of words in the list. (See **Note**.)

Read the sample sentences. Have students point to each spelling word as you read the sentence for it.

The Page Have students complete page 138. Then have volunteers write the answers on the board and have students correct their own work.

Follow-Up Suggest that students work at home with a family member or a friend to use each word correctly in a sentence and spell it aloud.

Checkpoint

Write a spelling word for each clue.
Then use the Checkpoint Study Plan on page 224.

1. Something often worn with a blouse is a ___.
2. Another word for allow is ___.
3. The opposite of clean is ___.
4. Another word for sure is ___.
5. Two is to second as three is to ___.
6. The act of helping or assisting others is ___.
7. Another word for solid or hard is ___.
8. To fill a room with chairs, tables, and shelves is to ___.
9. Something without any mistakes or flaws is ___.
10. An apple is a kind of fruit, a chair is a piece of ___.
11. To be given money for working is to ___ a living.
12. It wasn't an accident, it was on ___.
13. Another word for a pleasing scent is ___.
14. Twelve comes before ___.
15. A kind of jewel is a ___.
16. The opposite of late is ___.
17. My diary is private and ___.
18. If you listened, you ___ the bell.
19. Education and instruction are part of ___.
20. This word comes from an old German word, *hurten*. *Hurten* meant to butt like a ram. The French borrowed this word. In Old French it meant to strike or knock. Then the English took the word. In Old English it meant to strike. Today its meaning has changed. It does not mean to strike or hit. But it tells what sometimes happens as a result of being struck or hit. Today, it means a wound or injury. Can you guess the word? ___

skirt
permit
dirty
certain
third
service
firm
furnish
perfect
furniture
earn
purpose
perfume
thirteen
pearl
early
personal
heard
learning

hurt

139

Objectives

- To write spelling words in response to clues: definitions, synonyms, antonyms, analogies, and context.
- To develop the critical thinking skills of making inferences and sequencing.
- To appreciate the diversity of sources of the English language and to understand that word meanings often change over time.

Spelling Strategy

If students misspell the vowel sound in heard, it may be helpful to point out to them that heard contains the words hear and ear.

Preparation The clues on this page are like crossword puzzle clues. Explain to students that the response to each clue is a spelling word. Use the following examples to illustrate the types of clues used:

Definition	Something without any mistakes or flaws is (*perfect*).
Synonym	Another word for sure is (*certain*).
Antonym	The opposite of clean is (*dirty*).
Analogy	An apple is a kind of fruit, a chair is a piece of (*furniture*).
Context	My diary is private and (*personal*).

The final clue explains how the meaning of hurt has changed over time.

The Page Have students complete page 139 using the words on page 138. When students have finished, have them read each clue and spell the answer aloud. Check each response twice: once for the correct answer and a second time for spelling accuracy.

Follow-Up Guide pupils in using the **Checkpoint Study Plan** on page 224 to take a self-test. Then have them use the plan for independent study.

Objectives

- To write words with /û/ in continuous text.
- To write each spelling word once.
- To integrate reading with spelling.

Use each list word once.

A Pearl of a Problem

Every time our family tells "remember when" stories, the story of Mom's missing ring is ___certain___ to come up. That afternoon Mom was getting ready to roast a chicken and bake a pumpkin pie. She put an apron on over her new ___skirt___, took off her beautiful ___pearl___ ring, and laid it on the kitchen table. Just then the doorbell rang, and our neighbor came in. She likes to ___earn___ extra money selling ___perfume___ and soap to her friends.

When the neighbor left, Mom started supper. I ___heard___ someone at the front door. It was the delivery man with a new piece of ___furniture___ that Mom and Dad had bought. I showed him where to put it and went upstairs to write in my ___personal___ diary. I have a ___firm___ rule: I don't ___permit___ anyone to read my diary but me!

A little while later my brother Jake came home with some friends from the school band. They began practicing. One boy was so bad that I began to count his mistakes. He made ___thirteen___ mistakes in one song. My ears began to ___hurt___. I complained to Mom, but she said, "They're only ___learning___, dear. And if you're finished with your diary, you can help in the kitchen."

140

Preparation Have students turn to pages 140 and 141. Let them look at the story and the pictures. Call their attention to the word list. Have the students say the words. Then explain that each spelling word belongs in one of the blanks in the story.

Write the title "A Pearl of a Problem" on the board. Then tell students that in this story a pearl ring is missing.

The Pages Have students complete pages 140 and 141 independently by silently reading the story and writing the missing spelling words. Or you may read the story aloud, supplying the missing words as students follow along in their texts; then have the students complete the pages on their own.

When students have finished, you may wish to discuss the story. Ask a student to summarize the plot of the story. When did they discover that the ring was missing? (*while the narrator was washing the dishes*) Why was the ring valuable? (*It was a pearl ring, and Dad had given it to Mom on their anniversary.*)

It was after I started washing the ___dirty___ dishes that Mom noticed her ring was gone. We looked on the table, on the floor, in the sink, and everywhere. Mom was really upset. Dad had given her the ring for their anniversary. She kept saying, "I'm sure no one took it on ___purpose___. Someone must be playing a joke."

We had dinner ___early___ that night. I dished out the chicken and dressing. Jake laughed and said, "Now that's what I call ___service___."

Then we all tried to solve the mystery. But no one could ___furnish___ any clues. We couldn't believe that one of the people there that day took the ring.

We finished dinner, and Mom brought in dessert. The pumpkin pie was ___perfect___. I had eaten all my lima beans to make sure that I'd be allowed a big slice. Mom gave the first piece to me and the second to my brother. She gave the ___third___ piece to Dad. We all started eating. Then Dad yelled, "Ouch!" He put his hand to his mouth and out came the pearl ring. We all cheered. And Dad got another piece of pie.

certain
service
perfect
permit
perfume
personal
dirty
thirteen
firm
skirt
third
earn
early
learning
heard
pearl
purpose
furnish
hurt
furniture

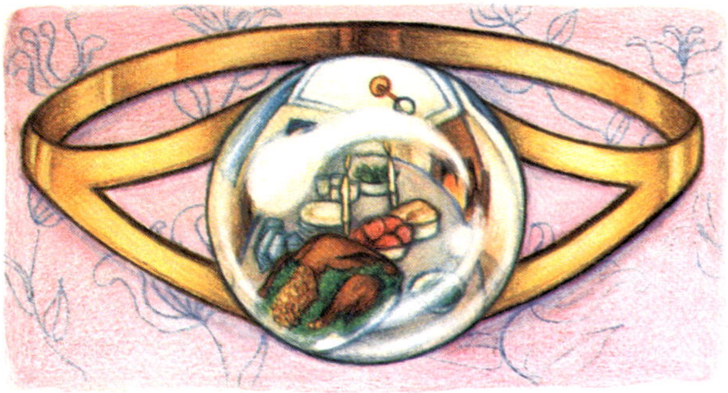

141

Have a volunteer read each paragraph in the story, supplying each missing spelling word and spelling it aloud. Have other volunteers write the answers on the board and have students correct their own work. Check students' responses for the accurate spelling of each answer.

Follow-Up Have students use each of the spelling words they missed in an original sentence that relates to the story.

As an additional follow-up activity, you may wish to have four students act out "A Pearl of a Problem" for the class—one child reading the narrator's part, one reading Mom's part, one reading Jake's part, and one reading Dad's part. When each student comes to a spelling word, have her or him spell the word aloud and then continue reading.

Enrichment

If you want to use the blackline activity masters for enrichment and additional practice, assign Lesson 26 activities at this time.

Maintenance and Review

OBJECTIVE

- To review words with /ô/ spelled: o, a, ou, oa.

ACTIVITIES

If you want to use the blackline activity masters for maintenance and review, assign Lesson 25 activities at this time.

You can also use the activity below to review Lesson 25 with students:

Write the following words on the board. Have students change one letter in each to form a word from Lesson 25. (Answers are in parentheses.)

soar *(roar)*
count *(court)*
barn *(warn)*
regard *(reward)*
scorn *(score)*
adorn *(adore)*
short *(shore)*
tire *(tore)*
wire *(wore)*
expert *(export)*

Objectives

- To relate spelling to another language skill.
- To review and identify adjectives.
- To write spelling words in the context of sentences.
- To practice proofreading.
- To use the **Spelling Dictionary**.

Adjectives

An adjective describes a noun or pronoun by telling what kind, how many, or which one.

A colorful bird was singing in the old tree.
A big, fat cat scared it away.

★ Write each sentence below, correcting each misspelled word. Then underline the adjectives.

1. I'm sertain today will be a beautiful, cool day.
I'm certain today will be a beautiful, cool day.

2. I herd there is a fantastic movie downtown.
I heard there is a fantastic movie downtown.

3. The earyl bird catches the worm.
The early bird catches the worm.

4. My perpus is to get a good grade on my report.
My purpose is to get a good grade on my report.

5. We made new ferniture for the tree house.
We made new furniture for the tree house.

6. I'd like to fernish my dark room with large, bright posters.
I'd like to furnish my dark room with large, bright posters.

7. I hert my foot when I dropped the heavy suitcase.
I hurt my foot when I dropped the heavy suitcase.

8. Jennifer wants a perl necklace for her birthday.
Jennifer wants a pearl necklace for her birthday.

9. That is the purfect costume for the wicked king in the play.
That is the perfect costume for the wicked king in the play.

10. Karen wore a wool skert.
Karen wore a wool skirt.

Preparation Have students read the title of page 142. Ask what an adjective is. (*a word that describes a noun or a pronoun*) Write this word on the board:

pearl

Have it identified as a noun. Have students name words that describe pearl. (*white*, *round*, *shiny*, *beautiful*) Ask what kind of word all these descriptive words are. (*adjective*) Point out that pearl can also be used as an adjective, as in pearl necklace.

The Page Have students do page 142. Then have volunteers write the answers on the board and review them orally.

Follow-Up Have students write each spelling word on a card (or small piece of paper), arrange the cards in alphabetical order, and underline the words that are adjectives. Have them look up the words in the **Spelling Dictionary** to check their work.

WORDS AT WORK

Challenge Yourself

conserve absurd earthenware virtual

Use your Spelling Dictionary to answer these questions. Then write sentences showing that you understand the meaning of each Challenge Word.

1. Do taking short showers and turning off the water while you brush your teeth help to conserve our water?
2. Would it be absurd to ride a bicycle while wearing ice skates or flippers on your feet?
3. Are cars and airplanes made out of earthenware?
4. Is a virtual fact a completely true fact?

Write to the Point

Do your family members like to retell any "remember when" stories about something funny or interesting that happened in the family? Put one of these stories into writing. Try to show your reader what made the story worth remembering. Use spelling words from this lesson in your story.

Challenge Use one or more of the Challenge Words in your story.

Proofreading

Use the proofreading marks to show the errors in the paragraph below. Write the five misspelled words correctly in the blanks.

(oval)	word is misspelled
≡	letter should be capitalized
! ^	exclamation point is missing

When Kate was thirteen, she did extra chores around the house to earn money. Her perpose was to buy grandma Rita a surtain kind of pirfume. The day she bought it, her baby brother spilled the whole bottle on her skurt. Good grief What a stink

1. thirteen
2. purpose
3. certain
4. perfume
5. skirt

143

Objectives

- To extend the vowel spellings presented in Lesson 26 to the Challenge Words.
- To use context and the **Spelling Dictionary** to enlarge students' vocabulary.
- To apply the vowel spellings presented in Lesson 26 in a writing activity.
- To practice proofreading for spelling, punctuation, and capitalization.

Dictation Sentences

1. You might hurt your back moving furniture.
2. It is still early, so I will wash these dirty dishes.
3. This school does not permit girls to wear perfume.
4. My mother's pearl ring was a personal gift from her father when she was thirteen.
5. I must earn a certain amount of money so that I can furnish my room.
6. What is the purpose of learning to sing?
7. I just heard that my pie came in third in the contest!
8. The service here is very slow.
9. The size nine skirt will be perfect.
10. She has a firm grip.

Challenge Yourself Answers

1. yes
2. yes
3. no
4. no

Students' sentences will vary.

Test Review these four ways to spell /û/: e as in certain; i as in dirty; ea as in earn; u as in hurt. Test words with /û/. Use one of these testing methods: (1) Say the word; read the sample sentence from page 138; say the word; have students write it. (2) Read each dictation sentence above; have students write the sentence. Correct the test with students.

Challenge Yourself The optional Challenge Words may be assigned to the entire class or limited to those students who do well on the test. Have students note the vowel spellings in the Challenge Words. Responses to this activity should be completed on separate paper. Answers to the questions are provided above.

Write to the Point Help students recall the selection "A Pearl of a Problem" on pages 140 and 141; then assign the "remember when" story. Encourage students to include vivid details about the people and events in order to bring the story to life for the reader. This activity should be completed on separate paper.

Proofreading The proofreading practice includes misspellings of words from this lesson as well as a capitalization error and punctuation errors.

LESSON 27

Objectives

- To hear and say words with /â/ and /ä/.
- To write words with /â/ and /ä/ with attention to letter sequence and sound/symbol relationships.
- To write each spelling word at least once.
- To recognize that /â/ may be spelled a.
- To recognize that /ä/ may be spelled a.

Sample Sentences

1. I wasn't aware that I was standing on your foot.
2. Let's prepare the soil for planting.
3. The bus fare has gone up to 60 cents.
4. It's not polite to stare at people.
5. Look carefully for the answer.
6. The sun burned Roscoe's bare shoulders.
7. I declare this meeting open for business.
8. You can often save money if you compare prices.
9. First, draw a square four inches long on each side.
10. Each student must share a book.
11. The sergeant will discharge the soldiers when they're done.
12. At harvest time we bring in the crops.
13. When the fire alarm rang, everyone left.
14. The South Pole is farther from here than the North Pole.
15. Boris and Lucy played a game of marbles.
16. The Fosters live in an apartment building.
17. David is in charge of getting the food.
18. I'm so hungry I feel like I will starve.
19. I'll write you a note in the margin of the paper.
20. The plane will depart in half an hour.

Note

- The sample sentences may be used for pretesting.
- Words are grouped according to the spelling of /â/ and the spelling of /ä/.

Lesson 27 Words with /â/ and /ä/

Listen for /â/ or /ä/ in each word.

aware
prepare
fare
stare
carefully
bare
declare
compare
square
share

discharge
harvest
alarm
farther
marbles
apartment
charge
starve
margin
depart

1. Which word begins with the letters ch? charge
2. Which word begins with the letters sh? share
3. Write the two words that begin with the letter f. fare farther
4. Write the three words that begin with the letter d. declare discharge depart
5. Which three words begin with a vowel? Circle the word that has a suffix. aware alarm (apartment)
6. Write two words that begin with the letters st and one that ends with st. stare starve harvest
7. Which word begins with /skw/? square
8. Write the two words that begin with /k/. carefully compare
9. Which word begins with the letters pre? prepare
10. Which word is pronounced exactly like bear? bare
11. Which word is pronounced exactly like fair? fare
12. Write the three words in which you hear /j/ but don't see the letter j. discharge charge margin
13. Which word ends with /z/? marbles

144

Preparation

Have students read aloud the title of the lesson on page 144. Write /â/ and /ä/ on the board. Have students say /â/ as in care and /ä/ as in father. Read each spelling word aloud. Have students repeat and then spell each word aloud.

Ask students to name the base words in carefully (*care*) and discharge (*charge*). Then have students identify the spelling of /â/ and of /ä/ in the groups of words in the list. (See **Note**.)

Read the sample sentences. Have students point to each spelling word as you read the sentence for it.

The Page

Have students complete page 144. Have volunteers write the answers on the board and have students correct their own work.

Follow-Up

Suggest that students write each word in two colors, using the same color for every other letter. Double letters should be written in the same color.

Checkpoint

Write a spelling word for each clue.
Then use the Checkpoint Study Plan on page 224.

1. The opposite of arrive is ___.
2. With great care means ___.
3. A shape with four equal sides is a ___.
4. To warn people, sound the ___.
5. To let go or fire is to ___.
6. The price of a bus ride is the ___.
7. I live in a house, she lives in an ___.
8. To get ready is to ___.
9. To show how things are alike is to ___.
10. The person who doesn't eat will ___.
11. If you know about something then you are ___ of it.
12. Little glass balls are ___.
13. To or at a greater distance is ___.
14. In the winter most trees are ___.
15. What was the ___ for fixing the bicycle?
16. A portion or a part of is a ___.
17. The border of a page is the ___.
18. To announce is to ___.
19. To look steadily for a long time is to ___.

20. Have you ever heard of a harrow? A harrow is a farm tool. It is used to break up lumps of earth. The harrow shares a common word history with our mystery word. They both come from the Viking word *harfr.* The German word for autumn, *herbst,* is also related to *harfr.* What do a harrow and autumn have in common with our mystery word? The mystery word names the act of gathering crops. A harrow is used to plow. Autumn is the time when crops are gathered. Can you guess the mystery word? ___

depart
carefully
square
alarm
discharge
fare
apartment
prepare
compare
starve
aware
marbles
farther
bare
charge
share
margin
declare
stare

harvest

145

Objectives

- To write spelling words in response to clues: definitions, antonyms, and context.
- To develop the critical thinking skills of making inferences and predicting outcomes.
- To appreciate the diversity of sources of the English language and to understand that a single word may be the origin of many newer words.

Spelling Strategy

You may want to alert students to the words in Lesson 27 that have familiar homophones: fare (fair), bare (bear), and stare (stair). Write the homophone pairs on the board and use each word in a sentence. Then have students write their own sentences using each word. Have them exchange papers with a partner and check each other's spelling and use of the words.

Preparation The clues on this page are like crossword puzzle clues. Explain to students that the response to each clue is a spelling word. Use the following examples to illustrate the types of clues used:

Definition	To look steadily for a long time is to (*stare*).
Antonym	The opposite of arrive is (*depart*).
Context	The person who doesn't eat will (*starve*).

The final clue gives the Viking and German origins of harvest.

The Page Have students complete page 145 using the words on page 144. When students have finished, have them read each clue and spell the answer aloud. Check each response twice: once for the correct answer and a second time for spelling accuracy.

Follow-Up Guide pupils in using the **Checkpoint Study Plan** on page 224 to take a self-test. Then have them use the plan for independent study.

Objectives

- To write words with /â/ and /ä/ in continuous text.
- To write each spelling word once.
- To integrate reading with spelling.

Note

Point out the use of the word starve in the story as a figure of speech meaning become very hungry.

Use each list word once.

THE BROADWAY LIMITED

"All aboard for the Broadway Limited to Chicago!"

Every day at 2:45 P.M., the conductor in New York's Penn Station gives the final call. The train to Chicago is about to leave.

You've paid your ___fare___. You check your baggage ___carefully___ to make sure you haven't forgotten anything. Then you get on board, and you ___prepare___ yourself for the 18-hour trip ahead. You unpack the snacks you've brought so you won't ___starve___ before dinner. You've even brought enough to ___share___ with the other passengers. And you set your ___alarm___ clock so you can wake up early tomorrow morning. The conductor comes by and punches holes in the ___margin___ of your ticket. As she moves on, she asks some children not to play with their ___marbles___ in the aisle. Then you settle back in your seat without a care in the world. (There's an extra ___charge___ for a bed, so you've taken a coach seat.)

As you ___depart___ from New York, you ride in a tunnel under the Hudson River. When you come out in New Jersey, you can see New York's offices and the tall ___apartment___ buildings. As the train rolls ___farther___ away from New York, factories give

146

Preparation

Have students turn to pages 146 and 147. Let them look at the story and the pictures. Call their attention to the word list. Have the students say the words. Then explain that each spelling word belongs in one of the blanks in the story.

Write the title "The Broadway Limited" on the board. Then ask if any students have taken a long trip on a train. If so, ask them what it was like, where they went, and what they liked and didn't like. Tell students that in the last century, before cars and airplanes were invented, trains were the most popular and best form of transportation.

The Pages

Have students complete pages 146 and 147 independently by silently reading the story and writing the missing spelling words. Or you may read the story aloud, supplying the missing words as students follow along in their texts; then have the students complete the pages on their own.

When students have finished, you may wish to discuss the story. Ask if this selection is fiction or nonfiction. (*nonfiction*) On a map of the United States, show students the train's route from New York to Chicago. If your students are familiar with any of the places along the way, have them tell what they are like.

way to hills and woods. In the winter, the trees will look cold and ____bare____. At first you ____stare____ at the scenery and ____compare____ the different areas of New Jersey and Pennsylvania. You become ____aware____ of hills and flatlands, farms and cities. In some cities, the train stops to take on and ____discharge____ passengers and freight.

As you go farther west into Ohio, you see lots of farms. Each field looks like a ____square____ in a giant patchwork quilt. If it's ____harvest____ time, you can watch as big machines cut the crops.

By this time, it's dark, and soon you fall asleep as the train speeds west through Ohio and Indiana. You wake up early, and you hear the conductor ____declare____ that the next stop is Gary, Indiana. Soon you can see the big steel-manufacturing town. By this time, you're almost in Chicago. And at 9:00 A.M. you arrive. You've traveled more than 700 miles in 18 hours, and you've seen a big piece of the United States.

aware
prepare
fare
stare
carefully
bare
declare
compare
square
share
discharge
harvest
alarm
farther
marbles
apartment
charge
starve
margin
depart

Ask how going by train is different from going by airplane. (*The train takes longer; you can see the countryside from a train.*) Ask students which form of transportation they would prefer and why. (*Answers will vary.*)

Have a volunteer read each paragraph in the story, supplying each missing spelling word and spelling it aloud. Have other volunteers write the answers on the board and have students correct their own work. Check students' responses for the accurate spelling of each answer.

Follow-Up

Have students use each of the spelling words they missed in an original sentence that relates to the story.

As an additional follow-up activity, you may wish to have students illustrate their favorite scene in the story. Tell them to copy the sentence from the story that best describes the action in their picture.

Enrichment

If you want to use the blackline activity masters for enrichment and additional practice, assign Lesson 27 activities at this time.

Maintenance and Review

OBJECTIVE

- To review words with /û/ spelled: e, i, ea, u.

ACTIVITIES

If you want to use the blackline activity masters for maintenance and review, assign Lesson 26 activities at this time.

You can also use the activity below to review Lesson 26 with students.

Write the following words on the board. Have students refer to the Lesson 26 word list and write the word that is an antonym for each word below. (Answers are in parentheses.)

late	(*early*)
unsure	(*certain*)
forbid	(*permit*)
soft	(*firm*)
clean	(*dirty*)
imperfect	(*perfect*)
impersonal	(*personal*)
teaching	(*learning*)

Objectives

- To relate spelling to another language skill.
- To review capitalization in a letter.
- To write spelling words in the context of a letter.

Capitals

Follow all the rules for capitalizing when you write a friendly letter. In addition, follow these rules for the heading, greeting, and closing.

HEADING: Capitalize the month of the year.
GREETING: Capitalize dear and the person's name.
CLOSING: Capitalize the first word of the closing.

Greeting		Heading / Closing
	April 5, 199__	Heading
Greeting	*Dear Sean,*	
	How would you like to go on vacation with me? Mother said I could ask you to come along on our Florida trip.	
	Give the idea some thought and call me next week.	
	Your pal,	Closing
	Paul	

★ Rewrite the friendly letter below, filling the blanks with these spelling words. Put capital letters where necessary.

carefully apartment charge square aware
starve compare bare share declare

september 14, 199__ (S)

dear cathy, (D C)

i was never __aware__ *of how expensive* __apartment__ *living can be! my cupboards are so* __bare__, *i am sure to* __starve__ *before the week is done. perhaps i should* __declare__ *myself poor and return home. i'll have to consider my choices* __carefully__.

my best bet is to find someone to help __share__ *my rent. i could* __charge__ *her half of the monthly expenses. and, if i can find a roommate whose cooking doesn't* __compare__ *with mine, i'm sure to get a* __square__ *meal!*

write soon. (W)

your big sister, (Y)
jeannie (J)

148

Preparation Have students read the title of page 148. Review that when we write a friendly letter, we always capitalize the first letter of certain words.

Ask students if they know where these words are found in a letter. If necessary, remind them that we capitalize dear and the person's name. Have a volunteer write this greeting on the board:

Dear Fay,

Remind students that we also start the first word of the closing with a capital. Have a volunteer write this closing on the board:

With love,

Finally, review that the name of the month in the heading begins with a capital letter. Have a student write today's date on the board.

The Page Have students do page 148. Then have volunteers write the answers on the board and review them orally.

Follow-Up Have students write an answer to either letter on page 148. Have them use at least six spelling words and remind them to capitalize correctly.

WORDS AT WORK

Challenge Yourself

bearable **precarious** **pecan** **sparse**

Write what you think each underlined Challenge Word means. Check your Spelling Dictionary to see if you were right. Then write sentences showing that you understand the meaning of each Challenge Word.

1. The aspirin didn't stop the pain, but it made it more bearable.
2. Standing at the top of the wobbly ladder, he was in a precarious position.
3. A pecan looks something like a walnut but with a smooth shell.
4. The grass that used to cover the yard like a thick carpet now grows in sparse patches.

Write to the Point

Think about a trip you have taken and write a description of the different sights you saw along the way. You may describe things you saw on a short trip, such as a bus ride to school or to someone's house. Or you might describe sights you saw on a longer trip to another city, state, or country. Use spelling words from this lesson in your description.

Challenge Use one or more of the Challenge Words in your description.

Proofreading

Use the proofreading marks to show the errors in the paragraph below. Write the five misspelled words correctly in the blanks.

(oval)	word is misspelled
(mark)	take out word
?‸	question mark is missing

Have you ~~have~~ been to the desert? The (farthur) we traveled, the more (awair) I became of its beauty. It is (bear) of trees, but nothing can (compair) to it. I took some pictures to share with ~~with~~ you. Sunday we (deppart) for home.

1. farther
2. aware
3. bare
4. compare
5. depart

149

Objectives

- To extend the vowel spellings presented in Lesson 27 to the Challenge Words.
- To use context and the **Spelling Dictionary** to enlarge students' vocabulary.
- To apply the vowel spellings presented in Lesson 27 in a writing activity.
- To practice proofreading for spelling, punctuation, and extra words.

Dictation Sentences

1. The apartment was bare when they moved out.
2. Are you aware that your alarm clock is going off?
3. You must prepare that report carefully so that I can write notes in the margin.
4. The children played with marbles.
5. The harvest is so poor that people may starve unless they share their food.
6. Don't stare at people.
7. The farther you travel, the more the fare is.
8. The charge for your haircut is cheap if you compare it to others.
9. The bus will depart from gate ten.
10. The army will discharge him if the doctors declare that he is not well.
11. The picture was square.

Challenge Yourself Answers

Possible definitions:

1. tolerable
2. dangerous
3. nut
4. thin; few and far apart

Students' sentences will vary.

Test Review this way to spell /â/: a as in share. Then review this way to spell /ä/: a as in charge. Test words with /â/ and /ä/. Use one of these testing methods: (1) Say the word; read the sample sentence from page 144; say the word; have students write it. (2) Read each dictation sentence above; have students write the sentence. Correct the test with students.

Challenge Yourself The optional Challenge Words may be assigned to the entire class or limited to those students who do well on the test. Have students note the vowel spellings in the Challenge Words, especially the following new spelling: ea as in bearable. Responses to this activity should be completed on separate paper. Answers to the questions are provided above.

Write to the Point Help students recall the selection "The Broadway Limited" on pages 146 and 147; then assign the description. Encourage students to use vivid descriptive words to describe the sights they encountered on their trips. This activity should be completed on separate paper.

Proofreading The proofreading practice includes misspellings of words from this lesson as well as a punctuation error and extra words.

LESSON 28

Objectives

- To hear and say compound words.
- To write compound words with attention to letter sequence and sound/symbol relationships.
- To write each spelling word at least once.

Sample Sentences

1. This hallway leads to the kitchen.
2. Betty's nose looks as red as a strawberry.
3. We got soaked in the thunderstorm.
4. Marie is having a party for her birthday.
5. Arnold ate a cheeseburger for lunch.
6. Last night I had a nightmare.
7. Please stay calm and don't get upset.
8. Felicity did a somersault and then a cartwheel.
9. Shine the flashlight into this corner so we can see.
10. Ella needs a new looseleaf notebook.
11. The teacher wrote his name on the chalkboard.
12. Sparky has a pet grasshopper.
13. Lester began to pack his suitcase.
14. When the snake escaped, there was quite an uproar.
15. Mary does her homework after dinner.
16. There's a blueberry patch behind the barn.
17. I like the smell of sawdust in the carpenter's shop.
18. Peter likes to eat cereal for breakfast.
19. Our club is going on a hike next weekend.
20. Rona is learning to sail a sailboat.

Note

The sample sentences may be used for pretesting.

Lesson 28 Compound Words

Say each word.

hallway
strawberry
thunderstorm
birthday
cheeseburger
nightmare
upset
cartwheel
flashlight
notebook
chalkboard
grasshopper
suitcase
uproar
homework
blueberry
sawdust
breakfast
weekend
sailboat

1. Write the three words that begin with the letter b.
   birthday blueberry
   breakfast
2. Write the four words that begin with the letter s.
   strawberry suitcase
   sawdust sailboat
3. Which word begins with the letters th?
   thunderstorm
4. Write the two words that begin with the letters ch.
   cheeseburger chalkboard
5. Write one word that begins with /k/ and two that end with /k/. Circle the letters that spell /k/.
   cartwheel notebook
   homework
6. Which word begins with the letter w? weekend
7. Which two words begin with the letter n?
   nightmare notebook
8. Which word begins and ends like flight? flashlight
9. Which two words end with the ay spelling of /ā/?
   hallway birthday
10. In which two words do you hear /o͞o/? Circle the letters that spell /o͞o/. suitcase blueberry
11. Which word has two pairs of double consonants?
    grasshopper
12. Write the two compound words made with each of these words: berry, up.
    strawberry blueberry
    upset uproar

150

Preparation Have students read aloud the title of the lesson on page 150. Ask what compound words are. (*words that are made up of two or more words*) Read each spelling word aloud. Have students repeat and then spell each word aloud.

Have students identify the two words in each compound word. Remind students that the meaning of a compound word does not always come from the meaning of each word in the compound word, as in strawberry. Ask them to identify the double letters in hallway, strawberry, cheeseburger, cartwheel, notebook, grasshopper, blueberry, and weekend.

Read the sample sentences. Have students point to each spelling word as you read the sentence for it.

The Page Have students complete page 150. Have volunteers write the answers on the board and have students correct their own work.

Follow-Up Suggest that students write all the words on cards (or small pieces of paper). Have them use these flash cards to study the words.

Checkpoint

Write a spelling word for each clue.
Then use the Checkpoint Study Plan on page 224.

1. A bad dream is a ____. — nightmare
2. To flip over on your hands is to do a ____. — cartwheel
3. To overturn or tip over is to ____. — upset
4. Saturday and Sunday make up the ____. — weekend
5. Pack your clothes into your ____. — suitcase
6. Noisy excitement and confusion make an ____. — uproar
7. A kind of insect is a ____. — grasshopper
8. Heavy rain with thunder and lightning is a ____. — thunderstorm
9. In class you need a pencil and a ____. — notebook
10. When you celebrate your age, it is your ____. — birthday
11. The morning meal is ____. — breakfast
12. From sawed wood comes ____. — sawdust
13. Pink ice cream may be ____. — strawberry
14. A boat moved by wind is a ____. — sailboat
15. Schoolwork done at home is ____. — homework
16. A corridor is a ____. — hallway
17. A fruit that's blue is a ____. — blueberry
18. A slate is a ____. — chalkboard
19. A hamburger with melted cheese is a ____. — cheeseburger

20. The English use different words from Americans for some things. For instance, what we call the hood of a car, the English call a bonnet. What we call an elevator, the English call a lift. The English word torch names a small electric light that we call by a very different name. This name is a compound with the word light. Can you guess it? ____ — flashlight

151

Objectives

- To write spelling words in response to clues: definitions and context.
- To develop the critical thinking skills of making inferences and drawing conclusions.
- To understand that two English-speaking cultures may have different words for the same thing.

Spelling Strategy

To help students remember the spelling of breakfast, remind them that the word fast means a period of time in which no food is eaten. Point out to students that when people eat their first meal of the morning, they are breaking their overnight fast. Thus, that meal is called breakfast.

Preparation The clues on this page are like crossword puzzle clues. Explain to students that the response to each clue is a spelling word. Use the following examples to illustrate the types of clues used:

Definition — The morning meal is (*breakfast*).
Context — Pack your clothes into your (*suitcase*).

The final clue explains that Americans and English people often use different words for the same thing and gives an example, flashlight.

The Page Have students complete page 151 using the words on page 150. When students have finished, have them read each clue and spell the answer aloud. Check each response twice: once for the correct answer and a second time for spelling accuracy.

Follow-Up Guide pupils in using the **Checkpoint Study Plan** on page 224 to take a self-test. Then have them use the plan for independent study.

Objectives

- To write compound words in continuous text.
- To write each spelling word once.
- To integrate reading with spelling.

Use each list word once.

STORMY WEATHER

My sister Bev is a singer. She sings in small restaurants and hopes someone will discover her. Last weekend she almost became a star, but . . .

Bev was singing at the Dew Drop Inn. The Dew Drop is a restaurant near the water. It has a small dock where you can leave your sailboat. Lots of boaters stop at the Dew Drop Inn for a bite to eat. You can get breakfast, lunch, or dinner. They have great pancakes and strawberry shortcake. You can get a plain hamburger or a cheeseburger made with cheddar cheese. Everything they serve is listed on a dusty chalkboard. At night they have live musical entertainment.

The owner had just introduced Bev to the audience when I saw a well-dressed man walk in the front door. I watched him walk down the hallway into the room. He stood in the back and listened to Bev for a few minutes. Then he took a spiral notebook out of his suitcase and began to take notes. I realized he was a talent scout! Bev must have sensed something special was happening. She really sang her heart out. My sister had done her homework. All that practicing was really paying off. I'd never heard her sound better.

Bev had just begun to sing "You Are My Sunshine" when there was a flash of lightning. A terrible, loud

152

Preparation Have students turn to pages 152 and 153. Let them look at the story and the picture. Call their attention to the word list. Have the students say the words. Then explain that each spelling word belongs in one of the blanks in the story.

Write the title "Stormy Weather" on the board. Then ask the students what they think the story is about. (*a storm*) Ask volunteers to tell what makes a storm. (*rain, wind, thunder, lightning*) Ask what kinds of things happen in a storm. (*trees fall, streets flood, lights go out*) Tell the students this story is about another kind of trouble caused by a storm.

The Pages Have students complete pages 152 and 153 independently by silently reading the story and writing the missing spelling words. Or you may read the story aloud, supplying the missing words as students follow along in their texts; then have the students complete the pages on their own.

When students have finished, you may wish to discuss the story. Ask students why they think the talent scout was so angry. (*He was embarrassed.*) Ask students how many of them would have kept singing when the lights went out. Ask them if they think Bev was right to change songs the next night. (*Answers will vary.*)

thunderstorm was under way. Within a few seconds the lights went out. Bev just kept singing, "You are my sunshine, my only sunshine . . ." Everyone was laughing. There was quite an uproar. The talent scout tried to move closer to the stage to hear Bev. In the dark, he bumped into a chair and slipped in the sawdust that covered the floor. Someone had just lit a flashlight and you could see the man's long legs go out from under him. He looked like a grasshopper doing a cartwheel. The man was still on the floor when the lights went on. The audience couldn't stop laughing.

I went over to Bev to tell her about the scout (Bev had wisely stopped singing by this time). She ran over to help the scout and to try to talk to him. The man said, "This has been a nightmare. I want to forget this place, forget you, and forget every song with the word 'sunshine.'" He was out the door before Bev could reply.

As you can imagine, Bev was very upset. But my sister's a trooper. The next night she was back on stage, even though she had changed her act. Her best number was "Stormy Weather"!

hallway
strawberry
thunderstorm
birthday
cheeseburger
nightmare
upset
cartwheel
flashlight
notebook
chalkboard
grasshopper
suitcase
uproar
homework
blueberry
sawdust
breakfast
weekend
sailboat

Have a volunteer read the story, supplying each missing spelling word and spelling it aloud. Have other volunteers write the answers on the board and have students correct their own work. Check students' responses for the accurate spelling of each answer.

Follow-Up

Have students use each of the spelling words they missed in an original sentence that relates to the story.

As an additional follow-up activity, you may wish to have one student read "Stormy Weather" for the class. When the student comes to a spelling word, have him or her stop and let the class spell the word aloud.

Enrichment

If you want to use the blackline activity masters for enrichment and additional practice, assign Lesson 28 activities at this time.

Maintenance and Review

OBJECTIVES

- To review words with /â/ spelled: a.
- To review words with /â/ spelled: a.

ACTIVITIES

If you want to use the blackline activity masters for maintenance and review, assign Lesson 27 activities at this time.

You can also use the activity below to review Lesson 27 with the students:

Write the following words on the board. Have students write the word from Lesson 27 that is a synonym for each word. (Answers are in parentheses.)

border	(*margin*)
naked	(*bare*)
release	(*discharge*)
arrange	(*prepare*)
leave	(*depart*)
say	(*declare*)
look	(*stare*)
fee	(*charge*)

Objectives

- To relate spelling words to a dictionary skill.
- To locate correct spellings of words in the **Spelling Dictionary**.
- To write spelling words in the context of sentences.

Finding Correct Spellings

Sometimes a dictionary is used to find the meaning of a word or the proper pronunciation. Other times, it is used to check on the spelling of a word.

> **sail·boat** | sāl′bōt′ | *n.* A boat that travels by wind blowing against its sails.

saleboat? sialboat? sailboat?

★ Kent wants to write a letter to a friend. He is not sure how to spell some words, so he has written three choices for them. Write the sentences with the correct spelling. Check your answers in the Spelling Dictionary, and write the page number for each word.

1. For a (berthday, burthday, birthday) present, I was given a trip.
   For a birthday present, I was given a trip. 198
2. When I found out, I could have turned a (kartwhel, cartwheel, cart wheel).
   When I found out, I could have turned a cartwheel. 200
3. I was to go away for the (weakend, wekend, weekend) with my friends.
   I was to go away for the weekend with my friends. 222
4. I can't say that anyone was (upset, upsit, up set) with the idea!
   I can't say that anyone was upset with the idea! 221
5. As a matter of fact, the prospect of no (hoamwork, homework, homeworc) didn't worry me at all! As a matter of fact, the prospect of no homework didn't worry me at all! 207
6. Once I packed my (suitcase, sootcase, sootkase), I couldn't wait.
   Once I packed my suitcase, I couldn't wait. 218
7. First Dad insisted that I have (brakefast, brecfast, breakfast).
   First Dad insisted that I have breakfast. 199
8. I finished my (blewberry, blueberry, bluberry) muffin and was on my way at last! I finished my blueberry muffin and was on my way at last! 198

154

Preparation Have students read the title of page 154. Ask them to name different reasons for looking up a word in a dictionary. (*to find the word's meaning, pronunciation, or spelling*) Tell students that a dictionary is a good place to find the correct spelling of a word. Sometimes you have to look in several places to find the spelling of a word. Say the word census, but do not write it on the board. Then ask under what two letters students might look to find the spelling of census. (*under c or s*) Point out that if you know the first letter of a word, it is easy to find it in the dictionary.

The Page Have students do page 154. Then have volunteers write the answers on the board and review them orally.

Follow-Up Dictate the spelling words to students or have students dictate them to each other. Students should write each word and check their spellings by looking up each word in the **Spelling Dictionary**.

WORDS AT WORK

Challenge Yourself

sweatshirt **tablespoon** **roommate** **handmade**

Use your Spelling Dictionary to answer these questions. Then write sentences showing that you understand the meaning of each Challenge Word.

1. What is one kind of measuring tool that you can find in most people's kitchen?
2. What piece of clothing might keep you warm on a chilly day?
3. What word might describe a sweater knitted by a person at home?
4. What person might you share a room with?

Write to the Point

A restaurant review is an article that tells what the writer likes and dislikes about a restaurant. Write your own review of a real or an imaginary restaurant. Tell what you liked and disliked about the food and how it was served. Use spelling words from this lesson in your review.

Challenge Use one or more of the Challenge Words in your review.

Proofreading

Use the proofreading marks to show the errors in the paragraph below. Write the five misspelled words correctly in the blanks.

⬭	word is misspelled
≡	letter should be capitalized
^	word is missing

The day I turned ten, Mom took me out ^for (brekkfast) at the Dew Drop Inn. What a (nightmair!) The (bluberry) pancakes were as dry as (saudust,) and the (strawbury) jam tasted like glue. Then all the waiters came out and sang "Happy b≡irthday" ^to me.

1. breakfast
2. nightmare
3. blueberry
4. sawdust
5. strawberry

155

Objectives

- To extend students' knowledge of compound words through the Challenge Words.
- To use clues and the **Spelling Dictionary** to enlarge students' vocabulary.
- To apply the compound words presented in Lesson 28 in a writing activity.
- To practice proofreading for spelling, capitalization, and missing words.

Dictation Sentences

1. I baked a blueberry pie for your birthday.
2. I made strawberry pancakes for breakfast.
3. I am upset because I have a lot of homework to do this weekend.
4. The animals were in an uproar because of the thunderstorm.
5. Copy the problems on the chalkboard into your notebook.
6. This cheeseburger tastes like sawdust.
7. Can you do a cartwheel?
8. I left my suitcase in the hallway back at the hotel.
9. The grasshopper jumped when we turned a flashlight on it.
10. I had a nightmare that I was on a sailboat that was sinking.

Challenge Yourself Answers

1. tablespoon
2. sweatshirt
3. handmade
4. roommate

Students' sentences will vary.

Test Review and test compound words. Use one of these testing methods: (1) Say the word; read the sample sentence from page 150; say the word; have students write it. (2) Read each dictation sentence above; have students write the sentence. Correct the test with students.

Challenge Yourself The optional Challenge Words may be assigned to the entire class or limited to those students who do well on the test. You may wish to have students work in pairs. Responses to this activity should be completed on separate paper. Answers to the questions are provided above.

Write to the Point Help students recall the selection "Stormy Weather" on pages 152 and 153; then assign the restaurant review. Discuss with students other aspects that a restaurant reviewer might comment on besides the food. Explain to them what the terms *service* and *atmosphere* mean when referring to a restaurant. This activity should be completed on separate paper.

Proofreading The proofreading practice includes misspellings of words from this lesson as well as a capitalization error and missing words.

LESSON 29

Objectives

- To hear and say space words.
- To write space words with attention to letter sequence and sound/symbol relationships.
- To write each spelling word once.

Sample Sentences

1. One revolution of the earth around the sun is one year.
2. Stars and planets are celestial bodies.
3. The sun is the center of the solar system.
4. The study of the stars and planets is astronomy.
5. The tail of a comet is made of gas.
6. The earth is always in motion.
7. The name of our galaxy is the Milky Way.
8. The earth twirls around on its axis.
9. Chunks of rock that fall from the sky are meteors.
10. No one knows for sure how big the universe is.
11. A light-year is the distance light goes in one year.
12. The earth makes one rotation every day.
13. The moon covers the sun in a solar eclipse.
14. You can see Neptune through a telescope.
15. The asteroids may once have been a planet.
16. The moon is the earth's only natural satellite.
17. The lunar surface has mountains and valleys.
18. A space shuttle will go back and forth to the moon.
19. A group of stars with a name is a constellation.
20. The moon is in orbit around the earth.

Note

The sample sentences may be used for pretesting.

Lesson 29 Space Words

Say each word.

revolution
celestial
solar
astronomy
comet
motion
galaxy
axis
meteors
universe
light-year
rotation
eclipse
telescope
asteroids
satellite
lunar
shuttle
constellation
orbit

1. Write the two words that begin with the letter m.
   motion meteors
2. Which word begins with /sh/? shuttle
3. Which three words begin with /s/? celestial
   solar satellite
4. Which three words begin and end with a vowel?
   astronomy universe
   eclipse
5. Which three words begin with a vowel and end with a consonant? axis asteroids
   orbit
6. In which words do you hear /o͞o/? Circle the letter that spells /o͞o/. lunar revolution
7. Which word begins and ends like comfort?
   comet
8. Which word begins and ends like telephone?
   telescope
9. Which two words begin and end like relaxation?
   revolution rotation
10. Which word has a hyphen? light-year
11. Write the words in which a double consonant spells one sound.
    ll satellite ll constellation
    tt shuttle
12. Which two words end with /ē/? Circle the letter that spells /ē/. astronomy galaxy
13. Write the word in which the letters ti spell /ch/, not /sh/.
    celestial

156

Preparation Have students read aloud the title of the lesson on page 156. Read each spelling word aloud. Have students repeat and then spell each word aloud.

Note the tion ending in revolution, motion, rotation, and constellation. Ask what two letters end solar and lunar. (ar) Point out that in both of these words, a stands for /ə/ in the last syllable: /sō′lər/, /lo͞o′nər/. Write the sample sentences on the board or read them and have students write them, underlining each spelling word. If students write the sentences, tell them to save their work to use with the Checkpoint and Story activities. If you write the sample sentences on the board, leave them there until students have completed work on Lesson 29.

The Page Have students complete page 156. For exercise 4, tell students that y can be a vowel. Have volunteers write the answers on the board and have students correct their own work.

Follow-Up Suggest that students write each word three times without lifting their pencils from the paper.

Checkpoint

Write a spelling word for each clue.
Then use the Checkpoint Study Plan on page 224.

1. Look at the stars through a ____. telescope
2. A kind of spacecraft is a space ____. shuttle
3. Light or heat from the sun is ____ heat. solar
4. If the moon blocks the sun, there is an ____. eclipse
5. To rotate once means to make a ____. rotation
6. A measurement of distance in space is a ____. light-year
7. The Big Dipper is a ____. constellation
8. All matter and space make up the ____. universe
9. Solid fragments from space are ____. meteors
10. To revolve around the sun once means to make a ____. revolution
11. The path of a planet around the sun is its ____. orbit
12. Of the moon is the meaning of ____. lunar
13. Something related to the sky is ____. celestial
14. Another word for movement is ____. motion
15. The study of heavenly bodies is ____. astronomy
16. A heavenly body with a long tail is a ____. comet
17. A large collection of stars is a ____. galaxy
18. The earth turns on its ____. axis
19. The moon is the earth's ____. satellite

20. This word names any of the many small planets between Mars and Jupiter. These small planets look like stars. Their name comes from the Greek words *astēr* and *eīdos*. *Astēr* meant star. *Eīdos* meant form. When these two words were put together they looked like this: *asteroeidēs*. *Asteroeidēs* meant star-like. Can you guess what these planets are called? ____ asteroids

157

Objectives

- To write spelling words in response to clues: definitions, synonyms, and context.
- To develop the critical thinking skills of making inferences and understanding cause and effect.
- To understand that words have come into the English language from other cultures and that words can be combined to form new words.

Spelling Strategy

Some students may have difficulty remembering how to spell the unaccented vowel sound in words such as solar, comet, and axis. It may be helpful to have them make flash cards for the words. On one side of the card, have them write the word but leave a blank for the troublesome letter or letters. On the other side, have them write the complete word. Suggest to students that they use the flash cards to quiz themselves on the words until they can spell each word correctly without hesitation.

Preparation The clues on this page are like crossword puzzle clues. Explain to students that the response to each clue is a spelling word. Use the following examples to illustrate the types of clues used:

Definition	Of the moon is the meaning of (*lunar*).
Synonym	Another word for movement is (*motion*).
Context	The earth turns on its (*axis*).

The final clue identifies the Greek words that make up asteroids.

The Page Have students complete page 157 using the words on page 156. When students have finished, have them read each clue and spell the answer aloud. Check each response twice: once for the correct answer and a second time for spelling accuracy.

Follow-Up Guide pupils in using the **Checkpoint Study Plan** on page 224 to take a self-test. Then have them use the plan for independent study.

Objectives

- To write space words in continuous text.
- To write each spelling word once.
- To integrate reading with spelling.

Use each list word once.

Star Light, Star Bright: The Story of Astronomy

The stars and planets are called celestial bodies. From very early times these ___celestial___ bodies have interested people. What did early people think when a ___comet___ blazed across the sky? What did they think when an ___eclipse___ made day become night? We know that they tried to predict eclipses of the sun and moon. These ___lunar___ and ___solar___ eclipses were wondrous and frightening to them. It's no wonder that the study of heavenly bodies, ___astronomy___, is one of the oldest sciences.

Early people did not understand that the earth rotates on its axis, or that the ___rotation___ of the earth on its ___axis___ causes day and night. People had their own explanations for what happened in the heavens. It seemed clear that a sun god drove a shining chariot across the sky. Shooting stars or ___meteors___ were thought to be messages from the gods. They made up stories to explain a group of stars or ___constellation___.

Note

Point out the pronunciation of the names: Thales /thā' lēz/, Pythagoras /pĭ thăg' ə rəs/, Galileo /găl ə lē' ō/, and Copernicus /kō pûr' nĭ kəs/.

Preparation Have students turn to pages 158 and 159. Let them look at the article and the picture. Call their attention to the word list. Have the students say the words. Then explain that each spelling word belongs in one of the blanks in the article.

Write the title "Star Light, Star Bright: The Story of Astronomy" on the board. Then ask if any students have studied astronomy or been to a planetarium. Have them tell about the things that most interest them in astronomy. Tell students that people have been interested in astronomy for thousands of years and that new discoveries about space are being made all the time.

Remind students to look in the **Spelling Dictionary** if they are not sure of the meaning of any of the spelling words.

The Pages Have students refer to the sample sentences from page 156 that you wrote on the board or had students write and tell them to complete pages 158 and 159 independently by silently reading the article and writing the missing spelling words. Or you may read the article aloud, supplying the missing words as students follow along in their texts; then have the students complete the pages on their own.

Early Greeks, however, had some surprisingly correct ideas about the heavens. Two men stand out. Thales is the man we call the father of astronomy. He observed that the moon moved in an orbit around the earth. He thought that the whole universe was always in motion. Pythagoras is another Greek who knew much about the stars. He believed that the earth was not the center of the universe. We know now that the earth revolves around the sun. But thousands of years ago, the idea of the revolution of the earth around the sun caused many fights!

Most people continued to believe that the sun and stars moved around the earth until the telescope proved that idea wrong. With the telescope, people such as Galileo and Copernicus were able to prove Pythagoras was right! The moon was the only satellite that circled the earth.

Technology improved our knowledge. New tools made it possible for scientists to gather new facts. They were able to watch the many asteroids between Mars and Jupiter. When astronomers realized the huge distances between stars, a light-year became a way to measure space.

We are already used to having people on the moon. The day when you can hop on an intergalactic space shuttle and visit another galaxy may not be far away.

159

revolution
celestial
solar
astronomy
comet
motion
galaxy
axis
meteors
universe
light-year
rotation
eclipse
telescope
asteroids
satellite
lunar
shuttle
constellation
orbit

When students have finished, you may wish to discuss the article. Ask students what idea caused many fights hundreds of years ago. (*the idea that the earth moves around the sun*) Tell students that today there are still arguments about how the universe works, such as how old the universe is, how it began, whether it is expanding and if so, how fast, and so on. Encourage students to find out more about astronomy and plan to have them report to the class on their findings.

Have volunteers read each paragraph on the pages, supplying each spelling word and spelling it aloud. Have other volunteers write the answers on the board and have students correct their own work. Check students' responses for the accurate spelling of each answer.

Follow-Up

Have students use each of the spelling words they missed in an original sentence that relates to the article.

As an additional follow-up activity, you may wish to have students make a scrapbook about astronomy using the information provided in the article "Star Light, Star Bright." Ask students to illustrate the scrapbook and use sentences from the article as captions.

Enrichment

If you want to use the blackline activity masters for enrichment and additional practice, assign Lesson 29 activities at this time.

Maintenance and Review

OBJECTIVE

- To review compound words.

ACTIVITIES

If you want to use the blackline activity masters for maintenance and review, assign Lesson 28 activities at th s time.

You can also use the activity below to review Lesson 28 with students.

Have students write one or two paragraphs about a birthday party using at least four of the spelling words from Lesson 28.

Objectives

- To relate spelling words to a dictionary skill.
- To compare entries from different dictionaries.
- To write spelling words in alphabetical order.

Dictionaries

Different dictionaries show entry words and definitions in different ways. The part of speech may be listed before or after the definition. The sound spelling may be set off in parentheses ( ) or in slashes: / / or | |. Sometimes example sentences are given. Sometimes a picture helps illustrate the meaning.

A.

eclipse The disappearance of the sun or moon behind another heavenly body.

e•clipse (ĭ klīps') *n., plural* **eclipses.**

B.

eclipse
Total eclipse of the sun.

e•clipse |ĭ **klĭps'**| *n.* **1. a.** The blocking by another celestial body of part or all of the light that reaches an observer from a given celestial body. **b.** The time during which such a blocking occurs. **2.** A decline; downfall: *His fame has suffered an eclipse.* —*v.* **e•clipsed, e•clips•ing. 1.** To block the light of: *as one of a pair of binary stars eclipses the other.* **2.** To obscure or overshadow the importance, fame, or reputation of; reduce in importance by comparison: *This news eclipses everything. Columbus was destined to eclipse his fellow navigators completely.* [SEE PICTURE]

★ Study these two dictionary entries. Then answer the questions.

1. Is the entry word the same for each of the entries? yes
2. What is the entry word? eclipse
3. Which entry contains example sentences? B
4. Where is the part of speech shown in example A? end of the entry
   in example B? after the sound spelling
5. Which entry has a picture? B
6. Which entry has the longer definition? B

★ Put these words in alphabetical order. Then look up each word in two different dictionaries and make notes about the differences you find.

solar galaxy axis comet lunar

	Word	Dictionary Notes
7.	axis	Answers will vary.
8.	comet	
9.	galaxy	
10.	lunar	
11.	solar	

160

Preparation Have students read the title of page 160. Ask if they think all dictionaries are the same. (*no*) Ask how dictionaries may differ. (*Some dictionaries contain more entry words than others; some give word histories, or etymologies; some have different styles of presenting information.*) Ask in what ways dictionaries are all alike. (*They list words in alphabetical order; they give the part of speech of each word; they show how a word is pronounced; they give the meaning or meanings for each word.*)

The Page Have students do page 160. Then have volunteers write the answers on the board and review the answers orally.

Follow-Up Have students make up their own dictionary entries for five spelling words not covered on page 160. Students may follow the style of one dictionary or make up their own style. Remind students to include the entry word, sound spelling, part or parts of speech, meanings, and at least one example sentence.

WORDS AT WORK

Challenge Yourself

hemisphere cosmos velocity aurora

Decide which Challenge Word fits each clue. Check your Spelling Dictionary to see if you were right. Then write sentences showing that you understand the meaning of each Challenge Word.

1. These lights are a beautiful sight to see in the night sky.
2. Everything in the universe is a part of this.
3. This is what each half of the earth is called.
4. How long it takes you to get somewhere depends on the distance you are traveling and this.

Write to the Point

Write an explanation like the ancient Greeks did for an event or thing in nature, such as "Why the Sun Sets" or "Why There Are Stars in the Sky." Make up a creative explanation. Use spelling words from this lesson in your explanation.

Challenge Use one or more of the Challenge Words in your explanation.

Proofreading

Use the proofreading marks to show the errors in the paragraph below. Write the five misspelled words correctly in the blanks.

⬭	word is misspelled
⊙	period is missing
≡	letter should be capitalized

As her small ship easily left the orbet of Mars, the captain looked through her telascope to view the distant galaxy. This new univers was many light-years away, and captain Yee feared that the shuttel might crash into astoroids on the way there

1. orbit
2. telescope
3. universe
4. shuttle
5. asteroids

Test Review and test space words. Use one of these testing methods: (1) Say the word; read the sample sentence from page 156; say the word; have students write it. (2) Read each dictation sentence above; have students write the sentence. Correct the test with students.

Challenge Yourself The optional Challenge Words may be assigned to the entire class or limited to those students who do well on the test. You may wish to have students work in pairs. Responses to this activity should be completed on separate paper. Answers to the questions are provided above.

Write to the Point Help students recall the selection "Star Light, Star Bright: The Story of Astronomy" on pages 158 and 159; then assign the creative explanation. You may wish to brainstorm possible topics with students before they begin. This activity should be completed on separate paper.

Proofreading The proofreading practice includes misspellings of words from this lesson as well as a capitalization error and a punctuation error.

Objectives

- To extend students' knowledge of space words through the Challenge Words.
- To use clues and the **Spelling Dictionary** to enlarge students' vocabulary.
- To apply the space words presented in Lesson 29 in a writing activity.
- To practice proofreading for spelling, punctuation, and capitalization.

Dictation Sentences

1. The satellite took pictures of asteroids and meteors in space.
2. A light-year is a unit of distance in astronomy.
3. Our solar system is in the Milky Way galaxy.
4. The telescope was used to discover the orbit of Mars around the sun.
5. A shuttle is being built for space travel.
6. The Big Dipper is a bright constellation.
7. A lunar eclipse may last for hours.
8. The earth's rotation on its own axis is not steady because of the pull of the moon.
9. A comet is a celestial body with a bright tail and a fuzzy head.
10. Earth makes one revolution around the sun each year.
11. Did you know that the universe is in motion?

Challenge Yourself Answers

1. aurora
2. cosmos
3. hemisphere
4. velocity

Students' sentences will vary.

LESSON 30

Objectives

- To review and reinforce vowel spellings for /ô/, /û/, /â/, and /ä/.
- To hear, say, spell, and write representative spelling words from Lessons 25–27.
- To write an explanation using the five steps in the writing process.
- To use a prewriting activity to generate information for an explanation.

Dictation Sentences

1. We have new furniture for our apartment.
2. Don't quarrel over a game of marbles.
3. I am certain I will starve if I don't eat soon.
4. She tore the margin of her paper.
5. We must prepare carefully for the test.
6. We want to get a perfect score in this course.
7. He likes to perform to the roar of a crowd.
8. It is important to be of service to others.
9. Help me compare this pearl with that one.
10. Mom works for a law firm.
11. Who will declare the winner?

Note

A review test blackline master in standardized format and an answer sheet have been provided on pages T39 and T41 of this Teacher's Edition. The answers to the review test are given below.

1–B	11–D
2–D	12–B
3–C	13–A
4–B	14–D
5–C	15–B
6–B	16–A
7–A	17–A
8–D	18–C
9–B	19–C
10–B	20–D

If words misspelled were from:	have students complete activities:
List A	1, 3
List B	2, 3
List C	4, 6
List D	5, 6

Lesson 30 Words in Review

A. quarrel
roar
tore
perform
course
important

B. service
furniture
firm
certain
perfect
pearl

C. prepare
carefully
declare
compare

D. marbles
apartment
starve
margin

★ You will need a piece of paper for these review activities.

1. In Lesson 25 you studied four different ways to spell /ô/: **o, a, ou, oa.** Write the words in list A.
quarrel roar tore
perform course important
2. In Lesson 26 you studied four different ways to spell /û/: **e, i, ea, u.** Write the words in list B.
service furniture firm
certain perfect pearl
3. ★ Use each review word from lists A and B in a sentence.
4. In Lesson 27 you studied one way to spell /â/: **a.** Write the words in list C.
prepare carefully
declare compare
5. In Lesson 27 you also studied one way to spell /ä/: **a.** Write the words in list D.
marbles apartment
starve margin
6. ★ Look up each review word from lists C and D in the Spelling Dictionary. Write the sound spelling of each.

Your teacher may give you a test. Answer these questions when you have finished.

7. Did you spell all the words correctly? Yes or No
8. Did you leave out a letter? Yes or No
9. Did you write the wrong letter? Yes or No
10. Did you miss the spelling of a vowel sound? Yes or No

162

Test

Pretest the review words on page 162 to determine which students need reinforcement. Use one of these testing methods: (1) Read the words and the dictation sentences; have students write only the spelling words. (2) Read the dictation sentences and have students write the entire sentences. (3) Have students complete the review test blackline master. (See **Note**.) Correct the pretest with students.

The Pages

Assign pages 162 and 163 according to students' needs.

- Students who have mastered all of the review words may go on to the **Writer's Workshop** on page 163.
- Students who have not mastered all of the review words should complete the activities on page 162 and take a post-test administered with one of the pretesting methods. After the post-test students can then go on to the **Writer's Workshop** on page 163. For students who have misspelled only a few of the review words, you may wish to use the list at left to determine the activities they should complete on page 162.

For students who have misspelled several of the review words, you may wish to assign all of the activities on page 162.

An Explanation

An explanation gives readers information. It might tell how to do something, why something happens, or what something is made of. Here is the beginning of Anna's explanation of the different kinds of roller-skates people wear. Note that she gives interesting facts about what roller-skates are made of and what they look like.

Kinds of Roller-Skates

Roller-skating is an exciting activity. It can be done indoors or outdoors, just for fun, or in races. Roller-skates used outdoors have metal wheels. They last longer on the rough surface of sidewalks and roads. Indoor skaters use skates with wooden or plastic wheels. These wheels do not scratch the wooden floors at the rinks.

Most roller skates have four wheels. The wheels form a rectangle on the boot or a straight line down the middle of the boot. Wheels in a rectangle are more stable. Wheels in a straight line go faster. Racers use skates with five wheels.

To write her explanation, Anna followed the steps in the writing process. She first used a list as a **Prewriting** activity. The list helped her think of all the facts she wanted to include about roller-skating. This graphic organizer also helped her to remember her ideas once she was ready to begin writing. Part of Anna's list is shown here. Study what Anna did.

Kinds of Roller-Skates

ones used outdoors
  metal wheels

ones used indoors
  wooden wheels
  plastic wheels

ones with wheels set in rectangle
in-line skates

Get ready to write your own explanation. You might explain how to play a favorite sport or game. Or you might give facts about your hobby or another activity. Just make sure that your explanation is clear and complete. After you have decided what to write about, make a list to note all the facts and details you will include. Then follow the other steps in the writing process—**Writing, Revising, Proofreading,** and **Publishing.**

Note

If students have difficulty deciding on a topic, you may wish to suggest one of the following:

Interesting facts about (dogs, cats, turtles, and so on)

A great hobby

My favorite game

Writer's Workshop Point out that in an explanation a writer often describes how to do something or gives facts to inform the reader about a person, place, object, or activity. Read the explanation "Kinds of Roller-Skates" with students and point out the words and phrases that Anna used to make her explanation clear and complete.

Allow students to study the portion of the list shown on the pupil's page and guide students to see how this graphic organizer helped Anna prepare to write her explanation.

It's Your Turn Review the steps in the writing process with students. If students are not satisfied with the result of their prewriting, allow them to revise it as often as necessary or to choose another topic and repeat the prewriting activity.

Process Writing Blackline Masters

- Steps in the Writing Process, page T44
- Proofreading Symbols/Checklist, page T45

LESSON 31

Objectives

- To hear and say words with /ə/.
- To write words with /ə/ with attention to letter sequence and sound/symbol relationships.
- To write each spelling word at least once.
- To recognize that /ə/ may be spelled a, e, i, o, and u.

Sample Sentences

1. Don pushed against the door until it opened.
2. George paddled a canoe across the lake.
3. I can't stand to hear that song again!
4. It's easy to slip on a banana peel.
5. Willie will join us if his parents approve.
6. Today the ocean is too rough to swim in.
7. If he's not on time, perhaps we will wait.
8. The President is the highest government leader.
9. It is dangerous to swim in rough water.
10. There is a beautiful waterfall up this river.
11. You must be 13 to qualify for the prize.
12. My aunt and my cousin are coming to visit.
13. Maxine tried to comfort the cat by petting it.
14. A mosquito bit me on the elbow.
15. Chris has a good memory.
16. The beach is crowded during the summer season.
17. Dale is giving Phil a surprise party.
18. Oranges, lemons, and limes are citrus fruits.
19. I don't know the verse, but I'll sing the chorus.
20. The making and selling of skates is a big industry.

Note

- The sample sentences may be used for pretesting.
- Words are grouped according to spellings of /ə/:
  a o
  e u
  i

Lesson 31 Words with /ə/

Listen for /ə/ in each word.

against
canoe
again
banana
approve
ocean

perhaps
government
dangerous

beautiful
qualify
cousin

comfort
mosquito
memory
season

surprise
citrus
chorus
industry

1. Which word begins with the letter p? perhaps
2. Which word begins with the letter a and ends with the letter n? again
3. Write the word that ends with o. mosquito
4. Which three words begin with /s/? Circle the letter that spells /s/. season surprise citrus
5. Which word begins with /kw/? Circle the letters that spell /kw/. qualify
6. Which four words begin with /k/? Circle the letters that spell /k/. canoe cousin comfort chorus
7. In which word does a double consonant spell one sound? approve
8. In which word do you hear /j/ but don't see the letter j? dangerous
9. Which word has the same vowel letter repeated three times? banana
10. Which word ends with the letters st? against
11. Which three words end with the letter y? Circle the words in which the y is pronounced /ē/. qualify memory industry
12. Write the two words that have the suffixes ment and ful. government beautiful
13. In which word do you hear /sh/ but don't see the letters sh? ocean

164

Preparation Have students read aloud the title of the lesson on page 164. Remind students that /ə/ is called the schwa sound and that it occurs only in the least stressed syllables. Have students find /ə/ in the pronunciation key on page 196 and say the words. Read each spelling word aloud. Tell students to repeat and then spell each word aloud.

Ask what two letters spell /oo/ in canoe. (*oe*) Ask what three vowels appear together in beautiful. (*eau*) Note that the letters qu spell /k/ in mosquito. Ask what letters spell /k/ in chorus. (*ch*) Note that ce in ocean spells /sh/. Have students identify the schwa sound in each word in the lesson and the letter that spells this sound. (See **Note**.)

Read the sample sentences. Have students point to each spelling word as you read the sentence for it.

The Page Have students complete page 164. Have volunteers write the answers on the board and have students correct their own work.

Follow-Up Suggest that students write all the words in the list in alphabetical order.

Checkpoint

Write a spelling word for each clue.
Then use the Checkpoint Study Plan on page 224.

1. A yellow fruit with easy-to-peel skin is a ____.
2. The opposite of ugly is ____.
3. Once more means ____.
4. Another word for maybe is ____.
5. One type of flying insect is a ____.
6. The opposite of safe is ____.
7. To make someone feel better is to give ____.
8. The water that covers 72 percent of the earth is the ____.
9. The President is the head of our ____.
10. Your aunt's child is your ____.
11. If you are not for something, you are ____ it.
12. Another word for business is ____.
13. A group of singers may be a ____.
14. Past events are stored in your ____.
15. July is a month, summer is a ____.
16. To consider right or good is to ____.
17. Something unexpected is a ____.
18. Trees that grow oranges or limes are ____.
19. To meet certain conditions is to ____.

20. When Christopher Columbus first came to the Americas, he landed in the West Indies. He met a group of Indians and took one of their boats back to Europe. People in Europe called the boat by its Indian name. This name is our mystery word. Can you name the boat? ____

banana
beautiful
again
perhaps
mosquito
dangerous
comfort
ocean
government
cousin
against
industry
chorus
memory
season
approve
surprise
citrus
qualify

canoe

165

Objectives

- To write spelling words in response to clues: definitions, synonyms, antonyms, analogies, and context.
- To develop the critical thinking skills of classifying, comparing, and contrasting.
- To appreciate the diversity of sources of the English language.

Spelling Strategy

Some students may leave out the first n when spelling government. Write government on the board and circle the base word. Provide a sentence such as "We elect a government to govern us." Also point out that government and governor have the same base word and that it is easier to hear n in governor. Have students practice pronouncing the first n distinctly when they say government.

Preparation The clues on this page are like crossword puzzle clues. Explain to students that the response to each clue is a spelling word. Use the following examples to illustrate the types of clues used:

Definition	Something unexpected is a (*surprise*).
Synonym	Another word for maybe is (*perhaps*).
Antonym	The opposite of ugly is (*beautiful*).
Analogy	July is a month, summer is a (*season*).
Context	One type of flying insect is a (*mosquito*).

The final clue explains how canoe came into the English language.

The Page Have students complete page 165 using the words on page 164. When students have finished, have them read each clue and spell the answer aloud. Check each response twice: once for the correct answer and a second time for spelling accuracy.

Follow-Up Guide pupils in using the **Checkpoint Study Plan** on page 224 to take a self-test. Then have them use the plan for independent study.

Objectives

- To write words with /ə/ in continuous text and related sentences.
- To write each spelling word once.
- To integrate reading with spelling.

Note

Point out the use of the word com-fort in the story as a noun meaning a condition of ease. Ask students for another meaning of comfort.

Use each list word once.

Oranges and Alligators

Every year, thousands of people escape the cold northern winter by going to Florida. Many go to the eastern coast. There they swim in the warm ocean and lie in comfort on the sandy beach.

But for those who want another kind of vacation, there is a different kind of Florida in the central part of the state, away from the coast. There you can visit the huge orange, grapefruit, and other citrus groves. The growing of these fruits is a large industry. There are miles and miles of trees as far as the eye can see.

The wildest part of Florida is the Everglades. The Everglades are in the southern part of the state. Everglades National Park was established in 1947 by the federal government. It is a huge swamp, full of strange plants and animals. In some places, you can paddle a canoe through the streams, if you don't mind getting a few mosquito bites. The swamp often looks still and beautiful. But it can also be dangerous. If your canoe bumps up against an alligator, you'll be in for a nasty surprise. In fact, before you go off on your own into the Everglades, the park rangers must approve your trip. In order to qualify, you must carry a snakebite kit and take other safety precautions. In summer, the wet season, you must be prepared for lots of rain.

166

Preparation Have students turn to pages 166 and 167. Let them look at the pages and the pictures. Call their attention to the word list. Have the students say the words. Then explain that each spelling word belongs in one of the blanks on the pages.

Write the title "Oranges and Alligators" on the board. Then ask what the selection is about. (*Florida*) Explain that the sentences on page 167 are related to the article and that students will write the missing spelling words for the sentences, too. On a map of the United States, show students the location of Florida. Then have students look at the map of Florida on page 166. Ask if any students have been to any of the places marked on the map. If they have, ask them to tell what each place was like and whether they liked it or not. Tell students that Florida contains several different climates and types of land and that they will read about a few of them in this selection.

The Pages Have students complete pages 166 and 167 independently by silently reading the pages and writing the missing spelling words. Or you may read the pages aloud, supplying the missing words as students follow along in their texts; then have the students complete the pages on their own.

However, many people love the Everglades, and they come back again and ___again___ to explore this area.

- My aunt, my uncle, and my ___cousin___ Herman took me to Everglades National Park.
- Because I have a good ___memory___, I can remember every detail of that trip to Florida.
- Herman and I turned on the car radio and sang the ___chorus___ of every song we knew.
- Once, when we stopped for lunch, I ordered a ___banana___ split. It tasted so good, I ordered another. Wow, did I have an upset stomach!
- Maybe I should have ordered just one. Or ___perhaps___ I shouldn't have had even one.

167

against
canoe
again
banana
approve
ocean
perhaps
government
dangerous
beautiful
qualify
cousin
comfort
mosquito
memory
season
surprise
citrus
chorus
industry

When students have finished, you may wish to discuss the pages. Ask students what part of Florida, if any, they would like to visit and why. Include in the discussion the geography of the eastern coast, the citrus growing area, and the Everglades as presented in the article. Compare these regions with your state. Encourage students to find out more about the different areas of their state and to report their findings to the class.

Have volunteers read each paragraph on the pages, supplying each missing spelling word and spelling it aloud. Have other volunteers write the answers on the board and have students correct their own work. Check students' responses for the accurate spelling of each answer.

Follow-Up Have the students use each of the spelling words they missed in an original sentence that relates to the article.

As an additional follow-up activity, you may wish to have students make a scrapbook about Florida using the information provided in the article "Oranges and Alligators." Ask students to illustrate the scrapbook and use the sentences from the article as captions.

Enrichment

If you want to use the blackline activity masters for enrichment and additional practice, assign Lesson 31 activities at this time.

Maintenance and Review

OBJECTIVE

- To review space words.

ACTIVITIES

If you want to use the blackline activity masters for maintenance and review, assign Lesson 29 activities at this time.

You can also use the activity below to review Lesson 29 with the students:

Write the following words on the board. Have students change one letter in each to form a word from Lesson 29. (Answers are in parentheses.)

scuttle	(*shuttle*)
notion	(*motion*)
axes	(*axis*)
polar	(*solar*)
comes	(*comet*)
notation	(*rotation*)
ellipse	(*eclipse*)

Objectives

- To relate spelling to another language skill.
- To understand capitalization of titles of books and movies.
- To write spelling words in the context of titles.
- To practice proofreading.

Capitals

The first word, the last word, and all other important words in a title are capitalized. Small words, such as a, the, in, to, and of are not capitalized when they are in the middle of a title. This is true for titles of books, stories, songs, movies, and television programs.

Butch Cassidy and the Sundance Kid
Newsweek
A Night to Remember

★ Write the following titles. Correct the spelling error in each title.

1. a seasun of song
   A Season of Song
2. ocaen life
   Ocean Life
3. the memery bank
   The Memory Bank
4. the most dangerus game
   The Most Dangerous Game
5. house beautifull
   House Beautiful
6. indutry and the u.s. goverment
   Industry and the U.S. Government
7. men agianst the sea
   Men Against the Sea
8. my cusin, my friend
   My Cousin, My Friend
9. play it agaen, sam
   Play It Again, Sam
10. the bananna cookbook
    The Banana Cookbook

168

Preparation Have students read the title of page 168. Ask them to name titles of favorite books or movies. Have volunteers write the titles on the board. Tell them to follow these rules in writing titles correctly. Capitalize the first letter of the first and last words of a title, and all other important words. Words such as and, the, in, and to in the middle of a title, are not capitalized. All nouns, pronouns, verbs, adjectives, and adverbs are capitalized, no matter how small. If necessary, correct the titles students wrote on the board.

Write this title on the board: **That's the Way It Is.** Ask why each word except the is capitalized. (*That is the first word; Way is a noun; It is a pronoun, Is is a verb and the last word.*)

The Page Have students do page 168. Then have volunteers write the answers on the board.

Follow-Up Have students make up 10 book or movie titles, using at least one spelling word in each. Remind them to capitalize correctly.

WORDS AT WORK

Challenge Yourself

tyrant **omen** **ultimate** **random**

Write what you think each underlined Challenge Word means. Check your Spelling Dictionary to see if you were right. Then write sentences showing that you understand the meaning of each Challenge Word.

1. We hoped the king would be just, but he turned out to be a tyrant.
2. Some people think finding a four-leaf clover is a good omen.
3. I have read ten pages, but my ultimate goal is to finish the book.
4. You can plan the colors of your design or simply choose random colors.

Write to the Point

If a friend of yours is visiting the area where you live for the first time, what would you want him or her to see? Write a short tourists' guide to your community or city. Describe some of the interesting or beautiful sights. Use spelling words from this lesson in your guide.

Challenge Use one or more of the Challenge Words in your guide.

Proofreading

Use the proofreading marks to show the errors in the paragraph below. Write the five misspelled words correctly in the blanks.

(oval)	word is misspelled
≡	letter should be capitalized
! ^	exclamation point is missing

Maine is a beautyful state in any seasen, but perhaps the best time to visit is october. the ocian crashes agenst the shore, and the brilliant colors of the trees will please and suprize you. What an awesome sight

1. beautiful
2. season
3. ocean
4. against
5. surprise

169

Objectives

- To extend the vowel spellings presented in Lesson 31 to the Challenge Words.
- To use context and the **Spelling Dictionary** to enlarge students' vocabulary.
- To apply the vowel spellings presented in Lesson 31 in a writing activity.
- To practice proofreading for spelling, punctuation, and capitalization.

Dictation Sentences

1. What a beautiful day it is to paddle down the river in a canoe!
2. The banana is not a citrus fruit.
3. The government will give money to the auto industry to make more jobs.
4. My cousin has a bad memory, and it is no surprise that he forgot your name.
5. During the summer season, we swim in the ocean.
6. If you open the window, perhaps the mosquito will fly out again.
7. You may qualify to join the chorus.
8. Does everyone approve of the plan to save energy?
9. I put the chairs against the wall before the party.
10. My dog is a comfort to me.
11. Sharks are dangerous.

Challenge Yourself Answers

Possible definitions:

1. harsh ruler
2. sign for the future
3. highest; final
4. without a plan

Students' sentences will vary.

Test Review these five ways to spell /ə/: a as in again; e as in perhaps; i as in cousin; o as in season; u as in chorus. Test words with /ə/. Use one of these testing methods: (1) Say the word; read the sample sentence from page 164; say the word; have students write it. (2) Read each dictation sentence above; have students write the sentence. Correct the test with students.

Challenge Yourself The optional Challenge Words may be assigned to the entire class or limited to those students who do well on the test. Have students note the vowel spellings in the Challenge Words. Responses to this activity should be completed on separate paper. Answers to the questions are provided above.

Write to the Point Help students recall the selection "Oranges and Alligators" on pages 166 and 167; then assign the tourists' guide. You may want to have students write their guide in the form of a list. Suggest that they write the name of each point of interest and a sentence or two explaining why it is worth seeing. This activity should be completed on separate paper.

Proofreading The proofreading practice includes misspellings of words from this lesson as well as capitalization errors and a punctuation error.

LESSON 32

Objectives

- To hear and say words with /ə/.
- To write words with /ə/ with attention to letter sequence and sound/symbol relationships.
- To write each spelling word at least once.
- To recognize that /ə/ may be spelled e and a.

Sample Sentences

1. Look at the next example in your textbook.
2. Marty eats a couple of oranges every day.
3. Do you like sweet or sour pickles?
4. Frank took a double helping of potatoes.
5. The earthquake made the ground shake and tremble.
6. Ray solved the crossword puzzle.
7. The salesperson gave Sam a sample.
8. You can hear the train whistle from here.
9. The leaves began to tumble in the wind.
10. The problem is quite simple if you do it step by step.
11. Alex is always getting into trouble.
12. If you sit on my jacket, you'll wrinkle it.
13. I need one more nickel for lunch money.
14. The rainwater dripped into the barrel.
15. The sixth grade is putting on a musical show.
16. What kind of animal would you like for a pet?
17. It's only natural to cry at a sad movie.
18. After the final day of school, we're going away.
19. Everyone can vote in the general election.
20. The traffic signal on the corner is broken.

Note

- The sample sentences may be used for pretesting.
- Words are grouped according to spellings of /ə/:
  e
  a

Lesson 32 Words with /ə/

Listen for /ə/ in each word.

example
couple
pickles
double
tremble
puzzle
sample
whistle
tumble
simple
trouble
wrinkle
nickel
barrel

musical
animal
natural
final
general
signal

1. Write the three words that begin with the letter s.
   sample simple
   signal
2. Which word begins with the letter f? final
3. Which word begins and ends like metal?
   musical
4. Write the two words that begin with a vowel.
   example animal
5. In which word do you hear /j/ but don't see the letter j?
   general
6. Write the word in which you see the letter w but don't hear /w/. wrinkle
7. Write the three words that begin with the letter t.
   tremble tumble
   trouble
8. Write the two words in which you see the letter t but don't hear /t/. whistle natural
9. Write the two words in which /k/ is spelled ck.
   pickles nickel
10. In which word is /z/ spelled zz? puzzle
11. In which word is /r/ spelled rr? barrel
12. Write the three words in which /ŭ/ is spelled ou.
    couple double
    trouble
13. Which two words end with the letters el?
    nickel barrel
14. Write the three words in which you hear /z/ but don't see the letter z. example musical
    pickles

170

Preparation

Have students read aloud the title of the lesson on page 170. Read each spelling word aloud. Tell students to repeat and then spell each word aloud.

Ask students to name the base words of musical (*music*) and natural (*nature*). Note that the letter e was dropped from nature before the ending al was added. Have students indentify the schwa sound in each word in the lesson and the letter that spells it. (See **Note**.)

Read the sample sentences. Have students point to each spelling word as you read the sentence for it.

The Page

Have students complete page 170 and then have volunteers write the answers on the board. Have students correct their own work.

Follow-Up

Suggest that students write each word in two colors. Have them begin each word with one color and write the le, el, or al ending with the other color.

Checkpoint

Write a spelling word for each clue.
Then use the Checkpoint Study Plan on page 224.

1. The clues fit together like pieces of a ____. puzzle
2. Difficulty is another word for ____. trouble
3. Another word for easy is ____. simple
4. To shake is to ____. tremble
5. A sample or model is an ____. example
6. The last one is ____. final
7. A fern is a plant, a cat is an ____. animal
8. Two people together make a ____. couple
9. Nation is to national as music is to ____. musical
10. A sound or small instrument used for a signal is a ____. whistle
11. When cucumbers are treated, they become ____. pickles
12. Start the race when I give the ____. signal
13. The opposite of specific is ____. general
14. To fall or roll over is to ____. tumble
15. A kind of large container is a ____. barrel
16. The opposite of man-made is ____. natural
17. Five pennies equal one ____. nickel
18. It's a new product, so take a free ____. sample
19. If it's twice as much, it's ____. double

20. The origin of this mystery word is uncertain. It may have come from the Old English word *wringan*. *Wringan* meant to twist. When cloth is twisted, it becomes creased. The mystery word means an unwanted crease. Can you guess the mystery word? ____ wrinkle

Objectives

- To write spelling words in response to clues: definitions, synonyms, antonyms, analogies, and context.
- To develop the critical thinking skills of making inferences, comparing, and contrasting.
- To understand that new words may develop from older ones and that the spelling and meaning of words in the English language may change over time.

Spelling Strategy

If students have trouble remembering certain letters such as the silent t in whistle or the silent w in wrinkle, suggest that they write each word on a sticky note, making the troublesome letter or letters larger than the others. Have them take the notes home and post them in a place they often look, such as the front of a dresser drawer or a bedroom mirror.

Preparation

The clues on this page are like crossword puzzle clues. Explain to students that the response to each clue is a spelling word. Use the following examples to illustrate the types of clues used:

Definition	A sample or model is an (*example*).
Synonym	Another word for easy is (*simple*).
Antonym	The opposite of man-made is (*natural*).
Analogy	A fern is a plant, a cat is an (*animal*).
Context	When cucumbers are treated, they become (*pickles*).

The final clue explains what may have been the origin of wrinkle.

The Page

Have students complete page 171 using the words on page 170. When students have finished, have them read each clue and spell the answer aloud. Check each response twice: once for the correct answer and a second time for spelling accuracy.

Follow-Up

Guide pupils in using the **Checkpoint Study Plan** on page 224 to take a self-test. Then have them use the plan for independent study.

Objectives

- To write words with /ə/ in continuous text.
- To write each spelling word once.
- To integrate reading with spelling.

Note

- Point out the use of the word general in the newspaper article as part of the phrase general store, which is a store that sells food, cloth, and other basic necessities.
- Point out that two of the names are puns: Del E. Catessen is a play on the word delicatessen, and John Darm is a play on gendarme, a French term for police officer.

Use each list word once.

The Goose Bay

THE CASE OF THE PILFERED PICKLES

Someone blew the whistle on Shifty Louie today. It solved a puzzle that has been bothering the police for weeks.

Shifty Louie had been causing trouble by stealing pickles. Pickle supplies across the country were dropping sharply. Just the name of Shifty Louie made grocery store owners tremble.

Upon hearing of his capture, Mr. Del E. Catessen, owner and manager of the general store in Goose Bay, was most relieved.

"I was down to the last pickle in my pickle barrel," Mr. Catessen said. "His capture means one less wrinkle on my forehead."

"What would a couple like us have done?" asked Mrs. Catessen. "Pickles cost a nickel apiece! We can't afford to have people taking a sample from our barrel whenever they want.

Captain John Darm, of the Goose Bay Police, was the principal person in the plan to catch the thief.

"As Chief of Police, it was only natural for me to try to end this crime wave. I wanted to make an example of Shifty Louie."

When asked how he managed to trap the thief, Captain Darm said, "It was simple! My first move was to double the number of officers working on the case. Then I put five police dogs on Louie's trail. We call them our Pooch Patrol."

Captain Darm went on to explain the Pooch Patrol and how the police use it. He explained that Mutt, who caught Shifty Louie, is the kind of dog the

172

Preparation Have students turn to pages 172 and 173. Let them look at the newspaper article and the picture. Call their attention to the word list. Have the students say the words. Then explain that each spelling word belongs in one of the blanks in the newspaper article.

Write the title "The Goose Bay Gazette" on the board. Then ask students what kind of selection this is. (*a newspaper article*) Ask if they think it is a fiction or nonfiction piece. (*fiction*) Ask students how this newspaper differs from the one on pages 134 and 135. (*This paper has only one article.*) Ask how the two selections are the same. (*They both contain front-page articles that report important "news."*)

The Pages Have students complete pages 172 and 173 independently by silently reading the newspaper article aloud and writing the missing spelling words. Or you may read the newspaper article aloud, supplying the missing words as students follow along in their texts; then have the students complete the pages on their own.

When students have finished, you may wish to discuss the newspaper article. Ask students what part of this article could really happen. (*The police could spend lots of time and energy looking for a thief; there could be a dog patrol.*) Ask which part is purely fiction. (*the pickle-stealing thief*)

Gazette

police use every day. This noble animal will even go on stakeouts. He is trained to wait without a sound until he is given a signal. Then he will make his move, corner the thief, and wait for help to arrive.

Shortly after 9:00 A.M. this morning, a citizen reported seeing "a funny-looking character who smelled like a delicatessen." In minutes Mutt, following the smell of dill pickles, sniffed Louie out on the far side of town. The dog chased him through the city streets. People saw pickle after pickle tumble out of Louie's pockets as he ran. Mutt finally cornered Louie in an alley. And soon after, neighbors heard the musical sound of sirens speeding to the scene.

Later that day at the police station, Shifty Louie's final statement was: "I am not a common thief! I prefer to be called a pickle-pocket!"

173

example
couple
pickles
double
tremble
puzzle
sample
whistle
tumble
simple
trouble
wrinkle
nickel
barrel
musical
animal
natural
final
general
signal

Enrichment

If you want to use the blackline activity masters for enrichment and additional practice, assign Lesson 32 activities at this time.

Maintenance and Review

OBJECTIVE

- To review words with /ə/ spelled; a, e, i, o, u.

ACTIVITIES

If you want to use the blackline activity masters for maintenance and review, assign Lesson 31 activities at this time.

You can also use the activity below to review Lesson 31 with students.

Write the following groups of letters on the board. Have students refer to the Lesson 31 word list and unscramble each word below to spell a list word. (Answers are in parentheses.)

tinydrus	(*industry*)
quoosmit	(*mosquito*)
stainga	(*against*)
regadnous	(*dangerous*)
verpopa	(*approve*)
fromcot	(*comfort*)
nessoa	(*season*)
rusrisep	(*surprise*)

Have a volunteer read each paragraph in the newspaper article, supplying each missing spelling word and spelling it aloud. Have other volunteers write the answers on the board and have students correct their own work. Check students' responses for the accurate spelling of each answer.

Follow-Up

Have students use each of the spelling words they missed in an original sentence that relates to the story.

As an additional follow-up activity, you may wish to have students make a mural illustrating the article in the newspaper. Attach a large piece of paper to the wall and have several students plan and draw the mural.

Objectives

- To relate spelling to another language skill.
- To review and identify adverbs.
- To write spelling words in the context of sentences.

Adverbs

An adverb is the part of speech that tells how, when, or where the action in a sentence takes place.

Jane skates gracefully.
Her brother dances beautifully.

★ Write the sentences below, and underline the adverbs.

1. The circus parade marches noisily past the general store.
   The circus parade marches noisily past the general store.
2. We tremble quietly with excitement.
   We tremble quietly with excitement.
3. The leader blows a whistle loudly.
   The leader blows a whistle loudly.
4. Each animal steps quickly into place.
   Each animal steps quickly into place.
5. The animals form a double line and march obediently behind the leader.
   The animals form a double line and march obediently behind the leader.
6. A couple of people busily sell souvenirs.
   A couple of people busily sell souvenirs.
7. A clown happily jumps out of a barrel.
   A clown happily jumps out of a barrel.
8. Acrobats tumble energetically on the streets.
   Acrobats tumble energetically on the streets.
9. Suddenly, the signal is given.
   Suddenly, the signal is given.
10. The parade makes a final turn on Main Street and disappears slowly from sight.
    The parade makes a final turn on Main Street and disappears slowly from sight.

174

Preparation Have students read the title of page 174. Ask them if they know what an adverb is. (*It is a word that tells how, when, or where something happens. An adverb can describe a verb, an adjective, or another adverb.*)

Write this sentence on the board:

Joseph ran quickly to the corner.

Have a volunteer underline the adverb in this sentence and ask if the adverb tells how, when, or where. (*Quickly tells how.*) Repeat the procedure with these sentences:

Rosita left yesterday.
We are staying here.
(*Yesterday tells when. Here tells where.*)

The Page Have students do page 174. Then have volunteers write the answers on the board, and/or review them orally.

Follow-Up Write these words on the board: **early, already, often, tomorrow, awhile, again**. Tell students to use each of these adverbs in a sentence that also includes a spelling word.

WORDS AT WORK

Challenge Yourself

spaniel vocal pedestal agile

Use your Spelling Dictionary to answer these questions. Then write sentences showing that you understand the meaning of each Challenge Word.

1. Would you keep your spaniel on your bookshelf?
2. When you give a speech, are you making a vocal presentation to your audience?
3. Is a pedestal something that might be found at the base of a statue in a museum or a garden?
4. Would it help to be agile if you were training to become a dancer or a gymnast?

Write to the Point

Write a funny story about a mystery involving food. For instance, you might write about "The Case of the Disappearing Doughnuts" or "The Missing Pizza Puzzle." Try to keep your readers guessing until the mystery is solved. Use spelling words from this lesson in your mystery.

Challenge Use one or more of the Challenge Words in your mystery.

Proofreading

Use the proofreading marks to show the errors in the paragraph below. Write the five misspelled words correctly in the blanks.

⬭	word is misspelled
≡	letter should be capitalized
?‸	question mark is missing

The Goose Bay police rushed to the generel store on bank street. What was the trubble at the store A couple of things had been stolen—for example, a dog wistle and a jigsaw puzzel. Clearly this would be no simpal crime for the police detectives to solve.

1. general
2. trouble
3. whistle
4. puzzle
5. simple

Objectives

- To extend the vowel spellings presented in Lesson 32 to the Challenge Words.
- To use clues and the **Spelling Dictionary** to enlarge students' vocabulary.
- To apply the vowel spellings presented in Lesson 32 in a writing activity.
- To practice proofreading for spelling, punctuation, and capitalization.

Dictation Sentences

1. Did you see the actors tremble when the monster appeared?
2. We are putting on a musical for our final show.
3. The pickles in the barrel made her wrinkle her nose.
4. When I whistle, it is a signal to my dog that I am in trouble.
5. This puzzle is simple!
6. A double scoop of ice cream costs a nickel more.
7. They are an example of a nice couple.
8. I thought it was a good movie in general.
9. The children like to tumble down the hill.
10. The sample questions show you how to fill out the answer sheet.
11. It's natural to like a friendly animal like our dog.

Challenge Yourself Answers

1. no
2. yes
3. yes
4. yes

Students' sentences will vary.

Test Review these two ways to spell /ə/: e as in nickel and puzzle; a as in final. Test words with /ə/. Use one of these testing methods: (1) Say the word; read the sample sentence from page 170; say the word; have students write it. (2) Read each dictation sentence above; have students write the sentence. Correct the test with students.

Challenge Yourself The optional Challenge Words may be assigned to the entire class or limited to those students who do well on the test. Have students note the vowel spellings in the Challenge Words, especially the following new spelling: i_e as in agile. You may wish to have students work in pairs. Responses to this activity should be completed on separate paper. Answers to the questions are provided above.

Write to the Point Help students recall the selection "The Case of the Pilfered Pickles" on pages 172 and 173; then assign the mystery story. Suggest to students that they plan their story "backward," first deciding how the story will end, then planning the events that will lead up to that ending. This activity should be completed on separate paper.

Proofreading The proofreading practice includes misspellings of words from this lesson as well as a punctuation error and capitalization errors.

LESSON 33

Objectives

- To hear and say words with /ər/.
- To write words with /ər/ with attention to letter sequence and sound/symbol relationships.
- To write each spelling word at least once.
- To recognize that /ər/ may be spelled er, ar, and or.

Sample Sentences

1. I'll go, but I'd really rather stay.
2. I'll go another day, but not today.
3. Ralph put a slice of bread into the toaster.
4. Evelyn is a member of the bicycle club.
5. Ms. Morris is a reading teacher.
6. Christopher Columbus didn't mean to discover a new world.
7. The main character in this story is a good witch.
8. The cat was trained to follow his master.
9. A lot depends on whether or not we win this game.
10. A crowd began to gather around the magician.
11. I'll answer your question in a minute.
12. Mrs. Sloan's watch is made of silver.
13. Step into the center of the circle.
14. Jamie looks quite similar to Johnny.
15. We keep old furniture down in the cellar.
16. Robin likes to put sugar on grapefruit.
17. The polar bear stayed cool by swimming.
18. José bought a calendar for next year.
19. I like riddles better than other kinds of humor.
20. Tony is going to be a movie actor someday.

Note

- The sample sentences may be used for pretesting.
- Words are grouped according to spellings of /ər/:
  er
  ar
  or

Lesson 33 Words with /ər/

Listen for /ər/ in each word.

rather
another
toaster
member
teacher
discover
character
master
whether
gather
answer
silver
center

similar
cellar
sugar
polar
calendar

humor
actor

1. Which word begins with the letters wh? whether
2. Which word begins with /sh/? sugar
3. Write the other two words that begin with the letter s. silver similar
4. Which two words begin with the letter c that is pronounced /s/? center cellar
5. Which two words begin with /k/? Circle the letters that spell /k/. (ch)aracter (c)alendar
6. Which three words begin with a vowel? another answer actor
7. Which word begins and ends like daughter? discover
8. Which word begins with the letter p? polar
9. Write the two words that begin and end like meter. member master
10. Write the two words that begin and end like timber. toaster teacher
11. Which two words have the same spelling of /ər/ as director? humor actor
12. Write the word in which you see the letter w but don't hear /w/. answer
13. Write the four words that contain the letters th. rather another whether gather

176

Preparation Have students read aloud the title of the lesson on page 176. Read each spelling word aloud. Have students repeat and then spell each word aloud.

Ask students to name the base words in toaster (*toast*), teacher (*teach*), discover (*cover*), and actor (*act*). Then have students identify the /ər/ sound in each word in the lesson and the letters that spell this sound.

Read the sample sentences. Have students point to each spelling word as you read the sentence for it.

The Page Have students complete page 176. Then have volunteers read the answers aloud or write them on the board. Have students correct their own work.

Follow-Up Suggest that students fold a piece of paper into thirds. Then have them write words with the er spelling of /ər/ in the first column, words with the ar spelling of /ər/ in the second column, and words with the or spelling /ər/ in the third column.

Checkpoint

Write a spelling word for each clue. Then use the Checkpoint Study Plan on page 224.

1. Alike but not the same is ___. similar
2. An animal's owner is its ___. master
3. A large, white animal from the north is a ___ bear. polar
4. A storage space beneath a house is a ___. cellar
5. Coins made of ___ are valuable. silver
6. The middle part is the ___. center
7. The opposite of question is ___. answer
8. A person in a book is a ___. character
9. If you would prefer, then you would ___. rather
10. A sweetener is ___. sugar
11. If you can laugh at yourself, you have a sense of ___. humor
12. She joined, so she is now a ___. member
13. If you don't like this one, then try ___. another
14. A person with a part in a play is an ___. actor
15. An instructor is a ___. teacher
16. You can heat English muffins in a ___. toaster
17. The opposite of scatter is ___. gather
18. Another word for if is ___. whether
19. To find is to ___. discover

20. The Latin word for months was *calendae.* Roman merchants called their monthly account books *calendārium.* The mystery word comes from *calendārium.* It names our system of dividing the year into twelve months. Can you find the word? ___ calendar

Objectives

- To write spelling words in response to clues: definitions, synonyms, antonyms, and context.
- To develop the critical thinking skills of drawing conclusions and making inferences.
- To understand that the meaning and spelling of words in the English language often change over time.

Spelling Strategy

Students who forget to include the w in answer may benefit from the following mnemonic device: "An answer is often given to a word that begins with w: who, what, why, where, when."

As an aid in remembering how to spell /ər/ in the words in this lesson, have students say each word aloud several times, replacing the /ə/ with a more distinct vowel sound. For example, have them pronounce actor as /ăk′ tôr/. Remind students that this pronunciation is incorrect, but tell them that if they hear it in their mind as they write the word, it will serve as a spelling reminder.

Preparation The clues on this page are like crossword puzzle clues. Explain to students that the response to each clue is a spelling word. Use the following examples to illustrate the types of clues used:

Definition	An instructor is a (*teacher*).
Synonym	Another word for if is (*whether*).
Antonym	The opposite of question is (*answer*).
Context	If you don't like this one, then try (*another*).

The final clue explains the Latin origin of calendar.

The Page Have students complete page 177 using the words on page 176. When students have finished, have them read each clue and spell the answer aloud. Check each response twice: once for the correct answer and a second time for spelling accuracy.

Follow-Up Guide pupils in using the **Checkpoint Study Plan** on page 224 to take a self-test. Then have them use the plan for independent study.

Objectives

- To write words with /ər/ in continuous text.
- To write each spelling word once.
- To integrate reading with spelling.

Use each list word once.

An Interview with Jamie Knight

Many people consider Jamie Knight to be the greatest movie ___actor___ alive today. However, not everybody knows that Jamie has held many different jobs. Here, Jamie tells My Magazine (MM) about his career.

MM: Jamie, when did you ___discover___ that you wanted to be an actor?

JK: When I saw my first play. I knew right away that I'd ___rather___ be in the ___center___ of the stage than be a ___member___ of the audience.

MM: What was your first acting job?

JK: Well, that's a hard question to ___answer___. When I was nine, my friends and I put on a play in the neighborhood. We held it downstairs in the ___cellar___ of my parents' house. There were lots of acts. I was the ___master___ of ceremonies.

But my first real acting job was in a TV commercial. I was a piece of bread popping out of a ___toaster___.

MM: I ___gather___ that you don't like doing commercials very much.

JK: It pays well, but I found myself doing one after ___another___. In commercials, I played a bowl of ___sugar___ and a ___polar___ bear, among other things. My ___teacher___

178

Note

Point out the use of the word humor in the interview as part of the phrase sense of humor, a person's ability to see the humor in his or her situation.

Preparation Have students turn to pages 178 and 179. Let them look at the interview and the pictures. Call their attention to the word list. Have the students say the words. Then explain that each spelling word belongs in one of the blanks in the interview.

Write the title "An Interview with Jamie Knight" on the board. Ask students what an interview is. (*an article in which a writer asks questions and the person being interviewed answers them*) Tell students that this is a fictional interview between a magazine writer and an actor. Ask students if they have ever read an interview in a magazine or newspaper. If so, have them tell what publication the interview was in, who was being interviewed, and what was said. Tell students that in an interview, the magazine writer is sometimes not identified because the focus is on the person being interviewed. Have students identify the interviewer by looking in the first paragraph. (*My Magazine*)

The Pages Have students complete pages 178 and 179 independently by silently reading the interview and writing the missing spelling words. Or you may read the interview aloud, supplying the missing words as students follow along in their texts; then have the students complete the pages on their own.

in acting school taught me to keep a sense of humor. But I used to wonder whether I'd ever get a real acting job.

MM: What is your favorite character to play on stage?

JK: Captain Hook in Peter Pan is my favorite role. I love playing a pirate. I've had many similar roles since. Having chests of gold and silver and roaring to scare people is great fun.

MM: What are you doing next, Jamie?

JK: Let me look at my calendar for next month. Oh yes! I'm opening in a new play in San Francisco. In this play, I have several roles. It will be interesting.

MM: It sounds unusual; that's for certain. Thank you, Jamie, for giving us your time.

JK: The pleasure was mine.

rather
another
toaster
member
teacher
discover
character
master
whether
gather
answer
silver
center
similar
cellar
sugar
polar
calendar
humor
actor

When students have finished, you may wish to discuss the interview. Ask students what kind of person Jamie Knight is. (*interesting, friendly, open, energetic, gracious, and probably a good actor*) Ask students whether or not they think the interviewer asked interesting questions. (*Answers will vary.*) Ask what kind of information about Jamie Knight's life you don't get from the interview. (*his age, where he was born, where he lives now, whether he is married or not, whether he has children*) You may wish to encourage students to interview a parent or another adult. Tell them to make up a list of questions based on the list above and the questions in the interview. Then have them write their results in the same format as that of the selection.

Have a volunteer read each paragraph in the interview, supplying each missing spelling word and spelling it aloud. Have other volunteers write the answers on the board and have students correct their own work. Check student responses for the accurate spelling of each answer.

Follow-Up Have students use each of the spelling words they missed in an original sentence that relates to the interview.

As an additional follow-up activity, you may wish to have pairs of students take turns reading the interview aloud to each other, pausing before each spelling word. The other student will supply the missing word by spelling it aloud at the appropriate time.

Enrichment

If you want to use the blackline activity masters for enrichment and additional practice, assign Lesson 33 activities at this time.

Maintenance and Review

OBJECTIVE

- To review words with /ə/ spelled e, a.

ACTIVITIES

If you want to use the blackline activity masters for maintenance and review, assign Lesson 32 activities at this time.

You can also use the activity below to review Lesson 32 with students:

Write the following words on the board. Have students write the word or words from Lesson 32 that are synonyms for each word. (Answers are in parentheses.)

easy	(*simple*)
mystery	(*puzzle*)
fall	(*tumble*)
shake	(*tremble*)
pair	(*couple, double*)
last	(*final*)
sign	(*signal*)
instance	(*example*)

Objectives

- To relate spelling words to a dictionary skill.
- To identify idioms.
- To write spelling words in the context of sentences.
- To practice proofreading.
- To use the **Spelling Dictionary.**

Idioms

An idiom is a phrase that may not be understood from the meanings of its separate words. Idioms are usually listed at the end of the entry for the main word in the idiom.

You make my blood boil when
you say things like that!

> **blood** | blŭd | *n.* **1.** The red liquid that is pumped through the body by the heart. **2.** Family relationship: *My cousin and I are related by blood.*
> ***Idioms.*** **make one's blood boil.** To anger. **make one's blood run cold.** To frighten.

★ Write the sentences below. Unscramble the spelling word in each sentence. Then underline each idiom.

1. John won't sanwre me because he's feeling down in the dumps.
   John won't answer me because he's feeling down in the dumps.
2. He's probably snowed under with homework from his math heactre.
   He's probably snowed under with homework from his math teacher.
3. Perhaps he has his hands full trying to become a bermem of the drama club.
   Perhaps he has his hands full trying to become a member of the drama club.
4. It is out of chtrraace for me to go poking my nose into his business.
   It is out of character for me to go poking my nose into his business.
5. We should put on our thinking caps to codsienr how to help him.
   We should put on our thinking caps to consider how to help him.
6. Let's tell some jokes to rhoum him and keep him on his toes.
   Let's tell some jokes to humor him and keep him on his toes.

Preparation Have students read the title of page 180. Write the following phrase on the board: **in the know**. Ask students what the phrase means. *(having inside information)* Have them look up know in the **Dictionary** and have a volunteer read the part of the entry that lists in the know. Ask what word comes before this phrase. *(idiom)* Tell students that an idiom is a phrase that the reader might not understand from the meanings of the separate words. Ask where students should look in the dictionary to find the meaning of an idiom. *(at the bottom of the entry for the main word in the idiom)*

The Page Have students do page 180. Then have volunteers write the answers on the board and review the answers orally.

Follow-Up Have students write what they think is the meaning of each idiom in exercises 1–6. Then tell them to look up each idiom in the classroom dictionary and write the meaning given.

WORDS AT WORK

Challenge Yourself

badger **muscular** **tutor** **razor**

Decide which Challenge Word fits each clue. Check your Spelling Dictionary to see if you were right. Then write sentences showing that you understand the meaning of each Challenge Word.

1. This might describe the legs of someone who climbs mountains.
2. If you are having difficulty with math or English, this person might be able to help you.
3. Many men use this every morning to remove hair from their face.
4. It has short legs and long claws for digging.

Write to the Point

Interview one of your classmates about his or her activities, plans, likes, and dislikes. Write your questions ahead of time, using spelling words from this lesson. Take notes as the answers are given. Then write a final draft of the interview, like the one on pages 178 and 179.

Challenge Use one or more of the Challenge Words in your questions.

Proofreading

Use the proofreading marks to show the errors in the paragraph below. Write the five misspelled words correctly in the blanks.

⬭	word is misspelled
^	word is missing
/	letter should be lower case

At first I didn't know (weather) to be an (acter) ^or a dancer. I finally decided I would (rathur) dance, even though ballet is hard to (mastor). My mother found me a good /Teacher, and I became a (membur) ^of a ballet company.

1. whether
2. actor
3. rather
4. master
5. member

Objectives

- To extend the vowel spellings presented in Lesson 33 to the Challenge Words.
- To use clues and the **Spelling Dictionary** to enlarge students' vocabulary.
- To apply the vowel spellings presented in Lesson 33 in a writing activity.
- To practice proofreading for spelling, capitalization, and missing words.

Dictation Sentences

1. The teacher found the answer in another book.
2. A good actor can play almost any character.
3. The master of the old house has a long silver beard and a good sense of humor.
4. She is a member of our club.
5. I do not know whether or not to put the flowers in the center of the table.
6. The sugar is next to the toaster.
7. You will discover that we have similar tastes in music.
8. After you gather up the old papers, put them in the cellar.
9. Would you rather go dancing than go to the movies?
10. I will write down our date on my calendar so that I don't forget.
11. Look at the polar bear playing!

Challenge Yourself Answers

1. muscular
2. tutor
3. razor
4. badger

Students' sentences will vary.

Test Review these three ways to spell /ər/: er as in answer; ar as in sugar; or as in humor. Test words with /ər/. Use one of these testing methods: (1) Say the word; read the sample sentence from page 176; say the word; have students write it. (2) Read each dictation sentence above; have students write the sentence. Correct the test with students.

Challenge Yourself The optional Challenge Words may be assigned to the entire class or limited to those students who do well on the test. Have students note the vowel spellings in the Challenge Words. You may wish to have students work in pairs. Responses to this activity should be completed on separate paper. Answers to the questions are provided above.

Write to the Point Help students recall the selection "An Interview with Jamie Knight" on pages 178 and 179; then assign the interview. Tell students to write questions that will get their interviewee to talk rather than to give a "yes" or "no" answer. This activity should be completed on separate paper.

Proofreading The proofreading practice includes misspellings of words from this lesson as well as a capitalization error and missing words.

LESSON 34

Objectives

- To hear and say words with ion.
- To write words with ion with attention to letter sequence and sound/symbol relationships.
- To write each spelling word at least once.

Sample Sentences

1. Alaska is the biggest state in the nation.
2. This movie has lots of fast action.
3. Next week I'm going on a vacation.
4. We will know who won the election soon.
5. The teacher read the last instruction.
6. In which direction are we going?
7. The electric light was an important invention.
8. The judges announced their selection.
9. Marvin has a collection of erasers.
10. This book has all the information you need.
11. Each car must pass an inspection before you drive it.
12. Please don't mention our fight to anyone.
13. Some industries cause pollution.
14. Rockets may soon be a common form of transportation.
15. What is the population of the earth?
16. Which radio station do you listen to?
17. In a fraction of a second, the rabbit was gone.
18. This is a good location for a bakery.
19. The records are kept in this section of the library.
20. Students in this school get a good education.

Note

The sample sentences may be used for pretesting.

Lesson 34 Words with ion

Say each word.

nation
action
vacation
election
instruction
direction
invention
selection
collection
information
inspection
mention
pollution
transportation
population
station
fraction
location
section
education

1. Write the four words that begin with the letters in.
   instruction invention
   information inspection
2. Write the three words that begin with the letter s.
   selection station
   section
3. Write the word that begins with /k/. collection
4. Which word begins with the letter d?
   direction
5. Which word begins with the letter m?
   mention
6. Which two words begin with the letter e?
   election education
7. Which two words begin with the letter p?
   pollution population
8. In which three words is /ā/ the first vowel sound?
   nation vacation
   station
9. In which word is /ō/ the first vowel sound?
   location
10. In which three words is /ă/ the first vowel sound?
    action transportation
    fraction
11. In which word do you hear /j/ but don't see the letter j?
    education
12. Write the two words in which /l/ is spelled ll.
    collection pollution

182

Preparation Have students read aloud the title of the lesson on page 182. Read each spelling word aloud. Tell students to repeat and then spell each word aloud.

Tell students that ion can be added to base words to form nouns. Ask students to identify the base words in action (*act*), election (*elect*), instruction (*instruct*), direction (*direct*), invention (*invent*), selection (*select*), collection (*collect*), information (*inform*), inspection (*inspect*), and transportation (*transport*).

Read the sample sentences. Have students point to each spelling word as you read the sentence for it.

The Page Have students complete page 182. Then have volunteers write the answers on the board and have students correct their own work.

Follow-Up Suggest that students write each word starting with very large letters, working down to tiny letters.

Checkpoint

Write a spelling word for each clue.
Then use the Checkpoint Study Plan on page 224.

1. To talk about briefly is to ____. mention
2. They waited for the train to pull into the ____. station
3. Another word for news is ____. information
4. All of the people in an area make up the ____. population
5. Director is to direction as inventor is to ____. invention
6. An instruction for doing something is a ____. direction
7. A rest from work is a ____. vacation
8. Smog is a type of air ____. pollution
9. Checking out or looking things over is an ____. inspection
10. Trains, cars, and skateboards are forms of ____. transportation
11. The process of doing something is ____. action
12. The process of learning is ____. education
13. Something that is taught is ____. instruction
14. Another word for country is ____. nation
15. Part of a whole unit is a ____. fraction
16. Another word for place is ____. location
17. A part or a division of an area is a ____. section

18. These three mystery words all come from the Latin verb *legere*. *Legere* meant to gather. It was used in many words. Three of these words were *colligere*, *eligere*, and *sēligere*. *Colligere* meant to gather together. Can you guess the mystery word that comes from *collectus*, a past tense form of *colligere*? ____ collection
19. *Eligere* meant to choose. Can you guess the mystery word that comes from *electus*, a past tense form of *eligere*? ____ election
20. *Sēligere* meant to choose from a number. Guess the word that comes from *selectus*, a past tense form of *sēligere*. ____ selection

Objectives

- To write spelling words in response to clues: definitions, analogies, synonyms, and context.
- To develop the critical thinking skills of making inferences and classifying.
- To appreciate the diversity of sources of the English language.

Spelling Strategy

Students who have difficulty spelling longer words such as population and transportation may benefit from dividing the words into syllables. Have students look up these words in the **Spelling Dictionary** and write them with extra space between the syllables. Then have them practice looking at each word, looking away and visualizing the word, and spelling the word aloud syllable by syllable.

Preparation The clues on this page are like crossword puzzle clues. Explain to students that the response to each clue is a spelling word. Use the following examples to illustrate the types of clues used:

Definition	A rest from work is a (*vacation*).
Analogy	Director is to direction as inventor is to (*invention*).
Synonym	Another word for place is (*location*).
Context	Smog is a type of air (*pollution*).

The final clue identifies the Latin verb that is the origin of collection, election, and selection.

The Page Have students complete page 183 using the words on page 182. When students have finished, have them read each clue and spell the answer aloud. Check each response twice: once for the correct answer and a second time for spelling accuracy.

Follow-Up Guide pupils in using the **Checkpoint Study Plan** on page 224 to take a self-test. Then have them use the plan for independent study.

Objectives

- To write words with ion in continuous text.
- To write each spelling word once.
- To integrate reading with spelling.

Note

- Point out that manatees are mammals that live in the water and look something like seals. Early sailors thought they were mermaids. In summer manatees live in the ocean, but in winter they go to the inland waterways of Florida.
- Point out that prairie chickens are not chickens but brown birds related to quail and grouse.

Use each list word once.

Public Service Announcements

1. It's time to start planning your next vacation.
Why not take a trip across the nation?
There are many means of transportation
To get to just about any location.
If you need more information,
Write to U.S. Travel Destinations
In care of this TV station.

★★★

2. Isn't it time you furthered your education
about the dangers of pollution?
Pollution upsets the animal population
in our wild areas. Isn't it time for each of us to take action? We can start in a new direction before it's too late for the manatees, the prairie chickens, and the last hundred foxes living in one small section of Texas.
If you would like to help, please take up a collection in your neighborhood or school club. You can help correct this sad situation.

★★★

3. It's election time again. Have you signed up to vote?

Preparation

Have students turn to pages 184 and 185. Let them look at the announcements and the picture. Call their attention to the word list. Have the students say the words. Then explain that each spelling word belongs in one of the blanks on the pages.

Write the title "Public Service Announcements" on the board. Then ask what kind of selection this is. (*a series of notices*) Tell students that these paragraphs are meant to be read on television by an announcer. Tell students that people broadcast such notices to give information, to tell where information is available, or to ask for other people's help.

The Pages

Have students complete pages 184 and 185 independently by silently reading the announcements and writing the missing spelling words. Or you may read the announcements aloud, supplying the missing words as students follow along in their texts; then have the students complete the pages on their own.

When students have finished, you may wish to discuss the announcements. Ask students which announcement gives information (*5*); which ones tell where information is available (*1, 2, 4, 5*); and which ask people to do something (*2, 3*). Ask if any students have posted similar notices in school. If so, have them tell what information the notice contained and whether or not people responded.

4. Starting your own business? Our book tells how to set up a business. Each ___instruction___ is clear and easy to follow. Do you plan to run an office? Or do you want to set up a factory for making clothes? This free book can help you. Write for The Business Manager's Guide. When you order our book, just ___mention___ this TV station, and we'll send you a gift that will aid in the ___selection___ of your office furniture.

★★★

5. Don't be fooled by a salesclerk's gift for fast talk. Be careful when he or she presents you with the latest new ___invention___ to cut your work to a ___fraction___ of its time.

All merchandise is inspected by our company. After ___inspection___, it is rated. Simply call us or write for our free book, Better Merchandise Rating.

nation
action
vacation
election
instruction
direction
invention
selection
collection
information
inspection
mention
pollution
transportation
population
station
fraction
location
section
education

Have a volunteer read each announcement, supplying each missing spelling word and spelling it aloud. Have other volunteers write the answers on the board and have students correct their own work. Check students' responses for the accurate spelling of each answer.

Follow-Up

Have students use each of the spelling words they missed in an original sentence that relates to the announcements.

As an additional follow-up activity, you may wish to have one student read the announcements aloud to the class, pausing before each spelling word. The other students will say the spelling word at the appropriate time.

Enrichment

If you want to use the blackline activity masters for enrichment and additional practice, assign Lesson 34 activities at this time.

Maintenance and Review

OBJECTIVE

- To review words with /ər/ spelled er, ar, or.

ACTIVITIES

If you want to use the blackline activity masters for maintenance and review, assign Lesson 33 activities at this time.

You can also use the activity below to review Lesson 33 with students.

Write the following words on the board. Have students refer to the Lesson 33 word list and write the word or words that rhyme with each word below. (Answers are in parentheses.)

tractor	*(actor)*
lather	*(rather, gather)*
solar	*(polar)*
preacher	*(teacher)*
coaster	*(toaster)*
faster	*(master)*
dancer	*(answer)*
speller	*(cellar)*
enter	*(center)*

Objectives

- To relate spelling to another language skill.
- To review the use of a colon in expressions of time and to introduce a list.
- To write spelling words in the context of sentences.

Colons

Use a colon between the hour and the minutes in expressions of time.

I leave the house at 7:15 every morning.

★ Write the following sentences, using colons and numbers in expressions of time. Use one of these words to fill in each blank.

station **vacation**

1. The train left the ___ in Boston at two thirty and arrived in New York at six forty-five. The train left the station in Boston at 2:30 and arrived in New York at 6:45.

2. We are leaving for our summer ___ promptly at nine in the morning. We are leaving for our summer vacation promptly at 9:00 in the morning.

Use a colon after a word that introduces a series or a list.

Be sure to pack everything you'll need: blankets, warm clothing, boots, and food.

★ Write each sentence below, putting a colon after the word that introduces the list.

3. Three topics will be covered on our test pollution, transportation, and why populations move. Three topics will be covered on our test: pollution, transportation, and why populations move.

4. There have been many important inventions the wheel, the gasoline engine, the telephone, and pizza. There have been many important inventions: the wheel, the gasoline engine, the telephone, and pizza.

5. There are three candidates running for election Mayor Hibbs, Mrs. Gold, and Mr. Santos. There are three candidates running for election: Mayor Hibbs, Mrs. Gold, and Mr. Santos.

186

Preparation Have students read aloud the title of page 186. Then write the following on the board: 9:15

Ask students what the punctuation mark between the numbers is called. (*a colon*) Ask a volunteer to tell where the colon goes in expressions of time. (*between the hour and the minutes*)

Write the following sentence on the board:

This bakery sells many things: cakes, cookies, milk, and ice cream.

Ask students why the colon is used here. (*to introduce a list*) Remind students that a comma belongs between each item in the list.

The Page Have students do page 186. Then have volunteers write the answers on the board and review the answers orally.

Follow-Up Write the following topics on the board. Have students write a sentence about each one, using a colon to introduce a list.

1 forms of transportation
2 steps in education
3 kinds of pollution
4. several nations
5. things to do on vacation

WORDS AT WORK

Challenge Yourself

consternation **pension** **friction** **audition**

Decide which Challenge Word fits each clue. Check your Spelling Dictionary to see if you were right. Then write sentences showing that you understand the meaning of each Challenge Word.

1. You might feel this emotion if your rowboat began to leak in the middle of the lake.
2. This wears down the heels of your shoes.
3. This might help someone pay the rent after retiring from a job.
4. You must do well at this if you want a part in a play.

Write to the Point

Write an announcement for an event at your school. Choose a real event or make up one. It could be a meeting, a show, a festival, a sports event, or anything you wish. Give all the information students will need, and tell them why they should attend. Use spelling words from this lesson in your announcement.

Challenge Use one or more of the Challenge Words in your announcement.

Proofreading

Use the proofreading marks to show the errors in the paragraph below. Write the five misspelled words correctly in the blanks.

(oval) word is misspelled
(circled dot) period is missing
(triple underline) letter should be capitalized

Tonight at City Hall on Oak Road, mayor Bond will discuss the acttion we must take to stop polution in our city and to provide better educasion for the entire popullation She will also mension the new train station.

1. action
2. pollution
3. education
4. population
5. mention

187

Objectives

- To extend students' knowledge of words with ion through the Challenge Words.
- To use clues and the **Spelling Dictionary** to enlarge students' vocabulary.
- To apply the vowel spellings presented in Lesson 34 in a writing activity.
- To practice proofreading for spelling, punctuation, and capitalization.

Dictation Sentences

1. There will be an inspection tomorrow.
2. I have to look up information on the brain.
3. Most of the population voted in the election.
4. Her children take dance instruction under the direction of a famous teacher.
5. The pollution here is bad because this town is the location of many factories.
6. The city is taking action to improve its transportation and education.
7. His invention is a radio that can pick up any station in the nation.
8. We have a wide selection of vacation plans.
9. This is just a fraction of the art collection.
10. Did I mention that we built this section of the house ourselves?

Challenge Yourself Answers

1. consternation
2. friction
3. pension
4. audition

Students' sentences will vary.

Test Review and test words with ion. Use one of these testing methods: (1) Say the word; read the sample sentence from page 182; say the word; have students write it. (2) Read each dictation sentence above; have students write the sentence. Correct the test with students.

Challenge Yourself The optional Challenge Words may be assigned to the entire class or limited to those students who do well on the test. You may wish to have students work in pairs. Responses to this activity should be completed on separate paper. Answers to the questions are provided above.

Write to the Point Help students recall the selection "Public Service Announcements" on pages 184 and 185; then assign the announcement. Remind students that an announcement about an event should include the date, time, and location. This activity should be completed on separate paper.

Proofreading The proofreading practice includes misspellings of words from this lesson as well as a punctuation error and a capitalization error.

LESSON 35

Objectives

- To hear and say homophones.
- To write homophones with attention to letter sequence and sound/symbol relationships.
- To write each spelling word at least once.

Sample Sentences

1. Ted threw the book to Sal.
2. Terry ran through the open door.
3. Touch your left elbow with your right hand.
4. Wilma began to write another story.
5. Herman crawled through a hole in the fence.
6. Willie ate a whole loaf of bread.
7. Trucks are not allowed on this road.
8. Rita rode a horse to Jan's house.
9. Paula wore a plain black dress.
10. Peter flew a plane to Mexico City.
11. Walter tied the scarf around his waist.
12. It's a shame to waste all that food, so I'll eat it.
13. An inchworm likes to crawl its way around.
14. Iris hopes it's not too late to call.
15. Toby is going to Toronto.
16. Tillie is going, too.
17. The two of them will visit friends.
18. They will also see their relatives.
19. An aunt and an uncle live there.
20. They're staying for a week.

Note

The sample sentences may be used for pretesting.

Lesson 35 Homophones

Say each word.

threw
through
right
write
hole
whole
road
rode
plain
plane
waist
waste
its
it's
to
too
two
their
there
they're

1. Write the five words that begin with the letters th. threw through their there they're
2. Which word ends with the letters ane? plane
3. Which word ends with the letters oad? road
4. Which three words begin with the letter w and end with the letter e? write whole waste
5. Write the two words that have an apostrophe. it's they're
6. Which word is spelled the same as another word on the list but doesn't have an apostrophe? its
7. Write the shortest word on the list. to
8. In which four words do you see the letter w but don't hear /w/? threw write whole two
9. In which word is /o͞o/ spelled oo? too
10. Which word has the same spelling of /o͞o/ as blew? threw
11. In which two words is /ā/ spelled ai? plain waist
12. In which three words is /ō/ spelled o-e? hole whole rode
13. Which word has the same spelling of /ī/ as might? right

188

Preparation Have students read aloud the title of the lesson on page 188. Ask what homophones are. *(words that sound alike but have different spellings and different meanings)* Read each spelling word aloud. Have students repeat and then spell each word aloud.

Note that the words through and right contain the silent letters gh. Ask why it's and they're have apostrophes. (*They are contractions.*) Then ask what two words each contraction stands for. (*it is; they are*)

Read the sample sentences. Have students point to each spelling word as you read the sentence for it. You may wish to spell aloud the spelling word in each sample sentence to avoid confusion.

The Page Have students complete page 188 and correct the answers by having volunteers write the answers on the board. Have students correct their own work. Suggest that students work at home with a family member or a friend to use each word correctly in a sentence and spell it aloud.

Checkpoint

Write a spelling word for each clue.
Then use the Checkpoint Study Plan on page 224.

1. The opposite of wrong is ___.
2. A highway is a kind of ___.
3. If you're finished, then you're ___.
4. Another word for also is ___.
5. A piece of pie is part of the ___.
6. The opposite of fancy is ___.
7. One and one make ___.
8. A belt goes around your ___.
9. Today I ride, last week I ___.
10. We flew over your house in a jet ___.
11. With a brush you paint, with a pencil you ___.
12. If you want to say it is, say ___.
13. Another word for tossed is ___.
14. You can use a shovel to dig a ___.
15. If you want to say they are, say ___.
16. He asked me to give this package ___ you.
17. The way to say belonging to it is ___.
18. It's not here. It's over ___.
19. The way to say belonging to them is ___.
20. The English word vast means very large. It comes from the Latin word *vastus*. In addition to meaning very large, *vastus* meant destroyed. From this second meaning of *vastus* comes another English word. This word as a verb means to destroy. As a noun it means something that has been destroyed. Can you guess this word? ___

right
road
through
too
whole
plain
two
waist
rode
plane
write
it's
threw
hole
they're
to
its
there
their

waste

Objectives

- To write spelling words in response to clues: definitions, synonyms, antonyms, analogies, and context.
- To develop the critical thinking skills of making inferences, analyzing, and sequencing.
- To understand that words have come to the English language from other languages and that a word may have more than one meaning.

Spelling Strategy

If students confuse homophones such as plane and plain or there and their, it may be helpful to have them write sentences containing the homophones, then exchange papers with a partner and check each other's spelling.

Preparation The clues on this page are like crossword puzzle clues. Explain to students that the response to each clue is a spelling word. Use the following examples to illustrate the types of clues used:

Definition	A highway is a kind of (*road*).
Synonym	Another word for tossed is (*threw*).
Antonym	The opposite of wrong is (*right*).
Analogy	With a brush you paint, with a pencil you (*write*).
Context	You can use a shovel to dig a (*hole*).

The final clue explains the origin of waste.

The Page Have students complete page 189 using the words on page 188. When students have finished, have them read each clue and spell the answer aloud. Check each response twice: once for the correct answer and a second time for spelling accuracy.

Follow-Up Guide pupils in using the **Checkpoint Study Plan** on page 224 to take a self-test. Then have them use the plan for independent study.

Objectives

- To write homophones in continuous text.
- To write each spelling word once.
- To integrate reading with spelling.

Use each list word once.

Important People

Jody loosened the seat belt around her waist. The experience of flying was completely new to her. She tried to act as if she rode planes as often as school buses.

Across the aisle two men were studying important-looking papers. Were they Representatives on their way to the Capitol building to vote on some law? The woman sitting next to her was trying to write something. Jody wondered what it was. She knew it was rude to look too much. But she was curious.

All week at school Jody had been Ms. Big Shot, the winner of the All-State Social Studies prize. Her prize was a trip to Washington, D.C., the capital of the country. Now as she rode through the skies, she didn't feel like such a big shot. Everyone else on the plane seemed so important and serious.

She looked through the window. She saw tiny cars on the road below. The buildings were tiny squares. Is that the way the whole world looks to birds, she wondered.

Jody glanced here and there around the plane. Then she threw a glance at what the woman next to her was writing. Written across the top of the page was SENATOR CLAUDIA GREEN!

190

Preparation Have students turn to pages 190 and 191. Let them look at the pages and the picture. Call their attention to the word list. Have the students say the words. Then explain that each spelling word belongs in one of the blanks on the page.

Write the title "Important People" on the board. Tell students that this is a story about a young girl who meets a senator. Ask students if they know what a senator is. (*one of one hundred people in the Senate who help make the laws in the United States*) Ask if they think a senator would listen to a young girl. Point out that people elect senators, and therefore it is the senators' job to listen to people's opinions. However, anyone under 18 is not eligible to vote, and it would depend on the individual senator.

The Pages Have students complete pages 190 and 191 independently by silently reading the story and writing the missing spelling words. Or you may read the story aloud, supplying the missing words as students follow along in their texts. Then have students complete the pages on their own.

When students have finished, you may wish to discuss the story. Ask why Jody felt important. *(She had a voice in her government.)*

"Wow!" said Jody out loud. "I mean wow!"

The woman looked up and smiled. "That's just what I'd like to say in this speech I'm writing. Would you like to know what it's about? It's about our country's energy problems. By the way, my name is Claudia Green."

"I'm Dody Javis. I mean Jody Davis." Poor Jody was so embarrassed she could have crawled into a hole.

"I'm pleased to meet you, Jody," said the Senator. "I'm concerned about what will happen if this country doesn't use its natural resources better."

"I know," said Jody. "All the kids at school are trying not to waste things like paper and electricity. If parents really thought about their kids, maybe they wouldn't drive their cars so much. What's going to be left when we grow up?"

"That's as plain as can be, Jody. I'd like to put what you just said in my speech. Is that all right with you?"

"Wow! The kids at school are never going to believe I got to talk to a real senator! And they're never going to believe something I said got into a speech."

"Well, how about some proof?" asked the Senator. She took out a card with her name on it. On the back she wrote, "Thanks for the help with my speech, Jody."

"Thank you, Senator," said Jody. "Thanks a lot!"

"We'll be landing in ten minutes," announced the flight attendant. "Please fasten your seat belts."

Jody touched the card in her pocket. Maybe she wasn't so unimportant after all!

191

threw
through
right
write
hole
whole
road
rode
plain
plane
waist
waste
its
it's
to
too
two
their
there
they're

Enrichment

Assign the Lesson 35 blackline activity masters for enrichment and additional practice at this time.

Maintenance and Review

OBJECTIVE

- To review words with ion.

ACTIVITIES

If you want to use the blackline activity masters for maintenance and review, assign Lesson 34 activities at this time. You can also use the activity below to review Lesson 34 with students.

Write the following word pairs on the board. Have students write a sentence containing each word pair.

inspection–pollution
nation–election
mention–location
population–section
vacation–transportation

Follow-Up Have students use each of the spelling words they missed in an original sentence that relates to the story.

As an additional follow-up, students may wish to find out who their senators and representatives are and write them a letter expressing their opinion about pollution or another important issue. Have them show their letters and the replies to the class. Emphasize that changes in the laws are sometimes made by people writing letters to their representatives in Congress.

Objectives

- To relate spelling words to a dictionary skill.
- To review and identify homophones.
- To write spelling words in context.
- To use the **Spelling Dictionary.**

Note

Homophone comes from the prefix homo, which means same, and phone, which means sound.

Homophones

Words that sound alike but have different spellings and meanings are called homophones (*homo* means same, and *phone* means sound).

They rode on the new road.

Some dictionaries list homophones at the end of an entry.

road |rōd| *n.* **1.** An open way for the passage of vehicles, persons, and animals. **2.** Any path or course; *the road to enlightenment*. **3.** A railroad. **4. roads.** An offshore anchorage area for ships; a roadstead: *ships lying in the roads.* **—modifier:** *road signs.* ¶*These sound alike* **road, rode.**

rode |rōd|. Past tense of **ride.** ¶*These sound alike* **rode, road.**

★ Look up plain and plane in the Spelling Dictionary. Write the sound spelling and first definition for each.

1. plain /plān/ 1. Something that is easy to hear, see, or understand.

2. plane /plān/ 1. A flat, level surface.

★ Write each sentence below, using the correct word in the blank.

3. We flew to San Diego in a jet ____.
We flew to San Diego in a jet plane.

4. My uncle likes ____ food with no rich sauces.
My uncle likes plain food with no rich sauces.

★ Use the Spelling Dictionary to answer the questions about these homophones:

its it's waist waste write right

5. Which word is the contraction of "it is"? it's

6. Which word names a part of the body? waist

7. Which word means "belongs to it"? its

8. Which word means the opposite of left? right

9. Which word means "to use carelessly"? waste

10. Which word names something you do with a pencil? write

192

Preparation

Have students read the title of page 192. Remind them that homophones are words that sound the same but have different meanings and different spellings. Ask students if they can think of any homophones not on their spelling list. If necessary, give them the first word in each pair below and have them spell aloud its homophone.

sun son groan grown
fir fur hey hay

Then have students use each homophone correctly in a sentence.

The Page

Have students do page 192. Then have volunteers write the answers on the board.

Follow-Up

Have students write each homophone in exercises 3–10 in an original sentence.

WORDS AT WORK

Challenge Yourself

alter **altar** **chili** **chilly**

Decide which Challenge Word fits each clue. Check your Spelling Dictionary to see if you were right. Then write sentences showing that you understand the meaning of each Challenge Word.

1. You may find this in a church or temple.
2. If you like spicy food, you might enjoy this dish.
3. This describes the kind of weather that makes you want to put on a sweater.
4. You do this to pants or a skirt when you put in a hem to make the pants or skirt shorter.

Write to the Point

Have you ever wanted to tell people about an issue you care about? Write a short speech about something that is important to you. You could write about honesty, animal rights, recycling, or whatever you wish. Include reasons and examples that will help your audience see your point of view. Use spelling words from this lesson in your speech.

Challenge Use one or more of the Challenge Words in your speech.

Proofreading

Use the proofreading marks to show the errors in the paragraph below. Write the five misspelled words correctly in the blanks.

(oval)	word is misspelled
≡	letter should be capitalized
(delete mark)	take out word

In there new book called It's Not Too late, the authors right that the future of the hole world depends on on our stopping the waist of natural resources. They say their is still time to save it our planet.

1. their
2. write
3. whole
4. waste
5. there

193

Objectives

- To extend students' knowledge of homophones through the Challenge Words.
- To use clues and the **Spelling Dictionary** to enlarge students' vocabulary.
- To apply the homophones presented in Lesson 35 in a writing activity.
- To practice proofreading for spelling, capitalization, and extra words.

Dictation Sentences

1. It's going to be a great day!
2. The two friends rode their horses along the beach.
3. My friends said they're taking the plane.
4. Is that life jacket too tight around your waist?
5. Take this road for one mile and then turn right.
6. The whole town tried not to waste energy.
7. I walked through the park to get to your house.
8. He threw the ball, and it fell into a hole over there.
9. Use a plain sheet of paper to write the letter.
10. The snake uses its tongue to smell.

Challenge Yourself Answers

1. altar
2. chili
3. chilly
4. alter

Students' sentences will vary.

Test Review and test homophones. Use one of these testing methods: (1) Say the word; read the sample sentence from page 188; say the word; have students write it. (2) Read each dictation sentence above; have students write the sentence. Correct the test with students.

Challenge Yourself The optional Challenge Words may be assigned to the entire class or limited to those students who do well on the test. You may wish to have students work in pairs. Responses to this activity should be completed on separate paper. Answers to the questions are provided above.

Write to the Point Help students recall the selection "Important People" on pages 190 and 191; then assign the speech. Encourage students to begin their speech in a way that will capture the interest of the audience and to end it in a way that will leave a strong impression. You may want to have students present their speeches to the class. This activity should be completed on separate paper.

Proofreading The proofreading practice includes misspellings of words from this lesson as well as a capitalization error and extra words.

LESSON 36

Objectives

- To review and reinforce vowel spellings for /ə/, /ər/, and ion.
- To hear, say, spell, and write representative spelling words from Lessons 31–34.
- To write a persuasive letter using the five steps in the writing process.
- To use a prewriting activity to generate reasons and examples for a persuasive letter.

Dictation Sentences

1. This whistle costs a nickel.
2. There is a picture of a beautiful dog on my calendar.
3. I have a happy memory of my trip to the ocean.
4. Your invention is similar to mine.
5. Do you know whether this road goes in the right direction?
6. This stamp is a good example from my collection.
7. His sense of humor was a surprise to me.
8. It's dangerous to lean against that fence.
9. That character is only in the final act of the play.
10. I want a good education.
11. There will be a general meeting of the club today.

Note

A review test blackline master in standardized format and an answer sheet have been provided on pages T40 and T41 of this Teacher's Edition. The answers to the review test are given below.

1–A	11–D
2–B	12–A
3–B	13–C
4–C	14–A
5–B	15–B
6–D	16–D
7–C	17–A
8–A	18–B
9–D	19–C
10–B	20–D

If words misspelled were from:	have students complete activities:
List A	1, 3
List B	2, 3
List C	4, 6
List D	5, 6

Lesson 36 Words in Review

A. memory, ocean, beautiful, surprise, against, dangerous

B. nickel, final, example, whistle, general

C. character, whether, similar, calendar, humor

D. direction, invention, collection, education

★ You will need a piece of paper for these review activities.

1. In Lesson 31 you studied five different ways to spell /ə/: **a, e, i, o, u.** Write the words in list A.
   memory ocean beautiful surprise against dangerous
2. In Lesson 32 you studied two different ways to spell /ə/: **e, a.** Write the words in list B.
   nickel final example whistle general
3. ★ Look up each review word from lists A and B in the Spelling Dictionary. Write the first definition of each word.
4. In Lesson 33 you studied three different ways to spell /ər/: **er, ar, or.** Write the words in list C.
   character whether similar calendar humor
5. In Lesson 34 you studied words with **ion.** Write the words in list D.
   direction invention collection education
6. ★ Use each review word from lists C and D in a sentence.

Your teacher may give you a test. Answer these questions when you have finished.

7. Did you spell all the words correctly? Yes or No
8. Did you leave out a letter? Yes or No
9. Did you write the wrong letter? Yes or No
10. Did you miss the spelling of a vowel sound? Yes or No

194

Test

Pretest the review words on page 194 to determine which students need reinforcement. Use one of these testing methods: (1) Read the words and the dictation sentences; have students write only the spelling words. (2) Read the dictation sentences and have students write the entire sentences. (3) Have students complete the review test blackline master. (See **Note**.) Correct the pretest with students.

The Pages

Assign pages 194 and 195 according to students' needs.

- Students who have mastered all of the review words may go on to the **Writer's Workshop** on page 195.
- Students who have not mastered all of the review words should complete the activities on page 194 and take a post-test administered with one of the pretesting methods. After the post-test students can then go on to the **Writer's Workshop** on page 195. For students who have misspelled only a few of the review words, you may wish to use the list at left to determine the activities they should complete on page 194.

For students who have misspelled several of the review words, you may wish to assign all of the activities on page 194.

Writer's Workshop

A Persuasive Letter

If you have a strong opinion that you want someone to share, you can try to convince the person by writing a persuasive letter. When you write your letter, it is important to state your opinion clearly and to let the reader know exactly what you would like for him or her to do. Your letter will be most convincing if you back up your opinion with solid reasons and give your reader all the important information he or she needs to know. Here is part of James's letter. In it he tries to persuade the school principal to have a covered bench installed at his bus stop.

> **Dear Dr. Bronstein,**
> **I feel that a covered bench should be built at the corner of Marshall Avenue and Broad Street. Right now we students don't have anywhere to sit while we wait for the bus. Many students sit on the curb. Sitting that close to the road is dangerous. When it rains, we get wet waiting on the bus. A covered bench set about ten feet back from the road would keep us safe and dry.**
> **My mom and dad say that a covered bench like we need would not be very expensive. Our school could even ask parents to give money toward the bench.**

To write his persuasive letter, James followed the steps in the writing process. He began with a cluster map as a **Prewriting** activity. On his cluster map he first wrote his opinion. Then he added reasons to support his opinion. The cluster map also helped James organize his ideas. Part of his cluster map is shown here. Study what James did.

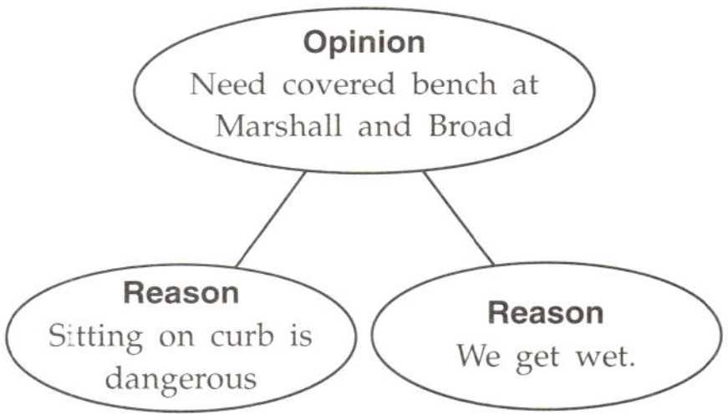

Get ready to write your own persuasive letter. You can write to a friend, a teacher, the mayor, or anyone else you wish. After you have decided what to write about, jot down your opinion and reasons in a cluster map. Then follow the other steps in the writing process—**Writing, Revising, Proofreading,** and **Publishing.**

195

Note

If students have difficulty deciding on a topic, you may wish to suggest one of the following:

Our community should have a public outdoor swimming pool.

The school day should include an hour for computer games.

My parents should let me have a bicycle (take guitar lessons, go to camp, etc.)

Writer's Workshop Explain that in persuasive letters writers try to convince others to do something or believe a certain way. Writers add force to their point of view by backing it up with reasons and examples. Often they use words and phrases that will appeal to the emotions of the reader. Have students read the letter that James wrote to the school principal and point out reasons, examples, words, and phrases that help to make his writing effective.

Allow students to study the sample cluster map shown on the pupil's page and guide students to see how this graphic organizer helped James prepare to write his persuasive letter.

It's Your Turn Review the steps in the writing process with students. If students are not satisfied with the result of their prewriting, allow them to revise it as often as necessary or to choose another topic and repeat the prewriting activity.

Process Writing Blackline Masters
- Cluster Map, page T49
- Steps in the Writing Process, page T44
- Proofreading Symbols/Checklist, page T45

SPELLING

Dic·tion·ar·y

Pronunciation Key

/ă/	**pat**	/î/	**pier**	/th/	**this**
/ā/	**pay**	/ŏ/	**pot**	/ŭ/	**cut**
/â/	**care**	/ō/	**toe**	/û/	**urge**
/ä/	**father**	/ô/	**paw, for**	/zh/	**vision**
/ĕ/	**pet**	/oi/	**noise**	/ə/	**about, item,**
/ē/	**bee**	/o͝o/	**took**		**edible,**
/hw/	**whoop**	/o͞o/	**boot**		**gallop,**
/ĭ/	**pit**	/ou/	**out**		**circus**
/ī/	**pie, by**	/th/	**thin**	/ər/	**butter**

A

ab•surd | əb **sûrd′** | *or* | **-zûrd′** | *adj.* Silly; foolish: *It is absurd to wear a heavy coat when it is very hot outside.*

a•byss | ə **bĭs′** | *n., pl.* **a•byss•es.** A hole or space so deep that it cannot be measured: *If you looked into an abyss, you probably could not see the bottom.*

act | ăkt | *v.* **1.** To do something: *A lifeguard must act quickly.* **2.** To behave: *act your age.* **3.** To play a part; perform: *Sean acted in the play.* —*n.* **1.** An action: *an act of kindness.* **2.** A part of a play: *Let's rehearse the third act.*

ac•tion | **ăk′** shən | *n.* **1.** Something that is done; a deed: *a brave action.* **2.** Motion; activity: *At half time, the cheerleaders jumped into action.*
Idiom. **take action.** To start to do something: *The mayor decided to take action to settle the strike.*

ac•tor | **ăk′** tər | *n.* A person who acts in a play, in a movie, on television, or on radio.

ac•tress | **ăk′** trĭs | *n., pl.* **ac•tress•es.** A girl or woman who acts in a play, a movie, on television, or on radio.

ad•dress | ə **drĕs′** | *n.* **1.** | *also* **ăd′** rĕs′ | The place where someone lives, works, or gets mail. **2.** | *also* **ăd′** rĕs′ | The information on the outside of an envelope that tells where the envelope is being sent. **3.** A formal speech. —*v.* **1.** To write the street, city, state, and zip code on an envelope or package: *address an envelope.* **2.** To make a speech to: *address a crowd.*

a•dore | ə **dôr′** | *or* | ə **dōr′** | *v.* **a•dored, a•dor•ing. 1.** To worship. **2.** *Informal.* To like very much.

a•gain | ə **gĕn′** | *adv.* Once more; another time.

a•gainst | ə **gĕnst′** | *prep.* **1.** In an opposite direction: *We sailed against the wind.* **2.** In contact with: *The rake is leaning against the fence.* **3.** In opposition to: *Our team will compete against yours and win!*

ag•ile | **ăj′** əl | *or* | **ăj′** īl′ | *adj.* Able to move easily and quickly; nimble: *The agile deer leaped over the fence and disappeared into the trees.*

a•gree | ə **grē′** | *v.* **a•greed, a•gree•ing. 1.** To have the same opinion. **2.** To say "yes"; consent: *She agreed to run for president.* **3.** To be the same: *Their stories about the accident do not agree.*

ail•ment | **āl′** mənt | *n.* A sickness or disease: *The doctor said that the ailment was not serious.*

a•larm | ə **lärm′** | *n.* **1.** Sudden fear caused by a feeling of danger: *The animals ran away in alarm.* **2.** A warning that danger is near: *It was only a false alarm.* **3.** A warning signal, such as a bell: *fire alarm.* —*v.* to frighten.

all right | ôl′ **rīt′** | *adj.* **1.** Acceptable; satisfactory: *The pizza was all right, but I've tasted better.* **2.** Correct: *His answers are all right.* —*adv.* **1.** Healthy; safe: *I feel all right.* **2.** Yes: *All right, we'll go with you.*

a•lone | ə **lōn′** | *adj.* Not near other people or things: *Sometimes I enjoy being alone.*
Idioms. **leave alone or let alone.** To not bother or interrupt. **let well enough alone.**

To be satisfied with things as they are and not try to change them.

al•read•y | ôl **rĕd′** ē | *adv.* By this time: *We are already 30 minutes late!*

al•tar | **ôl′** tər | *n.* A table or raised place that is used in religious services: *The altar was in the front of the temple. These sound alike* **altar, alter.**

al•ter | **ôl′** tər | *v.* To make or become different; change: *Mother had to alter my dress because I grew two inches taller. These sound alike* **alter, altar.**

am•a•teur | **ăm′** ə chŏŏr′ | *or* | -chər | *or* | -tyŏŏr′ | *n.* **1.** A person who does something for pleasure, not for money. **2.** A person who does something in an unskilled way.

a•mong | ə **mŭng′** | *prep.* **1.** In the company of: *a party among friends.* **2.** With a portion for each of: *We divided the clay among the class.* **3.** With or between one another: *Let's not argue among ourselves.*

an•gry | **ăng′** grē | *adj.* **an•gri•er, an•gri•est.** **1.** Feeling or showing anger: *an angry look; angry at him.* **2.** Stormy: *angry clouds in the sky.* **3.** Inflamed: *an angry cut on her knee.*

an•i•mal | **ăn′** ə məl | *n.* **1.** A living thing that isn't a plant. **2.** Any animal other than a human being.

an•noy | ə **noi′** | *v.* To make angry; bother.

an•oth•er | ə ***nŭth′*** ər | *adj.* **1.** Different: *Let's try another road.* **2.** One more: *May I have another glass of milk? —pron.* One of a group: *one problem after another.*

an•swer | **ăn′** sər | *or* | **än′**- | *n.* **1.** Something said or written in reply: *I received an answer to my letter.* **2.** The solution to a problem: *Did you get the answer to this math problem? —v.* To speak or write in reply to something: *Sarah likes to answer the telephone.*

a•part•ment | ə **pärt′** mənt | *n.* A room or group of rooms to live in, usually found in large buildings.

a•pol•o•gy | ə **pŏl′** ə jē | *n., pl.* **a•pol•o•gies.** A statement that one is sorry for being rude, doing something wrong, or making a mistake: *Juan gave his apologies to both the host and hostess of the party for being an hour late.*

ap•point | ə **point′** | *v.* **1.** To select for an office or position: *Jason will appoint a chairman.* **2.** To decide on; set: *We will appoint a time for the meeting.*

ap•point•ment | ə **point′** mənt | *n.* **1.** The act of naming someone for an office or position. **2.** An arrangement to meet someone at a certain time and place: *My appointment with the dentist is right after school.*

ap•prove | ə **prōōv′** | *v.* **ap•proved, ap•prov•ing.** **1.** To think or speak well of something: *My parents don't approve of my riding my bike on that busy street.* **2.** To agree or consent to something: *The mayor approved the new city budget.*

A•pril | **ā′** prəl | *n.* The fourth month of the year. April has 30 days.

a•rith•me•tic | ə **rĭth′** mə tĭk | *n.* The science of adding, subtracting, multiplying, and dividing numbers.

ar•row | **ăr′** ō | *n.* **1.** A thin stick, with a point at one end and feathers at the other, made to be shot from a bow. **2.** Anything shaped like an arrow, such as a road sign.

a•sleep | ə **slēp′** | *adj.* **1.** Sleeping: *Were you asleep when I called?* **2.** Numb: *My foot was asleep because I crossed my legs. —adv.* Into sleep: *She always falls asleep in a car.*

as•ter•oid | **ăs′** tə roid′ | *n., pl.* **as•ter•oids.** Any of the thousands of small objects that revolve around the sun. Most are between Mars and Jupiter.

as•tron•o•my | ə **strŏn′** ə mē | *n.* The science that deals with the sun, moon, stars, planets, and other heavenly bodies.

ath•lete | **ăth′** lēt′ | *n., pl.* **ath•letes.** A person who is trained to take active part in sports.

au•di•tion | ô **dĭsh′** ən | *n.* A short performance that shows the ability of an actor, speaker, singer, or other performer: *The audition for the play is tonight. —v.* To try out in an audition: *I plan to audition for the main part in the play.*

Au•gust | **ô′** gəst | *n.* The eighth month of the year. August has 31 days.

aunt | ănt | *or* | änt | *n.* **1.** The sister of one's mother or father. **2.** The wife of one's uncle.

au•ro•ra | ə **rōr′** ə | *n.* Shining bands of flashing light sometimes seen in the night sky.

au•then•tic | ô **thĕn′** tĭk | *adj.* **1.** Real; genuine: *Eduardo has an authentic autograph of a famous baseball player.* **2.** True: *The witness's story of the accident is authentic.*

au•to•mo•bile | ô′ tə mə **bēl′** | *or* | **-mō′** bēl′ | *or* | **ô′** tə mə bēl′ | *n.* A vehicle made to carry passengers; a car.

au•tumn | **ô′** təm | *n.* The season of the year between summer and winter; fall.

a•void | ə **void′** | *v.* To keep away from: *You should avoid ice cream and cake when you're on a diet.*

a•ware | ə **wâr′** | *adj.* Knowing; realizing: *Be aware of the dangers along the hiking trail.*

aw•ful | **ô′** fəl | *adj.* **1.** Causing fear; terrible: *the awful silence in the empty house.* **2.** *Informal.* Very bad: *an awful movie.* **3.** *Informal.* Very large; great: *an awful lot of dishes to wash.*

a•while | ə **hwīl′** | *or* | ə **wīl′** | *adv.* For a short time: *We studied awhile before supper.*

awn•ing | **ô′** nĭng | *n.* A cover that is like a roof over a window or door: *The awning kept the sun off the porch.*

ax•is | **ăk′** sĭs | *n., pl.* **ax•es** | **ăk′** sēz′ |. A straight line around which an object turns or rotates. The axis of the earth runs from the North Pole to the South Pole.

B

badg•er | **băj′** ər | *n.* An animal with thick grayish fur, short legs, and long claws: *Badgers live in holes that they burrow in the ground.*

bak•e•ry | **bā′** kə rē | *n., pl.* **bak•e•ries.** A place where bread, pies, cookies, cakes, etc. are baked or sold.

bal•loon | bə **lo͞on′** | *n.* **1.** A large bag filled with hot air or a gas that is lighter than air, used to lift heavy loads into the air. **2.** A child's toy made of brightly colored rubber that can be blown up by mouth. —*v.* To swell out like a balloon: *The sails ballooned in the wind as we raced through the water.*

ba•nan•a | bə **năn′** ə | *n.* A slightly curved fruit with yellow or reddish skin that peels easily: *Bananas grow in clusters.*

bare | bâr | *adj.* **bar•er, bar•est. 1.** Without covering or clothing: *bare feet.* **2.** Empty: *bare walls.* **3.** Just enough: *the bare necessities of life.*

bar•rel | **băr′** əl | *n.* A large wooden container with round, flat ends of equal size and sides that bulge out slightly.

base•ball | **bās′** bôl′ | *n.* **1.** A game between two teams of nine players each, played with a ball and bat. Baseball is played on a field with four bases that form a diamond pattern. Players score runs by touching all the bases. **2.** The ball used in this game.

bas•ket•ball | **băs′** kĭt bôl′ | *or* | **bä′** skĭt- | *n.* **1.** A game played with a large ball by two teams of five players each. The game is played on a rectangular court with a raised basket at each end. Players score by throwing the ball through the basket at the other team's end of the court. **2.** The large, round ball used in this game.

bear•a•ble | **bâr′** ə bəl | *adj.* Able to be put up with: *The hot day was bearable because the air conditioner kept us cool.*

beau•ti•ful | **byo͞o′** tə fəl | *adj.* Pleasing to hear or see: *beautiful music; a beautiful smile; beautiful weather.*

be•fore | bĭ **fôr′** | *or* | **-fōr′** | *adv.* Earlier; already: *I've read this book before.* —*prep.* Earlier than: *We finished before noon.* —*conj.* Sooner than the time when: *The soup started to boil before I finished making my sandwich.*

be•lieve | bĭ **lēv′** | *v.* **be•lieved, be•liev•ing. 1.** To think that something is true or real. **2.** To think; suppose: *I believe she went home.*

Idiom. **make believe.** To pretend.

bench | bĕnch | *n., pl.* **bench•es. 1.** A long seat: *park bench.* **2.** A heavy work table: *the carpenter's bench.* **3.** The seat for judges in a court of law. —*v.* To take a player out of a game: *The referee benched the player for bad conduct.*

be•neath | bĭ **nēth′** | *prep.* Below; under; underneath.

birth•day | **bûrth′** dā′ | *n.* **1.** The day on which a person was born. **2.** The anniversary of that day.

blind | blīnd | *adj.* **blind•er, blind•est. 1.** Not able to see: *a blind person.* **2.** Hidden: *a blind driveway.* **3.** Without reason or good sense: *a blind guess.* —*n.* Something that shuts out light or blocks sight, such as a window shade. —*v.* **1.** To take away sight: *The sun can blind you.* **2.** To take away reason: *Fright blinded him.*

bliss | blĭs | *n.* Great happiness; joy: *I think it is bliss to see my favorite baseball player hit a home run.*

blood | blŭd | *n.* **1.** The red liquid that is pumped through the body by the heart. **2.** Family relationship: *My cousin and I are related by blood.*

Idioms. **make one's blood boil.** To anger. **make one's blood run cold.** To frighten.

blue•ber•ry | **blo͞o′** bĕr′ ē | *n., pl.* **-ber•ries.** A small, round, dark blue, sweet berry that grows on a shrub.

blunt | blŭnt | *adj.* Having a dull point or edge; not sharp: *Even though a stick may have a blunt point, it hurts if you are poked with it.*

Blvd. Abbreviation of **Boulevard** | **bo͞ol′** ə värd′ |. A wide street usually lined with trees.

board | bôrd | *or* | bōrd | *n.* **1.** A flat, thin piece of lumber. **2.** A flat piece of hard material used for a special purpose: *a diving board; a game board.* **3.** A group of people who manage something: *a school board.* —*v.* **1.** To cover with boards. **2.** To get on a plane, train, ship, or bus.
Idiom. **on board.** Aboard.

boast | bōst | *v.* **1.** To brag. **2.** To take pride in owning: *This city boasts lovely lakes and parks.* —*n.* Bragging statement: *Don't believe all his boasts that he is the best player on the team.*

boil·er | **boi′** lər | *n.* **1.** A large tank for heating water and turning it into steam. **2.** A pot or kettle used for boiling liquids.

bois·ter·ous | **boi′** stər əs | *or* | **boi′** strəs | *adj.* Noisy and not having discipline; unruly: *The speaker asked the boisterous audience to be quiet.*

bor·row | **bŏr′** ō | *or* | **bôr′** ō | *v.* **1.** To take something from someone with the understanding that it must be given back: *borrow a pencil; borrow a library book.* **2.** To adopt: *The English language borrowed many words from other languages.*
Idiom. **borrow trouble.** To take on trouble unnecessarily.

both·er | **bŏ*th*′** ər | *v.* **1.** To trouble; disturb; annoy: *Don't bother me while I'm reading.* **2.** To take the trouble; to be concerned: *Don't bother waiting for me.* —*n.* Something or someone that is annoying: *Washing dishes is a bother.*

bot·tom | **bŏt′** əm | *n.* **1.** The lowest part: *the bottom of the well.* **2.** The under or lower part: *The bottom of the boat was covered with barnacles.* **3.** The ground under water: *The bottom is muddy here.* **4.** The basis; heart: *get to the bottom of the problem.*
Idiom. **from top to bottom.** Thoroughly: *The detective searched the house from top to bottom.*

bought Look up **buy.**

bowl[1] | bōl | *n.* **1.** A round dish used to hold things. **2.** Something shaped like a bowl.

bowl[2] | bōl | *v.* **1.** To play the game of bowling: *Carol likes to bowl after school.* **2.** To roll a ball in the game of bowling: *Who bowls first?*

bowl·ing | **bō′** lĭng | *n.* A game played by rolling a heavy ball down a wooden alley to knock over ten wooden pins at the opposite end.

brain | brān | *n.* **1.** The large mass of nerve tissue inside the skull of a person or animal. **2. brains.** Intelligence: *The pioneers had brains as well as courage.*
Idiom. **rack one's brains.** To try hard to solve something.

branch | brănch | *or* | bränch | *n., pl.* **branch·es.** **1.** A part of a tree or shrub that grows out from the trunk. **2.** Any part that grows out of a main part: *a branch of the river.* —*v.* To divide into branches: *Turn left where the road branches.*

break | brāk | *v.* **broke** | brōk|, **bro·ken** | **brō′** kən |, **break·ing.** **1.** To make something come apart by force; smash. **2.** To harm; damage. **3.** To fail to obey; break the law. **4.** To change: *break an Olympic record.* **5.** To fill with sorrow: *break a heart.* —*n.* **1.** A gap; opening: *a break in the fence.* **2.** A beginning: *the break of day.* **3.** A sudden change: *a break in the weather.*

break·fast | **brĕk′** fəst | *n.* The first meal of the day. —*v.* To eat breakfast.

breath | brĕth | *n.* The air inhaled into and exhaled from the lungs.
Idioms. **hold one's breath.** To wait anxiously or excitedly. **out of breath.** Breathing hard; panting. **save one's breath.** To refrain from useless talking: *Save your breath—he won't go.* **take one's breath away.** To excite or surprise greatly. **under one's breath.** In a whisper.

breathe | brē*th* | *v.* **breathed, breath·ing.** **1.** To inhale and exhale. **2.** To stop for a rest: *The athlete needed a minute to breathe.* **3.** To say quietly; whisper: *I won't breathe a word about the surprise party.*

bridge[1] | brĭj | *n.* **1.** Something built over a river, road, or other obstacle so that people can get across. **2.** The top part of a person's nose. —*v.* **bridged, bridg·ing.** To build a bridge over.

bridge[2] | brĭj | *n.* A card game for four people.

bring | brĭng | *v.* **brought** | brôt |, **bring·ing.** **1.** To carry along or escort: *Bring your sister to our party.* **2.** To cause to happen: *April showers bring May flowers.* **3.** To recall: *bring back happy memories.*

broad•cast | **brôd'** kăst' | *or* | -kăst' | *v.* **broad•cast** *or* **broad•cast•ed, broad•cast•ing.** **1.** To send out news, music, etc. by radio or television. **2.** To make known: *broadcast gossip.* —*n.* A radio or television program: *We listen to the news broadcast at noon.*

broil | broil | *v.* **1.** To cook directly over or under heat: *Dad likes to broil steak.* **2.** To be very hot: *We broiled in the hot sunlight.*

brooch | brōch | *or* | brōōch | *n., pl.* **brooch•es.** A large pin worn for decoration: *The woman wore a diamond brooch on her dress.*

brought Look up **bring.**

budg•et | **bŭj'** ĭt | *n.* A plan for using the money that one receives: *We have a budget so that we won't spend more money than we earn.* —*v.* **budg•et•ed, budg•et•ing.** To make a plan in advance for spending money: *I budget my allowance so that I can save a little each week.*

build | bĭld | *v.* **built** | bĭlt |, **build•ing. 1.** To make by putting parts together. **2.** To make gradually: *She wanted to build a good business.* —*n.* A person's physical make-up: *The athlete had a good build.*

built Look up **build.**

busi•ness | **bĭz'** nĭs | *n., pl.* **busi•ness•es.** **1.** What one does to earn a living; occupation: *Her family is in the jewelry business.* **2.** A factory or store: *They sold their business when they retired.* **3.** Concern, affair: *none of your business.*

bus•y | **bĭz'** ē | *adj.* **bus•i•er, bus•i•est. 1.** Active: *We are busy getting ready for a vacation.* **2.** Full of activity: *a busy day.* **3.** In use: *The phone is busy.*—*v.* **bus•ied, bus•y•ing, bus•ies.** To make busy: *busy yourself with homework.*

buy | bī | *v.* **bought** | bôt|, **bought, buy•ing.** To purchase. —*n.* A bargain: *This jacket was a good buy.*

by-line, also **by•line** | **bī'** līn' | *n.* A line at the beginning of a newspaper or magazine article giving the name of the writer.

C

cal•en•dar | **kăl'** ən dər | *n.* **1.** A chart that shows the days, weeks, and months of the year. **2.** A schedule; a list of things to be done arranged in order: *the school calendar.*

calf[1] | kăf | *or* |käf | *n., pl.* **calves** | kăvs | *or* | kävz |. **1.** A young cow or bull. **2.** A young whale, elephant, or seal. **3.** Leather made from the hide of a calf; calfskin.

calf[2] | kăf | *or* |käf | *n., pl.* **calves** | kăvs | *or* | kävz |. The fleshy back of the human leg below the knee.

cam•er•a | **kăm'** ər ə | *or* | **kăm'** rə | *n.* **1.** A machine for taking photographs or motion pictures. **2.** The part of a television system that changes an image into electronic signals.

can•did | **kăn'** dĭd | *adj.* Honest; frank; open: *Because the mayor wanted everyone to know all the facts, she gave candid answers at the town meeting.*

ca•noe | kə **nōō'** | *n.* A light, narrow boat with pointed ends that is moved with a paddle. —*v.* **ca•noed, ca•noe•ing.** To paddle or go in a canoe.

can•o•py | **kăn'** ə pē | *n., pl.* **can•o•pies.** **1.** A covering made of cloth or other material hung over a bed, throne, or entrance: *The canopy over the bed was made of white cloth.* **2.** A covering that is similar but found somewhere else: *In the rain forest, a canopy of leaves from the taller trees shades the smaller plants.*

care•ful | **kâr'** fəl | *adj.* **1.** Watchful; cautious: *Be careful crossing busy streets.* **2.** Done with care: *careful handling of the expensive equipment.*

cart•wheel | **kärt'** hwēl' | *or* | -wēl' | *n.* **1.** The wheel of a cart. **2.** A sideways handspring.

cas•sette | kə **sĕt'** | *or* | kă- | *n.* **1.** A small case that holds magnetic tape for use in a tape recorder. **2.** A case that holds a roll of film for a camera.

catch | kăch | *v.* **caught** | kôt |, **catch•ing.** **1.** To get hold of something that is moving. **2.** To be in time for: *catch a train.* **3.** To become infected: *catch a cold.* —*n.* **1.** The act of grabbing a ball: *The baseball player made a great catch.* **2.** The amount of something you have caught: *a catch of five trout.* **3.** A game in which a ball is thrown back and forth. ***Idiom.* catch one's breath**. To rest.

caught Look up **catch.**

ce•les•tial | sə **lĕs'** chəl | *adj.* **1.** Related to the sky: *The moon and stars are celestial bodies.* **2.** Heavenly; divine.

cel•lar | **sĕl'** ər | *n.* An underground storage room.

cen•ter | **sĕn'** tər | *n.* The middle point of a circle or a ball. **2.** The middle of anything: *the center of the table.* **3.** A center of activity: *a shopping center.*

cen•tu•ry | **sĕn'** chə rē | *n., pl.* **cen•tu•ries.** A period of 100 years.

cer•tain | **sûr'** tn | *adj.* **1.** Positive; sure: *I'm certain this is the right road.* **2.** Some: *Certain animals hibernate in winter.*

chalk•board | **chôk'** bôrd' | *or* | -bōrd' | *n.*

A hard surface used for writing on with chalk; a blackboard.

cham·pi·on | **chăm′** pē ən | *n.* A person or animal that wins first place in a contest.

chap·ter | **chăp′** tər | *n.* **1.** A main division of a book. **2.** A small division of a club.

char·ac·ter | **kăr′** ĭk tər | *n.* **1.** All the qualities that make a person or thing what it is. **2.** A person in a book, play, or story. **3.** *Informal.* A person who is different or funny.

charge | chärj | *v.* **charged, charg·ing.** **1.** To ask as a price. **2.** To delay payment: *We charged our new rug.* **3.** To attack: *charge the fort.* **4.** To give electricity to: *charge a flashlight battery.* —*n.* **1.** The price asked: *the charge for delivery.* **2.** Responsibility; supervision: *take charge of someone or something.* **3.** An amount of electricity.

check·er | **chĕk′** ər | *n.* **1. a. checkers** *(used with a singular verb).* A game played on a checkerboard by two players. **b.** One of the flat, round pieces used in this game. **2.** One square in a pattern of squares. **3.** An employee who checks out purchases in a self-service store.

cheese·burg·er | **chēz′** bûr′ gər | *n.* A hamburger sandwich with melted cheese on the meat.

chick·en | **chĭk′** ən | *or* | -ĭn | *n.* **1.** A hen or rooster. **2.** The meat of this bird. —*adj. Slang.* Afraid.

chil·i | **chĭl′** ē | *n., pl.* **chil·ies.** **1.** The pod of a red pepper that is often dried and ground to make a spicy seasoning. **2.** A spicy food made of chili powder, beef, tomatoes, and sometimes beans. *These sound alike* **chili, chilly.**

chill·y | **chĭl′** ē | *adj.* **chill·i·er, chill·i·est.** **1.** Cold enough to be somewhat uncomfortable: *Fall days are often chilly.* **2.** Unfriendly: *I was upset by the chilly greeting my friend gave me after our vacation. These sound alike* **chilly, chili.**

chim·ney | **chĭm′** nē | *n., pl.* **chim·neys.** An upright, hollow structure connected to a furnace, fireplace, or stove to carry away smoke.

choice | chois | *n.* **1.** The act of choosing: *make a choice between two things.* **2.** Someone or something that is chosen: *Your choices for a job are many.* —*adj.* **choic·er, choic·est.** Very good; excellent: *choice fruit.*

choose | chōōz | *v.* **chose** | chōz |, **cho·sen** |**chō′** zən|, **choos·ing.** **1.** To pick out: *choose a dessert.* **2.** To decide: *Do as you choose.*

cho·rus | **kôr′** əs | *or* | **kōr′**- | *n., pl.* **cho·rus·es.** **1.** A group of people who sing together. **2.** The part of a song that is repeated after each verse.

chose Look up **choose.**

cit·rus | **sĭt′** rəs | *adj.* Belonging to orange, lemon, lime, or grapefruit trees. —*n., pl.* **cit·rus·es** or **cit·rus.** One of these trees.

climb | klīm | *v.* To go up or move up. —*n.* **1.** The act of climbing: *the climb up the mountain.* **2.** A place to be climbed: *The rocky path is a difficult climb.*

clos·et | **klŏz′** ĭt | *n.* A small room or cabinet used for hanging or storing things.

cloth·ing | **klō′** *th*ĭng | *n.* Coverings worn on the body.

clue | klōō | *n.* Something that helps solve a mystery.

coach | kōch | *n.* **1.** A large carriage pulled by horses. **2.** A train car for passengers. **3.** A low-priced seat on a bus, train, or plane. **4.** A trainer: *a basketball coach; a voice coach.*

coast | kōst | *n.* The edge of land along the sea. —*v.* To move without power or effort: *coast down a hill.*

code | kōd | *n.* **1.** A set of signals that stand for letters and numerals: *Morse Code.* **2.** Secret writing: *The spy wrote the message in code.* **3.** A set of rules or laws: *a traffic code.* —*v.* **cod·ed, cod·ing.** To put into code.

coin | koin | *n.* A piece of metal issued by a government for use as money. —*v.* **1.** To make coins. **2.** To invent: *coin a phrase.*

col·lar | **kŏl′** ər | *n.* Something that is worn around the neck: *lace collar; dog collar.* —*v. Informal.* To capture: *collar a thief.*

col·lec·tion | kə **lĕk′** shən | *n.* **1.** A group of things gathered and kept together: *stamp collection.* **2.** Money that is gathered: *We took up a collection to buy him a gift.*

col·um·nist | **kŏl′** əm nĭst | *or* | -ə mĭst | *n.* One who writes a newspaper or magazine column.

com·et | **kŏm′** ĭt | *n.* A heavenly body with a bright head and a long tail. Comets travel around the sun.

com·fort | **kŭm′** fərt | *v.* To ease someone's sorrow. —*n.* **1.** A condition of ease: *They live in comfort.* **2.** A person or thing that gives relief: *He is a comfort to his mother.*

com•ma | **kŏm′** ə | *n.* A punctuation mark (,) that separates parts of a sentence, parts of an address, and dates.

com•mer•cial | kə **mûr′** shəl | *adj.* Relating to or engaged in business: *a commercial product.* —*n.* A radio or television advertisement.

com•mit | kə **mĭt′** | *v.* **com•mit•ted, com•mit•ting.** To do, carry out, or be guilty of: *commit a crime.*

com•mon | **kŏm′** ən | *adj.* **com•mon•er, com•mon•est. 1.** Shared by all: *common knowledge; common property.* **2.** Occurring often; usual: *Rain is common along the coast.* **3.** Average; ordinary: *common housefly.*
***Idiom.* in common.** Jointly: *interests in common.*

com•pa•ny | **kŭm′** pə nē | *n., pl.* **com•pa•nies. 1.** One or more guests. **2.** Companionship. **3.** A business firm. **4.** A group of actors.

com•pare | kəm **pâr′** | *v.* **com•pared, com•par•ing.** To show how things are alike or different: *Let's compare our answers.*

com•pass | **kŭm′** pəs | *or* | **kŏm′**- | *n.* **1.** An instrument used to show direction north, south, east, or west. **2.** An instrument used for drawing circles.

com•pel | kəm **pĕl′** | *v.* **com•pelled, com•pel•ling.** To force or make someone do something: *A big snowstorm might compel schools to close early.*

com•pete | kəm **pēt′** | *v.* **com•pet•ed, com•pet•ing.** To try hard against others to win something: *compete in a race; compete in business.*

com•pe•ti•tion | kŏm′ pĭ **tĭsh′** ən | *n.* **1.** A contest: *a diving competition.* **2.** The person or persons one competes with: *Is the competition any good?*

com•plain | kəm **plān′** | *v.* To say that something is wrong: *complain about a headache.*

com•plete | kəm **plēt′** | *adj.* **1.** Whole: *a complete set of the encylcopedia.* **2.** Finished; ended: *My report is complete.* **3.** Fully equipped: *a new car complete with power steering.* —*v.* **com•plet•ed, com•plet•ing.** To finish.

con•cept | **kŏn′** sĕpt′ | *n.* A general idea, notion, or understanding: *The concept of equal rights for all is important in the United States.*

con•demn | kən **dĕm′** | *v.* **1.** To strongly disapprove of: *I condemn cheating on a test.* **2.** To find someone guilty and give the punishment: *The judge condemned the robber to five years in prison.* **3.** To say something is unsafe: *The inspector may condemn the run-down apartment building.*

con•serve | kən **sûrv′** | *v.* **con•served, con•serv•ing.** To keep from loss, waste, or harm by using carefully: *Our class learned how to conserve the earth's natural resources.*

con•stel•la•tion | kŏn′ stə **lā′** shən | *n.* A group of stars, such as the Big Dipper.

con•ster•na•tion | kŏn′ stər **nā′** shən | *n.* Great fear, shock, or loss of courage: *Even though there was consternation when the fire alarm sounded, everyone got out safely.*

con•tain•er | kən **tā′** nər | *n.* A box, jar, or can used to hold something.

con•trol | kən **trōl′** | *v.* **con•trolled, con•trol•ling.** To have power over: *control a country; control a car.* —*n.* **1.** Authority or power: *the athlete's control over his body.* **2. controls.** Instruments for operating a machine.

cop•per | **kŏp′** ər | *n.* **1.** A reddish-brown metal. **2.** Small coin. —*adj.* Reddish brown.

cos•met•ic | kŏz **mĕt′** ĭk | *n., pl.* **cos•met•ics.** A preparation, such as powder, lipstick, or skin cream, used to make the face or body more beautiful.

cos•mos | **kŏz′** məs | *or* | **kŏz′** mōs′ | *n.* The universe thought of as an orderly and harmonious system.

cot•tage | **kŏt′** ĭj | *n.* **1.** A small house. **2.** A summer house at the beach.

coun•try | **kŭn′** trē | *n., pl.* **coun•tries. 1.** A nation or state: *Mexico is a country.* **2.** The land outside of towns and cities: *Farms are in the country.*

cou•ple | **kŭp′** əl | *n.* **1.** Two things of the same kind; a pair. **2.** A man and a woman who are engaged, married, or partners in a dance. **3.** *Informal.* A few: *a couple of months.* —*v.* **cou•pled, cou•pling.** To join together.

course | kôrs | *or* | kōrs | *n.* **1.** Onward motion; progress: *the course of history.* **2.** Direction; path: *the course of a river.* **3.** Lessons and classes in a subject. **4.** A piece of land laid out for a sport: *golf course.*
***Idiom.* of course.** Naturally; certainly.

court | kôrt | *or* | kōrt | *n.* **1.** An open place enclosed by buildings or walls. **2.** A place marked for a game: *tennis court.* **3.** A place for holding legal trials. —*v.* **1.** To seek the favor of. **2.** To try to win in marriage.

cous•in | **kŭz′** ən | *n.* The daughter or son of an aunt or uncle.

crack | krăk | *v.* To break with a sharp, snapping sound. —*n.* **1.** A sharp, snapping sound. **2.** A long, narrow opening; a narrow space.

crash | krăsh | *v.* **1.** To fall against or bump into noisily. **2.** To collide. —*n., pl.* **crash•es.** **1.** A loud noise like that made by things falling and breaking. **2.** A violent collision.

crawl | krôl | *v.* **1.** To move slowly on hands and knees or by dragging the body along the ground. **2.** To move very slowly: *The cars crawled up the crowded street.* —*n.* **1.** A slow movement. **2.** A swimming stroke.

crush | krŭsh | *v.* **1.** To press together so as to crumple or injure; squash. **2.** To break into small pieces: *crush ice.* —*n.* A dense crowd: *a crush of people.*

cy•cling | **sī′** klĭng | *n.* The sport of riding a bicycle or motorcycle.

D

dam•age | **dăm′** ĭj | *n.* Injury or harm. —*v.* To injure; harm; hurt.

dan•ger•ous | **dān′** jər əs | *adj.* Unsafe; risky; likely to do harm.

daugh•ter | **dô′** tər | *n.* A female child; a girl or woman, when thought of in relation to her parents.

dawn | dôn | *n.* The coming of daylight in the morning. —*v.* **1.** To begin to grow light in the morning. **2.** To begin to appear or develop: *A new age dawned.*

De•cem•ber | dĭ **sĕm′** bər | *n.* The 12th month of the year. December has 31 days.

de•cide | dĭ **sīd′** | *v.* **de•cid•ed, de•cid•ing.** To make up one's mind; come to a conclusion.

de•clare | dĭ **klâr′** | *v.* **de•clared, de•clar•ing.** **1.** To make known; announce: *The company declared a new policy.* **2.** To take a stand: *He declared himself in favor of building a new school.*

ded•i•ca•tion | dĕd′ ĭ **kā′** shən | *n.* The fact of giving oneself completely to something; devotion: *She shows her dedication to the violin by practicing two hours every day.*

de•feat | dĭ **fēt′** | *v.* To overcome; beat; win a victory over. —*n.* An overthrow.

de•gree | dĭ **grē′** | *n., pl.* **de•grees.** **1.** A unit of measuring temperature. **2.** A unit used in measuring angles: *a 90-degree angle.* **3.** A title given by a college or university. **4.** Amount, extent: *a high degree of skill.*

de•lay | dĭ **lā′** | *v.* To put off until later. —*n.* The act of putting off; a wait.

de•liv•er•y | dĭ **lĭv′** ə rē | *n., pl.* **de•liv•er•ies.** **1.** Distribution; handing over: *mail delivery.* **2.** Manner of speaking: *Her forceful delivery made us listen to her speech.*

de•part | dĭ **pärt′** | *v.* **1.** To go away; leave: *The bus departs in five minutes.* **2.** To change: *The builders departed from the original plan for the house.*

depth | dĕpth | *n.* **1.** The distance from the top to the bottom: *the depth of the lake.* **2.** Deepness of thought, tone, color, etc.

des•ert[1] | **dĕz′** ərt | *n.* A dry, sandy region.

de•sert[2] | dĭ **zûrt′** | *v.* To forsake; abandon: *She did not desert her friends when they needed her.*

de•stroy | dĭ **stroi′** | *v.* To ruin; make useless; lay waste.

dif•fer•ent | **dĭf′** ər ənt | *or* | **dĭf′** rənt | *adj.* **1.** Not alike: *Our paintings are different.* **2.** Separate; distinct; not the same: *We saw him at three different times today.* **3.** Unusual: *a different way of dressing.*

di•rec•tion | dĭ **rĕk′** shən | *or* | dī- | *n.* **1.** Management; guidance. **2.** The point toward which a person or thing faces, points, or moves. **3. directions.** Orders; instructions: *Read the directions before you begin the test.*

di•rec•tor | dĭ **rĕk′** tər | *or* | dī- | *n.* A person who directs or manages something.

dirt•y | **dûr′** tē | *adj.* **dirt•i•er, dirt•i•est.** **1.** Not clean: *dirty clothes.* **2.** Unfair: *a dirty trick.*

dis•charge | dĭs **chärj′** | *v.* **dis•charged, dis•charg•ing.** **1.** To let go; release. **2.** To remove; unload: *discharge cargo.*

dis•close | dĭ **sklōz′** | *v.* **dis•closed, dis•clos•ing.** To reveal or make known: *The teacher will disclose the answer to the puzzle later.*

dis•cov•er | dĭ **skŭv′** ər | *v.* **1.** To find out: *They discovered they were late.* **2.** To make known for the first time: *The explorer discovered the source of the river.*

dis•cuss | dĭ **skŭs′** | *v.* To talk over thoughtfully; consider.

dis•ease | dĭ **zēz′** | *n.* Sickness; illness.
dis•lodge | dĭs **lŏj′** | *v.* **dis•lodged, dis•lodg•ing.** To move out of a place or position: *It is hard to dislodge the big rock from the soil.*
dis•tort | dĭ **stôrt′** | *v.* **1.** To twist or bend out of the usual shape: *When I look in the lake, the ripples of the water distort my face.* **2.** To change the facts so that what one says is partly false: *Don't distort what really happened.*
di•vide | dĭ **vīd′** | *v.* **di•vid•ed, di•vid•ing.** **1.** To separate; keep apart. **2.** To share.
dol•lar | **dŏl′** ər | *n.* **1.** The unit of money in the United States and some other countries. **2.** A paper note or silver coin equal to 100 cents.
dou•ble | **dŭb′** əl | *adj.* **1.** Twice as much. **2.** In pairs: *double doors.* —*v.* **dou•bled, dou•bling.** **1.** To make twice as great. **2.** To fold over: *double the blanket.*
dou•bly | **dŭb′** lē | *adv.* In twice the amount or degree: *I wanted to win the bicycle race, so I pedaled doubly fast.*
dough | dō | *n.* A thick mixture of flour, water or milk, and other ingredients for baking into bread, cake, etc.
doz•en | **dŭz′** ən | *n.* A group of twelve.

E

ear•ly | **ûr′** lē | *adj.* **ear•li•er, ear•li•est.** **1.** Near the beginning: *the early evening.* **2.** Before the usual time: *The early bird catches the worm.* —*adv.* **1.** At or near the beginning of: *early in the morning.* **2.** Before the usual time: *to arrive early.*
earn | ûrn | *v.* **1.** To receive as payment in return for work: *earn $10 a week.* **2.** To gain through effort: *He earned good grades.* **3.** To deserve: *earn gratitude.*
ear•phone | **îr′** fōn′ | *n., pl.* **ear•phones.** A telephone, radio, TV, or stereo receiver that is held to the ear by a band over the head.
earth•en•ware | **ûr′** thən wâr′ | *n.* Pots, bowls, dishes, vases, and other like objects made from clay and baked at a low temperature.
ea•sel | **ē′** zəl | *n.* A tall stand or frame used to support, hold, or display things such as artists' paintings, chalkboards, or signs: *The artist put the canvas on the easel and began to paint.*
ech•o | **ĕk′** ō | *n., pl.* **ech•oes.** A repetition of sound, caused by the throwing back of sound waves. —*v.* To give back or repeat sound.
e•clipse | ĭ **klĭps′** | *n.* **1.** A complete or partial darkening of the sun caused by passage of the moon between it and the earth. **2.** A darkening of the moon by the earth's shadow. —*v.* **e•clipsed, e•clips•ing.** To overshadow: *Her performance eclipsed all the others.*
ed•i•to•ri•al | ĕd′ ĭ **tôr′** ē əl | *or* | **-tōr′-** | *n.* An article in a newspaper or magazine or a comment on a radio or TV station that gives the opinions of the editor, owner, or publisher.
ed•u•ca•tion | ĕj′ o͝o **kā′** shən | *n.* **1.** Training, schooling: *public school education.* **2.** Knowledge and skill.
el•bow | **ĕl′** bō | *n.* The joint in the arm between wrist and shoulder. —*v.* To nudge, jostle, or push: *elbow through the crowd.*
e•lec•tion | ĭ **lĕk′** shən | *n.* A choosing or selecting by vote.

el•e•phant | **ĕl′** ə fənt | *n.* A very large Asian or African animal with a thick, wrinkled hide, stout legs, long tusks, and a long, flexible trunk.
else | ĕls | *adj.* **1.** Besides; in addition. **2.** Instead. **3.** Otherwise.
em•ploy | ĕm **ploi′** | *v.* **1.** To hire; give work to. **2.** To make use of: *Employ your study time to good advantage.*
em•ploy•er | ĕm **ploi′** ər | *n.* A person or business that hires people to work for pay: *The employer gave everyone who worked for the company a raise.*
em•ploy•ment | ĕm **ploi′** mənt | *n.* **1.** Work; occupation; job. **2.** The act of putting to use: *The employment of harsh measures was necessary to save the city.*
emp•ty | **ĕmp′** tē | *adj.* **1.** Containing nothing. **2.** Without meaning: *empty promises.* —*v.* **emp•tied, emp•ty•ing, emp•ties.** To remove the contents of.
en•deav•or | ĕn **dĕv′** ər | *n.* A serious attempt; effort: *My endeavor to learn to swim paid off when I was able to swim in the ocean on our vacation.* —*v.* To seriously try; attempt: *Let's endeavor to get better grades.*
en•er•gy | **ĕn′** ər jē | *n., pl.* **en•er•gies.** **1.** The ability to do work. **2.** Force; strength.
en•joy | ĕn **joi′** | *v.* **1.** To take pleasure in: *enjoy the parade.* **2.** To have or benefit by: *enjoy good health.*
e•nough | ĭ **nŭf′** | *adj.* As much or as many as necessary or desirable: *There is enough paint for everyone in the art class.* —*n.* A sufficient amount: *We have had enough to eat.* —*adv.* Fully; quite: *I felt well enough to go to school.*

e•quip•ment | ĭ **kwĭp′** mənt | *n.* The things needed for a particular purpose: *garden equipment.*

es•cape | ĭ **skāp′** | *v.* **es•caped, es•cap•ing. 1.** To break loose; get free; get away: *escape from jail.* **2.** To avoid: *escape a storm.* —*n.* **1.** The act of escaping. **2.** A means of escape: *the fire escape.*

eve•ning | **ēv′** nĭng | *n.* The time between sunset and bedtime; early night.

ex•am•ple | ĭg **zăm′** pəl | *or* | **-zäm′-** | *n.* **1.** Sample. **2.** Someone or something that is a model. **3.** A warning: *Let this be an example.*
***Idioms.* for example.** Serving as a model. **set an example.** To be a model worthy of imitation.

ex•cel•lent | **ĕk′** sə lənt | *adj.* Extremely good; unusually high in quality.

ex•cept | ĭk **sĕpt′** | *prep.* Outside of; apart from: *everyone except me.* —*conj.* Only: *I could finish reading my book except I'd rather play the piano.*

ex•er•cise | **ĕk′** sər sīz′ | *n., pl.* **ex•er•cis•es.** Physical or mental activity that improves the body or mind. —*v.* **ex•er•cised, ex•er•cis•ing. 1.** To put into action: *exercise care.* **2.** To do exercise: *exercise your muscles.*

ex•ile | **ĕg′** zīl′ | *or* | **ĕk′** sīl′ | *n.* An enforced living away from one's country, often as punishment: *The spy's exile meant that he couldn't visit his native land.* —*v.* **ex•iled, ex•il•ing.** To send away from one's native land as punishment.

ex•pect | ĭk **spĕkt′** | *v.* **1.** To look forward to something that will probably happen. **2.** To wait for or feel sure of the arrival of: *I was expecting you.* **3.** To require: *You are expected to do a good job.*

ex•pert | **ĕk′** spûrt′ | *n.* A person who has special skill or knowledge. —*adj.* | ĭk **spûrt′** | *or* | **ĕk′** spûrt′ |. **1.** Having special skill or knowledge: *an expert swimmer.* **2.** Given by an expert: *expert advice.*

ex•plain | ĭk **splān′** | *v.* **1.** To make plain or clear; tell the meaning of: *explain directions.* **2.** To give the reason for: *explain your mistake.*

ex•ploit | **ĕk′** sploit′ | *v.* To make the best use of: *Maria wants to exploit her ability to get along with animals by becoming an animal trainer.* —*n.* A daring act: *The exciting book was about the exploits of the hero.*

ex•port | ĭk **spôrt′** | *or* | **-spōrt′** | *or* | **ĕk′** spôrt′ | *or* | -spōrt′ | *v.* To send or carry out goods to another country for sale or trade. —*n.* **1.** The act of exporting. **2.** Goods sold and sent to another country.

ex•tra | **ĕk′** strə | *adj.* More than what is usual or expected: *earn extra cash.* —*adv.* Especially: *an extra good dinner.* —*n.* Often **extras.** Something additional: *a car with all the extras.*

F

fac•to•ry | **făk′** tə rē | *n., pl.* **fac•to•ries.** A building or group of buildings where things are made.

fan•cy | **făn′** sē | *adj.* **fan•ci•er, fan•ci•est.** Not plain; elaborate: *fancy clothes.* —*n., pl.* **fan•cies. 1.** Imagination. **2.** A whim: *a sudden fancy for ice cream.* —*v.* **fan•cied, fan•cy•ing, fan•cies. 1.** To imagine. **2.** To like.

fare | **fâr** | *n.* The cost of a ride on a plane, bus, train, taxi, etc.

far•ther | **fär′** *th*ər | *adv.* To a greater distance: *She hiked farther than I did.* —*adj.* More distant: *He lives a mile farther down the road.*

fault | **fôlt** | *n.* **1.** Blame; responsibility: *It was my fault.* **2.** A weakness; shortcoming. **3.** A mistake.

Feb•ru•ar•y | **fĕb′** ro͞o ĕr′ ē | *or* | **fĕb′** yo͞o- | *n.* The second month of the year. February has 28 days except in leap years, when it has 29 days.

fe•male | **fē′** māl′ | *adj.* Having to do with women or girls; a female voice. —*n.* **1.** A girl or woman. **2.** A female animal.

feud | **fyo͞od** | *n.* A very long, unpleasant quarrel between two people, families, groups, or countries: *The feud lasted so long that people forgot why they were angry at each other.* —*v.* **feud•ed, feud•ing.** To carry on a long, bitter quarrel: *Let's not feud with each other.*

fight | **fīt** | *v.* **fought** | **fôt** |, **fight•ing.** To take part in a struggle or battle: *Doctors fight disease.* —*n.* **1.** A struggle; battle. **2.** A quarrel.

film | **fĭlm** | *n.* **1.** A thin strip or roll prepared for taking photographs. **2.** A motion picture; movie. —*v.* To make a movie of.

fi•nal | **fī′** nəl | *adj.* **1.** Coming at the end; last: *the final act of a play.* **2.** Settling the matter; deciding: *the final words on the subject.* —*n.* Often **finals.** The last game or last examination.

firm¹ | **fûrm** | *adj.* **firm•er, firm•est. 1.** Solid; not easily moved. **2.** Not changing: *a firm belief.* **3.** Steady: *a firm voice.*

firm² | **fûrm** | *n.* A group of persons who have joined in a business: *a law firm.*

flash•light | **flăsh′** līt′ | *n.* A small portable electric light.

float | flōt | *v.* **1.** To be held up by liquid or air. **2.** To move or drift freely. *—n.* **1.** Something that floats: *a float on a fishline.* **2.** An exhibit on a platform with wheels, used in a parade. **3.** A soft drink made with ice cream floating in it.

flood | flŭd | *n.* **1.** A great flow of water over land that is usually dry. **2.** A great outpouring: *a flood of tears; a flood of letters.* *—v.* **1.** To cover with water. **2.** To supply in large quantity.

fol•low | **fŏl'** ō | *v.* **1.** To come after; go after: *follow me.* **2.** To go along: *follow this road.* **3.** To accept as a guide; obey: *follow the rules; follow directions.*

fool•ish | **fo͞o'** lĭsh | *adj.* Without sense; unwise; silly; ridiculous.

foot•ball | **fo͝ot'** bôl' | *n.* **1.** A game played by two teams of 11 players each on a long field with a goal at either end. The object is to carry the ball across the opponent's goal line or kick it over his goal. **2.** The oval leather ball used in this game.

for•tu•nate | **fôr'** chə nĭt | *adj.* Favored; lucky.

fought Look up **fight.**

frac•tion | **frăk'** shən | *n.* **1.** A part of a fragment. **2.** A ratio: $^1/_2$; $^3/_4$.

fraud | frôd | *n.* An intentional trick or deception of someone in order to gain an unfair advantage or to cheat: *It is fraud to copy a video game and sell it as an original.*

fray | frā | *v.* **frayed, fray•ing.** To wear away and separate into loose threads, especially along the edge: *My favorite shirt began to fray at the collar.*

freeze | frēz | *v.* **froze** | frōz |, **froz•en** | **frō'** zən |, **freez•ing.** **1.** To change into ice. **2.** To make or become hard or solid with cold: *freeze meat in the refrigerator.* **3.** To become very cold: *I froze in that wind.* **4.** To become motionless: *freeze in terror.* *—n.* A frost; a condition of extreme coldness: *a sudden freeze.*

fric•tion | **frĭk'** shən | *n.* The rubbing of one thing or surface against another: *The friction of the tires and the road causes tires to wear out.*

Fri•day | **frī'** dē | *or* | -dā' | *n.* The sixth day of the week.

friend•ly | **frĕnd'** lē | *adj.* **friend•li•er, friend•li•est.** **1.** Like a friend; kind: *a friendly person.* **2.** Not hostile: *a friendly game.*

front-page | **frŭnt' pāj'** | *adj.* Printed on or important enough to be printed on the first page of the newspaper: *a front-page headline.*

fruit | fro͞ot | *n., pl.* **fruit** *or* **fruits.** The part of a plant that contains the seeds.

fur•nish | **fûr'** nĭsh | *v.* **1.** To equip with furniture: *furnish a house.* **2.** To supply; provide: *furnish cookies for the party.*

fur•ni•ture | **fûr'** nə chər | *n.* Articles, usually movable, to make a room fit for living or working, such as tables, desks, chairs, beds, etc.

fu•ror | **fyo͝or'** ôr' | *or* | -ər | *n.* An outburst or noisy commotion; uproar: *The closing of the popular zoo caused a furor in the town.*

G

gal•ax•y | **găl'** ək sē | *n., pl.* **gal•ax•ies.** **1.** A large group of stars, dust, and gas. **2. the Galaxy.** The Milky Way; the galaxy that contains our sun and solar system.

gar•bage | **gär'** bĭj | *n.* **1.** Scraps of food that are thrown away. **2.** Trash.

gath•er | ***găth'*** ər | *v.* **1.** To bring together; collect: *We gathered around the scoutmaster.* **2.** To conclude: *I gather you are excited about your new bike.* **3.** To pull cloth together with a thread: *gather a skirt.* *—n.* a small fold made by gathering cloth.

gen•er•al | **jĕn'** ər əl | *adj.* **1.** For everyone; for the whole: *a general meeting.* **2.** Common to most; widespread: *general interest in sports.* **3.** Not detailed: *Give us a general idea of how your invention works.* *—n.* A high-ranking officer in the Army, Air Force, or Marine Corps.

Idiom. **in general.** Usually; for the most part.

gen•tle | **jĕn'** tl | *adj.* **gen•tler, gen•tlest.** **1.** Mild: *a gentle hug.* **2.** Tame: *a gentle donkey.* **3.** Soft; low: *gentle lapping of the waves.* **4.** Gradual; not steep: *gentle slope of the hill.*

glue | glo͞o | *n.* A substance used to stick things together. *—v.* **glued, glu•ing.** **1.** To fasten together with glue. **2.** To hold firmly: *My eyes were glued to the clock.*

golf | gŏlf | *or* | gôlf | *n.* A game played outdoors over a large course. The course has 9 or 18 holes into which a player must try to hit a ball with a club. *—v.* To play this game.

gov•ern•ment | **gŭv'** ərn mənt | *n.* **1.** The group of people who rule a country, state, city, etc.: *We elect our government.* **2.** A way of ruling: *a democratic government.*

grass•hop•per | **grăs'** hŏp' ər | *or* | **gräs'-** | *n.* A winged insect with strong back legs for jumping.

greet | grēt | *v.* **1.** To welcome politely: *greet the guests.* **2.** To receive; to respond to: *Her arrival was greeted with joy.*

grind | grīnd | *v.* **ground** | ground |, **grind•ing. 1.** To crush into fine pieces: *grind wheat into flour.* **2.** To sharpen or smooth: *grind a knife.* **3.** To grate: *grind your teeth.*

groan | grōn | *v.* To make a deep, sad or annoyed sound. —*n.* A moan. *These sound alike* ***groan, grown.***

grow | grō | *v.* **grew** | gro͞o |, **grown** | grōn |, **grow•ing. 1.** To become bigger. **2.** To exist: *Moss grows in the shade.* **3.** To raise; produce: *grow vegetables.* **4.** To become: *grow cold.*

grown Look up **grow.** *These sound alike* **grown, groan.**

guide | gīd | *n.* Someone or something that shows the way or directs: *a museum guide.* —*v.* **guid•ed, guid•ing.** To direct; show the way; lead.

guilt•y | **gĭl′** tē | *adj.* **guilt•i•er, guilt•i•est. 1.** Having done wrong; deserving blame or punishment: *guilty of a crime.* **2.** Feeling that one has done wrong: *a guilty conscience.*

gui•tar | gĭ **tär′** | *n.* A musical instrument that has a long neck and a large sound box. Its six strings are played with the fingers or a pick.

H

half | hăf | *or* | häf | *n., pl.* **halves** | hăvz | *or* | hävz |. **1.** One of two equal parts. **2.** One of two equal periods of time in certain games: *the first half of the football game.*

Idioms. **in half.** Into two equal parts. **not half bad.** Good.

hall•way | **hôl′** wā′ | *n.* Corridor; passageway; hall.

hand•made | **hănd′** mād′ | *adj.* Made by hand rather than by a machine: *a handmade kite.*

har•vest | **här′** vĭst | *n.* **1.** The act of gathering in a crop: *Farmers expect an early harvest this year.* **2.** The crop that is gathered: *We store our harvest in large barns.* —*v.* To gather a crop.

head•line | **hĕd′** līn′ | *n.* Words printed in large, heavy type at the top of a newspaper or magazine article telling what the article is about.

health•y | **hĕl′** thē | *adj.* **health•i•er, health•i•est. 1.** Having good health: *a healthy body.* **2.** Giving good health: *healthy exercise.*

hear | hîr | *v.* **heard** | hûrd |, **hear•ing. 1.** To receive sound through one's ears: *hear music.* **2.** To listen to with care: *hear both sides of the argument.*

heard Look up **hear.**

hem•i•sphere | **hĕm′** ĭ sfîr′ | *n., pl.* **hem•i•spheres.** One half of the earth's surface as divided by either the equator or a meridian. The equator divides the Northern and Southern Hemispheres, and a meridian divides the Eastern and Western Hemispheres.

he•ro | **hîr′** ō | *n., pl.* **he•roes. 1.** A person admired for courage or special achievements. **2.** The main character in a story, play, movie, etc. **3.** A large sandwich served on a long roll.

hob•by | **hŏb′** ē | *n., pl.* **hob•bies.** An interesting activity that a person does for his or her own pleasure.

hock•ey | **hŏk′** ē | *n.* **1.** Also **ice hockey.** A game played on ice by two teams of six players each. The players wear skates and use sticks to try to hit a puck into the other team's goal. **2.** Also **field hockey.** A similar game played on a field with a ball and eleven players on a team.

hole | hōl | *n.* **1.** An opening: *hole in the ground; hole in a sock.* **2.** An animal's burrow: *a fox hole.* **3.** A hollow on a golf course into which a ball must be hit. *These sound alike* **hole, whole.**

hol•i•day | **hŏl′** ĭ dā′ | *n.* A day when people don't work, such as Thanksgiving or a vacation.

home•work | **hōm′** wûrk′ | *n.* School work assigned to be done outside the classroom.

hon•est | **ŏn′** ĭst | *adj.* Truthful; fair; sincere.

hon•or | **ŏn′** ər | *n.* **1.** A mark of distinction: *Winning the award was a great honor for her.* **2.** A sense of what is right; reputation; good name: *He is a man of honor.* —*v.* **1.** To show special respect to. **2.** To accept as payment.

Idiom. **on one's honor.** As a solemn promise.

hos•pi•tal | **hŏs′** pĭ təl | *or* | -pĭt′ l | *n.* A place where sick or injured people are cared for.

ho•tel | hō **tĕl′** | *n.* A public house where rooms and food are provided for pay.

hu•mor | **hyo͞o′** mər | *n.* **1.** The quality of being funny: *Clowns provide humor at the circus.* **2.** The ability to enjoy something funny: *a sense of humor.* **3.** State of mind; mood: *in a bad humor.* —*v.* To give in to someone's wishes: *humor a fussy child.*

hun•dred | **hŭn′** drĭd | *n.* The number 100; ten times ten.

hurt | hûrt | *v.* **hurt, hurt•ing. 1.** To cause pain to; injure: *hurt your foot.* **2.** To feel pain: *My eyes hurt after a day at the beach.* **3.** To have a bad effect on; harm: *hurt one's chances.* —*n.* An injury; pain.

hus•band | **hŭz′** bənd | *n.* A married man.

I

i·de·a | ī **dē′** ə | *n.* **1.** A thought or belief. **2.** The point or purpose of something: *The idea of this invention is to do away with homework.*

i·den·ti·cal | ī **dĕn′** tĭ kəl | *adj.* **1.** Exactly alike: *My sister and I wore identical blouses.* **2.** The very same: *Natasha recited the identical poem yesterday and today.*

im·port | ĭm **pôrt′** | *or* | **-pōrt′** | *or* | **ĭm′** pôrt′ | *or* | -pōrt′ | *v.* To bring in something from another country for sale, trade, or use. —*n.* | **ĭm′** pôrt′ | *or* | -pōrt′ |. Something imported from another country.

im·por·tant | ĭm′ **pôr′** tnt | *adj.* Having value; significant.

im·prove | ĭm **pro͞ov′** | *v.* **im·proved, im·prov·ing.** To make or become better: *improve your golf swing.*

in·crease | ĭn **krēs′** | *v.* **in·creased, in·creas·ing.** To make or become greater or larger. —*n.* |**ĭn′** krēs′ |. The amount by which something is increased: *an increase of 25 percent.*

in·dus·try | **ĭn′** də strē | *n., pl.* **in·dus·tries. 1.** Manufacturing, business, and trade: *a center of industry; the steel industry.* **2.** Hard work; steady effort: *It takes a lot of industry to become a doctor.*

in·for·ma·tion | ĭn′ fər **mā′** shən | *n.* **1.** Facts or knowledge about a subject. **2.** A service that gives facts: *Call information for his phone number.*

in·sect | **ĭn′** sĕkt′ | *n.* Any of a group of small animals without backbones, having wings, six legs, and a body divided into three parts.

in·sist | ĭn **sĭst′** | *v.* To make a firm demand; take a strong stand.

in·spec·tion | ĭn **spĕk′** shən | *n.* **1.** The act of examining. **2.** An official examination: *daily inspection of the soldiers.*

in·stead | ĭn **stĕd′** | *adv.* In place of someone or something.

Idiom. **instead of.** Rather than: *I went home instead of going to the library.*

in·struct | ĭn **strŭkt′** | *v.* **1.** To teach. **2.** To give orders to: *The crossing guard instructed us to remain on the sidewalk.*

in·struc·tion | ĭn **strŭk′** shən | *n.* **1.** Lessons: *music instruction.* **2. instructions.** Directions; orders.

in·tend | ĭn **tĕnd′** | *v.* **1.** To have in mind; plan: *to intend to go somewhere.* **2.** To mean for a particular use or person: *The surprise was intended for you.*

in·vent | ĭn **vĕnt′** | *v.* **1.** To think up and make for the first time: *invent a new machine.* **2.** To make up: *invent excuses.*

in·ven·tion | ĭn **vĕn′** shən | *n.* **1.** Something invented: *a new invention.* **2.** The act of inventing: *the invention of the wheel.* **3.** A false statement: *His story is only an invention.*

in·vite | ĭn **vīt′** | *v.* **in·vit·ed, in·vit·ing. 1.** To ask someone to go somewhere or to do something: *invite to a party.* **2.** To ask for politely: *invite questions.*

is·land | **ī′** lənd | *n.* **1.** A body of land that is surrounded by water. An island is smaller than a continent. **2.** Something that is different or separated from things around it: *There is a traffic island in the middle of the street.*

its | ĭts | *pron.* The possessive of **it:** *The bird flapped its wings. These sound alike* **its, it's.**

it's | ĭts |. The contraction for "it is" and "it has." *These sound alike* **it's, its.**

J

jab·ber | **jăb′** ər | *v.* To talk in a fast, silly, or mixed-up way; chatter: *Sometimes very young children seem to jabber to themselves.*

Jan·u·ar·y | **jăn′** yo͞o ĕr′ ē | *n.* The first month of the year. January has 31 days.

jave·lin | **jăv′** lĭn | *or* | **jăv′** ə- | *n.* A long, thin, light spear that is thrown for distance in an athletic track and field event: *It requires good balance to throw the javelin a long way.*

jos·tle | **jŏs′** əl | *v.* **jos·tled, jos·tling.** To bump, shove, and push against one another: *I was jostled by the big crowd as I entered the stadium.*

jot | jŏt | *v.* **jot·ted, jot·ting.** To write quickly or briefly: *Please jot down your telephone number, so I can call you later.*

jour·nal·ism | **jûr′** nə lĭz′ əm | *n.* The gathering, reporting, writing, and publishing of news in newspapers or magazines or on television or radio.

judge | jŭj | *n.* **1.** A public official who decides cases in a law court. **2.** A person who decides the winner in a contest. **3.** A person who can decide the value of something. —*v.* **judged, judg·ing. 1.** To hear and decide a case in a law court. **2.** To decide: *judge a contest.* **3.** To form an opinion: *Judge this book for yourself.*

juice | jo͞os | *n.* **1.** The liquid in fruit, vegetables, and meats. **2.** *Slang.* Electricity.

Ju·ly | jo͞o **lī′** | *n.* The seventh month of the year. July has 31 days.

June | jo͞on | *n.* The sixth month of the year. June has 30 days.

jun·gle | **jŭng′** gəl | *n.* **1.** Land with a thick growth of trees and plants in the tropics. **2.** A confused mass of objects.
Ju·pi·ter | **jo͞o′** pĭ tər | *n.* **1.** The largest planet in our solar system and the fifth closest to the sun. **2.** In ancient Roman mythology, the ruler of the gods.

K

kan·ga·roo | **kăng′** gə ro͞o′ | *n.* An animal from Australia and New Guinea that has short forelegs, long and powerful hind legs for leaping, and a long tail. The female carries her young in a pouch in front of her body.
kitch·en | **kĭch′** ən | *n.* A room where food is prepared.
knife | nīf | *n., pl.* **knives** | nīvz |. A thin blade used for cutting or spreading.
know | nō | *v.* **knew** | no͞o | *or* | nyo͞o |, **known** | nōn |, **know·ing. 1.** To understand: *know the answers.* **2.** To be acquainted with: *I know her well.* **3.** To have skill in: *know how to ride a bike.* ***Idiom.*** **in the know.** Having inside information.
known Look up **know.**
knuck·le | **nŭk′** əl | *n.* A joint of a finger.

L

land·slide | **lănd′** slīd′ | *n.* The sliding of rocks and soil down a steep slope: *Sometimes an earthquake may cause a landslide down the mountainside.*
laugh·ter | **lăf′** tər | *or* | **läf′**- | *n.* The act of making sounds to express happiness, amusement, or scorn.
lawn·mow·er | **lôn′** mō′ ər | *n.* Also **lawn mower.** A machine with revolving blades for cutting grass.
learn·ing | **lûr′** nĭng | *n.* Knowledge gained by study.
length | lĕngkth | *or* | lĕngth | *n.* **1.** How long something is from one end to another; its measured distance. **2.** How long something lasts from beginning to end: *the length of your visit.*
lib·er·ty | **lĭb′** ər tē | *n., pl.* **lib·er·ties. 1.** The state of being able to speak and act freely. **2.** Political freedom.
li·brar·y | **lī′** brĕr′ ē | *n., pl.* **li·brar·ies. 1.** A building where books, magazines, and reference material are collected. **2.** Any collection of books: *a library in the living room.*
light-year | **līt′** yîr′ | *n.* Also **light year.** A measure of distance equal to the distance that light travels in one year through space.
loathe | lō*th* | *v.* **loathed, loath·ing.** To dislike very much; hate: *Readers may loathe the cruel actions of some of the characters in the book.*

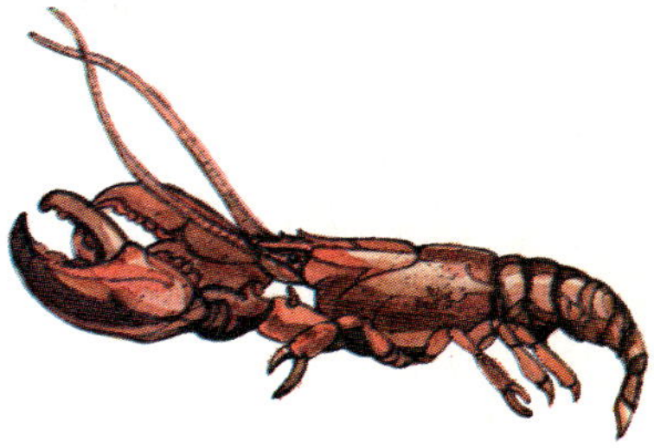

lob·ster | **lŏb′** stər | *n.* **1.** A large, hard shellfish with five pairs of legs having large claws on the front pair. **2.** The meat of this shellfish, used as food.
lo·ca·tion | lō **kā′** shən | *n.* A place where something is positioned: *the location of the restaurant.*
loose | lo͞os | *adj.* **loos·er, loos·est. 1.** Not fastened or firmly attached: *a loose cap.* **2.** Not closed in; free: *The dog was loose.* **3.** Not tightly fitted: *a loose pair of jeans.*
lose | lo͞oz | *v.* **lost** | lôst | *or* | lŏst |, **los·ing. 1.** To be without: *Don't lose the keys.* **2.** To be unable to keep: *to lose your temper.* **3.** To fail to win: *I won't lose this race.* **4.** To waste: *I'll lose an hour in this traffic.*
loy·al | **loi′** əl | *adj.* True and faithful.
loy·al·ty | **loi′** əl tē | *n.* The act of being true and faithful; faithfulness.
lu·nar | **lo͞o′** nər | *adj.* Having to do with the moon.
lyr·ics | **lĭr′** ĭks | *pl. n.* The words of a song: *The lyrics of the song came from a poem.*

M

mag·ic | **măj′** ĭk | *n.* Mysterious effects produced by tricks, usually as entertainment. —*adj.* Having magic power; done by magic: *a magic wand.*
mag·net | **măg′** nĭt | *n.* **1.** A piece of metal or ore that draws iron toward it. **2.** Anything that attracts.
male | māl | *adj.* Having to do with men or boys: *a male voice.* —*n.* **1.** A man or a boy. **2.** A male animal.
mar·ble | **mär′** bəl | *n.* **1.** A smooth, hard stone that is streaked or colored, often used in buildings. **2.** A small ball made of hard substance such as glass. **3. marbles.** A children's game played with small balls.
March | märch | *n.* The third month of the year. March has 31 days.

mar•gin | **mär'** jĭn | *n.* **1.** An edge or rim: *Water lilies grew along the margin of the pond.* **2.** A border around print or writing on a page: *Don't write in the margin of the book.* **3.** An extra amount beyond what is needed: *She gave herself a margin of ten minutes to catch the plane.*

ma•roon | mə **rōōn'** | *n.* A color that is dark brownish purplish red.

mas•ter | **măs'** tər | *or* | **mä'** stər | *n.* **1.** A person who has control of something: *the dog's master; the ship's master.* **2.** A person who has a great skill or ability: *a master of foreign languages.* —*adj.* **1.** Ruling over others: *the master switch.* **2.** Being expert at something: *master artist.* **3.** The original: *the master list.* —*v.* **1.** To bring under control: *to master your angry feelings.* **2.** To become skilled: *to master your spelling words.*

mast•head | **măst'** hĕd' | *or* | **mäst'-** | *n.* **1.** The top of a ship's mast. **2.** The section in a newspaper or magazine that gives its name, owner, chief editors, address, and other information about the publication.

May | mā | *n.* The fifth month of the year. May has 31 days.

mea•ger | **mē'** gər | *adj.* Hardly enough; very little: *The meager amount of water did not satisfy my thirst.*

meas•ure | **mĕzh'** ər | *n.* **1.** A device for finding length, size, time, etc., such as a foot ruler, a pint cup, a pound weight. **2.** A basis of judgment or comparison: *Deeds are a better measure than words.* —*v.* **meas•ured, meas•ur•ing. 1.** To find the length, size, contents, weight, or length of time of anything in standard units: *Let's measure these plants.* **2.** To be of a certain size, weight: *I measure five feet tall.*

med•dle | **mĕd'** l | *v.* **med•dled, med•dling.** To interfere in the business of other people: *Sometimes it is hard not to meddle in the affairs of others.*

mem•ber | **mĕm'** bər | *n.* **1.** A part of the body. **2.** A person or thing belonging to a group, society, etc.: *a club member; a class member.*

Me•mo•ri•al Day | mə **môr'** ē əl dā | *n.* A holiday in the United States that honors members of the armed forces who have died in wars. The official date is May 30, but it is observed on the last Monday in May.

mem•o•ry | **mĕm'** ə rē | *n., pl.* **mem•o•ries. 1.** The power of recalling something learned: *I have a poor memory for names.* **2.** A person or thing remembered: *Our old house is only a memory.*

men•tion | **mĕn'** shən | *v.* To speak or write about: *Don't mention our plans.* —*n.* A statement or reference: *You are worthy of mention.*

mer•ry | **mĕr'** ē | *adj.* **mer•ri•er, mer•ri•est.** Happy and cheerful; full of good spirits; jolly: *a merry twinkle in his eye.*

mes•sage | **mĕs'** ĭj | *n.* **1.** Any news or information sent from one person to another. **2.** A written statement or speech. **3.** The main subject or meaning of something: *After reading my note, did you understand my message?*

met•al | **mĕt'** l | *n.* **1.** A chemical element that is shiny when pure or polished and is a good conductor of electricity or heat. Gold, silver, copper, tin, iron, and aluminum are metals. **2.** An alloy made by mixing two or more metals.

me•te•or | **mē'** tē ər | *or* | -ôr' | *n., pl.* **me•te•ors.** A shooting star; a piece of matter that falls toward the earth at great speed from outer space. Meteors burn with a bright glow when they hit the air around the earth and usually burn up before they reach the ground.

met•ric | **mĕt'** rĭk | *adj.* Anything involving the system of weights and measures based on the meter for length and the gram for weight.

mi•cro•scope | **mī'** krə skōp' | *n.* An instrument which, by an arrangement of lenses, makes tiny things look large enough to be seen and studied.

mild | mīld | *adj.* **mild•er, mild•est. 1.** Gentle; kind; calm: *a mild person.* **2.** Not extreme, harsh, or severe: *a mild winter.*

mois•ture | **mois'** chər | *n.* **1.** Dampness; slight wetness: *There is still moisture in the ground from the spring rains.* **2.** Water vapor in the air or condensed on a surface: *Beads of moisture formed on the outside of the pitcher.*

Mon•day | **mŭn'** dē | *or* | -dā' | *n.* The second day of the week.

mon•key | **mŭng'** kē | *n., pl.* **mon•keys.** An animal that has hands with thumbs and usually has a long tail; not a gorilla, chimp, or other large ape. —*v.* **mon•keyed, mon•key•ing, mon•keys.** To play carelessly: *Do not monkey with that knife.*

mos•qui•to | mə **skē'** tō | *n., pl.* **mos•qui•toes** or **mos•qui•tos.** A slender, long-legged, blood-sucking insect with wings, the bite of which may cause swelling and itching. Some kinds carry yellow fever or malaria germs.

mo•tion | **mō′** shən | *n.* **1.** An action or movement; a changing from one place or position to another: *The motion of a boat on a rough sea makes some people ill.* **2.** Gesture: *He made a motion for silence.* **3.** A formal suggestion or proposal made at a meeting: *The secretary made a motion to select a program committee.* —*v.* To make a gesture or movement to express meaning; to signal: *He motioned to me to be quiet.*

mus•cu•lar | **mŭs′** kyə lər | *adj.* **1.** Having muscles that are strong and well-developed: *a muscular body.* **2.** Relating to or having to do with muscle.

mu•si•cal | **myo͞o′** zĭ kəl | *adj.* **1.** Having to do with music: *a musical instrument; a musical play.* **2.** Pleasing to the ear; melodious: *the musical song of a bird.* —*n.* A light, amusing play with songs and dances: *a musical comedy.*

mu•si•cian | myo͞o **zĭsh′** ən | *n.* A person skilled in music, especially one whose profession is playing music.

mu•tu•al | **myo͞o′** cho͞o əl | *adj.* **1.** Shared; held in common: *My friend and I have a mutual love of shopping.* **2.** Given and received equal in equal amounts: *Our friendship is mutual.*

mys•te•ry | **mĭs′** tə rē | *n., pl.* **mys•te•ries.** **1.** Something that is secret, strange, or unexplained: *The name of the thief is a mystery.* **2.** A story dealing with secret events.

N

na•tion | **nā′** shən | *n.* An independent country.

nat•u•ral | **năch′** ər əl | *or* | **năch′** rəl | *adj.* **1.** Belonging to by nature; inborn; native: *Eddie has a natural singing voice.* **2.** Formed or made by nature; not artificial: *There is the famous natural bridge.* **3.** According to the way things happen; ordinary: *Tiredness is the natural result of hard work.*

nau•ti•cal | **nô′** tĭ kəl | *adj.* Relating to or having to do with sailors, ships, or navigation: *Because I like to sail, I enjoy books with a nautical theme.*

nee•dle | **nēd′** l | *n.* **1.** A slender, pointed steel sewing tool with a hole or "eye" to hold a thread. **2.** A plain slender rod or a rod with a small hook at the end, used in knitting or crocheting. **3.** A device used by doctors and nurses to give shots. **4.** Any needle-shaped thing: *The ground was covered with pine needles.* —*v.* **nee•dled, nee•dling.** To tease or annoy.

neigh•bor | **nā′** bər | *n., pl.* **neigh•bors.** **1.** A person who lives nearby. **2.** A person, country, or thing that is near another: *Canada is our neighbor.* **3.** A fellow human being: *Love your neighbor.*

net•work | **nĕt′** wûrk′ | *n.* **1.** A system of arrangement of lines that cross: *a network of roads.* **2.** A chain of radio or television stations that carry the same programs.

news•pa•per | **no͞oz′** pā′ pər | *or* | **nyo͞oz′**- | *n.* A sheet of printed paper, or many sheets folded together, containing news, pictures, advertisements, etc.

news•stand | **no͞oz′** stănd′ | *or* | **nyo͞oz′**- | *n.* A place where newspapers and magazines are sold: *My father buys the newspaper at the same newsstand every morning.*

nick•el | **nĭk′** əl | *n.* **1.** A hard, silver-colored metal found in certain rocks; a chemical element. **2.** A coin in the U.S. that is worth five cents.

night•mare | **nīt′** mâr′ | *n.* **1.** A scary or bad dream. **2.** A scary or bad experience.

ninth | nīnth | *n.* **1.** Next after eighth. **2.** One of nine parts; $1/9$.

noise | noiz | *n.* **1.** An unpleasant sound. **2.** Any kind of sound: *The noise of the machine made study difficult.* —*v.* **noised, nois•ing** To tell or spread news: *He noised the rumor.*

no•mad | **nō′** măd′ | *n.* **1.** A member of a group of people who move from one place to another looking for food and water for themselves and their animals. **2.** A person who moves from place to place: *The nomad met many people in many different places.*

North Pole *n.* The farthest northern point on earth and the northern end of the earth's axis.

note•book | **nōt′** bo͝ok′ | *n.* A book with blank pages for writing.

no•tice | **nō′** tĭs | *v.* **no•ticed, no•tic•ing.** To see; observe: *I notice that you have a new car.* —*n.* **1.** Attention: *He escaped notice.* **2.** A statement or warning of what one intends to do: *We gave notice that we would move out of our apartment.* **3.** Written or printed announcement or description: *There are several notices on the bulletin board.*

Idiom. **take notice of.** To pay attention.

No•vem•ber | nō **vĕm′** bər | *n.* The eleventh month of the year. November has 30 days.

O

oak | ōk | *n.* **1.** Any acorn-bearing tree. There are nearly three hundred kinds of oak trees. **2.** The wood of these trees.

ob·ject[1] | **ŏb′** jĭkt | *or* | -jĕkt′ | *n.* **1.** A thing that has shape and can be touched and seen: *The only object rescued when the car sank into the lake was a tire.* **2.** Purpose; goal: *My object in life is to be a surgeon.*

ob·ject[2] | əb **jĕkt′** | *v.* **1.** To protest, to show disapproval: *Father objects to our walking barefoot in the living room.* **2.** To oppose; give reasons for disliking: *Do you object to our plan?*

o·cean | **ō′** shən | *n.* The vast body of salt water covering three fourths of the earth's surface.

Oc·to·ber | ŏk **tō′** bər | *n.* The tenth month of the year. October has 31 days.

of·ten | **ô′** fən | *or* | **ŏf′** ən | *or* | **ôf′** tən | *or* | **ŏf′**- | *adv.* Frequently; many times.

O·lym·pic | ō **lĭm′** pĭk | *adj.* Of or relating to the Olympics. —*n.* **Olympics.** **1.** A festival of ancient Greece with contests in athletics, music, and poetry. **2.** Modern sports competition held every four years in a different country: *Athletes from many countries compete in the Olympics.*

o·men | **ō′** mən | *n.* Something that is supposed to be a sign of a good or bad event to come: *When Kesha found a penny, she thought it was an omen of good luck.*

on·ion | **ŭn′** yən | *n.* A plant grown as a vegetable having a bulb, a strong odor, and a biting taste.

or·bit | ôr′ bĭt | *n.* **1.** The path in which one heavenly body moves about another. **2.** A circle of influence: *A famous person will often have many people following in his or her orbit.* —*v.* To travel in an orbit: *The earth orbits the sun.*

or·chard | **ôr′** chərd | *n.* A piece of land where fruit trees are grown.

owe | ō | *v.* **owed, ow·ing.** **1.** To have to pay; to be in debt. **2.** To have to do something because of the law, a promise, or a duty: *owe an apology.*

oy·ster | **oi′** stər | *n.* A soft-bodied animal that lives inside two rough half shells: *Many oysters have pearls.*

P

pack·age | **păk′** ĭj | *n.* A container or box that holds something. —*v.* **pack·aged, pack·ag·ing.** To put into a container or box.

paid Look up **pay.**

pa·rade | pə **rād′** | *n.* A public event for a special occasion: *the Thanksgiving Parade.* —*v.* **pa·rad·ed, pa·rad·ing.** **1.** To march. **2.** To walk proudly: *to parade around in new clothes.*

par·ty | **pär′** tē | *n., pl.* **par·ties.** **1.** An entertainment or social gathering: *a birthday party.* **2.** A group of people acting together: *A search party was sent out to find the missing child.* **3.** A political organization: *In an election, each party has a candidate.*

pay | pā | *v.* **paid** | pād |, **pay·ing.** **1.** To give money in return for things or work done. **2.** To give or make: *pay attention; pay a visit.*

peace | pēs | *n.* **1.** Freedom from fighting. **2.** Quiet; order.

pearl | pûrl | *n.* **1.** A small, round, white or grayish gem that is found inside the shell of certain oysters. **2.** Anything that looks like a pearl.

pe·can | pĭ **kän′** | *or* | **-kăn′** | *or* | **pē′** kăn | *n.* An edible nut that has a thin, smooth, oval shell and grows on a tree.

ped·es·tal | **pĕd′** ĭ stəl | *n.* The base or support on which a statue or column stands: *The statue stood on a pedestal made of concrete.*

pen·al·ty | **pĕn′** əl tē | *n., pl.* **pen·al·ties.** **1.** A punishment established by law. **2.** A disadvantage imposed by a referee upon a game player: *One more penalty and he's out of the game.*

pen·du·lum | **pĕn′** jə ləm | *or* | **pĕn′** dyə- | *or* | **pĕn′** də- | *n.* A weight that is hung from a fixed support, so that it can swing back and forth: *Pendulums are used to regulate the actions of some clocks.*

pen·sion | **pĕn′** shən | *n.* An amount of money that is paid regularly to a person who has retired from work or is disabled: *After teaching thirty years, Mrs. Mays retired and received a pension.*

per·fect | **pûr′** fĭkt | *adj.* **1.** Without fault; exactly right: *He got a perfect score on the test.* **2.** Complete; whole; thorough. —*v.* | pər **fĕkt′** |. To remove all flaws from.

per·form | pər **fôrm′** | *v.* **1.** To do or carry out: *to perform your obligations.* **2.** To act with skill: *She performed in the play.*

per·fume | **pûr′** fyo͞om′ | *or* | pər **fyo͞om′** | *n.* **1.** A sweet-smelling liquid: *a new perfume.* **2.** A sweet smell; fragrance: *The perfume from the roses is wonderful.* —*v.* | pər **fyo͞om′** |. To fill with a sweet smell.

per·haps | pər **hăps′** | *adv.* Maybe; possibly: *Perhaps it will rain today.*

pe•ri•od•i•cal | pĭr′ ē **ŏd′** ĭ kəl | *adj.* A magazine or other publication that is printed at regular intervals, such as every week, every two weeks, or every month: *I look forward to receiving my favorite periodical every month.*

per•mit | pər **mĭt′** | *v.* **per•mit•ted, per•mit•ting.** To allow. —*n.* | **pûr′** mĭt | *or* | pər **mĭt′** |. A written letter, license, or document giving permission.

per•son•al | **pûr′** sə nəl | *adj.* **1.** One's own; a private part of one's life. **2.** That which is done in person. **3.** Of a person's body or physical appearance.

pet•al | **pĕt′** l | *n.* One of the leaflike parts of a flower, usually brightly or lightly colored.

pi•an•o | pē **ăn′** ō | *n., pl.* **pi•an•os.** A large musical instrument with steel wire strings that sound when struck by felt-covered hammers operated from a keyboard.

pick•le | **pĭk′** əl | *n., pl.* **pick•les.** A cucumber that has been preserved by soaking in salt water or vinegar.

pic•nic | **pĭk′** nĭk | *n.* Food that is packed and eaten outdoors; a meal eaten in the open air. —*v.* **pic•nicked, pic•nick•ing, pic•nics.** To have a picnic.

pin•na•cle | **pĭn′** ə kəl | *n.* **1.** A tall pointed peak, as on a mountain. **2.** The highest point: *Being a star in the movie was the pinnacle of his career.*

pi•rate | **pī′** rĭt | *n.* A person who robs ships at sea.

pitch | pĭch | *v.* **1.** To throw or toss: *to pitch a baseball.* **2.** To set or put up: *to pitch a tent.* **3.** To fall forward. —*n.* **1.** A throw to a batter: *a good pitch right over home plate.* **2.** A degree of highness or lowness in music: *You have perfect pitch for this melody.*

piz•za | **pēt′** sə | *n.* An Italian dish made by baking a pie crust covered with tomato sauce, cheese, sausage, mushrooms, etc.

plain | plān | *adj.* **plain•er, plain•est.** **1.** Something that is easy to hear, see, or understand. **2.** Simple; without any decoration. **3.** Not rich or too spicy: *plain food.* —*n.* Flat, treeless land. *These sound alike* **plane, plain.**

plane | plān | *n.* **1.** A flat, level surface. **2.** An aircraft flown by an engine; airplane. *These sound alike* **plane, plain.**

plan•et | **plăn′** ĭt | *n.* One of the nine celestial bodies that move in a circular path around the sun: Mercury, Venus, Earth, Mars, Jupiter, Saturn, Uranus, Neptune, and Pluto.

plas•tic | **plăs′** tĭk | *n.* Any of many chemically made substances that are molded by heat and pressure and then shaped.

pleas•ure | **plĕzh′** ər | *n.* **1.** A feeling of happiness or enjoyment. **2.** Something that causes a feeling of delight and happiness.

pledge | plĕj | *n.* A serious promise: *The friends made a pledge to stay together.* —*v.* **pledged, pledg•ing.** To promise.

po•em | **pō′** əm | *n.* Writing in verse, often imaginative and in rhyme.

po•lar | **pō′** lər | *adj.* Anything to do with a region around a geographic pole such as the North or South Pole.

po•lite | pə **līt′** | *adj.* **po•lit•er, po•lit•est.** Having or showing good manners.

pol•lu•tion | pə **lo͞o′** shən | *n.* Contamination of the environment with waste.

pop•u•la•tion | pŏp′ yə **lā′** shən | *n.* **1.** The number of people who live in an area. **2.** People as a whole.

pore | pôr | *n.* A tiny opening in the skin of an animal or on the surface of a leaf, through which gases or liquids may pass.

pre•car•i•ous | prĭ **kâr′** ē əs | *adj.* Dangerous; unstable: *a precarious position.*

pre•pare | prĭ **pâr′** | *v.* **pre•pared, pre•par•ing.** To get ready or to plan and make.

pre•sume | prĭ **zo͞om′** | *v.* **pre•sumed, pre•sum•ing.** To think to be true, even without proof; take for granted: *I presume that everyone will be on time.*

pret•ty | **prĭt′** ē | *adj.* **pret•ti•er, pret•ti•est.** **1.** Pleasing; attractive. **2.** Appealing; charming.

prime time | prīm′ tīm | *n.* In radio or television, the evening hours that have the biggest audience, usually between 8 and 11 P.M.

pri•or | **prī′** ər | *adj.* Before or earlier in order, time, or importance: *Although she is now a nurse, her prior job was teaching.*

prob•lem | **prŏb′** ləm | *n.* A confusing question or situation; something difficult to figure out: *Finding a babysitter is a real problem.*

pro•duc•er | prə **dōō′** sər | *or* | **-dyōō′-** | *n.* **1.** The person, place, or organization responsible for making something: *Brazil is a producer of coffee beans.* **2.** A person who manages the making of a play, movie, or show: *I know a famous movie producer.*

pro•fes•sion•al | prə **fĕsh′** ə nəl | *adj.* **1.** Having a special knowledge or education for a job: *A doctor is a professional person.* **2.** Making money by doing what most people do for fun: *a professional tennis player.* —*n.* **1.** A person who has special knowledge or education. **2.** A person who makes money doing what most people do for fun: *We watched the professional ski down the mountain.*

pro•gram | **prō′** grăm | *or* | -grəm | *n.* **1.** A list of what is to be shown or done in a presentation, ceremony, etc. and who is to take part. **2.** The ceremony or presentation itself. **3.** An organized series of events: *What's the camp program for today?* —*v.* **pro•grammed, pro•gram•ming.** **1.** To plan a program: *A committee programmed the activities for the celebration.* **2.** To train to perform; to plan a series of operations: *The computers were programmed with the necessary information.*

prom•ise | **prŏm′** ĭs | *n.* **1.** A statement that one will or will not do something: *I gave a promise not to be late again.* **2.** A sign of future success: *She showed promise of becoming a good astronaut.* —*v.* **prom•ised, prom•is•ing.** **1.** To make a statement that one will or will not do something. **2.** To give hope or reason that one may expect something: *The thunder promised rain.*

proof | prōōf | *n.* Evidence; demonstration of truth.

prove | prōōv | *v.* **proved, proved** or **prov•en** | **prōō′** vən |, **prov•ing.** To show to be true; to demonstrate, or to give evidence: *She proved she knew how to do long division.*

pump•kin | **pŭmp′** kĭn | *or* | **pŭm′-** | *or* | **pŭng′-** | *n.* A large, round, orange-yellow fruit grown on a vine and often used in making pies.

pur•pose | **pûr′** pəs | *n.* The aim; intention; desired result.

***Idiom.* on purpose.** Not by accident.

puz•zle | **pŭz′** əl | *n.* **1.** Something that is confusing; a problem. **2.** A game or toy: *a crossword puzzle.* —*v.* To confuse: *The magic trick puzzled them.*

Q

qual•i•fy | **kwŏl′** ə fī′ | *v.* **qual•i•fied, qual•i•fy•ing, qual•i•fies.** **1.** To be fit or show ability in skill or knowledge: *They qualified for the football team.* **2.** To limit: *to qualify your comments.*

quan•ti•ty | **kwŏn′** tĭ tē | *n., pl.* **quan•ti•ties.** The number or amount: *Pens and pencils are needed in equal quantity.*

quar•rel | **kwôr′** əl | *or* | **kwŏr′-** | *n.* A fight with words; an argument. —*v.* **quar•reled, quar•rel•ing.** To have a fight with words.

ques•tion | **kwĕs′** chən | *n., pl.* **ques•tions.** **1.** Something asked for an answer or information. **2.** Matter to be discussed; problem or proposal: *The question of the class party was never settled.* —*v.* To ask for information.

***Idiom.* out of the question.** Unthinkable.

quick | kwĭk | *adj.* **quick•er, quick•est.** Fast; rapid; done with speed. —*adv.* **quick•ly.** Rapidly.

quit | kwĭt | *v.* **quit, quit•ting.** **1.** To stop: *quit work at five o'clock.* **2.** To leave; depart from: *quit college.*

quite | kwīt | *adv.* **1.** Completely; entirely: *You are quite right.* **2.** To a considerable degree: *It is quite cold today.*

quiz•zi•cal | **kwĭz′** ĭ kəl | *adj.* Showing confusion or puzzlement: *Because the student hadn't heard the question, she had a quizzical look on her face.*

R

rab•bit | **răb′**ĭt | *n.* A soft, furry animal with long ears and a short, fluffy tail.

rac•coon | ră **kōōn′** | *n.* A grayish-brown animal with black, mask-like markings on the face and a long, bushy, black-ringed tail.

raise | rāz | *v.* **raised, rais•ing.** **1.** To lift or move to a higher position: *to raise your hand.* **2.** To gather together; collect: *to raise money for charity.* **3.** To help grow or rear: *to raise children.* **4.** To bring up or ask: *to raise a question.* **5.** To build or erect: *to raise a barn.*

—*n.* An increase in amount, price, pay, etc.: *a raise in salary.*

ran•dom | **răn′** dəm | *adj.* Made or done without a definite plan or pattern: *I didn't know which package to open first, so I made a random choice.*

***Idiom.* at random.** With no method, purpose, or pattern.

rap•id | **răp′** ĭd | *adj.* Fast; quick.

rath•er | **răth′** ər | *or* | **rä′** *th*ər | *adv.* **1.** More willingly; preferably: *I'd rather see a movie.* **2.** More properly; justly: *This gift is for Sally rather than for Robin.* **3.** Somewhat; to a certain extent: *a rather silly idea.*

raw | rô | *adj.* **raw•er, raw•est.** **1.** Not cooked: *a raw potato.* **2.** Not artificially treated or processed; natural: *raw lumber.*

ra•zor | rā′ zər | *n.* An instrument with a sharp blade used to shave or cut hair: *Be careful not to cut yourself with the razor.*

rea•son | **rē′** zən | *n.* **1.** A cause or motive for acting or feeling a certain way: *I have a reason for being angry.* **2.** An explanation; an excuse: *Give me one good reason.* **3.** The ability to think logically and clearly: *Don't lose your power of reason.* —*v.* **1.** To think with a clear mind. **2.** To try to persuade; to attempt to change a person's mind: *I will reason with you.*

re•cede | rĭ **sēd′** | *v.* **re•ced•ed, re•ced•ing.** To move back or away: *After the flood the river water began to recede slowly from the field.*

re•cord•er | rĭ **kôr′** dər | *n.* **1.** Someone who takes notes. **2.** A machine that keeps sounds on magnetic tape: *My tape recorder can play the song.* **3.** A small musical instrument that sounds like a flute.

re•cy•cle | rē **sī′** kəl | *v.* **re•cy•cled, re•cy•cling.** To treat or process materials that might be thrown away so that they can be used again: *Our class project was to recycle newspapers, cans, and plastic bottles.*

ref•e•ree | rĕf′ ə **rē′** | *n.* An official in certain sports and games who enforces the rules and supervises the play: *The referee ruled that the team had scored a goal.*

re•lax | rĭ **lăks′** | *v.* To become less stiff; to loosen up; to be at ease.

re•main | rĭ **mān′** | *v.* **1.** To stay behind after others go: *remain after school.* **2.** To be left: *So much remains to be done!* **3.** To continue as before: *She remained my friend.*

re•mem•ber | rĭ **mĕm′** bər | *v.* **1.** To think of again; to recall or cause to remind: *I can remember my homework from yesterday.* **2.** To keep in mind: *to remember an appointment.* **3.** To present with a gift or reward: *You'll be remembered on your birthday.*

re•mind | rĭ **mīnd′** | *v.* To cause to remember; to recall to mind.

re•source•ful | rĭ **sôrs′** fəl | *adj.* Able to deal with new, difficult, or different situations effectively or imaginatively: *On our picnic we had to be resourceful because we forgot our knives and forks.*

re•view | rĭ **vyoo͞′** | *v.* **1.** To study. **2.** To think back in one's mind. **3.** To write or tell about a book, movie, play, or event: *review a book.* —*n.* **1.** A time of studying. **2.** A report of a book, movie, play, or event: *I read the movie review in the paper.*

re•vise | rĭ **vīz′** | *v.* **re•vised, re•vis•ing.** **1.** To look over and change in order to improve: *to revise a story.* **2.** To change or make different: *to revise an opinion.*

rev•o•lu•tion | rĕv′ ə **lo͞o′** shən | *n.* **1.** A complete overthrow of government: *the American Revolution.* **2.** A sudden or dramatic change: *the industrial revolution.* **3.** Movement in a circular path: *It takes a year for the earth to make a revolution around the sun.*

re•ward | rĭ **wôrd′** | *n.* **1.** Something given in return for a service or act. **2.** Money offered for the return of something lost. —*v.* To give something in return for something done.

rid•dle¹ | **rĭd′** l | *v.* **rid•dled, rid•dling.** To make holes in: *Mice had riddled the house.*

rid•dle² | **rĭd′** l | *n.* A problem or question that is not easy to understand: *Try to answer this riddle.*

ride | rīd | *v.* **rode** | rōd|, **rid•den** | **rĭd′** n |, **rid•ing.** **1.** To sit on something in order to make it move: *to ride a bicycle.* **2.** To be carried on or by; to travel: *I ride the bus.* —*n.* **1.** A short trip on an animal or vehicle. **2.** A structure at the amusement park used for pleasure: *The Ferris wheel is my favorite ride.*

right | rīt | *n.* **1.** On the side opposite the left: *Her house is on the right.* **2.** Just; good: *the difference between right and wrong.* —*adv.* **1.** Straight on; directly: *He looked right at the object.* **2.** Correctly: *John guessed right.* —*v.* **1.** To set something in order: *We had to right the capsized boat.* **2.** To make something good, just, or correct: *to right an injustice. These sound alike* **right, write.**

Idioms. **right of way.** The right to move first. **right away.** Immediately.

right•ful | **rīt'** fəl | *adj.* Having a just or lawful claim: *Louis is the rightful owner of the house.*

road | rōd | *n.* **1.** Pavement or cleared ground used to go from one place to another; a route or path: *Which road goes to town?* **2.** A direction toward something: *your road to success. These sound alike* **road, rode.**

roar | rôr | *or* | rōr | *n.* **1.** A loud, deep sound: *a lion's roar.* **2.** A loud laugh: *I could hear his roar next door.* —*v.* To make a loud, deep sound: *Please don't roar in my ear.*

roast | rōst | *v.* **1.** To cook by dry heat or over an open fire; to bake: *to roast a chicken.* **2.** To be extremely hot; to feel overheated: *You'll roast with your coat on indoors.* —*n.* A large cut of meat suitable for roasting.

rode Look up **ride.** *These sound alike* **rode, road.**

rook•ie | **ro͝ok'** ē | *n.* **1.** A person who is a first-year player in a professional sport. **2.** A beginner who lacks training or experience.

room•mate | **ro͞om'** māt' | *or* | **ro͞om'**- | *n.* A person who lives with others in a room or apartment: *My sister's roommate at college is from another country.*

roost•er | **ro͞o'** stər | *n.* A full-grown male chicken.

ro•ta•tion | rō **tā'** shən | *n.* Circular turning on an axis: *The rotation of the earth takes 24 hours.*

rough | rŭf | *adj.* **rough•er, rough•est.** **1.** Having an uneven surface; not smooth: *a rough road.* **2.** Violent; severe; not gentle: *rough games.*

roy•al | **roi'** əl | *adj.* **1.** Anything belonging to or having to do with a king or queen: *a royal palace.* **2.** Made for or acceptable for a king or queen: *a royal welcome.*

rum•mage | rŭm' ĭj | *v.* **rum•maged, rum•mag•ing.** To look for something thoroughly by turning things over or moving them around: *rummage through the closet.* —*n.* A thorough search.

S

sa•fa•ri | sə **fär'** ē | *n., pl.* **sa•fa•ris.** A hunting trip, especially in Africa.

sail•boat | **sāl'** bōt' | *n.* A boat that travels by wind blowing against its sails.

sal•ad | **săl'** əd | *n.* A combination of vegetables or fruit that is often served with a dressing.

sam•ple | **săm'** pəl | *or* | **säm'**- | *n.* A small piece of something that shows what the rest is like. —*v.* To try a part; to test.

sand•wich | **sănd'** wĭch | *or* | **săn'**- | *n., pl.* **sand•wich•es.** Two or more slices of bread with a filling of jelly, cheese, meat, egg, etc. —*v.* To fit between with little space: *Four of us were sandwiched in the back seat.*

sat•el•lite | **săt'** l īt' | *n.* **1.** A heavenly body that travels in orbit around another larger body. **2.** A man-made object that orbits the earth, the moon, or other bodies in space. **3.** A country that is under the control of a more powerful country.

Sat•ur•day | **săt'** ər dē | *or* | dā' | *n.* The seventh day of the week.

saw•dust | **sô'** dŭst' | *n.* The tiny pieces of wood that fall off during sawing.

scale[1] | skāl | *n.* An instrument used to find out how heavy something is.

scale[2] | skāl | *n.* **1.** Equally spaced marks on a line used to measure: *Your ruler is a scale.* **2.** Musical tones that go up and down in pitch: *to play the scales on the piano.* —*v.* **scaled, scal•ing.** To climb.

scale[3] | skāl | *n.* One of the layered plates on the outer covering of a fish, snake, etc.

scarf | skärf | *n., pl.* **scarfs** | skärfs | *or* **scarves** | skärvz |. A piece of cloth worn around the head, neck, or shoulders for decoration or warmth: *Scarves are good for keeping your face and neck warm in winter.*

sci•ence | **sī'** əns | *n.* **1.** Knowledge based on facts about nature and the universe. **2.** Any branch of knowledge about the universe: biology, astronomy, etc.

scold | skōld | *v.* To blame with angry words in an angry tone of voice.

score | skôr | *or* | skōr | *n.* **1.** A number of points in a game. **2.** A result on a test. —*v.* **scored, scor•ing.** To keep a record of points in a contest or exam.

score•board | **skôr'** bôrd' | *n.* A large board that shows the score and other important game or contest information to the spectators.

sea•son | sē′ zən | *n.* **1.** One of the four parts of the year: spring, summer, autumn, winter. **2.** A special time of the year: *Christmas Season.* —*v.* To give flavor to: *season food.*

sec•tion | sĕk′ shən | *n.* A separated part; a cut-off area of a whole. —*v.* To separate or cut into sections.

se•lec•tion | sĭ lĕk′ shən | *n.* The act of selecting or choosing.

self | sĕlf | *n., pl.* **selves** | sĕlvz|. One's own person separate from any other.

self•ish | sĕl′ fĭsh | *adj.* Caring too much for oneself and not for others.

sen•tence | sĕn′ təns | *n.* **1.** A group of words that expresses a complete thought. **2.** A decision by a judge in a court of law; a verdict.

Sep•tem•ber | sĕp tĕm′ bər | *n.* The ninth month of the year. September has 30 days.

serv•ice | sûr′ vĭs | *n.* A useful act. —*v.* **serv•iced, serv•ic•ing.** To provide or make ready for use: *I'll service your car.*

sew | sō | *v.* **sewed, sewn** | sōn | *or* **sewed, sew•ing.** To attach or fasten with a needle and thread.

shad•y | shā′ dē | *adj.* **shad•i•er, shad•i•est.** **1.** Sheltered from sun or light. **2.** Of questionable honesty or character: *a shady person.*

sham•poo | shăm po͞o′ | *n.* A preparation for cleaning. —*v.* To wash and clean with soap or detergent.

share | shâr | *v.* **shared, shar•ing.** **1.** To take part; join: *to share in the happiness.* **2.** To use, enjoy, or have in common: *to share the same room.* **3.** To divide or portion: *to share your lunch.* —*n.* Portion or part of something received, done, or enjoyed by a number of persons: *He took his share of the profits.*

sheet | shēt | *n.* **1.** Cloth used to cover a bed: *Fresh sheets are on the bed.* **2.** Thin, broad piece of something: *A sheet of ice is slippery.* **3.** A piece of paper: *Take out a new sheet of paper.*

shock | shŏk | *n.* **1.** A sudden or violent blow: *the shock of an explosion.* **2.** A sudden upset of the mind or emotions: *The bad news was a terrible shock to them.* **3.** Effect of electric current on the body: *a shock from a wire.* —*v.* To surprise, horrify, or disgust.

shoe | sho͞o | *n.* An outer covering for the foot often made of leather.

shore | shôr | *or* | shōr | *n.* The land at the edge of an ocean, sea, river, or lake.

shut•tle | shŭt′ l | *n.* **1.** The thread holder used in weaving to carry the threads back and forth through the yarn. **2.** A train, plane, bus, etc. that goes only between two places on a frequent and regular schedule. **3.** A space craft capable of carrying astronauts back and forth for short distances in space: *The astronauts took the shuttle from their spaceship to earth and back again.* —*v.* **shut•tled, shut•tling.** To move back and forth.

siege | sēj | *n.* The surrounding of an enemy town or fort and cutting off supplies to it for a long time in order to force a surrender.

sig•nal | sĭg′ nəl | *n.* **1.** A sign that warns, gives notice, or points out something: *a railroad signal.* **2.** An action that is used to start something: *a referee's signal to start the game.* —*v.* **sig•naled, sig•nal•ing.** To warn or point out.

sil•ver | sĭl′ vər | *n.* **1.** Soft, shiny metal that is easily shaped into jewelry, coins, etc. **2.** Coins; change: *to carry silver.* **3.** Forks, knives, and other tableware made with this metal; silverware. —*adj.* Having the color of silver.

sim•i•lar | sĭm′ ə lər | *adj.* Alike somehow but not the same.

sim•ple | sĭm′ pəl | *adj.* **sim•pler, sim•plest.** **1.** A task that is easy to understand or to do: *a simple test.* **2.** Anything plain; not fancy: *a simple white shirt.*

since | sĭns | *adv.* **1.** From a certain time in the past until now. **2.** Ago; before now. —*conj.* Because.

sixth | sĭksth | *n.* **1.** Next after fifth. **2.** One of six equal parts; $\frac{1}{6}$.

skate | skāt | *n.* A boot or shoe made with a blade or wheels on the bottom, used for moving on the ice, street, floor, etc.: *roller skate.* —*v.* **skat•ed, skat•ing.** To move by using a blade or wheels on the foot: *to skate home.*

ski | skē | *n., pl.* **skis** *or* **ski.** A long, thin piece of wood, plastic, or metal attached to a boot to glide on snow. —*v.* **skied, ski•ing, skis.** To travel on skis.

skill | skĭl | *n.* Knowledge or ability to do something well.

skin diving | skĭn′ dī′ vĭng | *n.* Swimming underwater for a long time by using a face mask, rubber flippers, and a snorkel.

skirt | skûrt | *n.* Clothing worn by girls and women, which hangs from the waist down. —*v.* To travel along the edge of: *The car skirted the puddle.*

smol•der *also* **smoul•der** | **smōl'** dər | *v.* **1.** To burn slowly with little smoke and no flame: *The coals will smolder for hours.* **2.** To continue in a hidden manner.

snack | snăk | *n.* A small amount of food eaten between meals; a light meal.

snake | snāk | *n.* A long, scaly, crawling animal without legs; serpent. —*v.* **snaked, snak•ing.** To crawl or twist like a snake.

soc•cer | **sŏk'** ər | *n.* A game in which two teams of 11 players each try to kick a round ball into the other team's goal. The arms and hands cannot be used for hitting the ball or stopping an opponent.

so•lar | **sō'** lər | *adj.* Of or having to do with the sun: *solar energy.*

sol•id | **sŏl'** ĭd | *adj.* **1.** Having a definite size and shape, not a liquid or a gas. **2.** Hard; firm; able to support weight: *solid ground.* **3.** Having a sound character; trustworthy: *a solid person.*

sol•i•tude | **sŏl'** ĭ to͞od' | *or* | **sŏl'** ĭ tyo͞od' | *n.* **1.** The state of being alone: *The author needed solitude in order to write the book.* **2.** A place away from people: *the solitude of the mountain cabin.*

span•iel | **spăn'** yəl | *n.* A small to medium-sized dog with drooping ears, short legs, and silky, wavy hair.

sparse | spârs | *adj.* Not crowded; widely scattered: *Plants are sparse in the desert.*

spe•cial | **spĕsh'** əl | *adj.* Uncommon, unusual; that which is different from others: *a special day.*

speech | spēch | *n., pl.* **speech•es. 1.** The act of speaking: *to burst into speech.* **2.** Words; remarks: *Her speech is full of slang.* **3.** A formal talk delivered in public: *a graduation speech.*

square | skwâr | *n.* **1.** A figure with four equal sides and four right angles. **2.** Anything that has this shape: *a square piece of paper.* **3.** An open space in a town or city surrounded on all sides by streets: *Trees were planted in the city square.* —*adj.* **squar•er, squar•est. 1.** Having four equal sides. **2.** Measure of a surface area: *a square foot.* **3.** Honest, direct, or fair: *a square deal.*

St. Abbreviation of **Street** and **Saint.**

stare | stâr | *v.* **stared, star•ing.** To look with open eyes for a long time. —*n.* A wide-eyed, fixed look held for some time.

starve | stärv | *v.* **starved, starv•ing. 1.** To become very ill or to die from extreme hunger. **2.** To be hungry: *I'm starving for chocolate chip cookies.*

sta•tion | **stā'** shən | *n.* **1.** A regularly scheduled stop on a train or bus route. **2.** A building used for such a stop: *a train station.* **3.** An assigned place or position for a certain person: *The lifeguard sat at his station.* **4.** A place that is used to send or receive radio or television programs: *How many television stations do you get?* —*v.* To put oneself at an appointed place: *The detective stationed himself nearby.*

steep | stēp | *adj.* **steep•er, steep•est. 1.** Having a sharp slope; almost straight up and down: *a steep cliff.* **2.** Very high: *steep prices.*

stom•ach•ache | **stŭm'** ək āk' | *n.* A pain in the stomach or abdomen.

sto•ry[1] | **stôr'** ē | *or* | **stōr'** ē | *n., pl.* **sto•ries. 1.** An account, oral or written, of something that has happened: *a newspaper story.* **2.** A tale of fiction. **3.** A lie: *Tell the truth, not a story.*

sto•ry[2] | **stôr'** ē | *or* | **stōr'** ē | *n., pl.* **sto•ries.** Any level or floor of a building.

stow•a•way | **stō'** ə wā' | *n.* A person who hides in a ship, airplane, or other vehicle in order to travel without paying for the trip: *The stowaway was found by the captain of the ship and made to buy a ticket.*

straw | strô | *n.* **1.** A narrow tube made of plastic or waxed paper used for drinking a liquid: *a soda straw.* **2.** Stems or stalks of grain that have been seeded and dried: *The animals in the barn sleep on straw.*

straw•ber•ry | **strô'** bĕr' ē | *n., pl.* **-ber•ries.** A sweet, red fruit with many small seeds on its surface: *Strawberries grow close to the ground.*

stu•di•o | **sto͞o'** dē ō' | *or* | **styo͞o'**- | *n.* **1.** An artist's workroom. **2.** A place where a film, TV, or radio program is made.

sug•ar | **sho͝og'** ər | *n.* A sweet substance obtained from sugar beets, sugar cane, maple trees, fruits, etc. —*v.* **1.** To sprinkle sugar or to sweeten with sugar: *to sugar berries.* **2.** To make pleasant; make less disagreeable: *He sugared his criticism with a few flattering words.*

suit•case | **so͞ot'** kās' | *n.* A flat, rectangular traveling bag.

Sun•day | **sŭn'** dē | *or* | -dā' | *n.* The first day of the week.

sup•pose | sə **pōz'** | *v.* **sup•posed, sup•pos•ing. 1.** To assume; expect; take for granted: *I suppose I'll see you at the party.* **2.** To imagine;

pretend: *The little girl liked to suppose she was a princess.*

sur•prise | sər **prīz′** | *v.* **sur•prised, sur•pris•ing.** **1.** To take someone unawares; to come upon unexpectedly: *He surprised me with a visit.* **2.** To cause to feel wonder or astonishment: *The mild man's fury surprised us.* —*n.* **1.** A catching unawares: *to be caught by surprise.* **2.** Something sudden or unexpected: *a surprise for Mom.* **3.** A feeling caused by something sudden or unexpected; astonishment: *Imagine our surprise when we saw our new bikes!*

sur•vey•or | sər **vā′** ər | *n.* A person whose job is to measure land: *The surveyor will tell us exactly how big our property is.*

swal•low[1] | **swŏl′** ō | *v.* **1.** To transfer food or drink from the mouth to the stomach through the throat: *to swallow cake.* **2.** To perform the act of swallowing: *I feel as if there is a lump in my throat, and I cannot swallow.* **3.** To engulf; destroy. **4.** To believe easily: *They'll swallow anything you tell them.* —*n.* **1.** The act of swallowing. **2.** The amount swallowed at one time.

swal•low[2] | **swŏl′** ō | *n.* A slender, fork-tailed bird with pointed wings and swift, graceful flight.

sweat•er | **swĕt′** ər | *n.* Knitted or crocheted garment, with or without sleeves, for the upper part of the body.

sweat•shirt | **swĕt′** shûrt′ | *n.* A heavy long-sleeved knitted pullover shirt usually made of cotton jersey.

swim | swĭm | *v.* **swam** | swăm |, **swum** | swŭm |, **swim•ming.** **1.** To pass through water by moving legs, arms, fins, etc. **2.** To cross by swimming: *The team swam the English Channel.* **3.** To be immersed in or covered by a liquid: *Their eyes began to swim with tears.* —*n.* The act or sport of swimming.

***Idiom.* in the swim.** Taking part in whatever is fashionable or current.

symp•tom | **sĭm′** təm | *or* | **sĭmp′**- | *n.* **1.** A sign in the body that is an indication of a disease or illness: *Tiredness was the first symptom that I had the flu.* **2.** A sign or indication of something.

sys•tem | **sĭs′** təm | *n.* **1.** A group of things that go together to make up a whole: *The trains, the tracks, the schedule, and the engineer are all parts of a railroad system.* **2.** A combination of parts of the body that work together and are dependent on one another: *the circulatory system.* **3.** Orderly method of doing things; routine: *Hugh has a system for his day's work.*

T

ta•ble•spoon | **tā′** bəl spo͞on′ | *n.* **1.** A measuring spoon equal to three teaspoons that is used for cooking. **2.** A large serving spoon.

tape deck | tāp dĕk | *n.* A machine that is able to play back magnetic tapes. It is used as a part of a high-fidelity sound system.

tar•dy | **tär′** dē | *adj.* **tar•di•er, tar•di•est.** **1.** Not on time; late: *We were all tardy because of the storm.* **2.** Slow: *a tardy growth of plants.*

taught Look up **teach.**

teach | tēch | *v.* **taught** | tôt |, **teach•ing.** To give lessons; to help someone or something to learn.

teach•er | **tē′** chər | *n.* A person who teaches.

tear[1] | târ | *v.* **tore** | tôr | *or* | tōr |, **torn** | tôrn | *or* | tōrn |, **tear•ing.** To pull apart.

tear[2] | tîr | *n.* A drop of water from the eyes.

tel•e•phone | **tĕl′** ə fōn′ | *n.* An instrument or system for sending and receiving speech and other sounds over electric wires. —*v.* **tel•e•phoned, tel•e•phon•ing.** To use this instrument to speak with someone; call: *Please telephone me.*

tel•e•scope | **tĕl′** ə skōp′ | *n.* An instrument for making distant things appear larger, especially a large instrument of this kind for studying heavenly bodies. —*v.* **tel•e•scoped, tel•e•scop•ing.** To fit a smaller object into a larger similar object; nest: *Let's telescope these boxes to save space.*

tel•e•vi•sion | **tĕl′** ə vĭzh′ ən | *n.* **1.** A system for sending and receiving moving pictures and sound. **2.** A machine that receives these pictures and sounds and presents them to a viewer.

ten•nis | **tĕn′** ĭs | *n.* A game for two players or two pairs of players who use rackets to hit a ball back and forth across a net.

their | *thâr* | *pron.* Of or belonging to them: *Their float won first prize. These sound alike* **their, there, they're.**

theme | thēm | *n.* **1.** A subject written or talked about; topic: *the theme of the discussion; the theme of a party.* **2.** Short essay: *Students write themes.* **3.** In music, a short tune or melody that occurs again and again in a composition.

there | *thâr* | *adv.* **1.** In or at that place: *Put it there, not here.* **2.** To or toward that place: *I can walk there in an hour.* —*n.* That place: *We came from there an hour ago. These sound alike* **there, their, they're.**

they're | *thâr* | The contraction for "they are." *These sound alike* **they're, their, there.**

think | thĭngk | *v.* **thought** | thôt |, **think·ing.** To use the mind to form ideas, opinions, beliefs, decisions, etc.

third | thûrd | *adj.* **1.** Next after second. **2.** One of three equal parts; ⅓: *He ate a third of the pie.*

thir·teen | thûr′ **tēn′** | *n.* Amount or quantity that is one greater than 12.

though | *thō* | *adv.* **1.** In spite of the fact that; although: *We kept on working though it was very late.* **2.** Even if: *Start the job now though you cannot finish it.*

thought Look up **think.**

thread | thrĕd | *n.* A fine cord of twisted silk, cotton, wool, or similar fibers from which cloth is woven or with which things are sewed. *—v.* To make one's way through obstacles: *We threaded our way through the crowd.*

threw Look up **throw.** *These sound alike* **threw, through.**

throat | thrōt | *n.* **1.** The passage running from the back of the mouth to the lungs and stomach: *a sore throat.* **2.** A narrow entrance or passage: *the throat of a cave.*

through | thrōō | *prep.* From one end to the other: *to go through a tunnel.* *—adj.* **1.** Going or extending from one end to another: *a through street.* **2.** Finished: *I'm through with this work. These sound alike* **through, threw.**

throw | thrō | *v.* **threw** | thrōō |, **thrown** | thrōn |, **throw·ing.** **1.** To fling with a motion of the arm; hurl: *to throw a ball.* **2.** To cause to fall; cause to lose balance: *One wrestler threw the other.* **3.** To cast; project: *The lamp throws a shadow on the wall.* *—n.* A flinging; a casting: *a throw of the ball.*

Idiom. **stone's throw.** Short distance.

thun·der·storm | **thŭn′** dər stôrm′ | *n.* A storm of lightning and thunder, usually with a downpour of rain.

Thurs·day | **thûrz′** dē | *or* | -dā′ | *n.* The fifth day of the week.

tim·id | **tĭm′** ĭd | *adj.* Lacking in courage; shy; easily frightened: *Frank was too timid to give his speech.*

to | tōō | *or* | tə *when unstressed* | *prep.* **1.** Toward; in the direction of: *on my way to school.* **2.** As far as: *going to Boston.* **3.** For the purpose of; for: *built to last; a key to the door.* **4.** Opposite: *face to face.* **5.** On; upon; against: *There is a sign tacked to the door.* **6.** Until; till: *The play lasts to 10:30.* **7.** Before: *five minutes to six. These sound alike* **to, too, two.**

Idiom. **to and fro.** Back and forth.

toast·er | **tō′** stər | *n.* An electrical device for browning and heating bread and rolls.

to·ken | **tō′** kən | *n.* **1.** Something that represents something else, such as an event, special occasion, fact, object, or feeling; symbol: *The postcard is a token of our trip.* **2.** A piece of metal that looks like a coin and is used in place of money, as in paying the fares on buses or subways.

to·mor·row | tə **mŏr′** ō | *or* | **-môr′** ō | *n.* **1.** The day after today: *Is tomorrow a holiday?* **2.** The near future: *the world of tomorrow.* *—adv.* On the day after today: *I will give this to you tomorrow.*

tongue | tŭng | *n.* **1.** The muscular, movable organ in the mouth used in tasting and also, in human beings, for talking. **2.** A language: *Her native tongue is Spanish.* **3.** A manner of speaking: *to have a sharp tongue.* **4.** Anything like a tongue in shape or use, such as leaping flame or the piece of leather under the laces of a shoe.

too | tōō | *adv.* **1.** Also; in addition; besides: *You are invited to the graduation ceremony and the party, too.* **2.** More than enough: *There was too much food. These sound alike* **too, to, two.**

tore Look up **tear.**

tor·na·do | tôr **nā′** dō | *n., pl.* **tor·na·does** *or* **tor·na·dos.** Violent, whirling wind that travels rapidly in a narrow path. It is seen as a twisting, dark cloud shaped like a funnel.

touch | tŭch | *v.* **1.** To be in contact: *Their heads touched as they whispered.* **2.** To feel with the fingers: *She touched the paint.* **3.** To strike lightly; tap: *He touched the glass bells.*

to·ward | tôrd | *or* | tōrd | *or* | tə **wôrd′** | *prep.* **1.** In the direction of: *We sailed toward Hawaii.* **2.** Close upon; near: *We camped toward sundown.* **3.** About; regarding: *What is your attitude toward the candidates?*

track | trăk | *n.* **1.** A mark left by something moving: *The animal left its tracks.* **2.** A path or trail: *The track is two miles long.* **3.** The rails on which a train moves. **4.** A racetrack. —*v.* To follow by sight or scent.

traf·fic | **trăf'** ĭk | *n.* **1.** The movement of people, automobiles, planes, ships, etc.: *There was much traffic on the road.* **2.** The exchange of goods; buying and selling. —*v.* **traf·ficked, traf·fick·ing, traf·fics.** To buy or sell.

trans·por·ta·tion | trăns' pər **tā'** shən | *n.* The means of moving anything from one place to another.

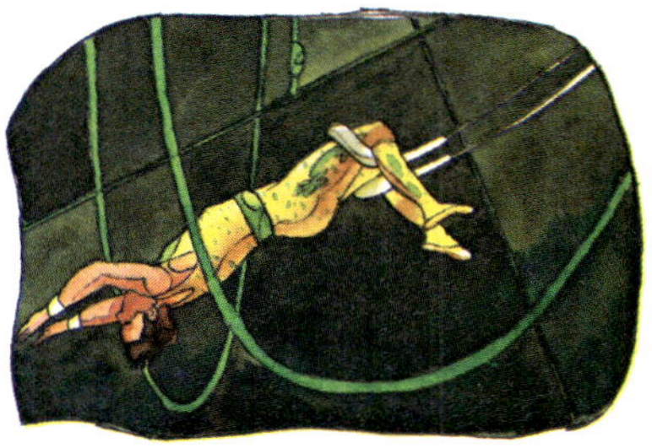

tra·peze | tră **pēz'** | *n.* A short bar placed between two hanging ropes, used by gymnasts and circus acrobats.

treas·ure | **trĕzh'** ər | *n.* Valuable thing or things such as jewels, gold, money, etc. —*v.* **treas·ured, treas·ur·ing.** To value; to think of very highly.

trem·ble | **trĕm'** bəl | *v.* **trem·bled, trem·bling.** **1.** To shake from fright, cold, anger, etc.: *Your hand is trembling.* **2.** To move or quake: *I think the building is trembling.* —*n.* A shudder.

tried. Look up **try.**

trou·ble | **trŭb'** əl | *n.* **1.** A dangerous situation: *The police rushed to the scene of trouble.* **2.** Extra effort or bother: *Please don't go to any trouble for me.* —*v.* **trou·bled, trou·bling.** **1.** To disturb or cause worry: *I'm troubled by your fever.* **2.** To bother: *May I trouble you for a minute?*

truth | trōōth | *n., pl.* **truths** | trōō*thz* | *or* | trōōths |. **1.** Something that is true; fact. **2.** Honesty or sincerity of speech and action.

try | trī | *v.* **tried** | trīd |, **try·ing, tries.** **1.** To make an effort: *I tried to finish in time.* **2.** To test or experiment: *Try out your new skates.* **3.** To examine or investigate in a court of law: *The case will be tried in court.* —*n.* An effort.

Tues·day | **tōōz'** dē | *or* | -dā' | *or* | **tyōōz'**- | *n.* The third day of the week.

tum·ble | **tŭm'** bəl | *v.* **tum·bled, tum·bling.** **1.** To fall or roll over. **2.** To perform acrobatics such as leaps, headstands, etc. —*n.* A fall.

tu·tor | **tōō'** tər | *or* | **tyōō'**- | *n.* A teacher who gives private instruction to a student: *My English tutor helped me three times a week.* —*v.* To teach privately.

tweed | twēd | *n.* A rough woolen fabric made with two or more colors of yarn that is often used to make coats and casual suits.

two | tōō | *n.* One more than one; **2.** *These sound alike* **two, to, too.**

ty·rant | **tī'** rənt | *n.* A person or ruler who uses power in a cruel and unjust way: *The people were very upset because the king had become a tyrant.*

U

ug·ly | **ŭg'** lē | *adj.* **ug·li·er, ug·li·est.** **1.** Unpleasant to look at: *ugly wallpaper.* **2.** Mean and disagreeable: *an ugly temper.*

ul·ti·mate | **ŭl'** tə mĭt | *adj.* **1.** Last; final: *Her ultimate goal is to be President of the United States.* **2.** Basic: *The ultimate cause of the accident was carelessness.*

um·pire | **ŭm'** pīr' | *n.* A person whose job is to rule on plays in sports, especially in baseball: *The umpire called the pitch a strike.* —*v.* **um·pired, um·pir·ing.** To act as an umpire for: *Jill umpired the game.*

u·ni·verse | **yōō'** nə vûrs' | *n.* Everything in existence: *the earth, the heavens, and all of space.*

up·roar | **ŭp'** rôr' | *or* | -rōr' | *n.* A loud noise caused by excitement or confusion.

up·set | ŭp **sĕt'** | *v.* **up·set, up·set·ting.** **1.** To overturn or knock over: *The kitten upset the fishbowl.* **2.** To interfere or cause disorder: *The holiday crowds upset the train schedule.* **3.** To disturb or worry: *Did I upset you?* **4.** To unexpectedly defeat in a contest: *Our soccer team upset the champions.* —*n.* | **ŭp'** sĕt' |. The act of overturning or causing a disturbance. —*adj.* | ŭp **sĕt'** |. **1.** Overturned: *an upset boat.* **2.** Disturbed; sick: *an upset stomach.*

u·til·i·ty | yōō **tĭl'** ĭ tē | *n., pl.* **u·til·i·ties.** **1.** A company that supplies a service to the public: *The company that provides electricity is a utility.* **2.** Relating to such a company. **3.** Usefulness: *The utility of computers is well known.*

V

va·ca·tion | vā **kā'** shən | *n.* Time of rest from a regular routine; freedom from school or work: *a summer vacation.*

veg·e·ta·ble | **vĕj'** tə bəl | *or* | **vĕj'** ĭ tə- | *n., pl.* **veg·e·ta·bles.** A plant whose seeds, leaves, or roots may be used as food: *Carrots are my favorite vegetables.*

ve·loc·i·ty | və **lŏs'** ĭ tē | *n., pl.* **ve·loc·i·ties.** The rate at which something moves in a particular direction; speed: *the velocity of sound.*

vil·lage | **vĭl′** ĭj | *n.* A group of houses and businesses forming a small community, usually smaller than a town.

vir·tu·al | **vûr′** cho͞o əl | *adj.* Being so for all practical purposes, though not in fact or name: *Kendall was the virtual star of the play even though she didn't have the biggest part.*

vo·cal | **vō′** kəl | *adj.* **1.** Relating to or made by the voice: *Because she had a sore throat, her vocal sounds were hoarse.* **2.** Relating to or made by singing: *I enjoyed the vocal music performed by the school choir.* **3.** Expressing opinions freely and often; outspoken: *She was vocal in her support of the new school building, making long speeches at every town meeting.*

voice | vois | *n.* A sound coming from the mouth made by speaking, shouting, singing, etc. —*v.* **voiced, voic·ing.** To give expression to: *He voiced his opinions.*

void | void | *n.* Empty space: *There was a void in the stadium after the teams and fans went home.* —*adj.* **1.** Empty. **2.** Worth nothing.

vol·ley·ball | **vŏl′** ē bôl′ | *n.* **1.** A game in which two teams try to bat a large ball back and forth across a net with their hands without letting the ball touch the ground. **2.** The ball used in this game.

vote | vōt | *n.* **1.** A formal expression of a choice: *a vote for student government.* **2.** The right or opportunity to express a choice: *I am too young to have a vote.* —*v.* To express a choice in an election.

voy·age | **voi′** ĭj | *n.* A long journey to a faraway place made by water or through space.

W

waist | wāst | *n.* **1.** The narrow part of the body between the ribs and the hips. **2.** Part of an object that is narrower than the rest of it: *the waist of a violin. These sound alike* **waist, waste.**

wal·low | **wŏl′** ō | *v.* To roll about in something such as mud or water: *Sometimes puppies will wallow in mud.*

wan·der | **wŏn′** dər | *v.* **1.** To roam without a particular purpose: *I wandered through the old gardens.* **2.** To get lost: *A search party was sent after the child who wandered from camp.* **3.** To ramble in speech or thought: *The speaker began to wander from the subject.*

warn | wôrn | *v.* **1.** To put on guard against danger; alert; caution: *The coast guard warned all ships of the hurricane.* **2.** To notify, signal: *Her look warned us it was time to leave.*

waste | wāst | *v.* **wast·ed, wast·ing.** **1.** To squander; use without profit: *I am afraid that my brother wasted his allowance.* **2.** To destroy; spoil; ruin: *The forest was wasted by fire.* —*n.* **1.** Useless expenditure; profitless use: *a waste of opportunity.* **2.** Discarded material; refuse; something left over: *Factory waste pollutes our river.* **3.** Wilderness; desert: *Nothing grows in that desolate waste. These sound alike* **waste, waist.**

watch | wŏch | *v.* **1.** To look carefully; be attentive; be on the lookout: *If you watch, you may see how I do this trick.* **2.** To see; look at: *to watch a parade.* **3.** To keep guard: *We watched all through the night.* —*n.* **1.** Close observation: *Keep careful watch and you'll see a falling star.* **2.** Wakefulness for the purpose of guarding or tending to: *a mother's watch over her sick child.* **3.** A small timepiece, usually worn on the wrist.

weak | wēk | *adj.* **weak·er, weak·est.** **1.** Lacking physical strength: *to be weak from hunger.* **2.** Likely to fail or break if placed under pressure, stress or strain: *a weak bridge.* **3.** Lacking in ability: *weak in math.*

wealth | wĕlth | *n.* **1.** A large quantity of money or possessions; riches. **2.** An abundance: *a wealth of ideas.*

wear | wâr | *v.* **wore** | wôr | *or* | wōr |, **worn** | wôrn | *or* | wōrn |, **wear·ing.** **1.** To have on the body: *wear clothes; wear a smile.* **2.** To cause damage by long use: *wear a hole in a sock.*

weath·er | **wĕth′** ər | *n.* The atmospheric conditions at any place at a particular time: *The weather is beautiful today.* —*v.* **1.** To come through safely or successfully: *to weather a storm.* **2.** To become bleached, dried, etc. by the action of the sun, wind, rain, etc.: *The shingles of the old house had weathered to a beautiful silver gray.*
Idiom. **under the weather.** Not feeling well; ill.

Wednes·day | **wĕnz′** dē | *or* | -dā′ | *n.* The fourth day of the week.

week·end | **wēk′** ĕnd′ | *n.* **1.** The end of the week, especially the time from Friday night to Sunday night. **2.** A visit, holiday, or house party during this period: *a weekend at the beach.*

weigh | wā | *v.* **1.** To find out the heaviness of something by means of a scale or balance: *to weigh a parcel.* **2.** To have a certain weight: *He weighs 90 pounds.* **3.** To turn over in the mind; ponder: *She weighed another plan.*

weight | wāt | *n.* **1.** The amount a thing weighs: *the weight of a feather.* **2.** An object, usually metal, of specific heaviness used to balance a scale: *a set of weights from one ounce to five pounds.*

***Idiom.* pull one's weight.** To do one's part.

weight•less | **wāt′** lĭs | *adj.* **1.** Having very little or no weight. **2.** Not affected by the pull of gravity: *The astronaut had to get used to being weightless in space.*

wheat | hwēt | *or* | wēt | *n.* **1.** A kind of grain. **2.** The seeds of this plant used to make flour.

wheth•er | **hwĕth′** ər | *or* | **wĕth′**- | *conj.* **1.** If: *I don't know whether you're telling the truth or not.* **2.** No matter if: *The race is beginning whether or not you are ready.*

whis•tle | **hwĭs′** əl | *or* | **wĭs′**- | *v.* **whis•tled, whis•tling. 1.** To make a shrill, piercing sound: *The train whistled.* **2.** To make a shrill sound with puckered lips or between the teeth: *We whistled for a taxicab.* **3.** To move with a speed fast enough to make a sharp, shrill, or piercing sound: *The wind whistled in the storm.* —*n.* **1.** A sharp, shrill, piercing sound: *the whistle of a quail.* **2.** A sound made by forcing air through puckered lips: *You have some whistle!* **3.** A device used to make a whistle: *The traffic officer blew her whistle.*

whole | hōl | *adj.* **1.** Not broken; having all parts: *The vase was dropped, but it is still whole.* **2.** The entire amount or extent: *We had trouble with the car the whole way home.* —*n.* **1.** Entire amount with all pieces; sum: *The whole is equal to the sum of its parts.* **2.** A complete system; unity: *The organs of the body work as a whole. These sound alike* **whole, hole.**

whom | ho͞om | *pron.* **1.** What person: *To whom am I speaking?* **2.** That (person): *This is the man whom I mentioned yesterday.*

whose | ho͞oz | *adj.* Possessive form of **who:** *the woman whose painting we bought.*

wife | wīf | *n., pl.* **wives** | wīvz |. A married woman.

wish | wĭsh | *n., pl.* **wish•es.** Something desired, needed, or wanted. —*v.* **1.** To crave; to want or feel a desire for. **2.** To express a hope for another: *I wish only the best for you.*

won•der•ful | **wŭn′** dər fəl | *adj.* **1.** Extraordinary; remarkable; causing wonder: *a wonderful trip.* **2.** Admirable; excellent: *a wonderful idea.*

wore Look up **wear.**

wreck | rĕk | *v.* To destroy or to take apart: *The building was wrecked because it was a fire hazard.* —*n.* **1.** Damage or destruction caused by wind, an accident, etc. **2.** Remains of anything ruined or destroyed: *The wreck was hauled away.*

wrin•kle | **rĭng′** kəl | *n.* A fold or ridge on a surface; crease: *a shirt full of wrinkles.* —*v.* **wrin•kled, wrin•kling.** To make a fold or to become creased.

wrist | rĭst | *n.* The joint connecting the hand and forearm.

write | rīt | *v.* **wrote** | rōt |, **writ•ten** | **rĭt′** n |, **writ•ing. 1.** To shape letters or words with a pencil or pen: *Write so that I can read.* **2.** To make up stories, poems, or books: *She writes stories.* **3.** To send a note or letter: *Write a thank-you letter. These sound alike* **write, right.**

wrong | rông | *or* | rŏng | *adj.* **1.** Incorrect; false: *a wrong answer.* **2.** Not right; bad, wicked: *It is wrong to steal.* **3.** Unsuitable; inappropriate: *to do or say the wrong thing.* **4.** Out of order; amiss: *There is something wrong with my watch.* —*v.* To treat unfairly.

Y

yolk | yōk | *or* | yōlk | *n.* The yellow part of an egg.

Z

zone | zōn | *n.* **1.** Any of five regions on earth divided by climate. **2.** Any area that is set off from others. —*v.* To divide into special areas.

THE CHECKPOINT

Study Plan

When you have finished a Checkpoint page and you know that you have the correct answers, use the Checkpoint page and this Study Plan to test yourself.

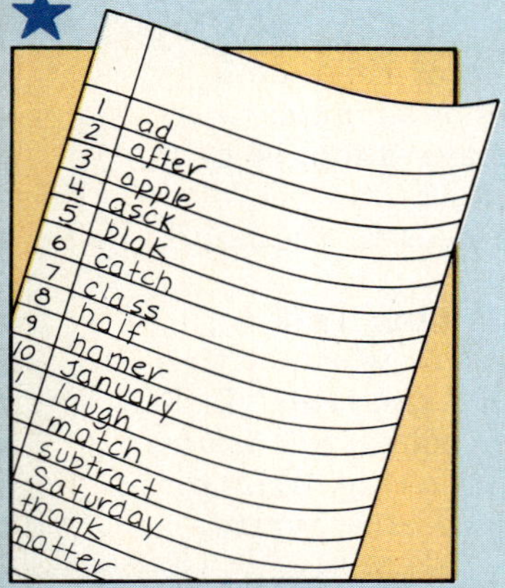

★ Cover your answers to the Checkpoint page with a piece of paper. Number the paper 1 through 16. For each spelling clue, do steps 1, 2, and 3.

1 Read the clue and say the answer.

2 Spell the answer aloud.

3 Write the answer.

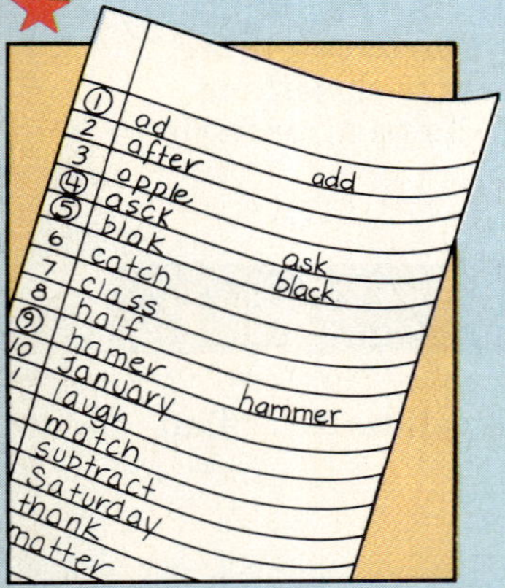

★ Uncover your first answers and do steps 4, 5, and 6.

4 Check your answers.

5 Circle the number of each misspelled word.

6 Write the correct spelling next to each incorrect word.

★ To study, cover your answers again, and fold the paper so that only the numbers show. For each circled number, repeat steps 1 through 6.

Review Test for Lesson 6

Directions: Read each sentence. Choose the correct spelling of the missing word. Mark your answer on the answer sheet by filling in the circle beside the correct letter. Do not write on this test.

Example:

1. The ___ is hot.
A. fier
B. fire
C. fyre
D. fir

1. Automobiles are made in a ___.
A. factory
B. factury
C. factery
D. faktory

2. Lightning split the tree in ___.
A. haff
B. haf
C. have
D. half

3. The crowd roared with ___.
A. luaghter
B. laughter
C. lafter
D. laughtar

4. I ordered a turkey ___.
A. sanwhich
B. sandwich
C. sandwitch
D. samwich

5. Our ___ has a big yard.
A. nayber
B. neyhbor
C. neighbor
D. nieghbor

6. The mirror will ___ if it falls.
A. brayk
B. brake
C. braek
D. break

7. The ___ sells French bread.
A. bakerie
B. bakery
C. baykery
D. bakary

8. The magician is an ___ artist.
A. escape
B. excape
C. escaep
D. eskape

9. Thanksgiving is an American ___.
A. holyday
B. holeday
C. holiday
D. haliday

10. Those children hardly ever ___.
A. complain
B. complane
C. complaine
D. cumplain

11. We weighed the fish on a ___.
A. skale
B. scael
C. scale
D. skayl

12. The dog was big and ___.
A. friendly
B. frendly
C. freindly
D. friendlie

13. I used a yardstick to ___ her height.
A. meazure
B. mesure
C. meshure
D. measure

14. The ___ system is used in Europe.
A. mettric
B. metric
C. metrick
D. metrec

15. The bridge was 1,573 feet in ___.
A. lenth
B. lengt
C. length
D. longth

16. The king had great ___.
A. waelth
B. welth
C. weath
D. wealth

17. We get ___ from the sun.
A. enirgy
B. energy
C. enurgy
D. energie

18. The cook makes ___ soup.
A. vegetable
B. vegtable
C. vegitable
D. vegtible

19. The divers found a ___ chest.
A. tresure
B. treshure
C. treasure
D. trezure

20. A birthday is a ___ occasion.
A. spechial
B. speshul
C. speciel
D. special

Review Test for Lesson 12

Directions: Read each sentence. Choose the correct spelling of the missing word. Mark your answer on the answer sheet by filling in the circle beside the correct letter. Do not write on this test.

Example:

1. The building is ____.
A. tawl
B. tall
C. tal
D. taul

1. Todd learned to play the ____.
A. peano
B. piyano
C. piana
D. piano

2. The puzzle is not easy to ____.
A. compleat
B. complete
C. compleet
D. cumplete

3. The mayor made a long ____.
A. speash
B. speech
C. speach
D. spetch

4. Don't ____ everything you hear.
A. believe
B. belief
C. beleave
D. beleive

5. The bottles are ____.
A. emty
B. empti
C. empty
D. emtie

6. They watch TV in the ____.
A. evening
B. efening
C. evenin
D. eavning

7. I have a good ____ for being late.
A. reson
B. reeson
C. reason
D. reasin

8. The colonists fought for ____.
A. liburty
B. liverty
C. liberty
D. libertie

9. We ____ the oxygen in the air.
A. breathe
B. brethe
C. breath
D. breethe

10. The lake will ____ in January.
A. frees
B. freeze
C. freaz
D. freese

11. The hurricane did a lot of ____.
A. damige
B. damege
C. damag
D. damage

12. The detective solved the ____.
A. mistary
B. mystery
C. mistery
D. mystory

13. Everyone ____ me went to the playground.
A. except
B. encept
C. escept
D. excipt

14. The buyers ____ on quality merchandise.
A. insist
B. insest
C. ensist
D. insised

15. Mr. Martin owns his own ____.
A. bisness
B. business
C. buisness
D. busyness

16. Let's ____ the book we read.
A. discuss
B. discus
C. descuss
D. diskuss

17. The plane wrote a ____ in the sky.
A. messige
B. mesage
C. message
D. messege

18. Each person has a ____ fingerprint.
A. differant
B. different
C. difrent
D. differnt

19. The criminal was ____.
A. giulty
B. gilty
C. guillty
D. guilty

20. The teacher will ____ the test.
A. reveiw
B. revue
C. review
D. revew

Review Test for Lesson 18

Directions: Read each sentence. Choose the correct spelling of the missing word. Mark you answer on the answer sheet by filling in the circle beside the correct letter. Do not write on this test.

Example:

> **1.** The ___ fell.
> A. rane
> B. rain
> C. rayn
> D. rian

1. Did Jo ___ which class to take?
A. deside
B. diside
C. decide
D. dicide

2. The stars ___ the sailors.
A. giude
B. gyde
C. gide
D. guide

3. We are studying plants in ___.
A. sience
B. siense
C. science
D. sciense

4. Puerto Rico is an ___.
A. island
B. iland
C. eyeland
D. islant

5. Many books are in the ___.
A. libary
B. librery
C. library
D. livary

6. The net caught a huge ___ of fish.
A. quantity
B. quanaty
C. quanity
D. quantaty

7. There is no cure for the ___ cold.
A. commin
B. common
C. comon
D. comman

8. Sick people are cared for in a ___.
A. hospitle
B. hospitel
C. hospitil
D. hospital

9. Don't make a ___ that can't be kept.
A. promice
B. pramise
C. promise
D. promiss

10. Someone who doesn't lie is ___.
A. honist
B. honest
C. onest
D. honess

11. The pilot is in ___ of the plane.
A. controll
B. controle
C. controol
D. control

12. Ralph knows how to ___.
A. soo
B. sew
C. so
D. seu

13. The hummingbird has a ruby-colored ___.
A. throte
B. troat
C. throat
D. throt

14. I heard an ___ in the canyon.
A. echo
B. eko
C. ecko
D. echoe

15. The dogs pulled the sled ___ the snow.
A. throo
B. threw
C. through
D. thrue

16. The ___ of an egg is yellow.
A. yolk
B. yoak
C. yoke
D. yok

17. I ___ my brother a quarter.
A. ow
B. oh
C. oew
D. owe

18. The ivy has ___ over the house.
A. grown
B. grone
C. groan
D. growne

19. We heard a mysterious low ___.
A. grown
B. grone
C. groan
D. groen

20. Alexander G. Bell invented the ___.
A. telefone
B. telaphone
C. telephone
D. teliphone

Review Test for Lesson 24

Directions: Read each sentence. Choose the correct spelling of the missing word. Mark your answer on the answer sheet by filling in the circle beside the correct letter. Do not write on this test.

Example:

> **1.** The ___ flew south.
> A. birdz
> B. birds
> C. burds
> D. berds

1. A ___ is used to indicate direction.
A. compas
B. cumpas
C. compass
D. compess

2. The ___ caused damage along the river.
A. flodd
B. flood
C. flud
D. flod

3. The ocean was ___ and choppy.
A. rough
B. rouh
C. ruff
D. ruogh

4. The ___ gave the gymnast a high score.
A. gudge
B. judge
C. juge
D. judg

5. The accident wasn't anyone's ___.
A. fawlt
B. falt
C. foult
D. fault

6. I write to my pen pal ___.
A. offen
B. often
C. ofen
D. oftan

7. The dogs ___ over a bone.
A. faught
B. faut
C. fought
D. fawt

8. I fell down but I'm ___.
A. all right
B. alright
C. all write
D. all rite

9. The movie was just ___!
A. aweful
B. awful
C. awfull
D. awfle

10. My sister's ___ is my niece.
A. dawter
B. daghter
C. daughter
D. daughtar

11. The detective found a ___.
A. klue
B. cloo
C. clue
D. clew

12. Marvin's ___ got stuck in the mud.
A. shue
B. shoo
C. shew
D. shoe

13. I try not to ___ my temper.
A. looz
B. lose
C. loose
D. looze

14. The door knob was ___.
A. loose
B. looss
C. lose
D. looze

15. Always tell the ___!
A. truth
B. trooth
C. truthe
D. trueth

16. To ___ is the package to be sent?
A. whume
B. hoom
C. whom
D. hume

17. The ___ is freshly squeezed.
A. juise
B. juice
C. joose
D. juess

18. The driver tried to ___ an accident.
A. aboid
B. avoyd
C. avoide
D. avoid

19. It was my ___ to take ballet lessons.
A. choyce
B. choice
C. choise
D. choiss

20. Insects ___ crops each year.
A. distroy
B. destroy
C. destroi
D. distroi

Review Test for Lesson 30

Directions: Read each sentence. Choose the correct spelling of the missing word. Mark your answer on the answer sheet by filling in the circle beside the correct letter. Do not write on this test.

Example:

1. The ___ is soft.
A. citten
B. kitten
C. kiten
D. kittin

1. They settled the ___ peacefully.
A. quarral
B. quarrel
C. quarel
D. quarrle

2. Tigers ___ when they are angry.
A. ror
B. rore
C. wroar
D. roar

3. The wind ___ the sail.
A. toar
B. tor
C. tore
D. tored

4. The actors ___ before an audience.
A. paform
B. perform
C. pirform
D. perfarm

5. The captain of the ship charted a ___.
A. cours
B. corse
C. course
D. coorse

6. I'm expecting an ___ phone call.
A. impordant
B. important
C. impertant
D. importent

7. She gave her ___ as a volunteer.
A. service
B. survice
C. surviss
D. servise

8. The ___ was made by hand.
A. furnisure
B. furnature
C. furnachur
D. furniture

9. The teacher was ___ with the students.
A. ferm
B. firm
C. furm
D. firn

10. The doctor was ___ the child would be well.
A. curtain
B. certain
C. certin
D. sertain

11. The diamond was ___ or flawless.
A. purfic
B. perfict
C. purfect
D. perfect

12. An oyster makes a ___.
A. purl
B. pearl
C. perl
D. perll

13. Help me ___ dinner.
A. prepare
B. perpare
C. prepair
D. prepaer

14. Walk ___ across the ice.
A. carefuly
B. cairfully
C. carfully
D. carefully

15. Presidents ___ national holidays.
A. declaer
B. declare
C. declair
D. daclare

16. The copy can't ___ to the original.
A. compare
B. compair
C. cumpare
D. compar

17. The children played ___.
A. marbles
B. marvles
C. marbels
D. marbils

18. The ___ had two bedrooms.
A. apartmint
B. apatment
C. apartment
D. apertment

19. The plants will ___ without fertilizer.
A. stave
B. storve
C. starve
D. starbe

20. Don't write in the ___.
A. magin
B. margen
C. marjin
D. margin

Review Test for Lesson 36

Directions: Read each sentence. Choose the correct spelling of the missing word. Mark your answer on the answer sheet by filling in the circle beside the correct letter. Do not write on this test.

Example:

1. The ____ is ten years old.
A. gurl
B. girl
C. gerl
D. girll

1. This was the worst storm in recent ____.
A. memory
B. memery
C. memry
D. memary

2. The ____ covers 70% of the earth's surface.
A. osean
B. ocean
C. oshun
D. oshin

3. The sunset was ____.
A. buetiful
B. beautiful
C. bewtiful
D. beautyful

4. The ____ party was a success!
A. suprise
B. surprize
C. surprise
D. saprize

5. Lean the ladder ____ the house.
A. againsed
B. against
C. aginst
D. agenst

6. Diving can be a ____ sport.
A. dangerus
B. dayngeros
C. dangarous
D. dangerous

7. A ____ is worth five cents.
A. nikel
B. nickle
C. nickel
D. nicle

8. The ____ exam was difficult.
A. final
B. fynel
C. fienle
D. finel

9. The honest boy set a good ____.
A. esample
B. exampel
C. ezampil
D. example

10. The train ____ blew loudly.
A. whisel
B. whistle
C. wisle
D. whistel

11. The statement was too ____.
A. generel
B. genarel
C. generil
D. general

12. The ____ in the play was funny.
A. character
B. charecter
C. caracter
D. charectar

13. I wonder ____ other stars have planets.
A. whethur
B. wether
C. whether
D. weather

14. The stories have ____ plots.
A. similar
B. simaler
C. similer
D. simelar

15. Circle the date on the ____.
A. calinder
B. calendar
C. calander
D. kalender

16. I have a good sense of ____.
A. huemer
B. humar
C. humer
D. humor

17. From which ____ is the wind blowing?
A. direction
B. derection
C. derecsion
D. direcshun

18. That ____ helps us to communicate.
A. invenshun
B. invention
C. inbention
D. invension

19. I have a butterfly ____.
A. colection
B. collecsion
C. collection
D. cullection

20. Everyone should have an ____.
A. edyoucasion
B. ejucation
C. edgecashun
D. education

Answer Sheet

Review Test for Lesson ____

Name ______________________________ **Date** ____________

Directions: Mark each answer by filling in the circle next to the correct letter. Be sure to fill in only one circle for each number.

Example:

1. A. ○ B. ● C. ○ D. ○

1. A. ○
B. ○
C. ○
D. ○

2. A. ○
B. ○
C. ○
D. ○

3. A. ○
B. ○
C. ○
D. ○

4. A. ○
B. ○
C. ○
D. ○

5. A. ○
B. ○
C. ○
D. ○

6. A. ○
B. ○
C. ○
D. ○

7. A. ○
B. ○
C. ○
D. ○

8. A. ○
B. ○
C. ○
D. ○

9. A. ○
B. ○
C. ○
D. ○

10. A. ○
B. ○
C. ○
D. ○

11. A. ○
B. ○
C. ○
D. ○

12. A. ○
B. ○
C. ○
D. ○

13. A. ○
B. ○
C. ○
D. ○

14. A. ○
B. ○
C. ○
D. ○

15. A. ○
B. ○
C. ○
D. ○

16. A. ○
B. ○
C. ○
D. ○

17. A. ○
B. ○
C. ○
D. ○

18. A. ○
B. ○
C. ○
D. ○

19. A. ○
B. ○
C. ○
D. ○

20. A. ○
B. ○
C. ○
D. ○

STECK-VAUGHN

Spelling

Dear Family of ______________________________ ,

This year your child will be learning to spell and write many new words. It will be exciting for your child to study the sounds and letters, check meanings, and use the new words.

You can support our classroom work in spelling by asking your child about the words he or she is currently studying and by making the study of words a shared experience at home. Here are some simple but fun ways to help your child build word power.

✔ Help your child study words when you are reading together. Look for clues to the meanings of words from the ways they are used in sentences, paragraphs, or passages.

✔ Make word search games using words in the spelling lessons. Write the letters of each word in the boxes on graph paper. The words can go across, up, down, backwards, or diagonally. Fill in the blank boxes with any letters. Trade papers; then find and circle the spelling words.

✔ Have your child spell the weekly spelling words aloud to you while you are engaged in daily tasks such as setting the table, preparing meals, or folding laundry.

Activities like these build spelling and vocabulary skills while promoting a lifelong love for learning.

Sincerely,

Teacher

STECK-VAUGHN

Spelling

Estimada familia de ____________________ ,

Este año su hijo(a) estará aprendiendo a deletrear y escribir muchas palabras nuevas. El estudio de los sonidos y de las letras, la verificación de significados y el uso de las nuevas palabras constituirán una fuente de emoción para su hijo(a).

El trabajo de deletreo que realizamos en el salón de clase puede complementarse mediante preguntas a su hijo(a) acerca de las palabras que está estudiando actualmente; así como también al hacer del estudio de palabras una experiencia compartida en el hogar. He aquí algunas maneras simples, mas sin embargo divertidas, de ayudar a su hijo(a) a adquirir habilidades con el uso de palabras.

- ✔ Ayudar a que su hijo(a) estudie palabras cuando estén leyendo juntos(as). Buscar pistas para el significado de las palabras a partir de la forma en que éstas han sido usadas en las oraciones, párrafos o pasajes.
- ✔ Participar en juegos de búsqueda de palabras en las lecciones de deletreo. Cada participante escribe las letras de cada palabra en los cuadritos de una hoja de papel cuadriculado. Las palabras pueden escribirse horizontalmente, hacia arriba, hacia abajo, hacia atrás; o bien, diagonalmente. Llenar los cuadritos en blanco con cualquier letra. Intercambiar hojas de papel; y a continuación, encontrar y encerrar en un círculo las palabras de deletreo.
- ✔ Hacer que su hijo(a) le deletree las palabras semanales de deletreo en voz alta mientras usted se dedica a faenas diarias tales como preparar la mesa, preparar las comidas, o doblar ropa lavada.

Actividades como éstas desarrollan destrezas de vocabulario y de deletreo, al mismo tiempo que fomentan un aprecio por el aprendizaje que dura toda una vida.

Cordialmente,

Maestro(a)

Steps in the Writing Process

Name ______________________________

1. Prewriting

Think about what you want to say.

- Make sure you know your reason for writing.
- Think about your reader.
- Make a plan.

2. Writing

Use your plan to make a first try.

- Don't worry about mistakes now.
- Add any new ideas you think of while writing.
- Keep your purpose and audience in mind.
- Leave plenty of room between lines so you can make changes later.

3. Revising

Look for ways to improve what you have written.

- Look for places that need more ideas or details.
- Get rid of sentences that don't belong.
- Find places where more colorful or exact words might be used.
- Revise until clear and complete.

4. Proofreading

Review your work for errors.

- Correct any misspelled words.
- Check for other errors.
- Make a clean, final copy.
- Proofread your work again. Make sure you have not made new errors.

5. Publishing

Share what you have written.

- Read it to the class or a friend.
- Add pictures or make a poster.
- Make a recording of your writing.

Proofreading Symbols/Checklist

Name ____

The chart below shows some proofreading marks and how to use them.

Mark	Meaning	Example
⬭	word is misspelled	Dogs are my (favrite) pet.
⊙	period is missing	I hear a dog barking outside ⊙
‸?	question mark is missing	Did the dog bark last night ‸?
‸!	exclamation point is missing	Look at the size of that dog ‸!
≡	letter should be capitalized	I love my dog buster.
/	letter should be lower case	On Saturdays I take him to the Park.
℘	take out word	He loves to ~~to~~ run and play there.
‸	word is missing	Buster is brown ‸and white.
‸,	comma is missing	He is loyal‸, brave, and smart.
’	apostrophe is missing	My sister’s puppy is very small.
“ ”	quotation marks are missing	“He can fit in my hand,” she said.
¶	first line of paragraph should be indented	¶ My family has always loved dogs. Ever since I can remember, we have had at least one dog to enjoy.

The checklist below will help you remember things to look for as you proofread. Place a check mark by each step when you have finished it.

- ☐ I have checked each word to make sure it is spelled correctly.
- ☐ I have used the correct punctuation mark at the end of every sentence.
- ☐ I have started every sentence with a capital letter.
- ☐ I have capitalized all proper names.
- ☐ I have lowercased all words that should not be capitalized.
- ☐ I have taken out all extra words.
- ☐ I have added all missing words.
- ☐ I have added all missing commas.
- ☐ I have added all missing apostrophes.
- ☐ I have added all missing quotation marks.
- ☐ I have indented the first line of each paragraph.

Chain of Events Chart

Name ______________________________ **Date** ____________

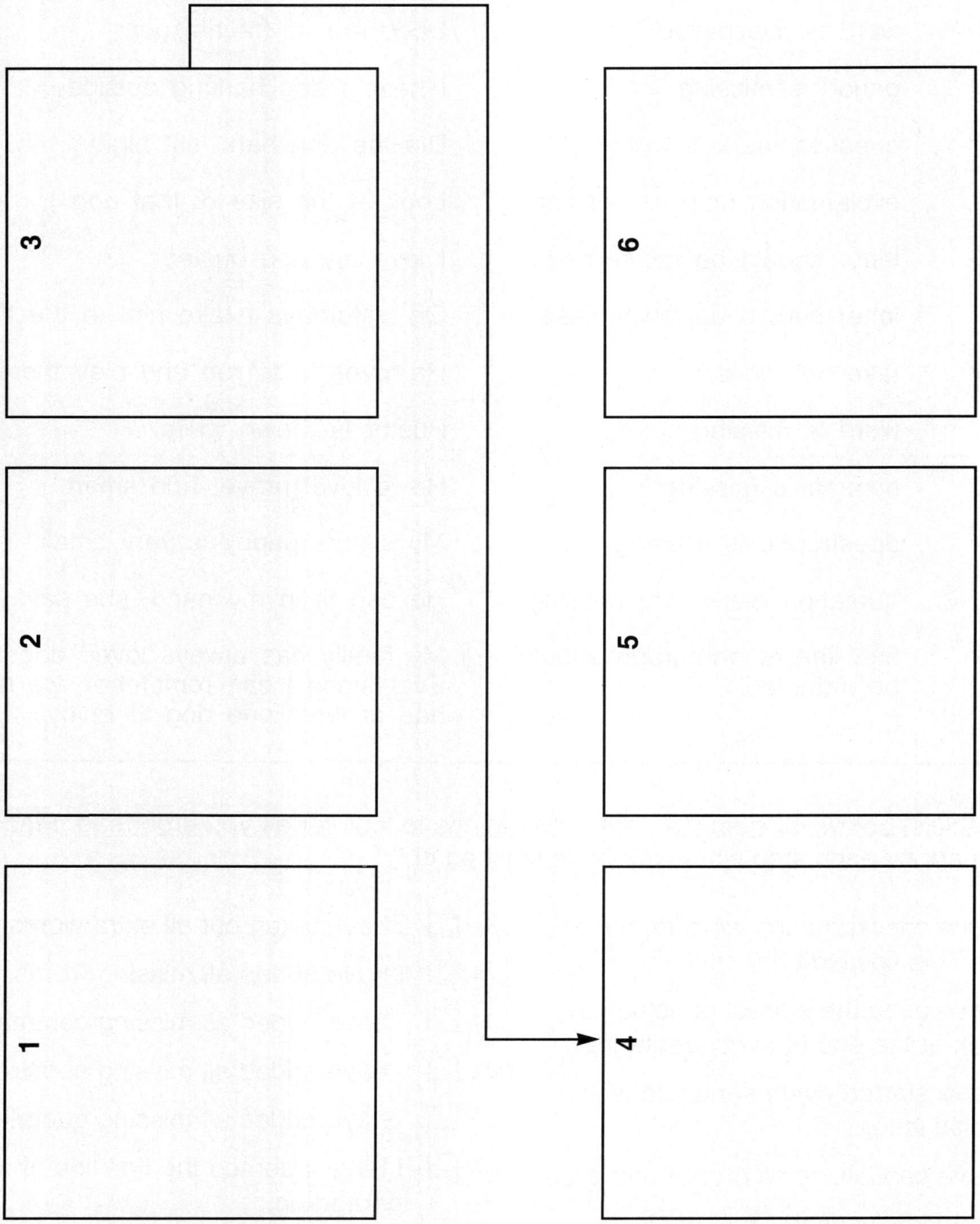

Story Map

Name ______________________________ **Date** ____________

Beginning

Middle

End

Senses Web

Name ______________________________ Date ____________

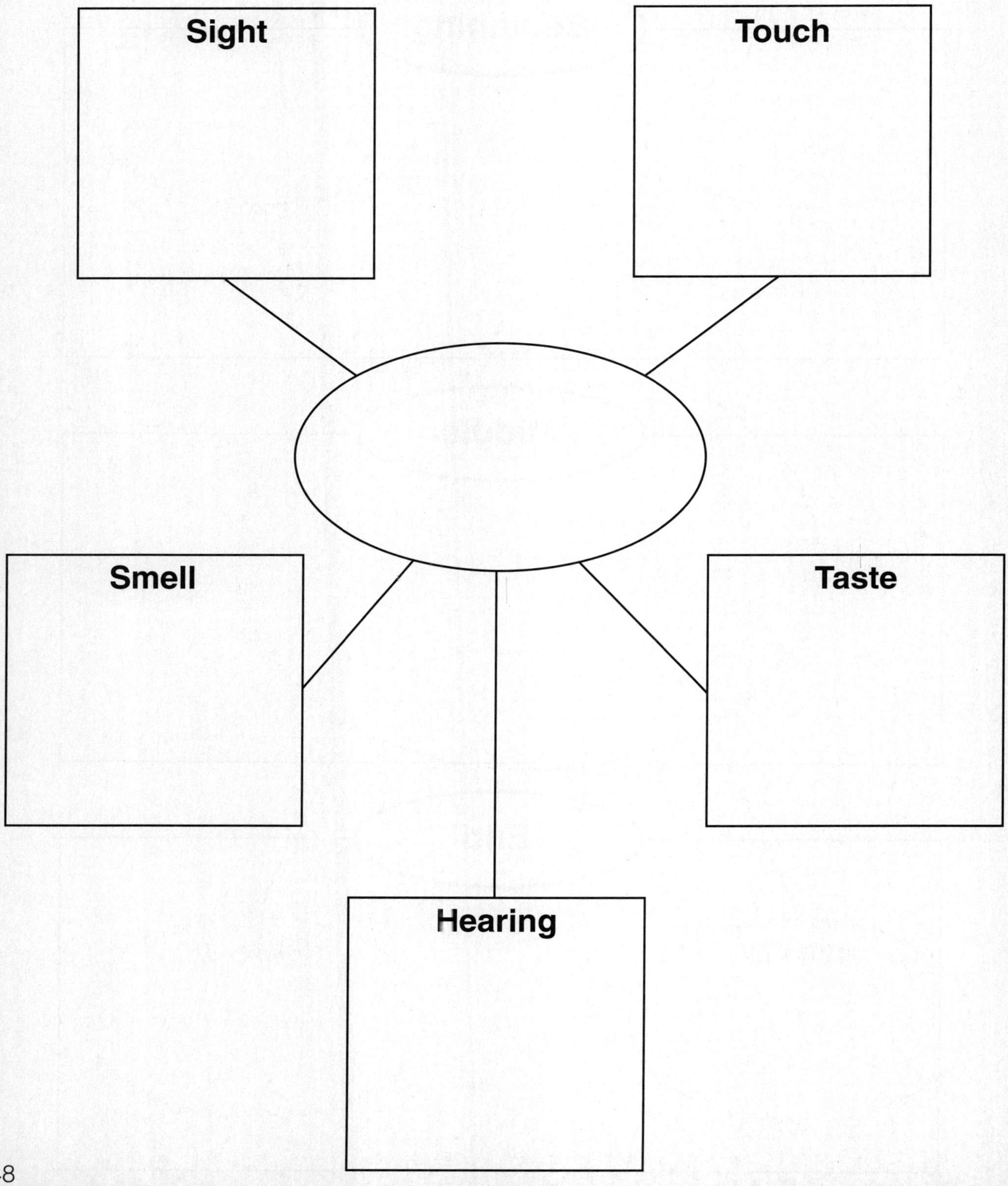

Cluster Map

Name ______________________________ **Date** ______________

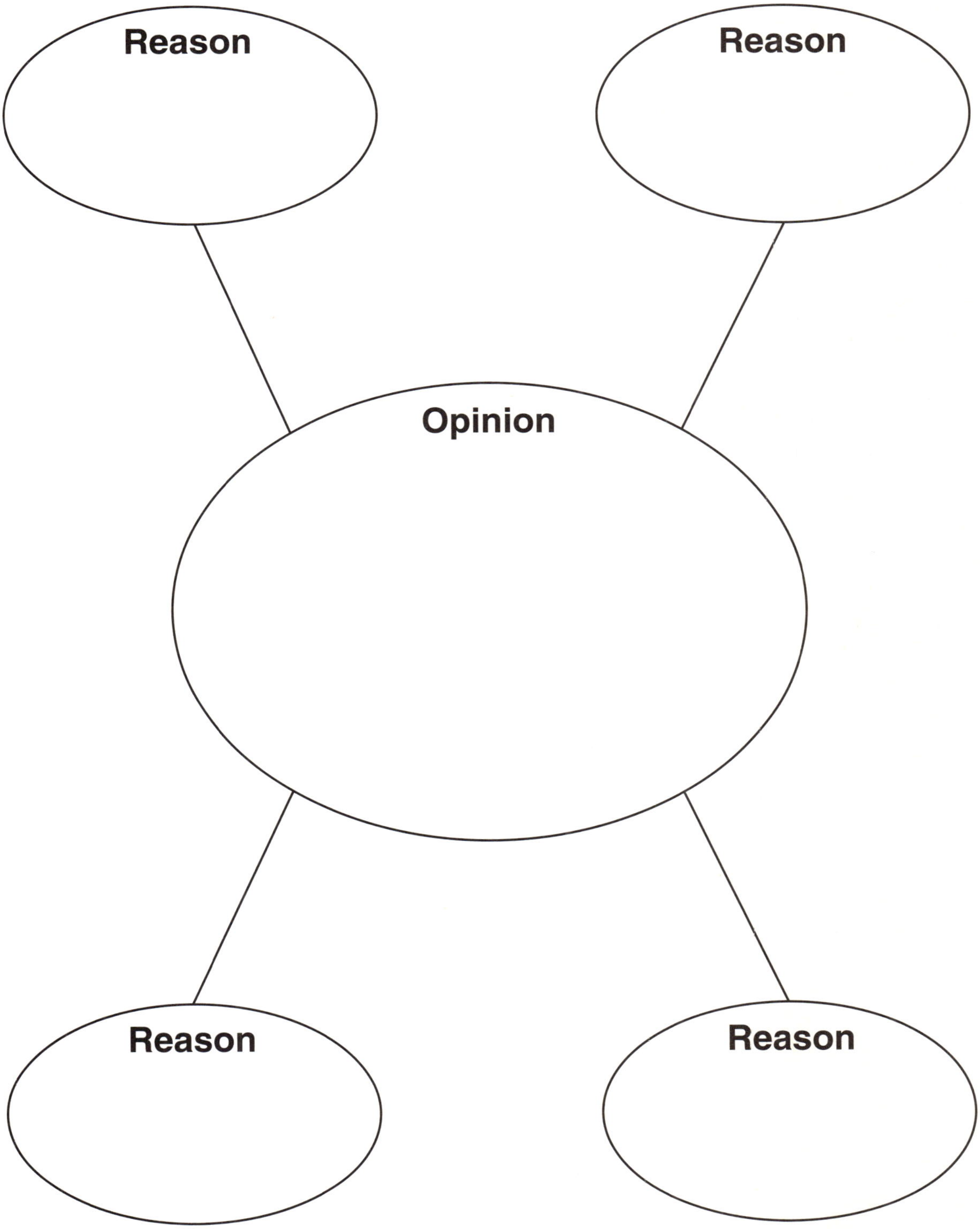